Readings in the Political Economy of Aging

Edited by Meredith Minkler and Carroll L. Estes

POLICY, POLITICS, HEALTH AND MEDICINE

Series

Baywood Publishing Company, Inc.
Farmingdale, New York 11735

Library of Congress Catalog Card Number: 84-20492
ISBN: 0-89503-042-X

© 1984 Baywood Publishing Company, Inc.

Library of Congress Cataloging in Publication Data
Main entry under title:

Readings in the political economy of aging.

  (Policy, politics, health, and medicine series; 6)
  Includes bibliographies.
  1. Aged—United States—Economic conditions. 2. Aged—
Government policy—United States. 3. Aged discrimination
—United States. I. Minkler, Meredith. II. Estes,
Carroll Lynn, 1938-   . III. Series.
HQ1064.U5R37   1984   305.2'6'0973   84-20492
ISBN 0-89503-042-X

Table of Contents

Preface

This book is based on three premises: 1) that the "aging problem" in our society cannot usefully be viewed or understood in isolation from the larger social, political and economic environment within which it is embedded; 2) that the political economy perspective presents a helpful theoretical framework within which to view the socially created aging problem; and 3) that viewed within a political economy perspective, the dependent position of the elderly and the public policies and institutional arrangements that affect them will be seen both to reflect and to reinforce the prevailing class structure of our society.

While the political economy of aging is relatively "underdeveloped" as a field, it provides an important contrast to the mainstream of gerontological theories and approaches which emphasize the individual as the appropriate unit of analysis. By viewing the problem of aging as a structural one, the political economy approach emphasizes the broad implications of economic life for the elderly and for society's differential treatment of the aged as a group, and of the elderly in different social classes. Such a perspective challenges many prevailing assumptions and in the process, forces a more critical analysis of the social construction of the problem of old age in America.

The introductory chapters in this volume will provide an overview of the political economy of aging, elaborating on the premises set forth above and briefly introducing the various interrelated topics examined in the book.

Subsequent chapters will present a multitude of subjects and perspectives within the broad area of the political economy of aging, including such key issues as the socio-political origins of retirement and social security; the "double jeopardy" of being old and female; the social production of mental illness; and public policy and the nursing home industry. The effects of the current politics of retrenchment on programs and policies affecting the elderly are presented and discussed by several contributors to this volume, and represent a particularly timely example of the utility of political economic analyses of the mislabeled problem of aging in America.

While the majority of the contributors to this volume are American and hence base most of their examples and analyses on the American experience, the problems and issues discussed will be seen to have broad universality with respect to other advanced industrialized nations. Moreover, as British scholar Alan Walker suggests in his chapter, the socially created "aging problem" is not simply a phenomenon of advanced capitalist societies. The British experience with structurally enforced dependency of the elderly under a socialist economy thus is seen as having some important parallels in advanced capitalist societies which must be examined if we are to comprehend the complexities of the "aging problem" in many parts of the advanced industrialized world.

Many chapters in this volume originally appeared in *International Journal of Health Services*. The other selections, reprinted from multiple sources, represent book chapters and articles that we believe are significant contributions to our understanding of a political economic analysis of aging. A variety of liberal and radical political perspectives are represented. This diversity is intentional and will, we hope, stimulate debate and contribute to the development of the political economy of aging as a major theoretical approach in gerontology and related disciplines.

Of at least equal importance, however, is the contribution which a well developed political economy of aging may make to praxis and to changing those conditions which underlie and reinforce the dependent position of the elderly in American society. It is toward the end of furthering such analysis and social action that this volume is presented.

Introduction:
Challenge to a New Age
MAGGIE KUHN

We live in a turbulent and exhilarating age of change, an age which reflects the potential for liberation and self-determination. The so-called "problems of age" in this new age are indeed the problems of our society: they reflect its malaise and also the distribution of power in American society. Yet every discipline, every institution, every nation-state, every human group cannot fail to be challenged by the profound issues of age in the 1980's.

Given the dramatic shifts in demography and an older America, there are three distinctive elements which seem to characterize this as a new age in contemporary society: the convergence of liberating forces, the intersection of biography and history, and the new critique of age-segregated services and life styles.

THE CONVERGENCE OF LIBERATING FORCES

The convergence and interaction of liberating forces at work in society against racism, sexism, ageism, and economic imperialism are all oppressive "isms" and built-in responses of a society that considers certain groups inferior. All are rooted in the social-economic structures of society. All deprive certain

Editor's Note: Maggie Kuhn is a scholar, an advocate and an activist widely heralded as the most effective change agent in our society's understanding of ageism and aging. In 1970, Maggie was at the height of a highly productive career with the WMCA and the national office of the United Presbyterian Church when she was confronted with the unwelcome prospect of mandatory retirement. With a group of like-minded friends, she began an action organization which was later to be named the Gray Panthers. Concerned with age discrimination against young as well as old, and with oppression in all its forms, the Gray Panthers took up opposition to the Viet Nam war as an initial focus for action. Its multiple issues today include nursing home reform, decent housing for all, development of a national health service for the United States, environmental protection and nuclear disarmament. The Gray Panthers currently boast a membership of 50,000 and 110 local affiliates around the nation. As founder and national convener of the Gray Panthers, Maggie Kuhn, age seventy-nine, remains the organization's most beloved and articulate spokesperson. The editors are grateful to Maggie for agreeing to write this special introduction to *Readings in the Political Economy of Aging.*

7

groups of status, the right to control their own lives and destinies with the end result of powerlessness. All have resulted in economic and social discrimination. All rob American society of the energies and involvement of creative persons who are needed to make our society just and humane. All have brought on indi·vidual alienation, despair, hostility, and anomie.

The civil rights struggles of the 1950's and 1960's focused largely on black-white issues and racial discrimination in education and employment. The struggle against ageism is a newer force. Only as public awareness of the growing numbers of Older Americans increased were age-segregated services and programs set up in every state. These services had little reference to the earlier liberation movements.

Today the oppressed are recognizing the need for sweeping economic and social change in society. They are beginning to form coalitions to deal with the root causes of social need and poverty, to oppose military expansion, to prevent the destruction of our environment by pollution, chemical and nuclear waste. It is wonderful to see grassroots groups coming together to deal with the problems of our society and attempt to solve them.

INTERSECTION OF BIOGRAPHY AND HISTORY

There is a growing awareness of interaction between personal troubles and public issues, between the private and public sectors and the societal causes of personal pain and need. C. Wright Mills wrote about the intersection of biography and history, as our personal lives are deeply affected by the history of our times. So many of us live intensely private, individualized lives, we do not recognize how our destinies are influenced by the forces and sweeps of history.

We cannot deal with public issues and policies like the arms race and U.S./Soviet relations without understanding that they affect the lives of trillions of individuals, innocent civilians, and the enormous waste of resources involved in the production of weapons. Mills makes clear that no personal problems can be fully revolved without some societal change. Many of the mental depressions which older people suffer are not organic. So-called senility is induced by despair and loss of status and selfhood in society.

When we the elders have a chance to reflect on our past, take stock of the changes we have seen, and the history we have lived through, we have a special perspective on life. When I was born in 1905 in my grandmother's front bedroom, we communicated only by telegraph or "wireless" and rode in carriages and horse cars, traveling distances by railroad. During my lifetime the western world has developed radio, television, world-wide telephone service, jet planes and trident missiles. I personally remember two devastating world wars, continued conflict in Korea and Vietnam, the Great Depression, the stock market crash, the landing on the moon, space exploration and the horrors of the near meltdown at the Three Mile Island Nuclear Plant.

Services are not enough to end discrimination and powerlessness. More and more people are realizing that society is sick and in need of social change. We see the powerful social forces that shape our attitudes and our lives and our roles in the world—forces that cannot be countered by individualistic approaches to help people as individuals. Services dull the pain, but they do not alter the conditions that have caused the suffering and created the need for the services. I call many of the services provided to help old people a form of novocaine.

AGE-SEGREGATED SERVICES AND LIFE STYLES

Age-segregated services have isolated the elders from the voting. The same ageism that makes old age lonely and despairing, robs youth of a future. The marginalization and ghettoizing of people by age and class must be challenged. As we look ahead to the year 2000, there is a serious danger of establishing a permanent underclass of older Americans if the present age-segregated policies and practices continue: roleless, powerless, living at the edge of poverty, out of the mainstream. There is the further danger that continued segregation will increase hostility and alienation between old and young who desperately need each other. Growing up is just as stressful as growing old in a technological society. As inflation increases, poverty threatens all but the very rich, and especially those who live on fixed incomes. And over all of these dangers and fears hangs the threat of nuclear annihilation. How do we change our present situation and counter this gloomy forecast?

The complexity of the issues and problems we consider here should not deter us from action. This is a new age requiring new attitudes, new structures and life-styles. There are positive trends which reflect the opportunity to change the future through the power struggles that accompany the uncertainty of our times. First, there is a view and understanding that old age is only part of a life cycle, a continuum of life and that the life chances of the old and of the young are tied together; aging is a socially constructed condition which awaits societal members and in which they must have a stake. Second, there is the emergence of a new vision which sees that there is something one can do and that we are the active makers of our own destiny, our own biography and history. Third, there is an understanding that health and social services must be designed to enable individual choice and social responsibility. Historical analysis points to the simple and important observation that our material conditions are the outcome not merely of personal opportunity or initiative, but largely the outcome of collective political action and struggle. Over the past century political action has taken the form of advocacy, community organizing, coalition building, developing leadership skills and political strategies to enable older people to realize a better life, a longer life, a healthier life. Rather than being a source of alarm, these advancements should be a cause of celebration.

CHAPTER 1

Introduction

MEREDITH MINKLER

A long tradition in the study of social problems has focused attention on issues which are not problems in and of themselves, but which are labeled as problems in response to larger societal difficulties and the successful efforts by key political and economic actors to divert attention from one set of issues to another. Aging in America is viewed in this volume as constituting one such mislabeled social problem.

In recent years, some encouraging attempts have been made to differentiate between the widely proclaimed problem of aging in America as a problem of individuals and the "problem behind the problem," namely the complex of societal, environmental, and other factors that have supported the view and treatment of virtually all people sixty-five and over as a single homogeneous group, labeled as a social problem.

While these efforts have been in the main unsystematic and atheoretical in nature, the emergence of a political economy of aging perspective has helped to provide a broad interdisciplinary framework for analysis within which the complexity of the "aging problem" is brought into focus. By rejecting the notion that aging or any other social problem can be viewed and understood in isolation from larger political, social, and economic issues, the political economy perspective requires us to take seriously the "problems behind the problem." Such an analysis enables and indeed forces us to examine such issues as:

- The socio-political nature of how our society views the elderly and what this means for older persons.
- The social, political, and economic bases of policies that determine how benefits, privilege, and power are distributed.
- The social creation of the dependent status of the elderly in our society, and the management of that dependency through public policies and health and social services.
- The social construction of reality concerning aging and old age which both underlies and reinforces those public policies and institutional arrangements through which aging is approached and managed in our society [1].

10

It is in requiring us to confront these more fundamental issues and questions that the political economy perspective can make a major contribution to gerontology and related disciplines.

POLITICAL ECONOMY DEFINED

For the purposes of this book political economy is defined as:

> The study of the interrelationships between the polity, economy, and society, or more specifically, the reciprocal influences among government . . . the economy, social classes, strate and, status groups. The central problem of the political economy perspective is the manner in which the economy and polity interact in a relationship of reciprocal causation affecting the distribution of social goods [2].

Such a perspective of necessity views the "problem" of aging in structural rather than individual terms. As Estes *et al.* note in Chapter 2, it further "starts with the proposition that the status and resources of the elderly and even the trajectory of the aging process itself are conditioned by one's location in the social structure and the economic and social factors that affect it."

The framework for inquiry provided through a political economy approach is importantly supplemented by the theoretical perspective of the social construction of reality. Social definitions of aging are important not only because they reflect the dominant values, ideologies, and class structure of the society, but further because they tend to become reified. The elderly are processed and commodified, and policies for the aged are developed which fail to address root causes or problems behind the problem. Such policies, moreover, create new problems through their focus on age segregation and isolation of the elderly from the rest of society and through their creation and perpetuation of a vast "aging enterprise" [3] dependent on such separatist thinking and approaches for its very survival. A major consequence of this enterprise, and of the health and social service policies which support and reflect it, may be seen in the perpetuation of existing social class differences. Yet such phenomena, including the socially constructed nature of the problem of old age, are seldom the subject of gerontological research.

LIMITATIONS OF THE DOMINANT
GERONTOLOGICAL THEORIES

In Chapter 2 of this book, the dominant theoretical approaches to the study of aging in the United States are examined, with particular attention to the reasons for their centrality in American gerontological thought. While on the surface, such approaches (e.g., disengagement theory, activity theory, and developmental or lifestyle approaches) differ significantly in substance, each tends to emphasize the individual as the appropriate unit of analysis and "adjustment" as the key to a successful aging experience. This micro level focus provides an important unifying dimension to otherwise disparate theoretical approaches and suggests why each of these traditional approaches has been relatively successful in legitimizing and reinforcing societal policies and problems for the elderly.

Disengagement theory, [4] for example, which posits the mutual and beneficial withdrawal of the elderly and society from one another, may be seen as legitimizing mandatory retirement policies and other public policies that foster the separation of the elderly from others in the society. Similarly, activity theory, [5] stressing the need for continued engagement over the life course, lends theoretical support to the Older Americans Act and to other policies stressing the provision, on an incremental level, of services and programs that primarily aim at social integration of the aged.

The symbolic interactionist perspective which gained popularity among some gerontologists in the 1960's [6, 7], has been important in challenging classical sociological approaches such as structural functionalism, and in suggesting that the interactional context and process (e.g., the environment, the person and their encounter) affect the way in which aging is experienced. Yet this theory too may be seen as more focused on how individuals *react* to aging than on the broad socio-structural factors that shape the experience and the management of aging in our society. Finally, Riley's theory of age stratification makes an important sociological contribution to the gerontology literature by focusing on the importance of age, period, and cohort effects on the social system of older individuals and by examining the effects of age stratification on the larger system [8]. As noted in Chapter 2, however, this theoretical approach does not specifically examine the independent effects of the political and economic structure on aging and old age.

AGE AND CLASS: A NEGLECTED AREA OF GERONTOLOGICAL RESEARCH

In analyzing the consequences of old age policy in Great Britain, Walker has described the economic and social situation of older persons as one of dependency and poverty which is socially created by the differential rewards in the labor market, by the pension system itself, upon retirement, and by the professionals in the service industry business [9]. The primary theories of aging in the United States give little or no theoretical attention to these social institutions or the functions they perform in society.

In an early exposition of this neglect, Simpson revealed that of 18,000 articles on old age published between 1936 and 1956, only a handful concerned both old age and social class and that handful added little to our knowledge of stratification among the aged [10]. More recently, McAdam noted that of 661 articles published in the *Journal of Gerontology* between 1972 and 1979, only twelve, or less than 2 percent, involved macro level analyses of political, social, or economic factors influencing and determining the position of the elderly in society [11].

The chapters in this volume present an alternative to the dominant paradigms in gerontological theory and research by virtue of their explicit focus on the structural conditions relevant to aging and to the development of social policies for this population segment. We are concerned especially with class structures as these relate to aging and to such issues as retirement, mental illness, the nursing home industry and the economics of aging, and with how these and other phenomena shape the experience of old age in our society.

Following an examination of the dominant and competing paradigms in gerontology presented in Chapter 2, we examine the political economy of aging in America with particular attention to the significance of the power structure and the creation, growth, and subsequent "crisis" of the welfare state. Explorations of the relationship between social class and age constitute a major theme running throughout the book. In these discussions, a political economic conception of class will be utilized in which our concern is not merely with what members of different classes derive from the system in income and resources, but also with their relative control (or lack thereof) over policy, resources, and other people [1].

The difficulties inherent in relating the concept of class specifically to the aged are discussed by Estes *et al.* in Chapter 2 and by Navarro in Chapter 3. As Navarro notes, a particular problem lies in the dominant notion that the main criteria dividing our society into differentially powerful groups are race, sex, and age. The large scale neglect of social class as a criteria—indeed as the *primary* criteria for how power is distributed in the United States—contributes to false notions of the relative "classless" nature of our society, obscuring a critical link between the majority of members of different ethnic, sex, and age groups.

As noted in Chapter 2, the issue of class and age becomes further clouded when it is realized that aging policy in the United States is based in part on the assumption that the elderly themselves constitute a distinct and relatively homogeneous class [3, 12]. Such an approach treats the aged as a dependent class of individuals, separate and apart from the productive sector of the economy. It further spawns age segregated programs and services that increase both the dependent position of the aged and the potential for intergenerational conflicts. Such policy does not deal seriously with class and other social differences and inequities among the elderly. Yet these differences are critical and must be confronted, just as we must confront the implications of retirement and other aspects of old age for class relationships.

The concept and reality of social control of the elderly is further developed and refined by Evans and Williamson in Chapter 4. As these authors note, any discussion of the relationship between the individual and society ultimately raises the question: "Whose interests are best served by a society's organizational arrangements and how do those not well served come to accept boundaries or controls on their options?" Whether one looks to Durkheim [13] or to Marx [14], social stratification and the consequent unequal distribution of resources and power are seen to constitute the major mechanisms by which individuals' options are differentially limited and controlled.

Without negating the existence of strong intra-group differences among the elderly, Evans and Williamson construct a strong argument that "the community whose interests are represented and served by existing social arrangements within American society is the community of adults under age seventy, to the detriment of those who are older." While acknowledging that the aged have benefitted economically as a consequence of programs like Social Security, Medicare, and Medicaid, they point out that such gains have not been without cost. Increased dependence on and control by the state and its caretakers are viewed as constituting a high price to pay for the material benefits derived through Social Security and the expansion of welfare programs in the 1960's and early 1970's.

Similarly, the rise of a bureaucracy of caregivers and the role of both caregivers and gerontologists as agents of social control are seen as problematic, since by their very existence they serve to underscore the separateness of older Americans with concomitant prolongation of their definition and labeling as a problem group.

SOCIAL CONTROL AND
CARE OF THE ELDERLY

While the social creation of the "problem" of old age is cast in sharpest relief in capitalist nations, the creation and reinforcement of the social dependency of the elderly may also be seen in state socialist countries. Indeed, as Walker notes in Chapter 5, structurally enforced economic dependency is a predominant characteristic of the elderly in industrial societies.

Drawing most heavily on the experiences of Great Britain, Walker examines the central role of the state in relation to dependency, the care of the elderly and the division of labor within the family. While the state is seen to provide some direct support where necessary in care of the elderly, it at the same time stigmatizes the poor and dependent in order to protect itself from more extensive demands from families, which remain the primary caregivers. Conflicts between the dependency of elders and changes in the status and aspirations of women are among the tensions seen to coincide with a period of sharp restrictions in state support for health and social services. Within this context, the future of community care and the assumptions underlying its provisions, must be carefully reevaluated.

The issues of structurally enforced dependency and social control of the elderly raised in Chapters 4 and 5 are further developed by Dowd, with specific attention to mental illness among the aged. Without discounting the utility of such notions as stigma and negative labeling, Dowd notes that these approaches are of little value to our understanding of aging if they fail to probe more deeply into the ways in which such labels "reflect and legitimate the marginal economic position of old people in modern society." Both the present economic position of the elderly and the earlier (pre-retirement) social class position of the older person have a major effect on mental health in old age. Consequently, a political economic approach to aging and mental health is seen as, of necessity, beginning with an understanding of the ways in which the nature and scope of mental illness is affected by the organization of work in capitalist societies.

Medicalization as a primary means of formal social control is discussed by Evans and Williamson and further by Dowd in his examination of the differential treatment of mental illness in young and old patients. The disproportionate allocation of mentally ill elders to custodial type treatments is, according to Dowd, "inevitable," as long as the physical and emotional decline observed in aged patients is viewed as a normal part of human aging, rather than as, in many cases, pathologically symptomatic of economic disadvantage.

The prevalence of biological and biomedical problem definitions of aging further reinforce conceptions of aging as an individual, and largely a medical problem. As noted by Estes [3], this "medicalization" of aging helps explain, in part, the genesis of health policies "that have benefitted doctors, hospitals, and insurance companies far more than they have the elderly."

In the United States, an understanding of those policies is best gained through an historical look at the half century of attempts to enact some form of national health insurance. In Chapter 7, Brown provides this historical context within which the country's Medicare and Medicaid programs are examined. Enacted in the mid-1960's, Medicare and Medicaid reflected in part a growing national concern with equity in health care. Yet there were, as Brown notes, "drastically different political responses" to these programs of "earned" and "public assistance" health insurance respectively. The unforeseen skyrocketting of costs associated with the Medicaid program in particular led cost containment to replace equity as the dominant concern of legislators in subsequent decision making surrounding both programs.

While Medicare and Medicaid did succeed in improving access to health and medical care for the elderly and the poor, a substantial "medi-gap" remained, with continued inequities in the health status of the nation's poor.

An unforeseen consequence of the passage of the Medicare and Medicaid legislation was a dramatic increase in the profitability of nursing homes. Indeed, as Vladeck has pointed out, the existing nursing home industry is "almost entirely a creation of public policy," with two-thirds of total nursing home revenues coming from government sources [15].

In Chapter 8, Harrington examines the nursing home industry in the United States, with particular attention to the influence of the profit motive on its growth and organization, and on quality of care issues and the lack of viable alternatives to institutional care of the frail elderly. As she notes, the multi-billion dollar nursing home business accounts for the fastest growing portion of the Medicaid budget. As a highly organized body with extensive lobbying and litigation capability, the nursing home industry has been able to promote weak regulations and other public policies favorable to its own interests. The phenomenal growth of nursing home corporations is particularly important in this regard, with current estimates suggesting that five to ten corporations will control 50 percent of all nursing home beds by 1990.

As Harrington points out, the demand for services continues to be artificially inflated by restrictive home care reimbursement policies which might otherwise provide humane options to institutionalization for many frail elders. Moreover, those alternatives which do exist (e.g., adult day health care) are in danger of themselves becoming simply another component of the nursing home industry as the latter moves to expand its influence over the entire long term care delivery system.

"COMPASSIONATE AGEISM"

In the mid-1970's public outrage over fraud and abuse in the nursing home industry played an important role in focusing attention on the plight of a small segment of the elderly population—the 5 percent to 6 percent of individuals aged sixty-five and above who reside in long-term care facilities. An unfortunate by-product of the increased visibility of the nursing home population, however, may have been the perpetuation of preexisting myths and generalizations concerning the aged as a decrepit and politically impotent social group.

In Chapter 9, Binstock examines the historical origins of scapegoating of the aged in America, noting that "compassionate stereotypes" of the elderly were erected as early as the Townsend movement of the 1930's to draw attention to the special needs of many elderly for income maintenance programs. Images of the aged as "poor, frail, objects of discrimination and above all deserving" were utilized by aging advocates from the 1930's through 1970's to help gain visibility for this group and to garner needed resources.

While such "compassionate ageism" succeeded to some extent in meeting its goals, it also led to an obscuring of individual and subgroup differences among the aged, who were viewed by the American public as an homogeneous group, to be dealt with through homogenized, age separatist policies and programs.

Not surprisingly, as Binstock notes, such "tabloid thinking" and its policy consequences set the stage for a new set of stereotypes about the elderly during the current era of fiscal crisis and retrenchment. The earlier stereotypes of the aged as frail, "deserving poor" individuals, impotent as a political force, gave way by the late 1970's to a new set of axioms: The aged, we are now told, are relatively well off, a potent political force and a costly burden on the rest of society. Binstock's careful analysis of the new axioms about the aged make clear their fallacious and dangerous nature. The scapegoating that they reflect and reinforce is seen to divert attention from more fundamental problems, such as unemployment, inflation and declining economic productivity, and to allow us to ignore the problematic aspects of existing public policies for the aged.

POLITICS OR DEMOGRAPHY?

Scapegoating of the aged and concern over their costliness to the rest of society is perhaps nowhere better demonstrated than in the arena of Social Security. As Myles notes in Chapter 10, however, the current concern over the future of old age security is, in reality, "a symptom of a larger conflict over the proper role of the democratic state in the market economy."

In both North America and Western Europe, optimism in the post-war welfare state gave way to radical reassessments by the mid-1970's in the wake of a protracted economic recession. Old age security programs, which in the United States comprised almost three-quarters of all income maintenance expenditures, came under particular scrutiny and attack.

Yet to equate the nature and scope of the backlash with the size of the elderly population or with levels of public spending on its behalf is an oversimplification. As Myles points out, capitalist countries with the proportionately largest elderly populations—Germany, Austria, and Sweden—have experienced among the least amount of popular resistance to rising welfare costs.

To understand the intense concern over the costs of Social Security in the United States, one must bear in mind Myles' contention that like all other old age policies, Social Security is distributional in nature, and hence reflects the "current arrangement for managing the contradictions of a democratic state in a market economy." As he further points out:

> Both the right to retire—and hence to become old—and the rights of retirement are today the product of national legislation. *Politics, not demography, now determines the size of the elderly population and the material conditions of its existence.* (Emphasis added.)

That "politics, not demography" determines how old age is defined in our society is further substantiated in Graebner's comprehensive history of retirement in the United States [16]. In Chapter 11, Graebner locates the origins of American age discrimination in the late 18th century, with its rise to prominence as a social phenomenon occurring a century later. The competitive nature of the economy and the move toward a shorter work week; subsequent continued technological change; the "youth cult" of the 1920's; and the unemployment of the Great Depression all increased the meaning and significance of discrimination against older workers in the American economy.

Beginning in the late 1800's, economic theorists, medical researchers, and the scientific management school of business and industry combined to provide an "empirical" rationale for the discriminatory practices of the day. While the positive attributes of older workers were recognized in some studies, the overriding consensus was that the labor force must be reconstituted, creating in the process a new social category: the superannuated elderly [17]. Indeed, retirement in advance of physiological decline was unpredecented in the history of industrial societies and only became institutionalized when employers saw this procedure as a simple and legal means to rid themselves of their most expensive workers.

DOUBLE JEOPARDY

While discriminatory practices and policies such as mandatory retirement affect the elderly on an aggregate level, they also differentially affect subgroups within the category of the aged. National sample survey data from the National Council on Aging reveal, for example, that the low income elderly are significantly more likely to have been forcibly retired than their wealthier counterparts [18]. Similarly, older women and ethnic minority group members face the "double jeopardy" involved in being old and non-white, or old and female—conditions which often translate into dramatically lower incomes and multiple societal disadvantages.

American's older women represent a critical case in point. Nearly three-quarters of all persons sixty-five and over who are below poverty line are women. In 1980, older women had the highest official poverty rate of any age group (19%), with their average annual income falling below $5,000. For older minority women, the picture is bleaker still. Two-thirds of elderly black women were officially below poverty line in 1980, with 83 percent either below or "near the poverty threshold." [19].

These kinds of statistics are not new, and given the deplorable picture they paint, Lewis and Butler were prompted to ask, back in 1972, "Why is Women's Lib Ignoring Old Women?" The original article in which they posed that question was submitted for publication to *MS* Magazine more than a decade ago and was rejected. It was subsequently published in an academic journal[1] [20] and is reprinted in this volume (Chapter 12) because the issues it raised remain of central importance to an understanding of the cultural, social, political, and economic meanings attached to being old and female in America today.

In Chapter 13 Estes, Gerard, and Clarke examine more deeply one particular facet of being old and female in their discussion of women and the economics of aging. The "feminization of poverty"—a phrase that gained currency in the late 1970's primarily with respect to young single mothers—here is seen to have at least equal applicability to older women in our society. The cumulative effects of wage discrimination over a lifetime, continued inequities in social security, and disincentives for community-based family support are among the facts of

---

[1] A slightly different version of this article also appeared in the *National Observer*, July 29, 1972.

life making inadequate income the most serious problem faced by America's older women. As the fastest growing segment in our society and the single poorest group in our population, women sixty-five and over are particularly symbolic of the poverty of policy in our nation with respect to equity, equality, and human dignity.

The particular inequities surrounding women's retirement are discussed in Chapter 14. Such phenomena as the dual labor market and the sexual division of labor are seen to importantly influence the ways in which retirement is experienced by women and the meaning which it consequently may hold.

Social class differences in women's retirement are examined in this chapter, as are the differences which may manifest themselves as a consequence of retirement under different societal economic conditions. Women's retirement thus is used both to further our understanding of structured gender inequities in old age, and to demonstrate the utility of a political economy perspective for understanding the differential impacts of retirement on sub-populations within society.

BUDGET CUTBACKS AND THE AGED

As numerous investigators have made clear [21-24], the inequalities resulting from public policy have worsened under the Reagan Administration. The final chapters of this collection, together with the earlier chapter by Navarro, focus on the major policy shifts under the Reagan Administration and their meaning and significance for the elderly.

As Navarro points out, these policy shifts do *not* represent, as is popularly argued, a "mandate" by the American people to cut back government programs and services for the aged. Rather, opinion poll data from 1970 to 1982 indicate "overwhelming and undiminished support" by the majority of Americans for such programs, and even for their expansion. To understand the genesis and the nature of cuts in programs for the elderly, one must look not to a public mandate, but rather to the power structure of the United States—a topic which, as Navarro argues, is all but ignored in most discussion of such phenomena.

In Chapter 15, Estes examines some of the specific social constructions of reality in the 1980's that have helped shape recent public policy for the aged. The political declaration of fiscal crisis at the federal level, the perception of decentralization as a partial "solution" to economic problems in the United States and the perception of old age as a social problem best approached through individual level interventions each is seen as having a profound effect on policy developments for the elderly during the current era of fiscal conservatism.

In Chapter 16, Minkler looks further at the tendency of many policy makers to scapegoat the poor and the elderly as "causes" of the "fiscal crisis." Unlike the victim blaming of the 1960's and early 1970's [25], which defined "the elderly" as a social problem and devised solutions (e.g., Medicare and Medicaid) for dealing with that problem, the victim blaming of the 1980's defines these earlier "solutions" as part of the problem: not only are the aged problematic, but ameliorative programs are "busting the federal budget" and in need of dismantling and/or shifting to other levels of government or to the private sector.

The new victim blaming, while bearing important similarities to the old, is seen as likely to prove more devastating in its effects on oppressed groups in American society including, importantly, the elderly.

CONCLUSION

The picture that emerges through this book is a sobering one. Aging in America has been labeled a social problem, and one whose origins lie primarily in the biological and physiological decline of the aging individual. The dependency of the elderly for the most part is not seen as socially created, but as rooted in individual problems or inadequacies, and hence as amenable to individual level interventions. Finally, the viewing of the aged as a class apart from the rest of society and the resultant development of age separatist policies and approaches, not only reinforce the dependent position of the aged, but also deflect attention from the more fundamental problems plaguing our society.

The political economy of aging perspective represents one attempt to turn current thinking about the problem of aging on its head, examining first and foremost the assumptions underlying our current problem definitions and our attempted solutions to those problems. Viewed in such a way, the problem becomes not "the aged" but the needs of capitalist society. "Solutions" such as mandatory retirement, Social Security, and Medicare and Medicaid legislation come into focus not simply—or even primarily—as humanitarian gestures, but rather as formidable instruments of social control designed primarily to meet the dominant needs of the economy. Indeed, even such largely unquestioned problems as mental illness in old age take on new meaning when viewed within the context of the exclusion of the aged from labor markets and their consequent special status as "strangers" in a capitalist economy.

The extent to which mental illness in old age, poverty in old women, and profitability in the nursing home industry each reflect the class structure of our society is reinforced as these and other facets of aging in America are examined within the context of broader historical, sociopolitical, and economic realities. The scapegoating of the aged and the magnitude and severity of recent budget cuts in policies and programs for the elderly (and particularly for those who are poorest) take on special meaning when viewed from a political economy perspective.

If this book succeeds in raising questions about the prevailing assumptions concerning aging and the nature, purposes, and consequences of aging policies in the United States, it will have been successful in reaching one of its objectives. If it stimulates debate and furthers the development of the political economy of aging as a major theoretical approach in gerontology and related disciplines, it will have accomplished another major objective.

It is our hope, however, that readers of this volume will also find that it contains some important messages for practice, and for helping to bring about change in those conditions that underlie and perpetuate the dependent position of the elderly in our society.

One such pivotal message centers on the need for developing educational strategies based on political-economic analyses and directed at those oppressed groups currently placed in competition with one another. As Navarro notes, interest group mentality and behavior must be replaced with a clear realization that the majority of male and female, young and old, white, black, and brown people in our society are members of the working class, and as such constitute a potentially powerful force for change. With Maggie Kuhn, we must recognize that such change requires both education and mobilization—and that the time is now.

REFERENCES

1. C. L. Estes, et al., *Political Economy, Health, and Aging*, Little-Brown and Company, New York, 1984.
2. J. Walton, Urban Political Economy, *Comparative Urban Research*, 7, p. 9, 1979.
3. C. L. Estes, *The Aging Enterprise*, Jossey-Bass Publishers, San Francisco, California, 1979.
4. E. Cumming and W. E. Henry, *Growing Old: The Process of Disengagement*, Basic Books, New York, 1961.
5. R. J. Havinghurst, Successful Aging, in *Process of Aging*, R. Williams, C. Tibbits, and W. Donahue (eds.), Atherton, New York, 1963.
6. A. M. Rose and W. P. Peterson (eds.), *Older People and Their Social Worlds*, Davis, Philadelphia, 1965.
7. J. E. Trela, Some Political Consequences of Senior Center and Other Age Group Memberships, *Gerontologist*, 2, pp. 118-123, 1971.
8. M. W. Riley, M. Johnson, and A. Foner, A Sociology of Stratification, in *Aging and Society*, Volume 3, Basic Books, New York, 1972.
9. A. Walker, The Social Creation of Poverty and Dependency in Old Age, *Journal of Social Policy*, 9, pp. 49-75, 1980.
10. A. P. Simpson, Social Class Correlates of Old Age, *Sociology and Social Research*, 45, pp. 131-139, 1961.
11. D. McAdam, Coping with Aging or Combatting Ageism?, in *Aging: Coping with Medical Issues*, A. Kolker and P. Ahmed, Elsevier Biomedical, New York, 1982.
12. J. J. Dowd, *Stratification Among the Aged*, Brooks/Cole Publishing Company, Monterey, California, p. 33, 1980.
13. E. Durkheim, *The Rules of Sociological Method*, translated by S. A. Soloray and J. H. Mueller, Free Press, New York, 1958.
14. K. Marx, *Selected Writings in Sociology and Social Philosophy*, T. B. Bottomore and M. Rubel (eds.), Penguin, Baltimore, Maryland, 1964.
15. B. Vladeck, *Unloving Care: The Nursing Home Tragedy*, Basic Books, Inc., Publishers, New York, p. 4, 1980.

16. W. Graebner, *A History of Retirement: The Meaning and Function of an American Institution 1885-1978*, Yale University Press, New Haven, Connecticut, 1980.
17. J. Myles, The Aged and the Welfare State: An Essay in Political Demography, paper presented at the meeting of the International Sociological Association, 1981.
18. Harris, Louis and Associates, *The Myth and Reality of Aging in America*, National Council on Aging, Washington, D.C., 1976.
19. National Women's Law Center, *Inequality of Sacrifice: The Impact of the Reagan Budget on Women*, Washington, D.C., March 16, 1983.
20. M. Lewis and R. Butler, Why Is Women's Lib Ignoring Old Women?, *Journal of Aging and Human Development*, *3*:3, pp. 223-231, 1972.
21. A. I. Blaustein (ed.), *The American Promise: Equal Justice and Economic Opportunity*, Transaction Books, New Brunswick, New Jersey, 1982.
22. V. Navarro, The Crisis of the International Capitalist Order and Its Implications for the Welfare State, *International Journal of Health Services*, *12*:2, pp. 169-190, 1982.
23. The Winners and Losers under Reaganomics, *The Washington Post* (United Auto Workers of America), *21*:33, pp. 1-3, 1981.
24. F. F. Piven and R. A. Cloward, *The New Class War: Reagan's Attack on the Welfare State and Its Consequences*, Pantheon Books, New York, 1982.
25. W. Ryan, *Blaming the Victim*, Random House, New York, 1976.

PART I. INTRODUCTION TO THE POLITICAL ECONOMY OF AGING

In this introductory section, several different approaches to the political economy of aging are presented. In Chapter 2, Estes, Swan and Gerard present the political economy perspective, broadly defined, as an important alternative to the dominant gerontological paradigm which focuses on the micro or individual level largely in isolation from broader political, social and economic realities. Under the new paradigm, the "problem" of aging is set forth in structural rather than individual terms, on the premise that the way in which aging is experienced is conditioned by one's location in the social structure and by the social and economic factors which affect that placement.

We next turn to a special application of the political economy perspective with Navarro's examination in Chapter 3 of the context and meaning of recent government cuts for the elderly. Written initially as a Keynote address for the 1982 annual meeting of the American Public Health Association, Chapter 3 locates the position of the elderly in American society, and the current economic crisis, squarely within a broad social class framework.

Current policies which have resulted in the weakening of the welfare state are seen to have had as their aim the division and weakening of the working class. To counteract such policies, the author suggests that the "interest group mentality" prevalent in the United States be replaced by an appreciation among the majority of Americans of their shared working class status and hence of their collective power.

The political economy of the current politics of retrenchment and its effects on the elderly is a topic to which we will return later in this volume. It is introduced here, however, both in view of its centrality to discussions of aging in the 1980's, and as an illustration of the usefulness of a political economy perspective to an understanding of this important phenomenon.

Implicit in each of the first three chapters in this section is an appreciation of the way in which existing social arrangements represent and best serve the interests of certain groups in the society to the detriment of others. The elaborate systems of social control, critical to the effective functioning of such arrangements, must be carefully examined if we are to understand how those not well served come to accept the limits placed on their options. In Chapter 4, Evans and Williamson trace the theoretical development of the concept of social control, and apply it to the position of the elderly in the United States. Using Social Security as a case in point, they demonstrate how what is widely perceived as a humanitarian reform was in fact fashioned at least as much as a formidable instrument of social control. The theme of social control of the elderly, introduced in some detail in this chapter, will be seen to run through much of the analysis presented in later chapters of this book.

CHAPTER 2

Dominant and Competing Paradigms in Gerontology: Towards a Political Economy of Aging

CARROLL L. ESTES
JAMES H. SWAN
LENORE E. GERARD

THE ORIGINS AND INFLUENCE OF SOCIAL SCIENCE PARADIGMS AND THEIR ROLE IN GERONTOLOGY

In tracking the development and elaboration of sociological theory, Alvin Gouldner persuasively argued that social theory develops as a consequence of the interaction between technical development (e.g., research methodologies, empirical findings, knowledge), and extra-technical sources (e.g., changes in sentiments, domain assumptions, and personal realities of the theorist and those around her or him) [1].

The conceptualization of old age, as well as the potential of the aged for securing power are "socially" created in that they are not determined solely by objective facts. Rather, they are created by: 1) the interpretation and ordering of perceptions of those facts into paradigms; and 2) the power and influence of the perceivers and interpreters of the data. In this sense, the aged do not have any problems or potential for political influence other than that which the experts, including the scientists, have "given" or defined as real for them. These are limited by available research technologies and current theories which channel the conceptualization, conduct, analysis, integration, and explanation of data, as well as the dominant social, economic, and political concerns and intellectual fashions of the day.

Little attention has been given in the U.S. to the socio-relational aspects of gerontological knowledge and to the technical and extra-technical sources underlying its development. Nor has much emphasis been given in gerontology to the

25

important role of social scientists and their perspectives in delimiting dominant world views of what is possible. For example, researchers contribute to "the social construction of reality" [2] about what growing old is like and about what changes and responses are likely to occur with age. As such, they provide central notions of what the social problem of old age "really" is and what the range of possible individual and social responses to aging may be. In this way, the development of scientific knowledge both facilitates and contains future action and social change.

UNDERSTANDING THE GERONTOLOGICAL FOCUS

Many U.S. social policies designed to meet the needs of the aged, receive support and legitimation from theoretical perspectives that have long dominated gerontological research and training in the United States. These perspectives include the disengagement, activity, and developmental life-cycle theories.

A brief review of these theories of aging and their policy implications is illustrative. Disengagement theory prescribes either no policy interventions that aid the withdrawal of the individual and society from each other. Under such a framework, retirement policies receive legitimation, as do other separatist approaches. Disengagement theory provides the rationalization for a purely symbolic policy because both society and the individual are seen as better off as a consequence of the exclusion of the aged. In contrast, activity theory, which is essentially a classless and universal prescription for continued activity in old age, supports policies that assist in the social integration of the aged. Policies focusing on recreational and social activities, are preferred under the tenets of activity theory. In a somewhat similar way, developmental theories, which are based on the "live and let live" principle, emphasize policies that would enable people to maintain continuity in status throughout the life cycle. This theory would endorse highly individualized social policies to meet each individual's needs.

Overall, social scientists in the United States have effectively legitimized incrementalist and individualistic approaches to public policy for the elderly, and both social and political gerontological thought in America reflects that. This emphasis has spawned a research tradition concerned with social integration, cohort effects, and biomedical models of aging. The biomedical approach that has gained ascendancy is reflected in the research priorities of the major federal research institutes that seek knowledge of hypothesized biological and physiological sources of decline with age. The biomedical theories not only individualize and medicalize old age, but also they overlook the relationship between socioeconomic status, the economy and health. Age stratification theory, although attending to structure via the notions of age cohort and generational succession, has spawned a research tradition focused on differentiating the effects of age, period and cohort.

The dominance of the biomedical approach has been offset somewhat by the contribution of social gerontology in studying the relationship between the elderly and society, particularly such structures as the family, community, and economy. Social gerontological theories, however, have focused largely on individuals and their role loss, economic dependence, adjustment, and isolation in old age [3-9]. Levin and Levin have shown how these theories have contributed toward blaming the aged for their condition [10].

American gerontological perspectives lend little support to social policies that might dramatically alter a distribution of resources in favor of the aged or of different classes of aged for such policies are irrelevant to gerontological theories. Such theories give little theoretical and empirical attention to the social creation of dependency through forced retirement and its functions for the economy, or to the production of senility and the economic, political and social control functions of such processes.

Emphasis on the individual is also represented by lacunae in U.S. political gerontology. The gerontological focus on power and politics has offered little critical direction to theory, research, or policy. In the U.S. there have been no unique theoretical issues of concern to political gerontology—these being drawn largely from the disciplines of political science, sociology and psychology. Apparent influences are the dominant 20th century American sociological and political science emphases on formal political institutions and democratic participation, and psychology's emphasis on the attitudinal and other psychological correlates of participation. These are reflected in studies of voting behavior, alienation, formal political participation and political socialization that have been reanalyzed in light of the aging question [11]. The individual has been the primary unit of analysis in most of this research—although the findings have been useful for "the system" as a barometer of citizen discontent and in validating democracy via legitimate political participation. To these orientations, the largely psychological concerns of social gerontology and emergent theories of aging have influenced studies of old-age politics.

Another thrust which sociologists and political scientists have drawn upon for political gerontology in the U.S. has been the study of interest groups, and the government/interest group interface [12]. Far less attention has been given to social movements and old age. There are a few exceptions [13-16]. These have been fragmentary and limited largely to case study approaches [17, 18]. There is a dearth of empirical research on the linkage of old age interests to the economic and political structure and on the political organization and consequences of old age interests at the state and local level [6].

TOWARDS A POLITICAL ECONOMY OF AGING

The central challenge of a political economy of aging is to move beyond a critique of conventional gerontology and to develop an understanding of the character and significance of variations in the treatment of the aged and to relate these to broader systematic trends. Another important task is to understand how the aging process itself is affected by the systematic treatment and location of the aged in society.

A political economy of aging emphasizes the broad implications of economic life for the aged and for societal treatment of the aged, and both for different classes of aged. Political economy is understood to be:

... the study of the interrelationships between the polity, economy, and society, or more specifically, the reciprocal influences among government ... the economy, social classes, strata, and status groups. The central problem of the political economy perspective is the manner in which the economy and polity interact in a relationship of reciprocal causation affecting the distribution of social goods [19].

Drawing upon the approach developed by Walton [19-20], the political economy of aging focuses on the nature of and intersections between aging status and class politics, which can be understood only in terms of their structural bases and how they are conditioned by the socio-economic and political environment.

The political economy approach is distinguished from the dominant gerontological perspective by viewing the problem of aging as a structural one. Walker provides an excellent summary of two views of the problem of aging and the consequences for social policy [21]. The individualistic view assumes the overriding importance of the market in distributing rewards and in determining socio-economic status. The dependency status of the elderly is explained by the individual and his or her lifetime (and work) behavior patterns. The theory, simply stated, is that "you get what you earned." Numerous U.S. studies on status and income maintenance adopt this approach [22-24]. Most policy interventions in the U.S. reflect this perspective and, in the case of the aged, promote age segregated policies and services for a detached and dependent minority.

In contrast, the structural view of aging starts with the proposition that the status and resources of the elderly, and even the trajectory of the aging process itself, are conditioned by one's location in the social structure and the economic and political factors that affect it. The dependency of the elderly is to be understood in the labor market and the social relations that it produces—and these as they change with age. Policy interventions from this perspective would be directed towards various institutionalized structures of society, in particular the labor market.[1]

Most social gerontologists share the individualistic perspective, with its

... emphasis on trying to explain individual aging within a structure, and especially class structure, (accepting it) without question rather than trying to explain that structure as a necessary precondition in the exposition of a theory about aging and the aged [25].

---

[1] This is not to say that structure must be seen as totally determining the individual as simply the victim of social forces. Our purpose, in this paper, however is to argue against the totally individualistic approaches which have dominated gerontology.

Over the past decade, a number of articles and books began to appear that laid the initial groundwork for the structural perspective in aging—Walker [21, 26] and Townsend [25, 27-29] in Britain; Myles [30-32] in Canada; Guillemard [33-35] in France; and Dowd [9], Estes [3], Evans and Williamson [36], Olson [37], and Tussing [38] in the U.S. The issue of the role and power of the state, constraints on state intervention and its legitimating function in the distribution of benefits has not been examined extensively to public policy for the aged, although Ginsberg [39], O'Connor [40], Gough [41], and others have addressed these issues indirectly in their analyses of the role and function of the welfare state. In the health field, major contributions to a political economy framework have been made [42-48].

THE RELATION BETWEEN CLASS AND AGE

In the gerontological literature, Dowd has examined exchange, power, and class issues in the negotiation of exchange rates between the aged and others in society, noting that:

> ... the individual experience of growing old and the nature of age relations vary so significantly by social class that there is a need for unified analysis in which both age *and* class are considered [9, pp. 21, 22].

Estes' analysis of the class basis of old age policies in the U.S. raises the question of who benefits and seeks to show that state health and social welfare benefits reflect and reinforce existing inequities among the aged [3]. Guillemard has examined similar issues in France, concluding that a new stage of life has been created by the necessity of capital to retire increased numbers of workers at an increasingly lower age [33, 34].

Relation to the means of production, the sector of the economy in which they work, and the duration and type of work performed all determine the relative status of the aged and their source of income [26]. It is not surprising then to learn that women and minorities are among the most disadvantaged elderly in the U.S. [49-51].

A crucial task for the political economy of aging is to examine the concept of class and how it relates more specifically to the aged. According to Giddens [52], there is widespread confusion and ambiguity in the use of the term "class." This seems particularly so for some who have attempted an analysis of aged and class [9, 53]. In the U.S., aging policy is based on the assumption that the aged themselves are a separate, distinct class. This approach treats the aged as a dependent class of individuals separate and apart from the productive sector of the economy of which they are no longer participants. In this sense, class refers to the aged as a social group who share one common denominator: they are all over sixty years of age and soon thereafter are summoned into retirement. The consequence of such a policy which fosters age segregated programs and services, is that it enhances both the dependency status of the elderly and intergenerational conflict [3].

The problem in relating Marxist class theory to the aged, according to Dowd, is that the aged are no longer in the productive sector of the economy [9]. Yet this is precisely the point of examination which is critical to a political economy approach [25, 26, 33, 34]. Many have observed that the plight of the aged, i.e., the economic inequality and dependency status, is a result of inadequate benefits and employment practices. Yet, benefit levels and employment policies are outcomes of the economic structure. The political economy perspective points to the structural dependency of the aged arising from conditions in the labor market and the stratification and organization of work and society. Walker specifically has argued that it is not age itself which determines retirement but the socially constructed relationship between age, the division of labor and the labor market [26].

The issue of class and age is an important one, both because of the need for class analysis in the political economics of aging, and because of the specific problems of social gerontology. Under this issue, we must consider both the differential implications by class of retirement and old age, and the implications of retirement and old age for class relationships. This is true, in part, because of retirement, and in part because of a wider disattachment of the aged from the productive process and from society in general, and the treatment of the aged as a group apart from society with different needs than other social groups. The fact that most of the aged must face life on a fixed income is itself both a reflection of class relations and an important factor to consider in an analysis of class and aging. Thus, the class analysis of aging may present different problems than does a more general analysis of the class dynamics of society; but a consideration of the class theory needed to "account for" the aged may throw light on class analysis in general—especially as it deals with other "non-productive" groups.

There are many Marxist expositions of the concept of class. Particularly useful for the present analysis are Wright [54-56], Ehrenreich and Ehrenreich [57], and Poulantzas [58]. Wright clarifies the present debates by distinguishing three basic features of Marxist definitions of class: 1) classes are defined in relational rather than in gradational terms; 2) the social relations that define classes are analyzed primarily in terms of the social organization of economic relations; and 3) class relations are primarily defined by the social relations of production rather than by the social relations of exchange [55]. Each of these themes are of importance to the consideration of class and age; and all of the following discussion is predicated upon the assumption of a relational rather than gradational definition of class.

Wright departs somewhat from a traditional Marxist view of class [53]. Wright puts the background as purely "juridical" the categories of "legal ownership of property," "legal status of being employer of labor power," and "sale of one's own labor power." The active "substantive processes comprising class relations" Wright finds to be: "control over investments and resources," "control over the physical means of production," and "control over the labor power of others." He further departs from the traditional view in his defining of "contradictory class relations":

> ... the three processes which constitute capitalist social relations of production do not always perfectly coincide. This non-coincidency of the dimensions of class relations defines the contradictory locations within class relations [54, p. 74].

Wright's approach is centered upon the labor process. Thus, whatever its utility in analyzing capitalism as a whole, its utility may be questioned for examining the political economy of aging. In particular, for those aged who have retired, Wright's "substantive processes" of class relations are not of immediate importance. Such processes were indeed parts of elders' class background before retirement; and they may define the class context of the families of many elders. But for the aged the major dimension of class relations, among those noted by Wright, is the "juridical" category of legal ownership of property. Although this is important to the class analysis of aging, such a one-dimensionality does not seem sufficient to the task of analyzing the wider social aspects of class and age.

Poulantzas argues that classes are determined not only by economic relations but also by political and ideological factors [58]. In addition to an economic dimension of "extortion of surplus value," classes are to be defined by relations of domination/subordination in political and ideological spheres. Poulantzas' approach has useful elements for the analysis of class and age. In particular, the dimensions of political and ideological domination might be of importance in considering class relations among the aged and of the aged with the non-aged [33, 34]. However, Poulantzas' focus is upon the labor process, and the terms are defined narrowly. In fact it could be argued that his criteria exclude all non-working aged from the working class; though the pre-retirement history of the aged could be seen to have defined their class positions in political and ideological terms. One would still wish for a definition of class which would take into account the social and economic dynamics which directly involved the aged qua aged.

Ehrenreich and Ehrenreich [57] propose a definition of class which, though it may be problematical in explaining the dynamics of capitalism [59] promises to be useful in defining class dynamics involving the aged. In addition to defining class in terms of a "common relation to the economic foundations of society," the Ehrenreichs define class as:

> ... characterized by a coherent social and cultural existence; members of a class share a common life style, educational background, kinship networks, consumption patterns, work habits, and beliefs [57, p. 11].

This definition of class may be of special importance to the analysis of class and age because it is concerned with dynamics which are still operating among those elders who are no longer in the workplace. In particular, it helps clarify the relationships of working class aged with the agents of public and private social welfare bureaucracies. Although the Ehrenreichs note that there is no way to simply define class for some categories of professional workers as a group, certain professional-client relationships can be seen as inherently class relationships.

Estes has argued that there exists an "aging enterprise" which assures that "the aged are often processed and treated as a commodity." [3, p. 2] Thus, the bureaucrats constituting the aging enterprise ensure that the aged will be dependent upon their services, and the class relationships fostered by their systems of services [60]. This dependency is a "unilateral dependency," in which bureaucratic structures "and the middle class bureaucrats by whom services usually are delivered, are the medium for interaction between members of lower social classes and the general society." [3, pp. 24-26] This system tends to isolate the aged from society because "the age-segregated policies that fuel the aging enterprise are socially divisive 'solutions' that single out, stigmatize, and isolate the aged from the rest of society." [3, pp. 2-3]

Thus, under the Ehrenreichs' definition of class, the relationships of working class elders with service bureaucracies can be seen as class relationships. And the functions of "middle-class bureaucrats," of the maintenance of social control over and of the dependency of the aged, can be seen as part of these class relationships. By this extension of the argument, the policies of the "aging enterprise" are not only class-based, rather they also constitute an important part of class relations, and of the reproduction of class relations, with respect to the elderly.

Given this discussion, a view of class and age may be considered. Any such view must be cognizant of a number of dynamics. As "being old" exists in the capitalist world, it is characterized by a disattachment from the productive process. Thus, retirement changes class dynamics by removing the aged from the immediate relations of the workplace. These relations, however, continue to "live" as a part of the individual retiree's personal history, and in the relationships among retirees with common working histories. Thus, as noted by Guillemard [33], the personal class history is of extreme importance to the aged—for example, affecting their post-retirement life expectancy. Nevertheless, this disattachment from the productive process means that the relations of the workplace do not constitute the primary dynamic of class relations for the aged.

Likewise, the dynamics of disattachment of the aged from the social relations of the productive process, dynamics which are broader than retirement alone, may divorce the aged from Wright's "substantive process" of class relations—including the control over investment and resources. Thus, the aged, even the wealthy aged, may be only involved in the "juridical" relationship of the ownership of property. The latter is in turn of extreme importance to the post-retirement lives of the aged in terms of their capacity to consume. Moreover, social welfare policy towards the aged further reproduces pre-existing class relationships, including those among the aged [3, 37, 61]. Therefore, the ownership of property, or of other sources of income, continue to be sources of class division among the aged; and these class divisions are reinforced by social welfare policy. But by Wright's argument, the ownership of wealth without the effective control over investment and over the physical means of production leaves even the wealthy elderly on the periphery of the class dynamics of the larger society.

The processes of disattachment from involvement in the productive process operate differently for the aged of different classes—a "differential process of devaluation." [61] Working class elders are more rapidly devalued in the labor market and in the society as a whole than are the aged of other classes. Thus, the relationship of class to age is itself dependent upon class status.

Finally, the dependent status of the aged subject them to a greater degree to the social relations of subordination to public and private agencies which act to reproduce capitalist culture and class relations. These agencies commodify the lives of the aged under the rubric of "services." Therefore, any analysis of class and age must concern itself with how the aged, whatever their previous background, are made dependent upon an aging enterprise and its agents, as well as how the aged are made differentially dependent according to their post-retirement class status.

CONCLUSION

Questions concerning the relation of age and class will require further investigation and analysis. Many other promising areas of inquiry from a political economy perspective, concern the role of aging policies within the context of capitalist development. For example, it will be important to examine the consequences of the segregation and devaluation of the aged via public policies, especially retirement policies in an era of economic decline. Another area would include the nature and outcomes of the intensifying conflict between the demands on the state arising from its function of facilitating accumulation; the pressure on the state to finance income and health costs for aged; the forms of fiscal austerity which will face governments for coming years (the effect on state services, the private economy, unemployment and social security); and the distributional impact of all these on different classes of aged.

It will be important also to take a critical look at the politics of aging, especially the politics and mobilization of the aged themselves. It will be important to distinguish empirically those conditions and situations under which class based coalitions emerge, overriding age interests, and those conditions in which status issues (e.g., age) dominate public policy. More complex, but equally significant, will be understanding the interconnections between class and status in political actions and social movements and their consequences for societal treatment of the aged and the aging process within it.

In summary, the political economy of aging proposed in this chapter as an alternative gerontological perspective would examine the structural conditions involved in aging and in the elaborations of aging policy. It would be concerned especially with class structures as they relate to aging, the isolation and alienation of the aged from society, their disengagement, senility, and institutionalization as a function of capitalism and the social relations it produces, and how all of these condition and shape the experience of old age itself.

REFERENCES

1. A. W. Gouldner, *The Coming Crisis in Western Sociology*, Basic Books, New York, 1970.
2. P. L. Berger and T. Luckmann, *The Social Construction of Reality*, Doubleday, New York, 1966.
3. C. L. Estes, *The Aging Enterprise*, Jossey-Bass, San Francisco, 1979.
4. _____, Political Gerontology, *Transaction Society*, *15*, pp. 43-49, July/ August 1978.
5. _____, Toward a Sociology of Political Gerontology, *Sociological Symposium*, *26*, pp. 1-27, Spring 1979.
6. C. L. Estes and H. E. Freeman, Strategies in the Design of Intervention, in *Handbook of Aging and the Social Sciences*, R. H. Binstock and E. Shanas (eds.), Van Nostrand, New York, 1976.
7. V. W. Marshall and J. A. Tindale, "Notes for a Radical Gerontology," paper presented at Gerontological Society, Louisville, Kentucky, 1975.
8. D. McAdam, "Coping with Aging or Combatting Agism?", paper presented at the Gerontological Society, San Diego, November 23, 1980.
9. J. Dowd, *Stratification among the Aged*, Brooks/Cole, Monterey, California, 1980.
10. J. Levin and W. C. Levin, *Ageism: Prejudice and Discrimination Against the Elderly*, Belmont, California, 1980.
11. A. Campbell, P. Converse, W. Miller, and D. Stokes, *The American Voter*, John Wiley, New York, 1960.
12. R. H. Binstock, Interest-Group Liberalism and the Politics of Aging, *Gerontologist*, *12*, pp. 265-280, 1972.
13. A. Pinner, P. Jacobs, and P. Selznick, *Old Age and Political Behavior: A Case Study*, University of California Press, Berkeley, 1959.
14. K. Putnam, *Old Age Politics in California*, Stanford University, Stanford, 1970.
15. S. L. Messinger, Organizational Transformation: A Case Study of a Declining Social Movement, *American Sociological Review*, *20*, pp. 3-10, 1955.
16. H. J. Pratt, *The Politics of Old Age*, University of Chicago, Chicago, 1976.
17. R. B. Hudson and R. Binstock, Political Systems and Aging, *The Politics of Old Age*, University of Chicago Press, 1976.
18. R. B. Hudson (ed.), *The Aging in Politics: Process and Policy*, Thomas, Springfield, Illinois, 1981.
19. J. Walton, Urban Political Economy, *Comparative Urban Research*, 7:1, p. 9, 1979.

20. _____, "Economic Crisis and Urban Austerity Issues in Research and Policy in the 1980's," paper presented at the Conference of Economic Crisis and Urban Austerity, Columbia University, New York, May 21-24, 1980.

21. A. Walker, The Social Creation of Poverty and Dependency in Old Age, *Journal of Social Policy*, *9*, pp. 49-75, 1980.

22. J. Henretta and R. Campbell, Status Attainment and Status Maintenance: A Case Study of Stratification in Old Age, *American Sociological Review, 41*, pp. 981-992, 1976.

23. R. J. Samuelson, Benefit Programs for the Elderly—Off Limits to Federal Budget, *National Journal*, October 3, 1981.

24. M. Baum and R. C. Baum, *Growing Old*, Prentice-Hall, New York, 1980.

25. P. Townsend, The Structured Dependency of the Elderly: A Creation of Social Policy in the Twentieth Century, *Aging and Society*, *1*, p. 6, 1981.

26. A. Walker, Towards a Political Economy of Old Age, *Ageing and Society, 1*, pp. 73-94, 1981.

27. P. Townsend, *The Last Refuge*, Routledge and Kegan Paul, London, 1962.

28. _____, *Poverty in the United Kingdom*, Penquin Books, Harmondsworth, Middlesex, 1979.

29. P. Townsend and D. Wedderburn, *The Aged in the Welfare State*, Bell, London, 1965.

30. J. F. Myles, "The Aged and the Welfare State: An Essay in Political Demography," paper presented at the International Sociological Association, Research Committee on Aging, Paris, July 8-9, 1981.

31. _____, The Aged, the State, and the Structure of Inequality, in *Structural Inequality in Canada*, J. Harp and J. Hofley (eds.), Prentice-Hall, Toronto, pp. 317-342, 1980.

32. _____, Income Inequality and Status Maintenance, *Research on Aging*, pp. 123-141, 1981.

33. A. M. Guillemard, "Retirement as a Social Process, Its Differential Effects Upon Behavior," communication presented to the 8th World Congress of Sociology, Toronto, Canada, August 21, 1974.

34. _____, "A Critical Analysis of Governmental Policies on Aging from a Marxist Sociological Perspective: The Case of France," Center for the Study of Social Movements, Paris, France, October 1977.

35. _____, The Making of Old Age Policy in France, in *Old Age and the Welfare State*, A. M. Guillemard (ed.), Sage, New York, International Sociological (forthcoming).

36. L. Evans and J. Williamson, Social Security and Social Control, *Generations*, pp. 18-20, Winter, 1981.

37. L. Olson, *Public Policy and Aging*, forthcoming.

38. A. Tussing, The Dual Welfare System, in *Social Realities*, L. Horowitz and C. Levy (eds.), Harper and Row, New York, 1971.

39. N. Ginsberg, *Class, Capital and Social Policy*, Macmillan, London, 1979.

40. J. O'Connor, *The Fiscal Crisis of the State*, St. Martin's, New York, 1973.

41. I. Gough, *The Political Economy of the Welfare State*, Macmillan Press, London, 1979.

42. S. Kelman (ed.), Special Section on Political Economy of Health, *International Journal of Health Services*, 5:4, pp. 535-642, 1975.
43. M. Renaud, On the Structural Constraints to State Intervention in Health, *International Journal of Health Services*, 5, pp. 559-571, 1975.
44. Review of Radical Political Economics, "Special Issue on the Political Economy of Health," 9, Spring 1977.
45. R. Alford, The Political Economy of Health Care: Dynamics Without Change, *Politics and Society*, 2, pp. 127-164, Winter 1972.
46. R. Lichtman, The Political Economy of Medical Care, in *The Social Organization of Health*, H. Dreitzel (ed.), New York, pp. 265-290.
47. V. Navarro, *Medicine Under Capitalism*, Prodist, New York, 1976.
48. V. Navarro (ed.), *Health and Medical Care in the U.S.: A Critical Analysis*, Baywood, New York, 1973.
49. M. Orshansky, "Poverty among America's Aged," testimony before the U.S. House Select Committee on Aging, Washington, D.C., August 9, 1978.
50. S. Crad and K. Foster, Income of the Population Aged 55 and Older, 1976, *Social Security Bulletin*, 42, pp. 16-32, 1979.
51. J. Abbott, Socioeconomic Characteristics of the Elderly: Some Black-White Differences, *Social Security Bulletin*, 40, pp. 16-42, 1977.
52. A. Giddens, *The Class Structure of the Advanced Societies*, Harper and Row, New York, 1975.
53. R. C. Atchley, Social Class and Aging, *Generations*, pp. 16-17, 34, Winter, 1981.
54. E. O. Wright, *Class, Crisis and the State*, Verso, London, 1978.
55. _____, Intellectuals and the Class Structure, in *Between Labor and Capital*, P. Walker (ed.), South End, Boston, p. 191, 1979.
56. _____, Varieties of Marxist Conceptions of Class Structure, *Politics and Society*, 9:3, pp. 323-370, 1980.
57. B. Ehrenreich and J. Ehrenreich, The Professional-Managerial Class, in *Between Labor and Capital*, P. Walker (ed.), South End, Boston, p. 5, 1979.
58. N. Poulantzas, *Classes in Contemporary Capitalism*, New Left Books, London, 1975.
59. A. Szymanski, J. Cohen, D. Noble, R. Schaeffer, and J. Weinstein, in *Between Labor and Capital*, South End, Boston, 1979.
60. G. Sjoberg, R. A. Brymer, and B. Farris, Bureaucracy and the Lower Class, *Sociology and Social Research*, 50, pp. 325-334, 1966.
61. G. Nelson, Perspective on Social Need and Social Services to the Aged, *Social Services Review*, (forthcoming).

Reprinted with permission of Cambridge University Press. From *Ageing and Society*, Vol. 2, Part 2, pp. 151-164, July 1982.

CHAPTER 3

The Political Economy of Government Cuts for the Elderly

VICENTE NAVARRO

In order to understand the meaning and significance of recent cuts in government expenditures for the elderly we must first comprehend: 1) the status of the elderly in American society, 2) the welfare state in the United States, and 3) the impact of the current economic crisis on both of the above. This chapter is designed to briefly introduce each of these topics, setting the stage for more detailed analysis in subsequent chapters.

STATUS OF THE ELDERLY

According to the government's official poverty index, about four million older persons, or roughly 15 percent of the elderly lived below poverty line in 1981 [1]. According to many authorities, however, this figure grossly underestimates the actual proportion of aged Americans who are poor. For example, Molly Orshansky, the original developer of the poverty index, now deems it an inaccurate reflection of current economic conditions [2]. Using her revised estimates, more than nine million elderly persons, or 36 percent of the aged, live below a more accurate poverty line.

For Americans confronted with the "double jeopardy" of being old and black in our society, these poverty figures rise even higher. The U.S. Census, thus, tells us that an estimated 44 percent of black elders live in poverty [1] and other analysts suggest that 60 percent may be a more accurate figure [3].

Women are also disproportionately found among the ranks of the elderly poor, accounting for 72 percent of all poverty in this age group. Single women, are at particular risk for poverty, with 87 percent of elderly women who are poor being either never married or separated, widowed or divorced [4].

The housing needs of America's elderly also should be noted. Estimates suggest that up to 30 percent of older persons in the United States live in substandard housing; that 40 percent do not have hot water baths or showers and that 54 percent have minimal winter heat [3]. While two thirds of all older people own their own homes, most of these houses were purchased forty to fifty years ago, and the high costs of maintenance, utilities and property taxes leave many of the aged on small fixed incomes with insufficient money left over for the meeting of other basic needs.

Unfortunately, programs such as Social Security, SSI, Medicare and Medicaid have helped to create the erroneous impressions that the needs of elders—for an adequate income for health care, etc.—have been well taken care of by government. In fact, Medicare covers only about 38 percent of the medical care costs incurred by persons sixty-five and over. And the 24 percent of elderly persons dependent on Social Security or SSI as their sole source of income live in poverty with a median annual income of only $3,248 in 1980 [5]. Finally, the poorest of the elderly in this country (about 1 in 10 elder persons) do not even qualify for Social Security benefits because they worked in occupations (e.g., domestic work) not covered by the system.

While employment should be an option for those elderly persons who choose to continue working for financial or other reasons, in reality, several factors make this an often unrealistic option. In particular, age discrimination in employment and Social Security penalties for those who earn more than a small amount are significant barriers to continued work in the later years [6].

The above mentioned indicators of major problems among many of our nation's elderly are not meant to suggest that there is not also much deserved joy and happiness among the aged. Rather, the indicators are designed to point up some of the pain and suffering which is experienced by far too many Americans sixty-five and over—pain and suffering which is for the most part preventable.

WHY DOES THIS SITUATION EXIST?

When confronted with the above picture of suffering among many of America's elderly, academic theorists and the lay public alike come up with a variety of explanations. One is that we, Americans, do not value the aged. We value youth. We as a group do not pay much attention to the elderly. Another answer given to that question is that the young in America do not want to pay for the elderly. The so-called productive ages—the age group of twenty to sixty— does not want to support the so-called unproductive age groups—those over sixty. Other explanations put forward by some leaders of our medical and political establishments is that we, Americans, lack compassion for the elderly and the poor. Moreover, it is assumed that there is a popular mandate to cut government programs for the elderly and the poor, a mandate which the current Reagan administration is implementing.

A common assumption behind all these arguments is that we, Americans, do not care that much for our elderly. But, let's analyze what it is generally meant by *"we, Americans."* If by *we* it is meant the majority of Americans, then I will show that there is plenty of evidence that this assumption and the arguments that reproduce it are wrong.

A survey of the major polls carried out from 1977 to 1982 about Americans' opinions on government expenditures shows an overwhelming and undiminished 1) support by the majority of Americans for government programs aimed at the elderly; 2) opposition to cuts in expenditures and services aimed at the elderly; and 3) a willingness to further expand those programs. It is worth stressing and repeating that while the Reagan administration has been cutting social expenditures that benefit the elderly (such as food stamps) and expanding military expenditures, the majority of Americans have repeatedly indicated that they would prefer cuts in military expenditures rather than cuts in services and expenditures for the elderly [7].

In summary, there is plenty of evidence that the majority of Americans are willing to provide our elderly with the secure and joyful retirement they well deserve. The majority of Americans are indeed compassionate and fair, *but their leaders are not.* Why? We have to keep asking 1) why, in spite of people's wishes to the contrary, the government programs for the elderly are being cut; and 2) why those cuts continue to be presented as being due to Americans' thoughtlessness and absence of compassion and fairness for our elderly—again, in spite of the overwhelming evidence that precisely the opposite is true. In order to be able to answer these questions, we need to understand who we, the Americans, are.

POWER IN AMERICA

The dominant interpretation of we, the Americans, is that we are a society divided into groups who have different degrees of power. Within that dominant interpretation, the main criteria for dividing us are race (black, white, Latinos, brown, Asian, etc.); sex (male and female); and age groups (young and old, etc.). The best characterization of that interpretation which I have seen appeared in a television program shown a few months ago entitled "I Love Liberty." It was billed as the liberal answer to the "moral majority." Appearing in the program were a white middle class man (the bigot), a black, an Indian, a Latino, a woman, an elderly person and a gay. American people in the program were presented as an aggregate of those different population groups, symbolically represented by those individuals.

What characterizes that interpretation of us, the American people, is the complete absence of social class as a criteria for dividing us. Indeed, Americans are not merely divided by biological characteristics (race, sex and age) but also—and primarily—by class. The majority of whites, blacks, Latinos, elderly, women and gays are indeed members of the working class. Thus a picture of the U.S. more accurate than the one presented in the program "I Love Liberty" would have been one presenting those individuals as workers, e.g., a white automobile worker, a black steelworker, an Indian construction worker, a female secretary, a retired hospital worker and a gay bank clerk. And, of course, a whole cast of characters should be added to that picture, i.e., the bosses—the members of the capitalist class—which were conspicuously absent in that interpretation of America. In other words, American people are divided into classes: the capitalist class, the petit bourgeoisie or middle class, and—the class of the majority of Americans—the working class; and power—political, economic, and social—in the U.S. is primarily distributed according to class.

This interpretation of American people, however, is continuously avoided and/or dismissed in normal and official analyses and discourses. Instead, the majority of Americans are presented as middle class individuals who are divided according to biological and social groupings. Everyone or almost everyone is middle class and, provided that he or she works hard, "can make it" ('where to' always being ambiguously defined). Of course, extremes are recognized—the wealthy on the one side and the poor on the other. But, they are presented as the exception, not the rule. Within this scenario, the majority of Americans—perceived to be middle class persons—express their wants, wishes and desires through their political institutions.

This interpretation of America carries its own discourse. By "we Americans do not value the elderly" it is meant that we, the majority of Americans—the U.S. middle class—do not value the elderly. It then follows that the political institutions, representative of the majority, act accordingly and cut services for the elderly. This interpretation is so prevalent and dominant that when Professor E. Ginzburg from Columbia University indicates that the cause for much misery among our elderly is because we Americans do not care so much for them, that statement is perceived as unrhetorical, factual and undressed of any ideological connection [8].

If, however, I make the statement that "the cause of that misery is 1) the overwhelming dominance which the U.S. capitalist class has over the U.S. political, economic and social institutions; and 2) the characterization of the elderly by the capitalist class as unproductive, i.e., do not contribute to production and capital accumulation," then I will most likely be dismissed by the current pattern of orthodoxy as rhetorical, predictable, ideological, biased and non-objective.

I would suggest, however, that Ginzberg's interpretation of the cause of our elderly's problem is profoundly ideological and political. It bears and reproduces the most important and functional form of discourse for the capitalist class: even its existence and power is ignored, denied, and not mentioned.

I have elaborated this point at some length to show that *language and discourse are not innocent. They are profoundly political.* To fully understand our reality, however, we need to question the pattern of class dominance that exists in U.S. language. Class is not an "Unamerican" concept and term. However it has been converted into a "silenced" category by the capitalist class (the most class-conscious class in America) and its organic intellectuals who define what is American or not. There is a great and urgent need to redefine the current discourse and the terms and concepts used in it. Indeed, to understand the nature of the cuts in programs for the elderly, we have to speak about capitalism, classes and class struggle—all of them terms and concepts dismissed or non-existent in dominant capitalist discourse.

THE CREATION OF THE WELFARE STATE

The period post World War II witnessed the establishment and extension of the welfare state in all the most developed capitalist countries, i.e., the expansion of social expenditures including sickness and disability programs, pensions, education, medical care, etc. The primary motor behind that expansion was *the strength of the working class*. The greater that strength, the greater was the expansion of social expenditures.

The U.S. does not compare very favorably with other developed capitalist countries in terms of social programs and benefits for the elderly. For example, a steelworker can retire in Sweden at fifty-five years of age (after 20 years of work) and get 90 percent of his/her salary. In the U.S., that individual will get only 60 percent of his/her salary.[1]

Let me stress that the limited nature of rights and benefits also applies to other social groups within the working class. For example, the average maternity leave that a woman worker is entitled to in the U.S. is two weeks. In Sweden it is nine months (at 90% pay). Similarly, at the workplace, shop stewards in Sweden can stop a factory if they see it harmful to the workers. This right is non-existent in the United States.

In summary, if we compare rights and benefits that the different "interest groups" (the elderly, women, workers, etc.) are entitled to in the U.S. and in Sweden we will see that they are far more limited here than there.

Why is there this situation? The reason is the differences in strength between the two working classes. By strength, I mean the possibility of acting and struggling as a class (as different from acting as an interest group) through its class instruments. Due to the enormous importance of those points, let me expand on each.

CLASS BEHAVIOR VERSUS
INTEREST GROUP BEHAVIOR

The working class in the U.S. is one of the few working classes in the western capitalist world that cannot act as a class. The Taft-Hartley Act, for example, forbids class solidarity, e.g., steelworkers' striking in sympathy with coal miners. Witness in contrast the British blue and white collar strikes in support of the nurses' demands in the NHS for better pay and working conditions. A sign of the strength of a class is its right and power to act as a class.

---

[1] All these figures are from V. Navarro's, "Work and Health in the U.S. and Sweden" (in preparation).

The other sign of strength of the working class is the existence of a working class party. The United States working class is the only working class in the western capitalist world that has not had its own political instrument to put forward and defend its class interests. For the most part, conscious elements within the U.S. working class have used the Democratic Party as their political instrument. But that instrument has not been the organic representative of that class. The Democratic Party is a multi-class party in which a strata of the capitalist class is the hegemonic force within the apparatuses of that party. The working class (and the black, the feminist and the ecological movements) have been the *junior* partners in a coalition that has established the New Deal and the New Society—the primary basis for the U.S. welfare state. The senior partners have been the enlightened strata of the U.S. capitalist class. The political instrument of that coalition has been the Democratic Party.

Still, the strength of the U.S. working class (however limited it might have been) was the primary motor behind the expansion of the welfare state, (i.e., Social Security, Medicaid, Medicare, etc.), using the Democratic Party as its instrument [9].

WHY IS THERE THIS CURRENT CRISIS?

The expansion of the welfare state was a symptom of the strength of the working class. That expansion also strengthened the working class as well. It made that class better able to carry on the struggle against the capitalist class. Consequently, the percentage of the national income going to individual, collective, and social wages increased and that going to profits declined [9]. The capitalist class resisted that expansion of the welfare state and feared the strength of the working class. Thus we are witnessing today a most brutal attack by the capitalist class against the working class, cutting and reducing the growth of social consumption, as a way of weakening that class. This attack is carried out at all levels—economic, political and ideological. It is carried out according to a discourse that aims at dividing the working class into its different components, such as young and old, or "unproductive." Let's focus, for example, on the current debate about the so-called "crisis of Social Security." It is said and repeated ad nauseum that the basic problem with Social Security is a demographic problem, i.e., there is an increasing percentage of elderly in our population. Thus a reduced number of productive workers have to pay for a growing percentage of the aged [10]. In that interpretation the interests of the young workers are seen in conflict with the interests of the elderly workers.

To comprehend the nature of the so-called Social Security problem, however, we need to break with the terms of the debate and see the events within a broader picture. What is important in the analysis of the totality of social expenditures (including Social Security) is the overall ratio of workers to non-workers in the population. Bear in mind, for example, that in terms of overall social

Table 1. WORKERS AND DEPENDENTS, 1950-2050 AND BEYOND

Year	Percentage of Total Population That Is:				Dependents Per Worker
	0-17	65+	18-64	Working	
1950	31.0	8.1	60.9	39.8	1.51
1960	35.7	9.2	55.1	37.8	1.65
1970	34.0	9.8	56.2	39.9	1.51
1979	28.4	11.2	60.4	44.9	1.23
2000	26.1	12.7	61.2	45.5	1.20
2025	24.0	18.2	57.8	43.0	1.33
2050	23.8	18.5	57.7	42.9	1.33
Long-Run Limit	23.4	19.0	57.6	42.8	1.34

Source: *Statistical Abstract of the United States*, 1980, p. 30-31, and *Economic Report of the President*, p. 264, January 1981.

expenditures, the young (from 0-20 years of age) consume more social resources than the aged (60+) [11]. Thus, the current demographic transition (from having less young to having more elderly) works *in favor, not against savings in social expenditures*. Moreover, the percentage of people working in the population (as is shown in Table 1) has been increasing and continues to increase all the way to the year 2050. Thus, the ratio worker-dependent has been increasing, rather than declining. There are increasingly more workers than non-workers in our populations [11].

Thus, in terms of overall resources, the demographic and employment transition is favorable to an expansion (not a reduction) of social expenditures for all sectors of the population, including the elderly.

The capitalist class, of course, denies this. It maintains the debate within a terrain in which the parameters of the discussion are not supposed to be touched upon or expanded. Seen in its totality, however, the demographic and employment arguments used to justify a weakening of Social Security do not have an explanatory value. They have an advocacy value for policies aimed at dividing and weakening the working class.

THE CURRENT REAGAN POLICIES

In the current analysis of the Reagan administration policies, a lot of attention is paid to the personal views, attitudes and behavior of the leader of that administration. For some that administration represents the epitomy of nastiness; for others an example of wisdom and foresightedness. I disagree with the interpretation of events that tries to explain leaders' behavior by looking at their motivations. History and reality are more complex than that. The Reagan administration represents the most extremist sectors of the capitalist class. They authentically believe that what is best for their class is best for the majority of

Americans. Thus, the defense of their class interests becomes the defense of the U.S. national and international interests. And they are willing to go to great extremes and lengths to defend their interests. That defense presupposes a most brutal weakening of the working class, with shifting of government resources from social expenditures (which benefit the majority of the U.S. population) to military expenditures (which benefit a minority—the extreme strata of the capitalist class currently in power) [12].

Needless to say, it is to the capitalists' advantage to present that shift of resources as responding to a popular mandate. Thus, an enormous avalanche of ideological messages is being put forward to justify that shift. Part of that message is that people are anti-government. But it is important that we not accept the discourse in the terms in which it is presented to us. The issue here is not government versus non-government, but *for whose benefit* government intervention occurs.

Let's not forget that Reagan is the most pro-government president we have had for a very long time. Indeed, he is the one who favors stronger government intervention in our economic, political and social lives. One cannot put 1.7 trillion dollars in military government expenditures in five years (as the current administration is in the process of doing) without militarizing the U.S. economy. Also, the current administration aims at legislating on all aspects of political and civil lives, including our morality. Indeed, greatly expanding the military budget; increasing government secrecy; closing off avenues of citizen participation in government; releasing the FBI and CIA from post-Watergate restraints; weakening the national defense against endemic polluters, monopolists and corporate defrauders; using government interventions to weaken unions and civil and political rights; legislating public morality; and invading citizens' privacy *can scarcely be viewed as a drive for smaller government.* These different types of interventions follow a predetermined project, i.e., the authoritarian state. Let me quote to you from an individual who should know well, Mr. H. Salvatori, the head of the transition team of the Reagan administration.

> In the history of man everyone has talked about expanding rights, having more and more freedom. But we have found that if you let people do what they want to do, you have chaos. We can't restore moral values, that's hopeless. What we have to do is restructure society, set minimum standards of respect and order. Frankly, *we need a more authoritarian state* [13]. (Emphasis added.)

Mr. Salvatori is on record indicating that all of the top Reagan appointments suggested by his team agree with his philosophy—which is Reagan's philosophy. President Reagan accepted almost all of Salvatori's task force recommendations [13]. Today we are witnessing the further development and strengthening of the authoritarian state needed to discipline the majority of the U.S. population, i.e., the U.S. working class.

WHAT CAN BE DONE?

The analysis presented here suggests a number of steps that progressive forces in the United States might take in order to bring about changes in this situation. Briefly, these steps are:

1. to break with the "interests groups" mentality, behavior and practice. The enormous ideological advantage of the capitalist class in this country has been to redefine 'majority' as an aggregate of minorities. We have to recover that majority and make our people realize that the majority of our white, black, Latino, brown, female, young and old people are working people, the components of the U.S. working class.
2. to encourage this majority to expect, demand and want far more where that 'more' is not merely measured by individual but rather collective consumption. In other words, we have to help clarify that U.S. society and its resources—including the most important resource, people—*can* afford to provide security and joy for the elderly; satisfaction, security and fun for the employed; equality and fairness for our women and national minorities; care and cure for our sick; rehabilitation for our disabled, and health and pleasure for us all.

The current position of the capitalist class is that the U.S. *cannot* afford this. What they actually mean is that U.S. *capitalism* can't afford it. But there is a need to differentiate one from the other. One is not the other. Capitalism is a specific form of production and distribution of resources that corresponds to a historical period in the development of humankind. It is not an eternal period. In the same way that feudalism was superseded by capitalism, capitalism will be superseded by a higher form of organization of production and distribution. It is, of course, in the capitalist class' interest to present the current system as the eternal and only one. But we need to question that. We need to redefine the terms of the discourse and redefine what is possible and impossible. We need *to be realistic and ask the impossible*. This is not an insoluble paradox. It is a result of redefinition of what is and what is not acceptable and possible.

3. to break with false dichotomies that progressive forces have been hung up on such as reform versus revolution. People do not ask for revolutions. Even those who have made one. People ask for bread, peace, social security and other reformist demands. It is only when the economic, political system cannot respond within the defined parameters of power that those parameters are broken. In the first socialist revolution, the Bolsheviks and the Russian people wanted peace with Germany, land and bread. In the latest revolution, the Sandinistas and the Nicaraguan people wanted bread and freedom.

In summary, we need to stress that indeed security, joy, health and fun are reachable. And they must be reached. Whether capitalism can or cannot afford it, it is not a predetermined situation. It depends on many forces and factors outside the capitalist class control.

Let me end by indicating that I am fully aware that this chapter will be perceived as political and ideological by those who define the parameters of the acceptable. My answer is that this chapter is not more political than the majority of theoretical contributions that appear in current academic journals and the general media. Rather, the terms of the "political" are different. And this is what gives it its difference. I consider the terms presented herein to be attuned and parallel to that saying from one of the founders of public health—that "public health and medicine are social sciences and politics is medicine on a large scale."

REFERENCES

1. Census Bureau, pp. 60, No. 134, Table 17.
2. United States House of Representatives, Select Committee on Aging, *Poverty among America's Aged*, U.S. Government Printing Office, Washington, D.C., 1978.
3. The Elderly Poor: An Example of What Happens to the Unproductive in Capitalist Society, in *Toward Socialism in America*, H. Freeman (ed.), Schenkman Publishing Co., second edition, pp. 5-13, 1982.
4. A. M. O'Rand, Women, in *Handbook of Aging in the United States*, E. Palmore (ed.), Greenwood Press, 1984.
5. United States Senate, Special Committee on Aging, *Developments in Aging, 1981*, Vol. 1, U.S. Government Printing Office, Washington, D.C., 1982.
6. R. M. Butler and M. I. Lewis, *Aging and Mental Health*, C. V. Mosley Co., St. Louis, 1982.
7. V. Navarro, Where Is the Popular Mandate?, *New England Journal of Medicine*, December 9, 1982.
8. E. Ginzberg, *The Limits of the Health Reforms*, Columbia University Press, 1979.
9. V. Navarro, The Crisis in the Capitalist Order and Its Implications in the Welfare State, *International Journal of Health Services*, *12*:2, 1982.
10. Guns and Butter: Special Report, *Business Week*, p. 68, November 29, 1982.
11. A Dependent by Any Other Name..., in, *Reagonomics: Rhetoric vs. Reality*, F. Adrerman (ed.), South End Press, Boston, p. 97, 1982.
12. V. Navarro, The Social Costs of National Security or Insecurity, *American Journal of Public Health*, 1981.
13. R. Nader, Introduction, in *Reagan's Ruling Class*, R. Brownstein and N. Easton (eds.), p. viii, The Presidential Accountability Group, Washington, D.C., 1982.

Plenary session address to the 110th Annual Meeting of the American Public Health Association, Montreal, Canada, November 16, 1982.

CHAPTER 4
Social Control of the Elderly
LINDA EVANS
JOHN B. WILLIAMSON

For centuries philosophers and social theorists have been concerned with the relationship between the individual and society. They have asked questions about how social order came to exist, why it persists, and whom it most benefits. Such theorists have been particularly attentive to the tension that exists between the desire for freedom and autonomy on the one hand and the desire for order and security on the other. Some philosophers such as Jean Jacques Rousseau (1712-1778) and John Locke (1632-1704) emphasized freedom; others such as Thomas Hobbes (1588-1679) emphasized social order.[1]

The work of Herbert Spencer (1820-1903) and other social Darwinists drew a Hobbesian picture of humankind as naturally animalistic and competitive. In this context, nineteenth century social theorists became interested in the study of specific mechanisms of social control whereby the group (society) constrains individual behavior.[2] These controls range from the use of police force, to the subtle transmission of values and norms through socialization. In all instances the question lurks: "Whose interests are best served by a society's organizational arrangements and how do those not well-served come to accept boundaries or controls on their options?"

---

[1] In *Leviathan* (originally published in 1598), Hobbes (1958) argues that in the so-called "state of nature" (that time prior to the establishment of any government or civil order), life was "solitary, poor, nasty, brutish, and short." [1] Thus he saw the "social contract" and with it the establishment of a strong government to preserve law and order as highly desirable. By contrast, in *The Social Contract* (originally published in 1762), Rousseau emphasizes the oppressive aspects of governments: they tend to best serve the interests of the wealthy [2]. Locke was yet another social contract theorist; he argued that people created government for the purpose of guaranteeing their freedom. If the government ceased to do so, the contract had been broken and the people had the right to rebel.

[2] The positivist school of thought underwent a major change with the application of Darwinism in its "social" form. In the eighteenth century, positivists assumed that the problems of humankind could be solved through rational thought. Once heredity and environment replaced free will and choice as the bases of action (per Darwinism), a Hobbesian description of nature resulted. Now a "struggle for existence" characterized relations between individuals, not a shared concept of social order [3]. For some of the early work dealing with the issue of social control as such, see the following: [4-7, pp. 195-210].

The evidence suggests that the community whose interests are best represented and served by existing social arrangements within American society is the community of adults under age seventy, to the detriment of those who are older. While Neugarten [8, pp. 4-9], Pratt [9], and Hudson [10, 11, pp. 30-33] are correct in suggesting that America's elderly as a group have made progress over the past fifty years in improving their standard of living and establishing legitimacy as an interest group, they fail to give adequate attention to the mechanisms of social control which have been evolving at the same time. To be sure, the elderly have achieved greater economic security; they have a national policy network in place, and they are growing in number. But these analysts have not adequately taken into consideration the growth of an elaborate system of social control by which the elderly are severely constrained. Furthermore, it is our contention that all of the helping and academic professions involved with elderly affairs are implicated in this tightening of controls.

We begin with an explication of the concept of "social control," exploring the forms it can take and noting that an increase in concern about proper social control of citizens was intimately linked with the rise of social casework and passage of Social Security. Because Social Security legislation was a harbinger of what was to come, we shall examine the causes of its enactment and outline some of the consequences for the elderly. Social Security led to an increase in autonomy with respect to intergenerational relationships; it became possible for millions of elderly Americans to remain economically independent of their middle-aged children. But this gain came at a cost: an increase in dependence on and control by the state and its representatives in various government bureaucracies. A case can be made that the bureaucratic structures established in connection with the Social Security program, and since expanded in response to legislation of the 1960's and 1970's, has increased the power and influence of the caretakers more than it has increased the power and influence of the elderly themselves.

WHAT IS SOCIAL CONTROL?

For centuries humankind has debated the extent to which—if at all—individuals need to forego some liberties and exercise of free will so as to benefit from order and predictability within their environment [1, 2]. With the onset of industrialization and the social disruptions it triggered, this debate intensified in Europe and the United States.

Emile Durkheim (1958) in advancing the idea that the total community is greater than the sum of its parts or members was clearly suggesting that the balance of control is held by the group, not recalcitrant members [12]. He went on to identify various means by which groups exert pressure on members to confine their behavior to acceptable boundaries. These include public opinion (reputation), law, belief systems, education, custom, religion, ceremony (rites of passage), and values—essentially all components of a social system. Indeed, the boundaries of acceptable behavior are often only defined through their violation. According to this argument, deviation from acceptable behavior may arouse group sentiment to the point where clear boundaries are identified or reaffirmed. Once a violator of norms is identified, he or she may be relegated to an "outgroup" status, and those not so-labeled can feel more strongly committed to the social order through their shared self-righteousness and conformity.[3]

Although Durkheim is credited with conceptualizing the magnitude of society's regulation of individual behavior, his analysis was not a justification for the status quo. His ideas are frequently contrasted with those of Marx (1964), but both in fact identified social stratification and the ensuing unequal distribution of resources and power as the major mechanism by which individuals' options are differentially limited and controlled.[4] Durkheim assumed a certain normative consensus among community members about what constitutes appropriate behavior, but it was American social scientists who went so far as to depict society as an organism whose equilibrium is constantly being maintained. Deviants should change, not existing economic and social arrangements.[5]

The idea that society is an organism whose parts or institutions are in balance came to be known as *functionalism* [12, 17-19]. Early American social scientists lamented the loss of a "natural order" inherent in small rural communities (upheld by white, Anglo-Saxon, and male values) and saw deviation from social norms as individual pathology or sickness [20, pp. 165-180]. According to this perspective, industrialism was the unavoidable wave of the future, and social selection of the fittest necessitated adjustment to this new order, assimilation (conformity) of immigrants, and amelioration of emerging social problems through correction of individual pathology. An order based on presumably shared sensibilities would be replaced with a legally based order. That which did not come "naturally" would be mandated through laws.

Concern among early social scientists about presumed animal drives within individuals and the desirability of social order has led to a dual approach in studying social control. On the one hand, efforts have been made to study and "rehabilitate" unadjusted individuals (i.e., deviants), and, on the other hand, some acknowledgement of structural strains within the social order has occurred. Theorists such as Merton have sometimes defined deviance as *adjustment* (not maladjustment) *to contradictions within the social system* [21]. Thus, some roles, values, and goals that people are socialized to aspire to are structurally

---

[3] See Erikson for a discussion of how boundaries are frequently defined through activities that transgress them [13].

[4] See Davis for an elaboration of this argument [14].

[5] For a discussion of European and American differences in approaching the subjects of stratification and social control, see Horton, as well as Pease, Form, and Rytina [15, pp. 283-300, 16].

frustrated, and, therefore, behaviors must be adjusted.[6] Functionalists assume that the more effective the socialization process (informal control), the less need will exist for legal or formal means of social control.[7]

While functionalists focus on society and seek to study how individual deviance from norms can be contained or accommodated so as to enhance the system's survival, labeling theorists are interested in how people define one another and how these definitions constrain behavior. Because they reflect the symbolic interactionist perspective [23, 24], which stresses the importance of symbols in creating social reality, labeling theorists view social control as the successful manipulation of labels. According to this line of thought, elites, bosses, ruling classes, adults, men, Caucasians, and other dominant groups exercise power through controlling how people define the world and what is possible [25]. Through the successful ascription of labels to people, a noncostly and *apparently* noncoercive type of oppression can be implemented and indeed eventually taken for granted.

Labeling theorists have traditionally studied deviant behavior in terms of legal definitions for creating social outgroups. Thus, deviance consists of 1) an act and 2) society's response to the act. Making certain behaviors "deviant" by law is a procedure by which a society literally creates its deviants (those who perform the outlawed act). And by labeling persons "deviant," a society sets up a process that can lead to further isolation and stigmatization of the offenders. With the deviant label society distributes stigma, and a self-fulfilling prophecy is set in motion—one which tightens the norm-breaker's outcast status.

Unlike interactionist theorists who emphasize the part labeling or social control plays in *creating* deviant or disvalued careers, conflict theorists are more interested in locating the conditions under which official labeling occurs and in identifying high-level agents of social control, not middle-level ones [14]. Rather than study how labeling can lead to a loss of autonomy and personal power, conflict theorists argue that the act of being labeled reflects *prior* powerlessness. According to this school of thought, the study of deviance is in itself an instrument of social control because system victims are targeted for analysis, not the system or those benefiting from present resource arrangements [26, pp. 103-120]. Social control is thus an active control involving the regulation of powerless groups [14, pp. 315-335]; economic stratification serves as the principal determinant of where power lies and what form laws will take. This emphasis upon structural inequalities underpinning social control is more derivative of early European social scientists (Durkheim and Marx), than early American ones who stressed individual pathologies.

---

[6] For example, within American society a structural tension can exist between the cultural goal of "success" and institutionalized means of attaining it, such as "working hard," "getting educated," etc. To the extent that the presumed means to the end do not work or are not available to all, individuals may find "innovative" ways of acquiring success or its symbols, that is, they may engage in criminal activities. Or in the case of some old persons who are denied access to the means, they may "retreat" from both the goals and the means.

[7] See Roucek for a discussion of this point [22, pp. 17-27].

Conflict theorists tend to believe that any political consensus that is reached is a manipulated consensus, not a communally based or pluralist one as functionalists imply. The state rather than being viewed as a neutral broker of interests is seen as using its legitimated authority to rationalize and supplement the exploitation of some groups by others. Market and political imperatives of elites determine the direction and scope of social changes, and the only reform proposals that are ever found acceptable to these elites involve technocratic solutions, such as creation of new bureaucracies, not redistributive ones [14, pp. 315-335]. Conflict theorists assert that "reforms" enhance state power over controlled groups and that they invariably solidify the security of economic elites. This solidification occurs through the *appearance* that something is being done to redress a problem and a resultant diffusion of any challenge to existing economic arrangements.

Keeping in mind each of these theoretical perspectives on social control, we now turn to an examination of the changes in the status of the elderly that preceded the rise of the pension movement and followed enactment of Social Security legislation. We will consider whether the Social Security program tended to increase or decrease the power of the elderly. Did it result in more autonomy for the elderly or more social control of the elderly? It is our contention that it increased autonomy in certain spheres, but increased the extent of social control within others. The pension benefits have increased the economic well-being of the elderly and in so doing have increased their autonomy. But Social Security legislation has also created jobs for a wide variety of caretakers who have come to play an increasing role in the management and control of the lives of the eldery.

THE RISE OF THE PENSION MOVEMENT

Many political analysts and gerontologists cite both normative and economic changes within American society as the causes of a pension movement forming at the turn of this century. The old-age pension movement was part of a campaign to institute compulsory social insurance. Sponsors of the social insurance goal believed that neither the poor laws nor private social work enterprises were sufficient to provide "indemnity against financial losses from . . . ordinary contingencies in the workingman's life." [27] [8] These included accidents, sickness, maternity, disability, unemployment, old age, and death—risks that could bring an end to a worker's wage-earning capacity or opportunity. Now that so many Americans were wage-dependent, social insurance sponsors believed laborers needed income protection. Activists on behalf of an old-age pension were particularly concerned because forced retirement had become widespread in the absence of private pensions, and the elderly appeared to occupy an increasingly precarious financial and social position within the community.

[8] See Graebner [28] and Lubove [29] for excellent discussions of the drive for Social Security and the various obstacles that were imposed.

Among those explanatory factors mentioned most often as indirect precipitators of the pension movement are an increase in secularism, an ethos of egalitarianism originally spawned by the American and French Revolutions, enlargement of the elderly population, Darwinism, industrialization, and eventually family difficulties in caring for senior members [30-33]. Concurrent with these various trends was the growth of "gerontophobia."[9] According to these accounts, early colonists—particularly Puritans—were heavily steeped in age hierarchy, and age was one indicator of being among God's elect [33]. The rarity of living till old age no doubt underscored its godly overtones.

By the late eighteenth century, the authority of age was already being challenged on several fronts. With the French and American revolutions, values such as independence, liberty, and equality began to filter through society. Young people and transcendentalists in particular began to challenge the familial and communal control held by their elders and claimed that liberty was a "prior condition" and equality at odds with age having preference over youth.[10]

In the mid-nineteenth century, the decline in status of the elderly got markedly worse with the appearance of social Darwinism and accelerating industrialization. As technology developed and medical advances occurred, old age became much more commonplace and increasingly linked with death. While social Darwinism was siring descriptions of society as continually "progressing" with time and age, this assumption was not extended to individuals. Progress had a decisively dualistic nature [34, pp. 26-35].

Indeed human development was finite, and society's evolutionary progress portended brutal problems for those older persons who could not hold their own in the struggle for existence. When this emphasis upon progress was reinterpreted by the managers of industrial facilities to mean higher and higher productivity, society's "best" came to be depicted as those who were in the prime of their productive powers. In a world where human mastery over every aspect of nature became a goal, youth was designated the most vital and creative source for accomplishing this mastery. As the age of workers went up, the age of the most valued workers went down; as education level rose, the relative education of the elderly declined. Employment problems among the elderly resulted in a rapid increase in poverty within their ranks, but the presumably productive younger family members who were living in congested urban areas and expected to be geographically mobile were not in a good position to lend assistance.

While old persons were increasingly portrayed as unfit for the "productive" world of work and frequently ejected, they were also being labeled with characteristics that had formerly been applied to other economically deprived and

[9] The term *gerontophobia* as commonly used refers to a fear of or aversion to old people and aging.

[10] Transcendentalism was a nineteenth century school of philosophy whose proponents argued that knowledge comes from intuition rather than objective experience. When this viewpoint caught on in America, it helped undermine the status of the elderly by minimizing the importance of experience (age). Both Emerson and Thoreau reflected this perspective.

nonmasterful groups. Specifically, old age during the Puritan era was pictured as good when it was associated with other virtues (such as a manly life), and patriarchs were portrayed as "commanding masculine figures." [33, p. 114] But the poor elderly carried the stigma of poverty, not the virtue of age, and impoverished older widows were treated with a contempt so strong that they were sometimes ostracized by entire communities. As older male workers were portrayed as not being up to the requirements of industrial "progress," they were increasingly ascribed with the characteristics of weakness—dependence, passivity, and femininity. Thus they joined the ranks of other stigmatized groups, and the most gracious version presented the Victorian patriarch as a "dummy figure . . . stowed away in the rocking chair, a male softened by the kindly touch of time." [33, p. 226] Stereotypes mirrored economic exigencies.

Assuming that all these normative and economically based pressures contributed to a drop in the elderly's fortunes, we might ask whether proposed corrective measures were as equally broad-based. As it turned out, pension plans proposed by protest activists were forcefully resisted by elites within all institutions, and claims of adherence to "American" values were invoked by proponents and opponents.

Functional theorists argue that "deviants" who want a change in economic and political order can be used to help stabilize the social order, if successfully managed. They do this by identifying problem areas that need some attention and by organizing into political groups. By forming some kind of secondary group, such as a protest movement, which allows some expression of alienated feelings, political deviants are easily located and can be insulated from the rest of society.

In American society, mere use of the word "radical" in describing a political group is a potent weapon among elites in repelling alternative claims to legitimacy and tends to insulate a group's impact. While the deviant or protesting group is being put on the defensive by elites for being "un-American," its members are often found asserting that they represent America's *real* values. For example, economic elites frequently invoke the "American" value of free enterprise to prevent any redistribution of income, while proponents of redistribution often speak of Americans' traditional concern for fair play, justice, and a decent life for all.

This claim among organized political deviants of being the true defenders of American values establishes a "bridge" whereby the group can be coopted [19]. By saying they are more American than elite defenders of the status quo, protesters are tacitly accepting the social order on the whole and are "set up" to settle for whatever minor accommodation to legitimacy their goals eventually receive. In this way, vested interests are not seriously threatened, and social order is strengthened through cooptation of alternative visions or ideologies. In the case of pension activists whose goals were eventually whittled down to social security legislation, this cooptation process of social control was followed to a tee.

SOCIAL SECURITY

By 1908, forced retirement was common, and since the net savings of most Americans approached zero, old age and poverty were unavoidably linked.[11] Even though most European nations had adopted a system of compulsory old-age insurance, the concept was perceived by America's institutional leaders as a repudiation of the American system of "volunteerism" and "individual liberty." Resistance to pensions came from elites of all major institutions, and each claimed that such a program would be a threat to American values. Religious leaders, economists, business persons, and union officers agreed that compulsory old-age insurance would be the corrupter of America's morals. Not only did such a plan represent socialist intentions and deferred wages, but it threatened the very underpinnings of national character. As one opponent summed up the situation, the prospect of old-age dependency is a "most powerful incentive which makes for character and growth in a democracy." Without such a threat we might revert to the behavior of our "barbarian ancestors." [3, pp. 367-390]

Even though the United States had a major public pension system already in operation for Civil War veterans, compulsory old-age pensions were described as "un-American." One Congressperson, in trying to reconcile this anomaly in thinking, proposed an "Old-Age Home Guard of the United States Army" in which all individuals sixty-five and above could "enlist" if their incomes were below $20 per month; their official responsibility would be to inform the War Department annually on the level of patriotism within their neighborhoods [33].

Opponents of pensions did not stop with attacking the concept as un-American; they also denounced those who supported compulsory old-age insurance as un-American. To the extent that many early proponents were immigrants or first-generation Americans from Eastern European countries and urban, they were not a part of the "natural order" frequently associated with Anglo-rural communities at that time. It was not until the 1920's when poverty among the elderly had become even more obvious that traditional or "American" institutions, such as the Fraternal Order of Eagles, promoted old-age insurance that proponents began to make any headway in their claims to legitimacy. Roosevelt and other New Deal architects nonetheless kept the first social insurance advocates, "un-American" upstarts that they were, at arm's length right through passage of the Social Security Act. These political "deviants" or "radicals" were never officially credited with the legislation, and indeed other than its establishment of the right—as opposed to privilege—

---

[11] The distribution of assets has changed very little over the past seventy years in America, and this negligibe savings level for all but the top economic stratum in 1908 has remained a characteristic feature [35-37].

of benefits for certain categories of workers, it bore no resemblance to their visions.[12]

While goals of political deviants were being successfully contained by the boundaries acceptable to elites, pension movement leaders themselves contributed to this eventual cooptation by relying heavily upon the appeal that sending elderly persons to almshouses violated American values and sentiments of justice. Rather than holding to a bold and positive vision of social insurance as an alternative to the survival of the fittest mentality, proponents implied that Americans' definition of fair play would be adhered to if the elderly were kept out of almshouses. This limited and negative tactical approach no doubt contributed to the skimpy, piecemeal, and categorical legislative product, but it is also a testimonial to how elites exercise social control through discrediting opponents of the status quo and thereby reduce political discourse to minor and unthreatening issues. Indeed, as exemplified by the Social Security Act, even an already compromised goal (in this case, keeping old people out of poor houses) is not necessarily met through the eventual legislative result.

Essentially what happened was that the original concept of a worker's right to an income through periods of disability was repeatedly cast into an issue of moral behavior. This was in keeping with the emphasis upon individual pathology and deviance control prevalent at the time. A plan that called for some redistribution of income became a regressive payroll tax that, as one disappointed activist put it, "actually decreases the purchasing power of the masses by depriving them of immediate purchases, by relieving the well-to-do from their share of the social burden, and by making the workers pay the expenses of a vast administration." [29, p. 179] [13]

This cooptation of goals occurred not only through pressure from business, religious, and government leaders, but also from social workers—a group that would eventually staff vast bureaucracies whose very existence could be traced back to passage of the Social Security Act. Unquestionably, the concept of state-mediated assistance as a "right" for the elderly that emerged with this legislation launched further modes of nonmaterial assistance whose distribution required social workers [39]. During the 1920's, however, social workers were self-consciously trying to become a "profession," and they along with psychiatrists and others in the "helping" professions were trying to understand the personality of deviants.

---

[12] Roosevent was careful to keep control of the drafting of the Social Security legislation in conservative hands. Persons such as Isaac Rubinow and Abraham Epstein were kept at arm's length despite the major role they had played as activists in the old-age pension movement. Upton Sinclair organized the "EPIC" movement (End Poverty in California), which originally proposed a modest $50 per month pension (which was eventually raised to $400 per month). More influential was the Townsend Plan, which called for a pension of $200 per month. In contrast, the old-age pension enacted by the Social Security Act of 1935 called for a pension of less than $25 per month. This is a far cry from what the old-age pension activists had in mind [9, 33, pp. 178-187].

[13] This statement was made by Abraham Epstein, a longtime advocate of the idea that pensions should be based on a concept of adequacy, not upon guidelines for moral behavior.

In focusing on individuals, social workers were attempting to stake out their area for skill monopoly by helping deviants "adjust" or change their personalities [29]. Most did not view economic security as a feasible goal of the public welfare sector and chose to emphasize a need for casework performed by social workers within private agencies. They did not directly address the issue of poverty and its objective causes—illness, injury, unemployment, death of a breadwinner, and old age. One thing upon which economic elites and social workers agreed was that individual workers should have those necessities that permitted a state of "physical efficiency" so that they could work [40], but neither wanted any major changes in the social order. One group wanted a legitimized mission within the order, and the other wanted a functional labor force at a cost that would not significantly reduce profits.

The core issues were never individual liberty or the desirability of volunteerism, but rather they were the imperatives of capital growth. In order to understand what occurred in the twentieth century with respect to employer control of workers, it is necessary to first examine the nineteenth century so that a comparison can be made.

During the nineteenth century, capitalism was dependent upon unskilled labor—an abundant commodity, but one requiring discipline and industriousness within the work force.[14] This need for discipline along with the emphasis upon increased productivity led to a situation where the state helped subsidize the costs of production (disciplining the labor force) by building almshouses, country poor farms, mental institutions, and municipal old-age homes where nonproductive members could be segregated from the rest of society [41]. Whether or not this change was humane as many reformers suggested, the segregation process definitely served many purposes simultaneously, all to the advantage of industrialists.

Individuals who were unproductive dependents could be removed from their families, thus freeing up other family members to work even more productively and to be ready for a move to where their labor was most needed. The discontent being expressed by poor families about the costs of caring for their unproductive members could be diffused without altering their wage rates. In addition, by making residence in these institutions most unpleasant and stigmatizing, those who were not contributing to the system would be properly punished, and those "poorer classes" who might be tempted to feign insanity or poverty to avoid work would be deterred from doing so. Furthermore, the concept of "outdoor relief" could be kept off the political agenda altogether.[15] Social participation within the community was thus prohibited in the absence of economic participation.

---

[14] For more elaboration on the argument being made here, see Scull [41].

[15] The term *outdoor relief* refers to assistance that is provided without the requirement that the recipient be confined to an almshouse or a workhouse.

This use of institutions to isolate nonproductive members of society only gave way to outdoor relief in the form of social insurance programs, such as Unemployment Compensation and Social Security, when the needs of capital changed. Accordingly, as the costs of labor increased due to rises in required skill and education levels for many jobs, industrialists became interested in maintaining the capacity and willingness to work among these costly employees. Social insurance programs constituted an investment in human capital, and with their passage the state got even more deeply committed to subsidizing production costs (maintaining workers in body and spirit).

In order to attract an ambitious, proficient, and fit workforce, industrialists deemed it necessary to show "good faith" by assuring some continuity in income during workers' less "fit" period [34, pp. 26-35]. It was presumed that removing "less efficient" old people from the labor force would boost morale, not to mention employment opportunities, for younger workers and enhance their commitment to work.[16] Retirement became a new and more subtle form of segregation and social control.

Whatever passage of Social Security legislation may say about how social control is exercised by elites through the government process, it unquestionably proved to be a "trump card" of social control over the elderly in many more ways than are commonly acknowledged. First, it is clear that Social Security was passed in order to "cool out" America's elderly without making any seriously distributive changes in the system and to regulate the labor market by removing older members. It is probably not accidental that political activity on behalf of and by the aged fell into what has been termed by one observer as the "dismal years." [9]   In this sense, Social Security can be compared with public assistance in that its stated purpose was humanitarian, but actually it helped stabilize the social order and thereby sustain the dominance of existent elites [43].[17]

Although the state had been involved in the subsidized segregation of the elderly to a limited degree before 1935 through maintenance of almshouses and municipal old-age homes, its role was greatly expanded with passage of Social Security legislation. Mandatory retirement was implicitly condoned, and the elderly became an official "problem" or target group of government policies.

---

[16] These types of rationales were given by those employers who supported industrial pensions. Pensions were seen by some as legitimate business expenditures that would reduce labor turnover, attract superior workers, and relieve employers of any obligation to keep individuals on the payroll in the absence of "real productivity." These inducements for enhanced worker cooperation and productivity were assumed to rest upon the worker's comprehension that a pension would be withheld if his output fell short of expectations [29, 42, p. 101].

[17] In the case of Social Security, America's old were "cooled off," and unemployment eased with payments and the expunging of the elderly from the work force that payments helped rationalize. With relief or public assistance, unemployed persons are "cooled" during periods of civil disorder resulting from severe economic decline with higher benefits and relaxed eligibility criteria. They are then expunged into the labor force during quiet periods through stringent eligibility requirements to assure an adequate supply of low-wage labor [43].

This formal labeling of people as "old" through Social Security eligibility along with the increased social distance between America's old and everyone else that Social Security payments permitted are appropriate issues for theorists of the labeling school.

A question debated by labeling theorists is whether society's fear of an act leads to labeling it deviant or whether the act of deviance leads to fear from society. We might ask what *act* America's elderly committed in order to become stigmatized, and the answer would be none in the sense that the word "deviance" is used by labeling theorists. It is important to make a distinction between occupying a "deviant" status in the legal order and a "devalued" one in the social order, although the labeling dynamics can be identical. As Cohen (1966) notes, all deviant roles are devalued—they are usually low-status and undesirable roles—but not all devalued roles (such as being an old person) are deviant in terms of being illegal [44]. While the deviant is usually assumed to choose violation of a norm, those occupants of a devalued role are seen as "unfortunate" and not "reprehensible." But once they are labeled or identified in some kind of segregating and stigmatizing way, their attempts to maneuver around the label or their failure to do so are similar to those of deviants.

The question raised about whether fear leads to the dispensing of stigma or vice-versa is relevant to the elderly. Just about the time that being old was labeled a "problem" to be dealt with legislatively, the elderly were becoming more numerous, and anxieties about how they were to be employed were growing. Thus, according to labeling theory, the "act" of being old—at least in large numbers—led to fear. Concurrently, medical scientists were busy studying senescence and turning out reports on the physical hardships of aging [34, pp. 26-35]. Negative descriptions of the aging process contributed to fear and to the devaluing of the older person role.

This dual aspect of society's fear of the elderly continues today. America's old are feared because their numbers are growing and because the process of aging is presumed to involve loss of highly valued attributes such as activity, productivity, and independence—attributes made ever more elusive through our constraints on the elderly. Whereas earlier generations feared the physical aspects of aging, we have created a situation where social aspects are to be feared too. This straitjacketing of the elderly can best be examined by tracing the "career" of an old person. A process that begins with the labeling of someone as "old," and reflects an expression of power by those who do the labeling, results in a loss of power for the elderly, particularly with respect to personal autonomy and choice.

THE CAREER OF AN OLD PERSON

The concept of a career path has been ascribed to deviant behavior by Goffman [45] and Becker [25].[18] Just as the term refers to a sequence of movements from one position to another within the world of work, with one step

---

[18] Goffman first wrote of the "moral career" of a mental patient to denote the public and private sides of an individual's identity transition pre-, mid-, and post-incarceration [45]. Becker uses the career concept when analyzing deviance to allow for the various contingencies involved and to underscore the chain-event aspect of labeling whereby a series of steps are set up, each partly anticipated by the previous event [25].

often predisposing another, Becker uses the term to describe a sequence of events which can follow the act of being labeled deviant or devalued. This sequential approach presupposes an interaction process between the labeled person and society whereby the deviant's career path is determined by both objective facts of social structure (e.g., discrimination) and subjective changes in his or her perceptions, motivations, and goals [25].

This process model of cause-effect is very different from the multivariate-type explanations offered by functionalist thought, and although functionalists and labeling theorists both assume a normative basis for the dispensation of stigma, labeling theorists emphasize its oppressive rather than system-sustaining properties. From this perspective a deviant career is often characterized by labeling, segregation, and ever-increasing constraints on individual options, autonomy, and power. To some degree most theories of aging to date can be seen as theories on how people adjust to the career of being an old person—how the self and perceptions of what is possible respond to predictable, though no inevitable, changes in their objective milieu.[19]

From the moment a person is publicly "caught" in the status "old," her career has begun. This labeling in terms of social consequences can first be manifest in different ways. She may have physical signs of age, such as wrinkles, a physical limitation, or the mere inclusion of chronological age on a required document or application. More frequently, reaching the age of eligibility for some elderly oriented service such as housing or Social Security payments can trigger the public labeling and certainly being retired does. To the extent that this public identification of being old results in a constriction of options, the person has moved into the second stage of her career. Or, in other words, she is beginning to have difficulties carrying on the routines of everyday life valued by the idealized community of nonelderly adults. Direct discrimination in gaining or keeping employment is one sanction; the requirement that wages not exceed a certain amount for those collecting Social Security pension benefits is a more indirect but potent exercise of social control at this stage.

Now that the old person can no longer work and has experienced a sizable drop in income, she may find that she has few social contacts, is engaging in less activity, and even has some new health problems. Thus, she might be exhibiting evermore socially expected signs of being an old person. At the point when the original public labeling and ensuing limitation of options lead to the acquisition of additional characteristics of the old-age stereotype, the person is in the third stage of her career path. Society is beginning to get the behaviors its structures promote.

If the elderly person manages to avoid succumbing to expected age-related behaviors, various familial and media-enforced weapons of social control will

---

[19] For an attempt to integrate exchange theory and symbolic interactionism in explaining the impact of elderly resources upon their social leverage, see [46].

assist her career "development." She can for example indulge her recently acquired penchant for passivity and need for cheap entertainment by watching television. There she will view "a rather gloomy picture of aging"—one where old persons are practically invisible (2.2% of prime-time characters) and where women such as herself are "quite likely to be hurt of killed and to fail." [47] And if these women are not hurt or killed, they along with their male counterparts are treated with disrespect and portrayed as stubborn, eccentric, or foolish. Our viewer will also notice a double standard of aging on television whereby male characters sixty-five and above play settled adult roles with romantic possibilities more often than women characters of the same age. Women are invariably cast as "old"—meaning inactive, nonproductive, and sexless—in case our elderly viewer had not gotten the message yet of what it means to be labeled old.

If older people need to move in with adult children or have frequent contact with them, they may experience certain costs for this relational dependence. Because most persons have needs for acceptance and nurturance, they often gear their behavior toward the expectations of others. Thus to the extent that an older person's relatives subscribe to age norms and try to get "appropriate" behavior from older family members, the elder's options may be constrained. For example, grandmother might be chastized for having a gentleman caller who is younger than herself, particularly if he is not as financially well-off and therefore automatically suspected of taking advantage of poor grandmother who must be feeling desperate or a little "crazy" to date a younger ne'er-do-well. Although age norms are restrictive for both men and women, they tend to be more confining for women—a form of social control which underscores the stereotype on television that older women have romantic adult roles less often than do older men. The stereotype both reflects reality and helps to sustain it.

If older individuals seek acceptance from their age peers, they may be confronted with equally strong age norms since many older Americans have internalized age as a reasonable criterion for evaluating behavior [48, pp. 710-717]. As labeling theorists suggest, when a stigmatized or oppressed group censors its own members, there is no need for dominant groups to resort to more openly coercive social control mechanisms.

Sometimes the costs for dependence on relatives are stronger than mere ridicule or ostracism. Reports of physical abuse of older members have begun to surface [49, 50, pp. 54-55]. Elderly abuse like child abuse involves someone who is dependent upon a caretaker, lives in a *presumably* loving environment, and can be a source of financial, physical, or emotional stress to the caretaker. Along with some wife abuse victims, the elderly often have such low self-concepts that they either think they deserve such abuse or fear the unknown outside the family (including nursing homes) more than the known within [51]. The mere existence of nursing homes and mental institutions can exert pressure on fearful old persons to put up with the alternatives, no matter what their form or personal cost.

Without a doubt the most coercive structural control mechanism that can be encountered by old persons relate to labels suggesting incompetence, mental illness, or incontinence. Short of institutionalization, it is possible for the elderly to lose the legal right to oversee their own affairs and to be assigned to the protective custody of a social worker or court appointee. The availability of such an alternative as a threat can augment the power of some family members over their elderly, and it clearly elevates the caretaker role of the state to an impressive level. With institutionalization in either a nursing home or a mental institution, the old person loses the last vestiges of personal autonomy or power.

Functionalists, labeling theorists, and conflict proponents all perceive medicalization as a primary mode of formal social control in American society today, and all argue that while such control is rationalized as humane, it results in the political castration of the deviant or devalued person [41, 52, pp. 609-617, 53]. As Goffman points out, when medicalization ends in confinement to a "total institution," the patient is exposed to a closed and rigidly administered life-style that reduces the individual to the symbolic antithesis of what is presumed to constitute "adulthood." [45] Self-determination and freedom of action disappear as options, and for all practical purposes the old person drops through to the bottom of the age-grading system.

As confining as age norms can be for the elderly, being treated as a child at the age of seventy-five facilitates a complete degradation of self. Forced communal living, regimentation, infantilism, segregation from the outside world, staff impersonalism, and task orientation all conspire to stigmatize the identity to the point of nonpersonhood. If the resident does not submit to this institutional routine, he or she may encounter the use of chemical or mechanical constraints.

One of the most insidious aspects of the medicalization mode of social control is the disciplinary use of medicine under the guise of the medical service model [45]. Just as drugs have been employed to manage hyperactive school children, so are they used as a means of deterring potentially "disruptive behavior" within total institutions such as nursing homes and mental institutions. Also, to the extent that such drugs are used on an outpatient basis with the elderly so as to help them "adjust" or cope with any isolation, hostility, or alienation they are feeling, they are coercive on two levels. First, they focus corrective measures on the victim rather than the system, and second, even though the older person is still in the community, he or she is being managed or controlled. Tranquilizers used in any setting tend to "dampen, sedate, diminish, and dehumanize social interaction" and thus reduce personal autonomy [54, p. 182].

So far we have focused on the structural or objective aspects of the control edifice experienced by the elderly as they assume their careers as old persons. As we have seen, these range from material sanctions—unemployment or reduction in income—through media, family, and peer pressures to act as an old person and can take on visibly coercive proportions with institutionalization. Chronological age serves as a triggering mechanism for inclusion in any and all of these transitions, and it is not surprising that many older Americans try to avoid being "caught" and labeled as an old person. The gerontophobia that accompanies these structural controls may originate as a prejudice against others but often ends up as a hating of oneself.[20] Thus the career of an old person is embued with subjective dimensions as well.

Unlike individuals who are labeled deviant due to homosexual or delinquent behavior and who may possibly shed the label (though with much difficulty after it is publicly affixed), persons labeled "old" are usually stabilized in that role, and this is due to its castelike properties. People respond differently to the ascription of a role they did not actively seek.

Some older persons react as though they have what Goffman calls "a spoiled identity" and maneuver their presentation of self so as to play down this undesirable role. Typical of this response is the older individual who goes to great lengths to participate in activities with middle-aged or younger cohorts and avoid association with aged peers. Older politicians who never identify themselves with elderly constituents reflect one form this avoidance can take. Such persons tend to be hypersensitive to any reference to age by others and feel on the defensive. Shame of being old is implied, and sometimes those affected engage in "secret deviance" [25]; that is, they try to avoid being publicly labeled old by falsifying documents or consistently misrepresenting their age.

Others view their age as a hard-earned medal of survival and make no attempts to maneuver around any labeling as old. By and large though, studies indicate a reluctance among America's elderly to identify with being "old," even when they are seventy or more years of age [57, 58].[21] Gerontophobia does indeed have an impressive and controlling effect upon the elderly's self-concepts and identities.

A second subjective component in the career of an old person can be withdrawal into a subculture based on age. Although Rose's theory of the old as a subculture has positive overtones for eventual political activity among the elderly, the concept of subculture connotes negative dynamics as well [60, pp. 3-16]. When a person joins an organized group (subculture) of similarly labeled and devalued individuals, he or she has taken the final step in the career path. The negative part of this step is the assumption that it was forced. After labeling the person as old, setting a series of structural changes in motion (e.g., retirement, reduced income) and thereby limiting the older person's options within the community, the social control network has maneuvered the older person into a situation where he or she only feels free to be "old" among other old

---

[20] There is evidence that this loathing and fear is an extension of individuals' attitudes toward disabled people. This link exists among geriatric workers as well as the general public [55, pp. 347-353, 56].

[21] In a study based on a national sample, Cutler found that only 38 percent of persons over age sixty identified as being old as opposed to young or middle aged. Ward reports that in another study only 61 percent of those age seventy-one to seventy-nine identified as being old [59].

persons. Within the elderly subculture, the devalued role of being old can be carried out with a "minimum of trouble." [25]

In addition to factors mentioned earlier, fear of criminal victimization or familial abandonment could contribute to participation in an aged subculture to the extent that it takes the form of a retirement community. After being singled out as different by the larger community on the basis of age, those so-labeled can reach the point where this label becomes their superordinate basis for identity and behavior. Thus there is nowhere further to go in the career of being old, and that which society originally labeled important (being old) has fulfilled the prophecy and become the ultimate source of identity to the labeled victim as well.

Labeling theorists implicate all social levels in the stigmatizing process and stress *people*, not abstract institutions, as the principal agents of social control. As Hughes puts it, "good people" allow others to do their "dirty work," and the greater social distance they want to place between themselves and the stigmatized, the more they allocate their handling to "caretakers." [61, pp. 23-36] Degrees of segregation from the economic mainstream and social isolation reflect degrees of stigma tolerated by the community toward the labeled group.

According to this perspective, those performing society's "dirty work" with respect to the elderly would include legislators, social workers, Social Security administrators, nursing home entrepreneurs, psychiatrists, and interpreters of pension guidelines, to name just a few categories. These specialists in elderly care are akin to undertakers who protect Americans from their dead, only in this case the "loved one" is conscious. If Hughes is correct about the relationship between relegation of care and social distance, then this evidence of an increase in the number and types of specialists dealing with the elderly suggests an increase in gerontophobia in contemporary society. The act of these older members against the social order seems to have been growing old in the land of the young.

There have been at least two additional results of Social Security legislation that have had a tremendously constraining effect upon the well-being of the elderly. One is the deinstitutionalization of many state inmates of late, and the other is the huge network of caretakers and gerontologists which has flowered to deal with the "problem" group identified by Social Security. We not only increased old people's economic resources with enactment of Social Security, but we also created huge bureaucracies and what conflict theorists call "regimes of experts" to assess, regulate, advise, and ultimately control the elderly. We shall now examine each trend for its relevance to containment of the elderly within our society today.

DECARCERATION: A CHEAP WAY TO PROTECT SOCIETY FROM ITS OLD?

The connections made earlier between the changing needs of capital and passage of Social Security legislation are important because we are witnessing repercussions today. As the state has absorbed more and more costs of production through subsidizing the employed and unemployed work forces, it has gotten into a fiscal bind so great that dismantling an earlier means of social control—institutionalization of deviants—has become politically desirable. Decarceration, as the dismantling process is called, is possible *only* because social insurance and welfare payments exist. In many ways this decarceration trend parallels the decentralization approach to the provision of social services that has evolved over the past ten years, and in both cases social control of deviant or devalued populations at lower costs is the goal, if not the outcome. The elderly in particular have been adversely affected by these changes.

The most striking feature of institutionalized care of the elderly during the 1960's was enactment of the Medicare and Medicaid programs in 1965 and the subsequent mushrooming of the nursing home industry. Because of the form in which this legislation passed—conforming to the entrepreneurial concerns of physicians, the drug industry, and nursing home operators—it quickly led to an avalanche of abuse, scandal, and fraud. Profiteering was manifest in various ways, ranging from skimping on food, charging privately paying patients extra fees for "bedsore," "incontinent," and "senile" care, to billing Medicaid patients after discharge and sometimes death [62-65].

After hearings on abuse were held and reforms instituted, the elderly joined other categories of the population being victimized by a wave of decarceration. Although this decarceration trend, which began in the 1960's for mental hospital and penal populations, was hailed at the time as a reform that would lead to more integrated life-styles and quality community care for deviant populations, it has resulted in a number of serious problems. Hundreds of thousands of persons—including many elderly—have been discharged from state mental facilities, for example, into communities where resources have never been allocated for their care. Screening procedures for identifying the best candidates for release have been nonexistent in numerous instances [66], and many of the released elderly have ended up in nursing homes. Further, when the Supplementary Security Income was introduced and the definition of "long-term" care was loosened to include boarding houses, these sprang up everywhere; in one case even taking the form of a converted chicken coop [67].

Some have charged that this "dumping" of stigmatized populations into the community is a new type of social control intended to cost less than institutionalization; and the recently decarcerated who lack adequate incomes, work, and in many cases basic coping mechanisms comprise "deviant ghettos" right in the heart of cities [41]. Many cannot move or travel, and thus their whereabouts can be known. Also they tend to be dangerous only to one another. Essentially, older individuals are easy marks for crimes committed by other outcasts and for profiteering by adult home operators. Originally, adult homes in the community were intended for the frail elderly, but in states such as New York they have been opened to released mental patients who are eligible for Supplemental Security Income (SSI) funds. Because psychiatric hospitals are eager to release these persons and cut costs (with the guise that local communities will pick them up), they do not always mention a releasee's propensity for violent behavior if it exists, and the frail elderly have sometimes been criminally victimized by the mentally ill [66].

The reason nursing homes are still relied upon for elderly care in an era of decarceration is that they are privately run operations and do not constitute the same fiscal drain on the state that other total care facilities do.[22] The elderly in mental hospitals are finding themselves on the streets along with other devalued groups, sometimes with nothing more than a piece of paper inscribed with the name of a half-way house. Not only do many old persons never locate such residences, but also some never collect their Supplementary Security Income payments—their "ticket" to the streets—because they do not know (or do not remember having been told) about them.

The state is subsidizing care providers by contracting out work to them, but it is also having enormous difficulties assuring any kind of quality for its investment. For example, in Massachusetts many private providers who "came to the state's rescue" with alternative treatment models for the deinstitutionalized populations now resist state "interference" with their operations. This has been a dilemma with physicians and nursing home operators since the introduction of Medicare and Medicaid. As one provider put it, "I could be running a zoo here, and they wouldn't care as long as I filled in the little blocks on the form." [68] By the time the states hire enough persons to enforce quality guidelines for their contracted work, they may well spend as much money as they did when incarcerating most deviants, particularly where entrepreneurs resist their "interference."

Although the elderly who are unloaded from mental institutions onto the streets are a minority, the fact that such situations have been made possible by "reforms" authorized by the state raises serious questions about what the past fifty years of legislation have meant for older Americans. Whether we speak of social control as the exercise of legitimized authority in the form of laws (functionalism), constraint of personal autonomy (labeling theory), or dominance of one group by another (conflict theory), the elderly are a heavily controlled segment of the population. With enactment of Social Security and official recognition of the elderly as a dependent population, an "aging enterprise" [69] has evolved to service this group. Social Security not only helped to stabilize the social order and ensure the positions of elites, it also created the conditions whereby legions of "experts" would come to speak on behalf of the elderly; technocratic rather than redistributive policies were found. Indeed, if the number of specialists in caretaker roles for the elderly connotes social distance from the rest of society, ageism is worse today than it was one hundred years ago. If regimes of experts (researchers and policymakers) help control the claims of the

[22] Because of the way nursing home legislation was passed, numerous inflated costs do exist as well as many remaining questions about the quality of care delivered. For a thorough examination of nursing homes see [65].

nonexpert by advising them of what is "good" for them, the elderly are in serious trouble on two fronts.

CARETAKERS AND GERONTOLOGISTS AS AGENTS OF SOCIAL CONTROL

One indication of the elderly's controlled position is the "legitimized" status of the aging network that is now in place. This network is accepted by political elites and delimited as well. Goals are incremental and never seriously challenge the existing distribution of income and wealth. Leaders of senior organizations want to be "respected" and accepted by Washington's insiders and pride themselves on "playing the game." The more these individuals move in an out of private and public positions as other clientele group leaders do, the more vested their interest will become in being accepted by Washington peers and invoking these "working relationships" to justify not rocking the boat [9]. Just as union leaders have at times been charged with aligning with the objective interests of business at the expense of rank and file members in order to enhance their own respectability, so too are senior organization leaders similarly suspect as they become politically entrenched.

Evidence of their coopted status comes from supposed victories which have been claimed for the elderly. The Older Americans Act of 1965 established the Administration on Aging, which was to herald a new era in advocacy for the elderly; nonetheless, many observers describe this administration as virtually impotent. Some of its problems stem from having to deal with aged-related divisions of other federal departments and agencies rather than being authorized to center all elderly services within the Administration on Aging. Another problem is in funding. Despite substantial expansion since its inception, present funding levels severely restrict the scope of the social service programs supported by the Administration on Aging.

National elderly advocates have been constrained by the New Federalism put into effect in the 1970's to cut costs and put control of elderly services in the hands of local authorities [69]. As was noted earlier, this decentralization of planning and resource control paralleled the decarceration movement, and in both instances money was the bottom line. Not only does this decentralized strategy limit potential coordinating faculties of the Administration on Aging (as it was no doubt intended to do), but it has also fostered a situation where providers of indirect services for the elderly have increased, while direct services have received low priority. Thus Congress has made aging affairs so decentralized that some say almost everyone but the elderly is benefitting; and this occurred either in spite of or because of the regime of experts standing by in Washington to represent the interests of the elderly. Older persons may speak at public hearings or serve as consultants to local agencies, but their actual input is usually held to "technical matters"—not anything that would threaten agencies' bureaucratic rationales or the control of staff [69].

America's elderly are not only contained within the political arena by Congress and advocates on their behalf (including organizational leaders, entrepreneurs, and service providers), but they are also kept under close tabs by their benefactors in the local community as well. The elderly have been set aside as a "problem" group in need, and their resource deprivation must be maintained in order for their caretakers to justify their own continued existence. This may be a reason why so much money and effort is going toward indirect services such as referral agencies at the local level rather than into direct services, such as housing or adequate income maintenance—either of which requires a limited number of bureaucrats to operate. Amelioration of the elderly's difficulties is possible, it would seem, as long as their dependency as a group is not seriously dissipated.

It is important to note that gerontologists—including academically based ones—are implicated in the social control of the elderly. As a group that studies and services a social category called "the elderly," they are by their very existence underscoring the *separateness* of older Americans and prolonging their definition (label) as a problem group. The trouble with being a "special topic" or "problem group" in American society is that the group tends to be done to, is discouraged from doing, and becomes increasingly dependent through its separateness. To be a problem category is to carry a stigma whether the label is delinquent, welfare recipient, poor person, or old person. Also, to study the aging process so as to try and control it, as some researchers do, implies that the process is intrinsically negative and to be avoided. Gerontologists thus reflect the very values which they criticize at times.[23]

Second, although it is fashionable among social gerontologists to lament how policies to date have been piecemeal and of least assistance to the most disadvantaged elderly,[24] these observers do not tend to be in the vanguard of efforts to dissociate Social Security eligibility and funding from employment. Clearly those who are most socially devalued and therefore disadvantaged in the work world (e.g., women and nonwhites) are going to remain that way into old age. It would seem that gerontologists, just like most Americans, do not want to get caught on the side of an issue that is opposed by elites, who might label them "radicals" or withhold research funding.

Also, the incremental approach of Congress in subsidizing elderly well-being has been paralleled by a piecemeal and individualistic orientation among gerontologists themselves. For the most part, theories on aging have focused upon individual adjustment (called pathology in earlier days) to problems associated

[23] In this regard they are like poverty theorists, who argue that no such thing as a culture of poverty exists, and then proceed to study "the poor" as though they constituted a special or unique group.

[24] Reference has been made to the most disadvantaged elderly being excluded from many policies by several contributors to the July/August, 1978 issue of *Society* devoted to political gerontology and before that by Hudson and Binstock in their overview of the politics of aging [70].

with aging, not on the structural creation of the problems.[25] Gerontologists have shown even more reticence in aggressively investigating, analyzing, and unmasking the insidious social control elements involved with medicalization, institutionalization, and decarceration of the elderly and in asking and exposing who ultimately benefits from these trends. The most critical analyses of "reforms" applicable to the elderly have by and large not been done by gerontologists,[26] nor directed at mass audiences.

To the extent that gerontologists are conducting research funded by the government, are read by policymakers, or serve as advisors to the government, they are part of the regime of experts who presumably know more about the elderly than do the elderly. When their research, commentary, or advice deals with predicting future behavior of the elderly, particularly in the political realm as this book does, complicity in the political containment and control of older Americans is undeniable. Other forms this social control has taken among gerontologists include downplaying the potential of the elderly to bloc vote [71, pp. 50-53], predicting a political backlash against the elderly if they pursue further age-based gains [11, pp. 30-33], and suggesting that incremental goals are the only feasible ones [9]. All of these ideas underpin the status quo and the existing distribution of society's resources. In fact, taken collectively, they promote defeatism about the desirability or possibility of significant change occurring—a situation that presumably would necessitate the continued services of the growing cadre of gerontologists on behalf of that special, segregated, and controlled group known as "the aged."

In this chapter we have highlighted the social control aspects of a variety of welfare programs for the aged. Many readers will, no doubt, question the propriety of being so openly critical of these programs, particularly in this era of welfare state retrenchment. Our goal has not been to suggest that today's elderly would be better off without these programs. To the contrary, they would most definitely be a great deal worse off without them. But if we are to design future programs in such a way as to minimize their most oppressive social control aspects, we must admit that a problem does exist, and only then will we begin to directly address this issue.

Similarly, it would be inappropriate to interpret our discussion of gerontologists as agents of social control as a call for gerontologists to fold up their tents and return whence they came, leaving the elderly alone. Gerontologists are presently performing a wide range of valuable services to those who are elderly.

[25] Even the recent work of Dowd speaks of the need for elderly persons to manage their interaction processes with others so they are not perceived as victims [46]. This solution does not address the problem of limited exchange resources available to the elderly, which Dowd himself goes to great lengths to delineate earlier in his analysis.

[26] A major exception to the generally noncritical approach of gerontologists to the meaning of their work is Carroll Estes [69]. Although Estes does not speak in terms of social control, the events and dynamics she discloses do indeed reflect various aspects of the control apparatus.

We would hardly argue that the elderly would be better off if professional gerontologists did not exist. Rather, our goal is to sensitize gerontologists to the social control aspects inherent in many of their activities. Those who are aware of these ramifications will be in a better position to do something about it.

REFERENCES

1. T. Hobbes, *Leviathan*, Liberal Arts Press, New York, (1598), 1958.
2. J. J. Rousseau, *The Social Contract*, E. P. Dutton, New York, (1762), 1950.
3. H. S. Hughes, *Consciousness and Society: The Reorientation of European Social Thought 1890-1930*, Vintage, New York, 1958.
4. C. H. Cooley, *Two Major Works: Social Organization and Human Nature and the Social Order*, Free Press, Glencoe, Illinois, 1956.
5. E. Durkheim, *The Elementary Forms of Religious Life*, (translated by J. W. Swain), Free Press, New York, 1947.
6. E. A. Ross, *Social Control: A Survey of the Foundation of Order*, Macmillan, New York, 1928.
7. W. G. Sumner, The Absurd Effort to Make the World Over, in *War and Other Essays*, Yale University Press, New Haven, 1911.
8. B. L. Neugarten, The Future and the Young-Old, *Gerontologist*, *15*, 1975.
9. H. J. Pratt, *The Gray Lobby*, University of Chicago Press, Chicago, 1976.
10. R. B. Hudson, The "Graying" of the Federal Budget and Its Consequences for Old-Age Policy, *Gerontologist*, *18*, 1978.
11. _____, Emerging Pressures on Public Policies for the Aging, *Society*, *15*, 1978.
12. E. Durkheim, *The Rules of Sociological Method*, (translated by S. A. Solovay and J. H. Mueller), Free Press, New York, 1958.
13. K. T. Erikson, Notes on the Sociology of Deviance, in *The Other Side*, H. S. Becker (ed.), Free Press, New York, 1964.
14. R. D. Davis, Television Communication and the Elderly, in *Aging: Scientific Perspectives and Social Issues*, D. Woodruff and J. Birren (eds.), Van Nostrand, New York, 1975.
15. J. Horton, The Dehumanization of Anomie and Alienation, *British Journal of Sociology*, *15*, 1964.
16. J. Pease, W. H. Form, and J. H. Rytina, Ideological Currents in American Stratification Literature, *American Sociologist*, *5*, 1970.
17. H. Spencer, *The Principles of Sociology*, Appleton, New York, 1896.
18. T. Parsons, *The Structure of Social Action*, McGraw-Hill, New York, 1937.
19. _____, *The Social System*, Free Press, New York, 1951.
20. C. W. Mills, The Professional Ideology of Social Pathologists, *American Journal of Sociology*, *49*, 1943.
21. R. K. Merton, *Social Theory and Social Structure*, Free Press, New York, 1957.
22. J. S. Roucek, *Social Control*, Van Nostrand, New York, 1947.
23. G. H. Mead, *Mind, Self, and Society: From the Standpoint of a Social Behaviorist*, C. W. Morris (ed.), University of Chicago Press, Chicago, 1934.

24. H. Blumer, *Symbolic Interactionism: Perspective and Method*, Prentice-Hall, Englewood Cliffs, New Jersey, 1969.
25. H. S. Becker (ed.), *Outsiders*, Free Press, New York, 1973.
26. A. Liazos, The Poverty of the Sociology of Deviance: Nuts, Sluts, and Preverts, *Social Problems, 20*, 1972.
27. L. D. Brandeis, *Workingmen's Insurance–The Road to Social Efficiency*, Proceedings of the National Conference of Charities and Corrections, 1911.
28. W. Graebner, *A History of Retirement*, Yale University Press, New Haven, 1980.
29. R. Lubove, *The Struggle for Social Security 1900-1935*, Harvard University Press, Cambridge, Massachusetts, 1968.
30. W. A. Achenbaum, *Old Age in the New Land*, Johns Hopkins University Press, Baltimore, 1978.
31. D. O. Cowgill and L. D. Holmes, *Aging and Modernization*, Appleton-Century-Crofts, New York, 1972.
32. E. W. Burgess, Human Aspects of Social Policy, in *Old Age in the Modern World*, E. and S. Livingston, Edinburgh, 1955.
33. D. H. Fischer, *Growing Old in America*, Expanded Edition, Oxford University Press, New York, 1978.
34. W. A. Achenbaum, *Old Age in the New Land*, Johns Hopkins University Press, Baltimore, 1978.
35. B. E. Vanfossen, *The Structure of Social Inequality*, Little, Brown, Boston, 1979.
36. H. P. Miller, *Income Distribution in the United States*, U.S. Government Printing Office, Washington, D.C., 1966.
37. G. Kolko, *Wealth and Power in America: An Analysis of Social Class and Income Distribution*, Praeger, New York, 1962.
38. F. L. Hoffman, State Pensions and Annuities in Old Age, *American Statistical Association Quarterly Publications, 11*, 1909.
39. R. B. Calhoun, *In Search of the New Old: Redefining Old Age in America, 1945-1970*, Elsevier, New York, 1978.
40. R. Hunter, *Poverty*, Torchbook/Harper and Row, New York (1904), 1965.
41. A. T. Scull, *Decarceration: Community Treatment and the Deviant–A Radical View*, Prentice-Hall, Englewood Cliffs, New Jersey, 1977.
42. National Industrial Conference Board (NICB), Industrial Pensions in the United States, New York: National Industrial Conference Board, 1925.
43. F. F. Piven and R. A. Cloward, *Regulating the Poor: The Functions of Public Welfare*, Random House, New York, 1971.
44. A. K. Cohen, *Deviance and Control*, Prentice-Hall, Englewood Cliffs, New Jersey, 1966.
45. E. Goffman, *Asylums*, Anchor/Doubleday, Garden City, New York, 1961.
46. J. J. Dowd, *Stratification among the Aged*, Brooks/Cole, Monterey, California, 1980.
47. L. Brown, *Study Finds Stereotyping in TV Casts*, New York Times, October 30, 1979.
48. B. L. Neugarten, J. W. Moore, and J. C. Lowe, Age Norms, Age Constraints, and Adult Socialization, *American Journal of Sociology, 70*, 1965.

49. S. K. Steinmetz and M. A. Straus (eds.), *Violence in the Family*, Harper and Row, New York, 1974.
50. S. K. Steinmetz, Battered Parents, *Society*, *15*:5, 1978.
51. M. R. Block and J. D. Sinnott, *The Battered Elder Syndrome: An Exploratory Study*, University of Maryland, Center on Aging, College Park, Maryland, 1979.
52. T. Parsons, Illness and the Role of the Physician: A Sociological Perspective, in *Personality in Nature, Society and Culture*, 2nd Edition, C. Kluckhohn and H. A. Murray (eds.), Knopf, New York, 1955.
53. T. S. Szasz, *Law, Liberty and Psychiatry: An Inquiry into the Social Uses of Mental Health Practices*, Macmillan, New York, 1963.
54. A. Bernstein and H. L. Lennard, Drugs, Doctors, and Junkies, in *Social Problems: The Contemporary Debates*, 3rd Edition, J. Williamson, L. Evans and A. Munley (eds.), Little, Brown, Boston, 1981.
55. J. Drevenstedt and G. Banziger, Attitudes toward the Elderly and toward the Mentally Ill, *Psychological Reports*, *41*, 1977.
56. J. F. McCourt, A Study of the Acceptance of the Geriatric Patient among Selected Groups of Hospital Personnel, unpublished doctoral dissertation, Boston University, Boston, 1963.
57. M. W. Riley and A. Foner, *Aging and Society*, Volume 1: An Inventory of Research Findings, Russel Sage, New York, 1968.
58. N. E. Cutler, The Impact of Subjective Age Identification on Social and Political Attitudes, paper presented at the Annual Meeting of the Gerontological Society, Portland, Oregon, 1974.
59. R. A. Ward, *The Aging Experience*, J. B. Lippincott, New York, 1979.
60. A. M. Rose, The Subculture of Aging: A Framework for Research in Social Gerontology, in *Older People and Their Social World*, A. M. Rose and W. A. Peterson (eds.), F. A. Davis, Philadelphia, 1965.
61. E. C. Hughes, Good People and Dirty Work, in *The Other Side*, H. S. Becker (ed.), Free Press, New York, 1964.
62. M. A. Mendelson, *Tender Loving Greed*, Knopf, New York, 1974.
63. C. H. Percy, *Growing Old in the Country of the Young*, McGraw-Hill, New York, 1974.
64. J. B. Williamson, L. Evans, and A. Munley, *Aging and Society*, Holt, Rinehart, and Winston, New York, 1980.
65. B. C. Vladeck, *Unloving Care: The Nursing Home Tragedy*, Basic Books, New York, 1980.
66. R. Herman, *Mental Patient Release Program Leaves Many to Harsh Fate*, New York Times, November 18, 1979.
67. U.S. Senate Special Committee on Aging, *The Role of Nursing Homes in Caring for Discharged Mental Patients (and the Birth of a For-Profit Boarding Home Industry)*, Supporting Paper No. 7, U.S. Government Printing Office, Washington, D.C., 1976.
68. J. Dietz, *Social Services: Big Business*, Boston Globe, July 15, 1980.
69. C. L. Estes, *The Aging Enterprise: A Critical Examination of Social Policies and Services for the Aged*, Jossey-Bass, San Francisco, 1979.

70. R. B. Hudson and R. H. Binstock, Political Systems and Aging, in *Handbook of Aging and the Social Sciences*, R. H. Binstock and E. Shanas (eds.), Van Nostrand Reinhold, New York, 1976.
71. P. K. Ragan and W. J. Davis, The Diversity of Older Voters, *Society, 15*, July-August, 1978.

Reprinted with permission of Charles C. Thomas, Publisher. From *The Politics of Aging*, John B. Williamson et al., Charles C. Thomas Publishers, Springfield, Illinois, pp. 214-244, 1982.

PART II. INSTITUTIONS AND STRUCTURED DEPENDENCY: SOCIAL CONTROL AND MARKET ECONOMY HEALTH CARE

The social control and management of the elderly is perhaps most dramatically played out in the medicalization and treatment of old age. At the same time, health policies affecting the elderly, (e.g., Medicare and Medicaid in the U.S.) often are instituted in part out of a genuine concern with increasing access to needed health and medical care services. The "double edged sword" which health policies and programs for the elderly represent is thus particularly important to view from a broad political economy perspective.

Whether in capitalist or state socialist economies, a characteristic of health and social policies for the elderly is their emphasis on the family as the primary provider of care. This section begins with Walker's examination of the theory and the reality of community care and the elderly in Great Britain. Contradictions between the meaning of community care in statements of public policy, in actual policy implementation and in the rhetoric of administrators and politicians are seen as "a classic example of 'words that succeed and policies that fail'". Concurrently, the changing role and status of women is seen as severely taxing the limits of the family's ability to provide care, at the same time that governments in much of Western Europe and the United States sharply restrict health and social service resources.

Following this more general introduction to dependency and social policy in care of the elderly, we turn to the specific case of mental illness. Dowd's examination of this topic focuses in particular on the ways in which the social and economic class position of the elderly effect mental health in old age. Following a critique the dominant mental health paradigms within social gerontology, Dowd presents a social control approach to these issues, arguing that the fact of growing old in capitalist societies brings with it increased risks of mental illness due to both the elderly's exclusion from labor markets and their assignment, by society, to a position as "stranger" within that society.

Following Dowd's analysis, we turn in Chapter VII to an historical look at the genesis and metamorphosis of two programs which constitute both mechanisms of social control and positive attempts to improve the access of the elderly and the poor to health and medical services. As Brown notes, the United States' enactment of Medicare and Medicaid in the mid 1960's grew out of a half century of fighting for (and against) national health insurance. While the programs finally implemented *did* help to increase access to care for the elderly and the poor, they also were frought with ideological and fiscal problems, and failed to end inequities in health status and health care between rich and poor.

Medicare and Medicaid also had major unanticipated consequences, among them dramatic growth in size and profitability of the nursing home industry in the United States. This section ends with Harrington's analysis of public policy and the nursing home industry, focusing on the influence of the profit motive on its growth and organization, on quality of care issues, and on the lack of viable alternatives to institutional care of the frail elderly. The nursing home industry is seen as constituting a particularly vivid example of the social control of the elderly, and of the way in which social, economic and political forces within a society shape and determine the ways in which problems are defined and managed, to whose benefit, and at whose expense.

CHAPTER 5

Community Care and the Elderly in Great Britain: Theory and Practice

ALAN WALKER

In Great Britain, as in other advanced industrial societies, much has been written and spoken about the recent growth of the "dependent" sectors of the population—particularly the elderly—and the "burden" they represent to the concomitantly shrinking productive population [1]. The rise in the numbers of elderly people[1] has indeed created difficult problems for families, health services, and social service departments. However, insufficient attention has been paid to the mechanisms by which some states of dependency are created, the motives underlying state intervention in the provision of community care, and how far these policy responses have fulfilled the explicit goals of successive governments, and the extent to which these community care policies[2] rely on an unequal sexual division of labor within the family. The analysis is based on experience in postwar Britain, but the conclusions will have relevance to policy on aging in other industrial societies.

It is necessary, as a prelude to this account, to make a few brief comments on the meaning of dependency in old age. The term "dependent" is often used loosely to describe those groups not taking part in productive work [3]. Primarily this applies to young children and elderly people, but can also include the disabled, handicapped, and unemployed. Some of these periods of dependency, especially childhood and old age, have been explained on the basis of a life-cycle approach to family need [4]. Typical patterns of family development are superimposed on a chronological age scale and it is assumed that periods of need are the natural result of age itself. This, in turn, has been translated into social policy and the provision of services, as well as the practice of social workers and others dealing almost exclusively with the "dependent population." The resulting

---

[1] The numbers of those aged seventy-five or more will rise by 23 percent between 1976 and 1996 in Great Britain. The very elderly (age 85 and over) will increase by 42 percent in the same time period [2].

[2] State community care policies have traditionally taken the form of the provision of help and support in non-institutional settings, usually in an individual's own home. They are intended to keep the individual in the community and out of an institution.

policies and popular perceptions of dependency help to reinforce the low status of those concerned.

It is important for policy makers and practitioners to recognize that this process of assigning dependent status on the basis of age is a *social*, not a biological construct. I have argued in detail elsewhere [5] that there is no necessary relationship between chronological age and dependency. Even at the extremes of age, dependency is associated with functional ability rather than with age as such. And this relationship between disability and physical dependency is by no means clear cut, because financial resources, aids, and adaptations may mitigate this need to some extent. The essentially social nature of dependent status can be underlined by recalling that as late as the mid-nineteenth century it was common for children to work long hours in factories [6]. In some parts of the world this practice continues today [7]. At the other end of the age scale, between 1931 and 1978 the proportion of men over sixty-five in Great Britain who were at work fell by more than one half [8]. Moreover, in recent years there has been a growing trend toward early retirement, a trend that with the exception of France, is common to other advanced industrial societies [9].

The "dependency" of the vast majority of elderly people consists of structurally enforced social status inferior to that of the working population and financial dependence on the state. Although old age is often characterized by physical dependency, *economic* dependency is a predominant characteristic of the elderly in industrial societies [10]. Altogether, eight million elderly people in Great Britain receive a retirement pension (including five million women, of whom 40 percent are eligible through their own contributions). For significant proportions of elderly people this dependency is characterized by poverty and generally low incomes in relation to the non-elderly population [11]. Ever since such statistics have been collected socially, elderly people have been shown to comprise the majority of those living in poverty. In Great Britain currently, they form just under one half of all persons living in households with incomes on or below the poverty line. In all, nearly two thirds of the elderly (just over five million people) live in or on the margins of poverty[3] compared with one fifth of the non-elderly [12]. In the United States, about 20 percent of elderly people have incomes below the federally established minimum [13]. In Japan, 90 percent of the elderly have incomes in the lower half of the income distribution [14].

As in the preretirement population, poverty in old age is socially divided, being more likely to affect those from the lower than higher social classes. The ownership of other resources, such as wealth, housing, basic amenities, and consumer durables, which with income determine standard of living, is distributed along lines broadly similar to income [15]. Large sections of elderly people are

[3] The poverty line is defined by the appropriate supplementary benefit scale rate. Those whose net incomes do not exceed 140 percent of this minimum state income are considered on the margins of poverty.

also deprived of the rising standard of living being enjoyed by succeeding generations [5, 16]. Many live and die in abject poverty [17].

SOCIAL DEVALUATION OF THE ROLE OF THE ELDERLY

Old age, for many, is a period of contradictions. Experience gained through a life's work can be rejected by social institutions at a fixed retirement date and the individual consigned, for a period potentially of near equal length to that of working life, to dependency. The increased opportunities for leisure and escape from monotonous tasks, provided in theory by retirement, are often accompanied in practice by poverty and inadequate resources. Senior citizenship status, perhaps supported by familial deference, is denied by the collective judgment of economic and social systems which create dependency, and implicitly suggest inferior status. One small illustration of this collective judgment is the fact that in official statistics, all those over retirement age are grouped with those under sixteen as the "dependent population." A dependency ratio is then calculated as the basis of the ratio of this dependent group to the "working population" (the latter is itself spuriously based on the age range sixteen to retirement age) [18].

More significant perhaps is the institutionalization of early retirement through the job-release scheme, which has been in operation in Britain since 1977. Under this scheme, workers within one year of National Insurance pension age are offered a tax-free allowance if they agree to withdraw prematurely from the labor market to make room for a younger person. By March 7, 1978, applications totalled 24,303 [19]. Some income maintenance policies have also contributed to the tendency for the elderly to be non-participants in the labor force, and have at the same time failed to alleviate poverty [20].

Viewed from the rather narrow perspective of individual responses to aging, it could be concluded on the basis of an analysis of poverty among elderly people that they are detaching themselves from social institutions and relationships. But in the context of the wider structure of resource distribution and the economic and social values which may create dependent status, it can be argued, rather, that the elderly in general, and certain low status groups in particular, are being detached *by* society, through its failure to provide adequate resources and its apparent desire to remove many of them from the labor market [5, pp. 70-74].

It is hardly surprising, therefore, that some gerontologists have concluded that aging is an "inevitable mutual withdrawal of disengagement." [21] Similarly, it is quite obvious that in the face of poverty and the contradictions of old age, many of the elderly cannot participate fully in society. For example, in the absence of an analysis of falling relative income with distance from retirement, the conclusion that the elderly are "disengaging" from society could follow from the finding that twice the proportion of women over eighty-five living in the community as those aged between sixty-five and seventy-four have no regular weekly expenditure commitment such as credit payments or television rental [22]. Such conclusions, however, fail to give sufficient attention to the link between industrial and administrative policies, income maintenance, and other social policies, and their influence on individual responses to aging.

In view of the close relationship between dependent status and poverty in old age, it is important for policy makers to be wary of increasing retirement in an attempt to solve the growing social problem of unemployment [23]. Increasing dependency, resulting from a further reduction in the retirement age, would reinforce the existing tendency for the social costs of the failure of industrial societies to provide enough work of a pleasant and rewarding kind to be partly transferred from the unemployed to the retired. This tendency, already at work, is itself part of a much wider discrimination against elderly people in industrial societies [24]. This discrimination stems in part from the detachment of elderly people from the processes of production, but is also reinforced by the social construction of a dependent minority through social policies and by the officials and experts who administer them [25]. This devaluation of the worth of elderly people in relation to productive processes may have important implications for primary relationships within the family and, therefore, for the pattern of care that is provided by the family.

DEPENDENCY AND SOCIAL POLICY

The cumulative effect of policies in the spheres of industrial organization and income maintenance is to disengage many of the elderly from the working population (whether by bureaucratic regulations or normative coercion) and from useful participation in society. On the one hand society defines work as the main device for establishing a normal family life, and on the other it denies access to work to some groups, including the elderly. Yet in the face of this *social* creation of dependency, our categorization of, and response to, "the problem of the elderly" are individually based. So for example, the official British government publication on the elderly [26] talks of the measures taken *to care for* the elderly who "for the purpose of this pamphlet are defined as those aged sixty years and over." Stress is placed on an individual response to aging through different social service agencies, rather than on the structural relationships between the elderly and the rest of society, the link between dependency and poverty and the creation of need. This approach stems from the fact that social policies reflect ideological assumptions concerning industrial and social values, values which also underlie the growth in dependency.

Individually based responses through social and other agencies to the disengagement of the elderly from society also serve important social functions, such as control and the neutralization of conflict. By defining the problem of dependency in old age in individual terms, it becomes manageable in theory and more easy to solve. Of course it is not, but by concentrating on individual problems and techniques of intervention, social service agencies perform the function of depoliticizing the issues, such as the relationship between the elderly and the rest of society and the extent of poverty among the elderly. Similarly, use of apparently neutral terms such as "helping" hides the fact that social definitions are *imposed* on elderly people by social policies and the agencies which apply them [27]. In fact, government social policies have both failed to counteract the imposition of the social costs of change on the elderly and other groups, and have not compensated the elderly (at least sufficiently to eradicate poverty) for bearing these costs. If such costs are continually shifted to the elderly in the form of increased dependency, this may have several important implications for the family and the care of the elderly.

The observation that the majority of elderly people do not live with their relatives is sometimes taken to be conclusive evidence of a disintegration of the family [28]. But many older people do not have close relatives living [29]. Furthermore, research such as the cross-national survey by Shanas and her colleagues [30], has shown that elderly people often live alone by choice (although the authors did not explore how open the "choice" was). The desire on the part of elderly people for independence and "intimacy at a distance" with their relatives is an enduring finding in social research [31].

Despite exaggerated claims for the break-up of the family and the abrogation of family responsibilities, the family remains an important social institution and certainly the main basis of social support for the elderly in industrial societies [30, 31]. In Great Britain there are between two and three times as many bedridden and severely disabled people living in their own homes as in institutions. In the U.S., for each older person living in an institution there are two elderly persons with a similar impairment residing with a relative [33]. However, there are increasing proportions of very elderly people living in isolation without relatives; due to long periods of dependency, low life-long status, and the likelihood of disablement, they are also prone to poverty. Policies for community care are therefore dependent to some extent for their success on policies to counteract poverty.

One quarter of elderly people in Britain are visited less often than once every month (28 percent for those who are bed-ridden and housebound) [22, p. 95]. The extent of support and care provided by the extended family depends on a number of factors, including the cohesiveness of the family network. Of fundamental importance is the geographic proximity of children, which in turn rests on the interaction between family cohesiveness and the employment and opportunity structure. A recent locally based study found that the number of elderly people with two or more children living nearby was relatively small [34]. Thus the burden of "community care" fell predominantly on one child: "In terms of the ability of family members to provide informal help of one sort or another for an elderly relative, there is normally only one 'provider'—the child who lives nearby." [34] This supports Townsend's finding of some twenty years earlier that old people, particularly women, with daughters and other female relatives living nearby make least claims on the social services [32, p. 214].

Part of the rationalization of the social depreciation of the worth of the elderly is the fact that they are often characterized in public policies as a passive minority, a dependent burden to be *helped* or *cared for*, the recipients of a one-way transaction. Clearly this grossly oversimplifies social relations and, in fact, there is a great deal of reciprocity between elderly people and their offspring. In the small area-based study referred to earlier, for example, almost two thirds of those elderly people with children were actively engaged in helping them by babysitting, shopping, lending money, and caring or cooking for school-age children [34, p. 48]. Obviously the extent of reciprocity is related to some extent to age: in the official survey 27 percent of the elderly aged sixty-five to seventy-four, 14 percent aged seventy-five to eighty-four, and 7 percent aged eighty-five or more said they were able to do things for their relatives when they visited [22, p. 100].

Social policy for the elderly is based on the continued willingness of the family to care for dependent relatives. It is primarily where older people have no living relatives or none living nearby that social services play a major role in caring for the elderly or that the elderly are institutionalized. The state in modern British society occupies a central role in relation to dependency, the care of the elderly, and the division of labor within the family, and it is to an examination of the operation of community care policies and the assumptions underlying them that I now turn. While the state has engaged in policies which have contributed to the dependency of older people, its support for relatives and others providing the bulk of care has been, to say the least, ambiguous. Moreover, through the failure to recognize social inequalities in caring roles *within* the family, state social policies have tended to support the unequal sexual division of labor in caring for the elderly.

THE STATE AND COMMUNITY CARE

Community care has been an explicit policy goal in Britain since the end of World War II. But the development of opinion against institutional care and in favor of community care in the immediate postwar period was primarily concerned with children. The Children Act of 1948, which followed the famous Curtis Report of 1946, spelled out the new principle of policy for the treatment of deprived children. It was not until the late 1950's that a critique of institutions for older people and a policy of community care for the elderly developed. In 1958 the Minister of Health stated that the "underlying principle of our services for the old should be this: that the best place for old people is their own homes, with help from the home services if need be." [35] The Hospital Plan of 1962 [36] was officially said to rest on the expansion of community care services for its success. The report *Health and Welfare*, published in the following year, described the needs of the elderly in the following terms [37]:

> Elderly people living at home may need special support to enable them to cope with their infirmities and to prevent their isolation from society. As their capabilities diminish, they will more often require such services as home help, laundry services, meals cooked ready for eating and chiropody. Loss of mobility brings the need for friendly visiting, transport to social clubs and occupation centres, and arrangements for holidays. When illness is added to other infirmities, they need more home nursing, night care, and help generally in the home. In terminal illness, an elderly person may for a limited period need considerable help from many of the domiciliary services.

Local authority services were increased considerably in the late 1960's and early 70's, following the critical Seebohm Report and the important government survey of handicapped people carried out by the Office of Population Censuses and Surveys [38]. The latter confirmed the findings of independent researchers concerning the lack of domiciliary services: only 16 percent of the very severely handicapped (the majority of whom were elderly) were getting home help assistance [39]. Between 1972 and 1975, the number of cases covered by the home help service[4] increased by 30 percent [40], but this of course does not imply that individual elderly people received more help.

The 1976 consultative document, *Priorities for Health and Personal Social Services in England* [41], repeated the state's explicit commitment to community care: "The general aim of policy is to help [the elderly] maintain independent lives in their own homes for as long as possible. The main emphasis is then on the development of the domiciliary services...." In *The Way Forward* [42], published in the following year, the Department of Health and Social Security (DHSS) announced the diversion of £6 million from capital revenue in 1977-1978 to domiciliary services in response to comments on the previous document. In addition, hope was expressed for a slightly higher rate of growth in such services for the elderly than had been envisaged in 1976.

The goal of community care has also been enshrined in various acts of Parliament since the 1946 Children Act. These include the National Assistance Act of 1948, Mental Health Act of 1959, Health Services and Public Health Act of 1968, and Chronically Sick and Disabled Persons Act of 1970. But despite the reiterated commitment of successive governments, the policy of community care remains a precarious one [43]. In other words, while the explicit goal has been impressive, it has at the same time been ambiguous, and insufficient means have been provided to achieve the goal. (The latter point is illustrated briefly below by reference to expenditure on community care by local authorities.)

[4] There are about 95,000 home helps employed by the local authorities in Great Britain who provide partial help with tasks such as washing, cooking, and shopping.

It is important to examine the concept of community care on which public policy has been based, since one of the most striking features of the continued official commitment to this end has been the confused relationship between the meaning of community care in public policy statements, its meaning in the actual policy carried out, and the sense in which politicians and administrators use it—a classic example of "words that succeed and policies that fail." [27]

As Abrams has pointed out, the possibility of community care in the sense of help, support, and protection provided by lay members of society recedes as state capitalist societies develop [44]. Community care is reinterpreted in public policy as care *in* the community supported by welfare workers [45, 46]. But even this goal has been reinterpreted from care in the family home to care in a range of settings "in the community," including certain types of residential and hospital care [41]. According to one authority [47], community care becomes total care "provided by the service or person most appropriate to the patients' needs regardless of administrative boundaries and definitions."

Rather than reflecting a policy of deinstitutionalization, therefore, the concept of community care has been broadened to encompass residential institutions. It now also includes institutional treatment, institutional care, and community treatment [44, p. 125]. Thus, community care policies themselves may create very limited social constructions of "community" and "care." These limited definitions in turn constrain possibilities for change beyond the boundaries defined by policies. Encouraged by officials and experts, the elderly themselves adopt the restricted definitions of community care implied by policies.

Despite its various reinterpretations, some politicians still use community care in the sense of care *by* the wider community. The policy was most recently restated in the last government's discussion document on elderly people, *A Happier Old Age* [23, pp. 4-5]. As part of a three-point strategy toward the elderly, it was the government's third aim to keep elderly people active and independent in their own homes. With the growth in the proportion of very elderly people in the population, this goal depends, of course, on increasing the level of the resources that are devoted to community services. However, in this green paper the last government appeared to be complacent about its role in providing such services: "There is no doubt that as time goes on, growing demands will fall on the relatives of elderly people." [23, p. 6] While questioning the ability of families to carry the *whole responsibility* for caring for the growing numbers of very old people, the government had little to offer beyond looking to the "wider community."

Turning to the actual provision of community care facilities and personnel, there is a great deal of research in Britain showing a wide gulf between intentions and practice [48]. In the face of rising need for domiciliary services, created by rising numbers of very elderly people and the expectations of clients and service providers encouraged by official proclamations, the government has starved local authorities of resources to meet even existing needs. The home help service is the most important form of domiciliary care provided by local authority social service departments (which are predominantly centrally funded) and elderly people comprise about 80 percent of home help cases. In 1962 Townsend suggested that the ratio of home helps to elderly people should be increased, to meet outstanding need, to 15 per 1000 and then to 20 per 1000 by 1973 [48]. But even on the basis of the official guideline of 12 per 1000, the shortfall of home helps in England in 1977 was 54 percent, or 37,126 home helps [49]; in 1978-1979, the shortfall was 48 percent, or 29,835 home helps [50]. Moreover, research has revealed a very wide variation between local authorities in the provision of home helps, meals on wheels, and other support services per head of population age sixty-five and over [51].

The widening gap between the need for and provision of domiciliary services has been met with expressions of alarm from independent and quasi-independent authorities. The Association of Metropolitan Authorities has expressed doubts concerning the ability of local authorities to meet the guidelines on community care set out by the DHSS in *The Way Forward* [52]. The Personal Social Services Council recently expressed concern that unless additional resources were made available, local social services would be unable to maintain standards of assistance for the elderly, quite apart from making the much needed improvement to services. One authority has even referred to domiciliary care as the "neglect" of the elderly, arguing that unless substantial additional financial allocations are made for such care, it will be increasingly "economic" simply because it is inadequate [53].

The social costs of this failure to provide sufficient resources to carry out community care policies fall on those least able to bear them. Townsend and Wedderburn reported in 1965 that of those elderly people in social classes one and two (highest) who were severely incapacitated, only half already had a paid or local authority home help and nearly half of the remainder said that they needed it. But only one sixth of those in social class five (lowest) who were severely incapacitated had a home help and only one fifth of the remainder felt the need for it [48, p. 31]. Comparison with a recent official survey of older people living at home suggests that, despite a doubling of the coverage of the home help service between the two surveys, it is still the case that those in the higher social classes are more likely to provide themselves with assistance when they are incapacitated [54]. In addition, it has been suggested that an expansion in the coverage of the home help service has been carried out at the expense of the amount of service received by each elderly person: the jam has been spread thinner. In 1976, 42 percent of the elderly had some help visits more frequently than weekly compared with 64 percent in 1962 [54, p. 116].

Successive ministers of health and social security have reaffirmed their commitment to a policy of community care for old people. In 1978 DHSS policy was categorically spelled out as follows [55]:

> The primary objective of the departmental policies towards the care of the elderly is to enable old people to maintain independent lives in the community for as long as possible. To help achieve this, high priority is being given to the development of domiciliary provision and the encouragement of measures designed to prevent or postpone the need for long-term care in hospital or residential homes.

Unfortunately, when set against the needs of the elderly outlined in the earlier quotation from *Health and Welfare*, the performance of community care policy in the postwar period has not matched the promise of this and similar pieces of political rhetoric [56]. In fact, there is no evidence to suggest that the policy of community care for the elderly (even in the restricted sense of preventive support provided by welfare workers) is any less precarious or ambiguous than it was in the early 1960's when Titmuss questioned the government's commitment to carry it out [57]. One of the main reasons the state has not provided the political commitment or resources for the realization of a consistent policy of community care has been its reluctance to intervene openly in the provision of care by the family, and its desire to maintain the existing stucture of relationships within the family.

COMMUNITY CARE AND THE FAMILY

The growth of the welfare state and the varying degrees of state intervention in community life are obviously built on implicit assumptions about family structure and culturally approved life styles. Foremost among these are assumptions concerning the role of the family in caring for its dependents and the sexual division of labor *within* the family.

Despite recent increases in legislation concerning the family and the existence of a community care policy over the last thirty years, the direct involvement of the state in family life remains small. Social services departments are primarily concerned with crisis intervention, short-term support, and, only in cases of severe breakdown, long-term residential care. In fact, the state has a dual role in relation to community care: it may provide direct support where this is absolutely necessary, but its main concern is to ensure the continuance of the practice whereby prime responsibility for the support and care of its own members rests with the family. So, as Moroney has pointed out [58], by presenting traditional family responsibilities for dependents and the division of labor between the sexes and between generations as "normal" or "natural," ". . . the state supports and sustains these relationships without appearing intrusive, thus preserving the illusion that the family is a private domain."

What are perhaps less readily recognized are the reasons underlying the role of the state in sustaining the particular social construction of family life in Great Britain and other industrial societies. Primarily it is the family which reproduces the labor force and provides care and education to the workers of the future. In addition, although many dependencies are created by the state (through, for example, unemployment, inflation, and age-barrier retirement), families bear a large proportion of the social costs of these dependencies privately, and, of course, far more cheaply than the state could. By stigmatizing the poor and dependent, the state protects itself from demands from "normal" families. For example, social service provision for the elderly is usually confined to those without immediate families living nearby [59].

As noted previously, the concentration by the state, through its local agents, on individual problems diverts attention from the underlying political issues. Crisis intervention in issues such as nonaccidental injury to children raises questions concerning the best social work response to individual problems but not the role of the state and society in creating such crises. Social service interventions also reflect a broad hierarchy of values in British society: nonaccidental injury to children is the most important reason for emergency social work intervention; at the same time, thousands of elderly people die of hypothermia every year, often in isolation with little or no social service support [60].

Turning to the sexual division of labor within the family, the implicit assumption of policies promoting community care is that such care will be provided, within the family, by women, usually themselves of dependent status. Community and family in this context therefore can often serve as euphemisms for women [61]. Moreover, as Land has pointed out, men are not expected to look after themselves to the same extent that women are, nor are they expected to look after elderly or infirm relatives: "their primary commitment must be to the labour market and when they have retired from it they are not expected to acquire domestic skills." [62, p. 268] For the same level of incapacity, men are more likely than women to receive home help support [59, p. 178]. In a survey of women's employment in 1968, Hunt found that 5 percent of women aged sixteen to sixty-four were responsible for the care, to a varying extent, of at least one elderly or infirm person in their households, and 6 percent were responsible for at least one person outside of the household (for over half of the women "caring" meant doing virtually all of the household tasks) [63]. In her later study of the home help service, Hunt suggested that between the ages of thirty-five and sixty-four roughly one half of all housewives could expect at some time or another to give help to elderly or infirm persons [59, p. 424]. And in her most recent report on the elderly at home, Hunt concluded that ". . . this survey therefore provides further evidence that the burden of caring for sick or elderly relatives most often falls on women and makes it impossible for them to work." [22, p. 63]

Townsend found that old people more often lived with married daughters than married sons, and that others were more likely to have contact on a regular basis with daughters than sons [32, pp. 23, 37]. Furthermore, elderly husbands helped their wives less often when daughters or other female relatives lived at home or nearby [32, pp. 86-88, 120-123]. While the population of old people's homes includes a disproportionately large number of unmarried persons and married persons without children, new residents with surviving children are more likely to have sons than daughters [64, p. 171]. Other research in Great Britain has shown that it is female members of families who bear the brunt of care for those with terminal illness [65]. Similarly in the U.S., elderly men are much more likely than elderly women to receive help with housework, meal preparation, and shopping from their spouse when they are ill in bed. Women are much more likely to get help from their children or to receive none at all [30, p. 172].

Women are demonstrably an essential feature of the current community care policy in Great Britain and other industrial societies. They are the main source of family and community support and, not surprisingly in view of the social construction of sex roles in capitalist societies, women also predominate in the "caring" professions. (This may be part of the reason why such work is often not treated seriously as productive labor.) The fact that caring or servicing functions, such as housework, are as much a part of the productive apparatus of society as work on more easily quantifiable outputs has been recognized by many authorities, including liberals such as Beveridge, since the 1940's [61, p. 61]. But this recognition has never implied that the sexual division of labor within and outside of the family was anything other than natural and incontravertable. It has been assumed, moreover, that the dominant form of the family in industrial societies, the nuclear family and its traditional divisions of paid and unpaid labor, would survive unaltered in perpetuity.

In fact, the family is not a static institution. It changes not only over the lives of its individual members [66], but also in the longer term. It has changed considerably from the earlier form of "family economy," with reduced dependence of women at childbirth and in the early years of childhood, due to a fall in family size, and the increased dependence of children and elderly people. It is likely that the unequal sexual division of labor will be increasingly challenged by women as the family continues to adapt to the needs of developing capitalism. The costs of these developments in the structure of society and the family are socially divided, with, for example, some women and families in the upper social classes being able to buy community care for themselves or for their relatives, while those in the lower classes bear the full burden with the state's meager assistance. Who will care for the charlady or nurse in her old age?

The first half of the twentieth century was marked by a massive expansion of women's employment. In the early part of the century the activities of reformers such as Tawney coincided with the social aspirations of the middle classes and changes in the state's attitude to children, necessitated by the developing needs of industry to institutionalize primary and later secondary education for all. Thus families could rely less and less on the earning power of children: "The pattern characteristic of the industrialising period was reversed. In the past children had worked so that their mothers could remain at home fulfilling domestic and reproductive responsibilities. Now, when families needed additional income, mothers worked instead of children." [67]   Because the male head's wages remained unrelated to his family's needs, part of this necessity for increasing married women's labor outside the home was the economic cost of keeping children at school, most of which families have had to bear privately.

Thus, the pattern of labor force participation of married women has changed considerably in the last 130 years. Since the mid-nineteenth century the constant rather than spasmodic employment of married women has become more common. The activity rate for all women increased from 32 to 43 percent between 1921 and 1971, while that for married women rose from 9 to 42 percent [68]. Underlying this changing pattern has been the changing structure of industry, broadly the reduction in importance of primary industries such as agriculture, forestry, and fishing as employers and the rise of the service sector, which now employs just over one half of the labor force. Related to this changing structure has been the growing demand for part-time labor, in the distribution, public and manufacturing sectors. Between 1971 and 1976 the number of part-time employees increased by 28 percent [6, p. 528]. Eighty percent of the four million part-time employees in Britain are women. Two fifths of female workers are employed on a part-time basis, two thirds of them in three sectors—professional and scientific, distribution, and miscellaneous services. They tend to be concentrated in low-skilled jobs and are more likely than their full-time counterparts to be low paid [70].

So, the changing needs of industrial society have coincided with its failure to provide wages to meet adequately the growing needs of families, needs which were in turn partly generated by the economic system itself. It is important to note here that the rise in married women's employment did *not* result from their liberation from family responsibilities. Working wives continue to carry a double burden [71]. Nor did it result from an increasing proliferation of labor-saving devices. On the contrary, these were a part of the process of the social construction of needs. With a concentration on the production of consumer durables for the home market, pressure is put on families to increase their purchasing power to buy the ever expanding range of such goods.

Contrary to a popular tendency to devalue the contribution of women's labor as temporary, stop-gap employment for "pin-money," research has shown the vital role of female earnings in keeping families out of poverty. On the basis of surveys of subemployment in two local labor markets, it was concluded, "The truth of the matter is that for families with children where the man has below average earnings (not necessarily particularly low earnings) a reasonable standard of living can now only be attained when the wife goes out to work." [69, p. 415] The difference between a mother's full-time and part-time earnings can have a dramatic impact on family income [62, p. 261]. In the longer-term, employment significantly reduces the woman's chances of experiencing poverty in old age [16]. Moreover, employment is important in reducing the risk of depression among women, and particularly so for working class women [72].

There is further an *income gap* between the wages of the semiskilled and unskilled workers (who are also among the most vulnerable to unemployment) and their needs. At the root of the problem is the economic system itself, which defines and promotes relative needs, but at the same time does not pay the individual wage earner enough to meet them. The state has failed to fill this income gap through its "family policies" and has failed even to maintain living standards during the recent period of rapid inflation [73]. For example, the combined value of child benefits (family allowances until 1976) and child tax allowances (for children under age eleven) for families with one child was £2.43 in 1946 and £2.02 in 1976. For families with four children the difference was even wider: £12.38 compared with £9.95. These allowances represented 4.9 percent of incomes *after* tax for one-child families in 1964-1965 and 3.5 percent in 1977-1978. For four-child families the proportions were 18.5 percent compared with 14 percent [74]. Therefore, many married women in the lower social classes, wedged between the traditional and powerful sexual division of labor within the home and growing family needs, are pushed into low-skilled part-time work, often for very low wages.

Changes in the social structure and in social values towards the emancipation of women may in the near future collide with opposing trends and result in a significant change in the division of family and social responsibility. On the one hand, there is the increasing proportion of very elderly people and the growing dependency partly caused by the superannuation and redundancy of older workers; and on the other, there is a campaign for sexual equality coupled with an increase in married women's employment in an attempt to redress the erosion of living standards over the recent periods of inflation and wage restraint. A continuation of the long overdue change in the status and aspirations of women and their increased employment will pose some difficult questions for families, and men in particular, concerning the division of caring functions, and for the state on the extent of investment in community care. So far this policy has rested primarily on the willingness of women to forfeit other activities, including careers, and provide care for elderly relatives who need it. Because of continued improvements in life expectancy, the period of dependency in old age frequently exceeds that of childhood. While community care policies are left predominantly to individual families, unsupported by the state except in crises, the implicit expectation is that some women will quit or seriously reduce their employment and suffer loss of pay, career prospects, and fringe benefits, and reduced social contact and longer-term financial security. In addition, it is assumed that women will continue to care, despite what is often considerable stress, until this becomes intolerable and crisis intervention is necessary.

CONCLUSION

Despite the fact that research has shown that the family remains by far the most important source of care in the community, Moroney found that in the opinion of "scores" of civil servants and social welfare practitioners throughout England and Wales and in Denmark and the Federal Republic of Germany, families are now less willing to provide this care [28, p. 125]. Civil servants and planners cited the increase in demand for social services as an indication of this trend. However, increasing demand is not necessarily an indication of less willingness to care, but perhaps reflects both the increasing burden on, and changing roles within, the family. Many needs are socially generated, and perhaps the modern family is beset by greater needs than previously: needs created, for example, by superannuation, redundancy, unemployment, and inflation. Thus, it is not that the welfare state is breaking down family responsibility, but that more support is necessary if the family is not to be overburdened.

Although many of its policies are aimed at family substitution, whether in the short or long term, rather than family support, the state does operate, in part at least and however inadequately, to sustain the family and its caring and reproductive functions. The social definitions implied by community care policies are one aspect of this maintenance of the status quo. But the family may not necessarily be the only, or indeed always the best, vehicle for social support—the neighborhood or local community may be more effective in sharing care. Moreover, government social policies are aimed at supporting a particular form of family unit. But it may reasonably be asked, first, why it operates to sustain a traditional social unit that is based on inequality between the sexes, when it could encourage alternative forms, such as families based on sexual equality or community groups, which may provide necessary care to the elderly as effectively. Secondly, in view of the overwhelming importance of the family to community care policies, why does the state devote such meager resources to family support?

The implication of these questions concerning dependency and care for social service provision is that consideration must be given to the implicit models of the family and "correct" life-style in providing care. Agents of the state locally, social workers, nurses, health visitors, and so on, must consider the appropriateness of their input: What is the goal and purpose of their agency, rather than the "best" method of intervention? Would their time be better spent encouraging community or neighborhood support? This is not to imply that the family unit is not worth supporting in most cases. On the contrary, a closer partnership between families and social services is urgently needed. Nor does it imply that social workers and other local agents have such a clear-cut choice. But discussions within and between agencies may promote collective pressure for change. At the very least, social workers and other agents of community care may act as educators of their own agencies and local political elites to the possibility of alternative forms of care and support to those defined by institutionalized social policies.

Some of the questions raised above appear at their sharpest in a period of restriction on social service resources. At such times the fundamental role of the family in care and the insensitivity of the state are clearly demonstrated. At the same time, as increasing pressure is placed on individuals and families through, for example, industrial relocation, housing policies, unemployment, poverty, inflation, and increasing longevity, the state in Britain is actually withdrawing resources from families and family support [75]. It is complacently assumed that "the family" will continue to care regardless of how much pressure it is put under and how little support it is given.

ACKNOWLEDGMENTS

I am extremely grateful to Anne-Marie Guillemard, Dulcie Groves, Harold Orbach, Tony Rees, Adrian Sinfield, Gillian Stewart, and Peter Townsend for their helpful comments on an earlier draft of this chapter.

REFERENCES

1. Sir F. Anderson, Ageing Population May Cause Social Disaster. *The Times* [London], November 27, 1976, quoted in Bosanquet, N. *A Future for Old Age*, Maurice Temple Smith, London, 1978.
2. M. Abrams, *Beyond Three Score and Ten*, Age Concern, London, 1978.
3. B. Rodgers, A. Doron, and M. Jones, *The Study of Social Policy: A Comparative Approach*, Allen and Unwin, London, 1979.
4. B. S. Rowntree, *Poverty: A Study of Town Life*, Macmillan, London, 1901. See also Wynn, M., *Family Policy*, Penguin Books, Harmondsworth, 1972.
5. A. Walker, The Social Creation of Poverty and Dependency in Old Age, *Journal of Social Policy*, 9:1, pp. 49-75, 1980.
6. F. Collier, *The Family Economy of the Working Classes in the Cotton Industry 1785-1833*, Manchester University Press, Manchester, 1964.
7. *The Observer*, London, November 11, 1979.
8. P. Lewis, Off the Scrap Heap, *New Society*, February 6, 1975. See also Office of Population Censuses and Surveys, *General Household Survey 1978*, Her Majesty's Stationery Office, London, 1980.
9. M. Tracy, *Retirement Age Practices in Ten Industrial Societies 1960-1976*, International Social Security Association, Geneva, 1979.
10. A. Walker, The Concept of Dependency and Its Application to Old Age, *Social Policy and Administration*, in press.
11. P. Townsend, *Poverty in the United Kingdom*, Allen Lane, London, 1979.
12. R. Layard, D. Piachaud, and M. Stewart, *The Causes of Poverty*, Royal Commission on the Distribution of Income and Wealth, Background Paper No. 5, Her Majesty's Stationery Office, London, 1978.
13. J. Hendricks and C. D. Hendricks, *Aging in Mass Society*, Winthrop, Cambridge, Massachusetts, 1977.
14. D. Maeda, Ageing in Eastern Society, in *The Social Challenge of Ageing*, D. Hobman (ed.), pp. 45-72, Croom Helm, London, 1978.
15. P. Townsend, Poverty as Relative Deprivation, in *Poverty, Inequality and Class Structure*, D. Wedderburn (ed.), Cambridge University Press, London, 1974.
16. A. Walker, Towards a Political Economy of Old Age, *Ageing and Society*, 1:1, 1981.
17. *Found Dead*, Age Concern, Mitcham, 1978.

18. Office of Population Censuses and Surveys, *Population Trends 11*, Her Majesty's Stationery Office, London, 1978.
19. Department of Employment, *Employment Gazette*, p. 422, April 1978.
20. M. Reddin, National Insurance and Private Pensions, in *The Yearbook of Social Policy in Britain 1976*, K. Jones, et al. (eds.), pp. 74-93, Routledge and Kegan Paul, London, 1977.
21. E. Cumming and W. Henry, *Growing Old*, Basic Books, New York, 1961.
22. A. Hunt, *The Elderly at Home*, Office of Population Censuses and Surveys, Her Majesty's Stationery Office, London, 1978.
23. Department of Employment, *Employment Gazette*, March 1978, pp. 283-285. See also Department of Health and Social Security, *A Happier Old Age*, Her Majesty's Stationery Office, London, 1978; and J. Harris, From Cradle to Grave: The Rise of the Welfare State, *New Society*, p. 129, January 18, 1979.
24. R. N. Butler, *Why Survive? Being Old in America*, Harper and Row, New York, 1975.
25. C. Estes, *The Aging Enterprise*, Jossey-Bass, London, 1979.
26. Central Office of Information, *Care of the Elderly in Britain*, Her Majesty's Stationery Office, London, 1974.
27. M. Edelman, *Political Language*, Academic Press, New York, 1977.
28. R. M. Moroney, *The Family and the State*, Longman, London, 1976.
29. J. Tunstall, *Old and Alone*, Routledge and Kegan Paul, London, 1966.
30. E. Shanas, P. Townsend, D. Wedderburn, H. Friis, P. Milhoj, and J. Stehouwer, *Old People in Three Industrial Societies*, Routledge and Kegan Paul, London, 1966.
31. L. Rosenmayer and E. Kockies, Propositions for a Sociological Theory of Ageing and the Family, *International Social Science Journal, 15*:3, pp. 410-427, 1963. See also Shanas, E., the Family as a Social Support System in Old Age, *The Gerontologist, 19*:2, pp. 169-174, 1979.
32. P. Townsend, *The Family Life of Old People*, Pelican Books, Harmondsworth, 1963.
33. C. Tavani, Meeting the Needs of the Oldest of the Old, *Ageing*, pp. 2-7, January 1979.
34. H. Butcher and D. Crosbie, *Pensioned Off*, Cumbria Community Development Project, York, 1978.
35. P. Townsend, *The Last Refuge*, Routledge and Kegan Paul, London, 1964.
36. *A Hospital Plan for England and Wales* (Cmdn. 1604), Her Majesty's Stationery Office, London, 1962.
37. *Health and Welfare: The Development of Community Care* (Cmdn. 1973), Her Majesty's Stationery Office, London, 1963.
38. *Report of the Committee on Local Author:.y and Allied Personal Social Services*, Her Majesty's Stationery Office, London, 1968.
39. A. Harris, *Handicapped and Impaired in Great Britain*, Part 1., Her Majesty's Stationery Office, London, 1971.
40. *Personal Social Services: Basic Information*, Personal Social Services Council, London, 1976.

41. Department of Health and Social Security, *Priorities for Health and Personal Social Services in England*, Her Majesty's Stationery Office, London, 1976.
42. Department of Health and Social Security, *The Way Forward*, Her Majesty's Stationery Office, London, 1977.
43. A. Sinfield, Meeting Client Need—An Ambiguous and Precarious Value, paper presented at the Second OECD-WZB Conference, Berlin, June 13-16, 1978.
44. P. Abrams, Community Care: Some Research Problems and Priorities, *Policy and Politics, 6*, pp. 125-151, 1977. See also Hirsch, F., *Social Limits to Growth*, Routledge and Kegan Paul, London, 1977.
45. W. Jaehnig, Domiciliary Services for the Mentally Handicapped and Their Families: Beyond "Community Care," paper presented at conference on The Mentally Handicapped: An Effective Service, Liverpool, 1972.
46. M. Bayley, *Mental Handicap and Community Care*, Routledge and Kegan Paul, London, 1973.
47. M. Warren, Talk Given at the Oxford Conference on the Concept of Community Care, quoted in Personal Social Service Council, *Collaboration in Community Care—A Discussion Document*, Her Majesty's Stationery Office, London, 1978.
48. P. Townsend and D. Wedderburn, *The Aged in the Welfare State*, G. Bell and Sons, London, 1975. See also Goldberg, T., and Connelly, N., Reviewing Services for the Old, *Community Care*, pp. 27-30, December 6, 1978.
49. S. Clark, Where Have all the Home Helps Gone?, *New Society*, pp. 578-579, December 7, 1978.
50. *Personal Social Service Statistics 1978-79 Estimates*, Chartered Institute of Public Finance and Accountancy, London, 1978.
51. *Home Help Services in Great Britain*, National Council of Home Help Services, Cambridge, 1979. See also Stapenhurst, D., *The Home Help Service in Greater London*, Greater London Association for the Disabled, London, 1978; and Department of Health and Social Security, *Local Authority Personal Social Services Summary of Planning Returns 1976-77 to 1979-80*, Her Majesty's Stationery Office, London, 1979.
52. *Services for the Elderly: A Metropolitan View*, Association of Metropolitan Authorities, London, 1978.
53. L. J. Opit, Domiciliary Care for the Elderly Sick, *British Medical Journal, 1*, pp. 30-34, 1977.
54. A. C. Bibbington, Changes in the Provision of Social Services to the Elderly in the Community Over Fourteen Years, *Social Policy and Administration, 13*:2, pp. 114-123, 1980.
55. Department of Health and Social Security, The DHSS Perspective, in *Social Care Research*, J. Barnes and N. Connelly (eds.), Bedford Square Press, London, 1978.
56. W. Jaehnig, *A Family Service for the Mentally Handicapped* (Fabian Tract 450), Fabian Society, London, 1979.
57. R. M. Titmuss, *Commitment to Welfare*, George Allen and Unwin, London, 1971.
58. R. M. Moroney, The Family as a Social Service: Implications for Policy and Practice, *Child Welfare, 4*, pp. 211-220, 1978.

59. A. Hunt, *The Home Help Service in England and Wales*, Her Majesty's Stationery Office, London, 1970.
60. M. Wicks, *Old and Cold*, Heinemann Educational Books, London, 1978.
61. C. Cockburn, *The Local State*, Pluto Press, London, 1977.
62. H. Land, Who Cares for the Family?, *Journal of Social Policy*, 7:3, pp. 257-284, 1978.
63. A. Hunt, *Women's Employment*, vol. 1., Her Majesty's Stationery Office, London, 1968.
64. P. Townsend, The Effects of Family Structure on the Likelihood of Admission to an Institution in Old Age: The Application of a General Theory, in *Social Structure and the Family*, E. Shanas (ed.), pp. 163-187, Prentice-Hall, New Jersey, 1965.
65. A. Cartwright, J. Hockey, and E. Anderson, *Life Before Death*, Tavistock Publications Limited, London, 1973.
66. C. Bell, Occupational Career, Family Cycle and Extended Family Relations, *Human Relations*, 24:6, pp. 463-475, 1971.
67. L. A. Tilly and J. W. Scott, *Women, Work and Family*, Holt, Rinehart and Winston, New York, 1978.
68. Central Office of Information, *Occupations and Conditions of Work*, Her Majesty's Stationery Office, London, 1976.
69. P. J. Sloan, Evidence Presented to the Royal Commission on the Distribution of Income and Wealth, in *Selected Evidence Submitted to the Royal Commission for Report No. 6: Lower Incomes*, Her Majesty's Stationery Office, London, 1978.
70. J. Hurstfield, *The Part-Time Trap*, Low Pay Unit, London, 1978.
71. C. T. Adams and K. T. Winston, *Mothers at Work*, Longman, London, 1980.
72. C. Brown and T. Harris, *Social Origins of Depression*, Tavistock Publications Limited, London, 1978.
73. Royal Commission on the Distribution of Incomes and Wealth, *Report No. 6: Lower Incomes*, Her Majesty's Stationery Office, London, 1978.
74. F. Field, *Children Worse Off Under Labour?*, (Poverty Pamphlet 32), Child Poverty Action Group, London, 1978.
75. A. Walker, P. Ormerod, and L. Whitty, *Abandoning Social Priorities*, Child Poverty Action Group, London, 1979.

CHAPTER 6
Mental Illness and the Aged Stranger
JAMES J. DOWD

In his study of institutionalization for insanity between 1870 and 1930 in California, Fox found that aged women were especially likely to be committed. In explaining this peculiar finding, Fox pointed to the greater vulnerability of the aged to social control by the state. "It was a simple matter," Fox argues, "... to demonstrate that almost any aged person was insane, since senility was increasingly equated with old age." [1, p. 132] Further, he continues, "almost any personality quirk in an aged person was taken as evidence of senility. Suspiciousness, failure of memory, or slowed reflexes were signs of deterioration." [1, p. 133]

This analysis by Fox raises a set of troubling issues concerning mental illness in old age. The implication from his work is that older women may have been no more likely to have been "insane" than either younger women or men but may have been simply less able to resist the imputation by others that they were indeed insane. But why were such imputations made? And by whom? Contrary to the judgment prevailing among social gerontologists today that affectual "vertical bonds" exist within families that protect and nurture the aged, Fox concludes that the insane aged "probably became intolerable to their families" [1, p. 179] and were, as a consequence, institutionalized.

Their problematic status resulted from two factors. First, these older people probably *did* evidence some "behavioral idiosyncrasies" that, over time, became intolerable. They may have, in other words, exhibited real and severe symptoms of mental illness that their families could not (or would not) manage. Secondly, according to Fox, these older people were given over by their families to state institutions for the insane "because they were unable to contribute their share to family 'production.'" [1, p. 180] A stable social order, in effect, required that older women be institutionalized.

This historical documentation carries considerable importance for current investigators of aging and mental illness. It requires that we ask again the critical questions of what is mental illness and what causes it. More importantly, however, Fox's analysis requires that we be especially attendant to those groups, such as aged women or the poor, who demonstrate a disproportionate incidence of mental illness. Indeed, the lack of attention paid by sociologists to mental illness in old age has allowed a reductionistic medical/psychiatric understanding of the phenomenon to develop as the conventional wisdom in this area. That is to say, the recurrent focus of research into the causes and treatment of mental illness has been the individual.

The problem with this approach is not that it fails to discern the mentally ill from the mentally fit or that it fails to treat effectively the symptoms of the illness. The problem, rather, is that the prevailing research paradigms in the area of mental illness and aging take us to the periphery of the problem, but not its center. We are led to consider among stress, or role loss, or lowered income, or labeling as the principal social factors involved in the production of mental illness in old people. To control the symptoms of the illness (that is, to "treat" the illness), we seek to modify the behavior of·the sick individual with ECT, psychotherapy, or with drugs such as one of the phenothiazines. And, finally, we have attempted to prevent or to limit further incidence of the illness by emphasizing the importance of individual "coping skills," social support systems, and adaptation. Left untreated, indeed left practically unnoticed, is the structure of capitalism itself.

It is the argument of this chapter that mental illness among old people needs to be considered within the present historical moment of late capitalism. The stress, role loss, and susceptibility to negative labeling that are frequently posited as the causes of depression or poor morale or negative self-concept observed in older populations, are themselves outcomes of a larger structure of capitalist social and economic relations among age groups and social classes. One *purpose* of this chapter, then, is to synthesize some existing threads of a political economy approach to the mental health of old people. I will argue that growing old in capitalist societies brings increased risk of mental illness primarily because of the exclusion of older workers from labor markets and the consequent diminution in their ability to "consume."

It is important that we emphasize at the outset of this analysis that it would be as incorrect to consider this problem solely as one of social structure as it would be to consider it solely as an individual one. Both approaches are equally undialectical. The economic forces of production, regardless of how ultimately basic in some sociological sense they may be argued to be, reproduce themselves in the lives of individuals only through the differentiating filter of culture [2]. And, culturally, the aged are different than younger cohorts. This difference is only partially understood, however, by the actors themselves as well as by the social scientists who observe the unfolding drama, presumably from a disinterested distance. The "only partially understood" aspect of the generational differences in culture to which I refer here is the *ideological* difference. Participation in a different historical epoch gives birth to an ideological coloring that one may describe as a "generational Weltanschauung." Apart from the physical, social, and psychological differences that separate the generations and that help to sustain the age stratified access to labor markets, this ideological difference also serves as a boundary that keeps separate young and old. Lacking opportunity for routinized social contact and lacking as well any common basis with which to enrich the contact, the generations in modern capitalism have come to view one another as *strange*. The second purpose of the chapter is to examine the ways in which the perception of the aged as strangers may contribute to beliefs concerning their mental illness. Sanity is a concept that refers, as Berger has written, "to socially relative situations. . . . One adjusts to a particular society, one matures by becoming habituated to it. One is sane if one shares its cognitive and normative assumptions." [3, p. 64] The "insanity" of the aged stranger has roots in their strangeness: not only are they different from the accepted cultural models of youthful health and physical vigor, their superfluous economic position also disallows their full sharing in the "cognitive and normative assumptions" of consumer capitalism.

MENTAL ILLNESS AND THE AGED

The Medical/Psychiatric Model

Gerontological studies of mental illness, while sharing many of the same conceptual and methodological problems of mental illness research generally, must contend as well with a set of issues specific to older populations. The underlying rationale for the present analysis of the aged stranger was developed in part from a consideration of these common and unique problems.

Let us consider first those factors that distinguish mental illness in old age from those disabilities occurring earlier in life. There are at least *two* such factors. The first is an increased incidence of dementia, or brain syndrome. In addition to the functional psychoses, neuroses, personality disorders and alcoholism that appear throughout the adult life span, the period of old age is also marked by the increased prevalence of both acute and chronic organic brain syndrome. Characterized by "widespread development of senile plaques, neurofibrillary tangles, and granulovascular change," [4, p. 138] Alzheimer's disease and other types of organic brain syndrome constitute one of the two most common psychiatric disorders in late life (along with depression)." [5, p. 961]

The second factor that distinguishes mental illness in old age is the custodial treatment of aged mental patients. Older mental patients constitute only 2 percent of those treated in psychiatric, *outpatient* clinics but approximately 30 percent of all public mental hospital patients, a fact that Lowy attributes to psychiatrists' perceptions of old people "as unattractive patients." [6, p. 828] Treatment for specific illnesses like, for example, depression have been found to differ across age groups. While younger patients are treated with psychotherapy or with minor tranquilizers, older patients tend to be diagnosed as psychotic and/or endogeneously depressed and, therefore, are "likely to be treated with drugs and ECT." [7, p. 321] Others charge that diagnostic criteria applied to aged patients are too gross to serve as the basis for appropriate treatment. As a result, the aged tend to appear disproportionately in those classifications, like organic brain syndrome or melancholia, that "result in custodial-type treatment." [8, p. 457] Such custodial care is inevitable as long as the physical and emotional deterioration observed in aged patients is presumed to be a normal correlate of human aging rather than as a pathological symptom due in part to economic disadvantage in many cases [4].

These two issues are not unrelated. Part of the reason for routine custodial care offered to the aged is the mistaken belief that symptoms of mental illness reflect an underlying condition of senile dementia or other type of organic brain syndrome that presumably accompanies old age. It is not surprising, then, that psychiatric surveys report approximately 15-20 percent of the noninstitutionalized aged have at least mild or moderate degrees of psychiatric impairment. While agreement has been reached in the medical profession as to the need to distinguish those impairments that are organically-based from those that "originate in the older person's personality structure or living situation," [6, p. 828] in the public consciousness this is hardly a difference that matters. With some justification, diagnoses like "senile confusion" or "senile dementia" are widely understood to be "medical expression[s] of despair applied to socially isolated old people for whom nobody will accept responsibility." [9, p. 40]

In addition to these unique problems, gerontological mental health research must concern itself as well with those controversies that spill over from the research agenda of the more general mental health field itself. A discussion of these issues is necessary in order that we may place the social gerontological research effort in better perspective. The major controversies drawn from this broader context involve: 1) the nature of mental illness; 2) the causes of mental illness; and 3) the inverse relationship between socio economic status and prevalence of mental illness symptoms, especially those associated with schizophrenia.

The Nature of Mental Illness

Concerning the nature of mental illness, three general positions have evolved over the years: 1) the *medical model*, which views mental illness as a disease like any other disease, that is, as having an etiology, pathogenesis, course, prognosis, and outcome; 2) the *social psychiatric model*, which accepts as the source of the psychiatric symptoms a variety of possibilities, including genetic, biochemical, psychological, or social-environmental factors; and 3) the *myth of mental illness* view, most closely associated with Szasz, which argues that mental illness is not an illness at all but, rather, an unresolved personal or social problem in living [10].

Of these three views, the social psychiatric model is most widely accepted among mental health practitioners. Very few in the medical field take seriously the opinion of Emil Kraepelin that dementia praecox, or schizophrenia, is to be considered in similar terms as diabetes or arteriosclerosis. Similarly, Szasz's argument that "mental illness" describes not illness but an inability to live competently has little support within the medical profession. Instead, the most common conceptualization of mental illness, the one that is able to tolerate total disagreement as to the causes of the illness (requiring agreement only as to the need to treat the illness *with professional care*), is the social psychiatric perspective. This apparent catholicity, however, of the social psychiatric view is achieved only with considerable cost. Because of the "fuzziness" that distinguishes both schizophrenic and affective disorders, for example, it is widely acknowledged that the intermediate "schizo-affective" state "cannot be precisely defined." [11] It has become commonplace for researchers operating within the positivistic constraints of the social psychiatric model also to lament their inability to better understand the dynamics affecting mental illnesses like depression [12] or paranoid illness [13].

As to the precise nature of schizophrenia, "there is no agreement" according to Stenback [14, p.627]. Post hypothesizes that "there is no schizophrenia, only schizophrenics" or those who display "deviant, maladaptive, and sometimes even 'psychotic' personality features to varying degrees." [15, p. 612] The problems experienced by the aged schizophrenic (primarily lack of social skills) are due less to the "illness," according to Zarit, than "to a syndrome of social inadequacy that was induced by the institution." [4, p. 250] Such views suggest that mental illness would indeed be better conceptualized as a "problem in living" that while manageable by the state through either drug therapy, electro-shock therapy, or institutionalization, remains shrouded in surmise and misunderstanding [16].

The strategy of those who remain committed to the social psychiatric model has been to concede some ground to their critics (like Szasz) by redefining the boundaries of mental illness. By so doing, the ambiguous terrain of *organic brain syndrome* and *personality disorders* has been given up to whomever wishes to claim it. This is the approach, for example, of Gove and Tudor who see mental illness as [17]:

> . . . a fairly specific phenomenon—a disorder that involves personal discomfort (as indicated by distress, anxiety, depression, etc.) and/or mental disorganization (as indicated by confusion, thought blockage, motor retardation, and, in the more extreme cases, by hallucinations and delusions) and that is not caused by an organic or toxic condition. The two major categories of mental illness that fit our definition are

neurotic disorders and functional psychoses and the minor categories
are transient situational disorders and psychophysiologic disorders.

Gove and Tudor eliminate the personality disorders from consideration because
such people "do not experience personal discomfort, being neither anxious nor
distressed." Those with personality disorders are better categorized, it is now
argued, as social deviants who may be "forced into treatment because their behavior is disruptive to others." [17, p. 1328] In the revised categorization,
those with personality disorders are no longer mentally ill but merely anti-social
or asocial. The need to modify continually definitions of mental illness points to
both the obvious lack of agreement among practitioners and researchers in this
field as well as the tenacious commitment among mental health professionals to
the *social psychiatric* understanding of mental illness.

Gove's view of mental illness is a very narrowly circumscribed one: it should
be precipitated by stress and it should make the person unhappy. The narcissistic
or schizoid personality cannot be mentally ill since he or she does not seem in
sufficient distress. This is an interesting correlate of the traditional American
postulate that "one could not be judged to be mentally healthy if one were not
happy [18, p. 6]. Conversely, then, one could not be diagnosed as mentally ill
if one were not unhappy. Both notions are, of course, misguided. The well-
adjusted, happy individual cannot be considered healthy if the society itself is
undemocratic. "In adjusting to the mad whole," Adorno writes, "the cured
patient becomes really sick. . . . His integration would be a false reconciliation
with an unreconciled world. . . ." [19, 20]

Adorno's position emphasizes the necessity of approaching the problem dia-
lectically. Certain types of mental sickness, like schizophrenia—"the most extreme consequence of the subject's alienation from the objective social order"
[19] —do indeed mirror the sickness of the larger society. It is a mistake, then, to
consider mental illness as suggested by either unhappiness or a non-conformity
to social expectations. Mental health is better considered as a human potential in
the spheres of love and work. It involves the potential for intimate social relationships and for creative productivity. Mental illness, then, is the outcome of
the repression or perversion of this potential. Organic brain syndrome, insofar
as it disables the individual from joining in intimate social contact or disallows
creative productivity, is rightly categorized as mental illness. Organic brain syndrome, irrespective of its etiology, does produce symptoms of confusion that to
use Gove and Tudor's own words, "are the ones that historically and cross-
culturally seem to be considered as mental illness." [17, p. 1327] The same
reasoning applies to narcissistic personality disorders or to schizophrenia.

The Causes of Mental Illness

A second area of controversy within the mental health field concerns
the causes of mental illness. The two principal approaches to the causation issue

emphasize either genetic or social-psychological factors,[1] although a consensus of sorts has emerged concerning the likelihood that at least several factors are implicated in the production of mental illness.

The basis of the *genetic* argument can be traced to studies of biological relatives, especially identical twins raised apart, in which one of the relatives, or siblings, is a chronic schizophrenic, for example. These studies presumably demonstrated a significant concentration of the illness among biological relatives [22]. In a comprehensive review of research conducted between 1938 to 1981 that involved identical twins raised apart in which at least one twin was schizophrenic, Ratner uncovered ten studies involving twenty-seven pairs of identical twins [23]. Of the twenty-seven pairs, fourteen were concordant and thirteen discordant. While the sociologist Kohn interprets such data as demonstrating "beyond any reasonable doubt that some genetic mechanism must be involved in the etiology of schizophrenia [24, p. 178], Ratner is not quite so certain. Ratner concludes, Kohn to the contrary notwithstanding, that the genetic hypothesis is *not* supported since "physical separation does not establish genetic causation unless social causes can be shown to be insignificant." [24, p. 178] The most recent evidence supports Ratner's cautiousness concerning the genetic component in schizophrenia. In studies that used the DSMIII diagnostic criteria for schizophrenia, the evidence for genetic or familial transmission was very weak. The authors of one such study conclude that, if genetic transmission does occur, "it is either limited to a subgroup yet to be defined or transmission is weak with a . . . population prevalence of the illness that is low enough (.2% or less) to qualify as a rare disease." [25, p. 175]

Among those who still accept some form of genetic involvement in the production of mental illness, the modified argument based upon the less-than-compelling evidence of the MZ twin studies is that while there may be no defined genotype that causes an illness like schizophrenia, it is instead "the predisposition of schizophrenia that is genetically determined rather than the disease itself." [26, p. 516] Given the enormous and perplexing variation in the degree of twin concordance across studies, the geneticists further acknowledge that the environment must "also play an important role."

The *social-psychological* explanation of mental illness centers on the ideas of stress and change. Change of any type, but especially change that leads to a negative end-state (as that produced by certain life events, such as the death of child or unemployment), causes *stress* that, in people with a diminished capacity to cope, results in personal confusion and psychiatric symptoms of depression. Brenner's (1973) analysis of economic fluctuation and mental illness in New York

---

[1] While genetics and social psychological stress or socialization theories constitute the two poles of the nature/nurture argument, other explanations for mental illness have also been proffered. As part of their socio-medical explanation for schizophrenia, Rushing and Ortega posit that a slow virus may be the underlying cause [21]. This possibility exists, according to the authors, because a disproportionate number of schizophrenics are born during the height of the virus season (viz., January through April).

state shows, for example, that for each 1 percent increase in unemployment, admissions to mental hospitals increase 4.3 percent for men and 2.3 percent for women [27]. Suicide, homicide, as well as stress-related disorders like alcoholism, anxiety, and heart disease are similarly affected by recession and unemployment. Basic to this type of research is the idea that "status frustration," denied opportunity, and unfulfilled aspirations are the source of the stress [28].

Stress is frequently cited as a contributing factor in the mental illness observed in older populations. The aged are particularly likely to suffer stress-related mental disorders because of their exposure over long periods of time "to continuous adverse or stressful influences." [4, p. 112] Given "the rising frequency of somatic illness, physiological decline, physical debilities, malnutrition, overmedication . . . , sensory deficits, reduction in mental agility, economic deprivations, social losses, and the increasing proximity of death," Jarvik wonders why every old person is not profoundly depressed [29, p. 326]. Other writers see the personality disorders among the aged as a behavioral reaction to the stress associated with age-related role loss [30, 31].

Whether stress is indeed distributed unevenly across the life cycle is not as obvious as Jarvik and others apparently believe. In terms of the stresses associated with work, it is the younger person who, according to Pearlin, experiences the greater stresses and strains. It is the younger worker who has to "confront the changes associated with the establishment, interruption, or advancement of career" and who is, therefore, susceptible to insecurity and disruption [32, p. 181]. It is true, however, that the strains in the lives of younger people tend to dissipate after a time. Those faced by older people, in contrast, may be *scheduled* (that is, expected) and fewer in number but they are also "more irreversible in their character and, consequently, arguably more stressful [32, p. 182].

Among sociologists, the issue of stress as a causative factor in mental illness is nested within the related concern of why symptoms of mental illness are more prevalent among the unemployed and the working class. Because of the large volume of research generated by this problem, I treat it separately here although there is indeed some overlap with the more general question of what causes mental illness. In the following section I shall discuss the three major approaches to the class-illness problem (i.e., selection/drift; stress; and labeling) and then review a fourth approach that has only recently begun to enter the mainstream of sociological discussion, the Marxist/political economy position.

THE RELATIONSHIP BETWEEN SOCIAL CLASS AND MENTAL ILLNESS

The relevance of the sociological enterprise to social policy is perhaps no where better seen than in the area of mental health. Sociologists occupy positions of influence within the National Institutes of Health and are responsible as well for much of the research effort in mental health. Consequently, a primary focus of both social policy and social research in the mental health field has been directed towards a predictably "sociological" concern, viz., why is there variation by social class (or, as it is more often phrased, socio economic status) in the incidence of mental illness? The answers proposed to this question are several and varied. The nature/nurture dichotomization of approaches is again present here as it was earlier with the causation question. In the present context, the nature argument is referred to as either *social selection or drift*, while the nurture position is contained in the *stress/socialization* hypothesis.

"Drift" and "selection" have been neatly defined by the NIMH researcher Eaton. According to Eaton, *selection* is "the process whereby the insidious onset of schizophrenia handicaps an individual in the social class system so that his ultimate social class attainment is not as high as that of persons from the general population with similar background characteristics." [33] *Drift*, on the other hand, is "the process whereby schizophrenics undergo downward class mobility after the onset of schizophrenia due to disability in the competition for employment." [33, p. 149] Both processes are consistent with the genetic explanation of mental illness, a view that Eaton finds compelling. As evidence supporting the drift/selection hypothesis, it has been found that marital status is related to schizophrenia with single men hospitalized for schizophrenia more often than married men. The reason for this difference, the authors argue, is that "the more symptomatic and/or ineffective an individual, the less likely he will find a marital partner, achieve higher class levels, . . . and the more likely he will spend extended periods in the hospital." [34, p. 370] In sum, the drift/selection position interprets the concentration of schizophrenia among the economically marginal segments of the population as a function of social incompetence. Schizophrenics are "poor performers" who drift downwards to their ultimate lower-class distinction.

In contradistinction to the drift interpretation is the understanding that "lower-class life somehow contributes to risk for schizophrenia," most likely through *stress* and/or *socialization* [33, p. 149]. Lower-class members presumably have *more* stress than those in the middle class (i.e., differential exposure) as well as being more susceptible to stress than their middle-class counterparts because of less adequate coping skills or resources (i.e., differential impact). It is not genetics but social structural conditions, then, that "not only discriminate in placing more strain on some groups of people than on others, but . . . seem as well to cause the very segments of society that are under the greatest strain to have less effective coping repertoires." [35, p. 18]

Such coping repertoires are broadly defined by some to include the biological and psychological adaptive capacities of the individual that are developed from both experiential *and* genotypic givens [29]. For the most part, however, coping resources typically are restricted to what are, in another context, described as *power resources*, that is, resources like money, a supportive social network, certain personal characteristics and so on [36, 37]. Stress presumably has greater impact on the aged and working class because of less dense social networks that operate not only to prevent isolation [38-40], but also to "act swiftly and in a supportive way to deal with the initial unusual behaviors of their members [41, p. 4]. The unusual behavior is not seen as something beyond the control of friends and family but, rather, as a "solvable problem requiring treatment."

Although the stress hypothesis is usually considered antithetical to the drift/ selection view, the two positions have come much closer together as the genetic position has evolved away from an argument of genotypic inheritance to one of phenotypic "predisposition." Kohn, for example, has attempted to explain the disproportionate schizophrenia present within the lower class as a function of genetic vulnerability and the experience of great stress that, considered in conjunction with "conceptions of social reality that are so limited and so rigid as to impair their ability to deal resourcefully with the problematic and the stressful . . . could be disabling and result in schizophrenia." [24, p. 176]

The argument by Kohn is the most ambitious and individualistic of those proposed to date. Kohn does not simply repeat the drift argument that schizophrenics are incompetent and consequently drift downwards in the social hierarchy. Rather Kohn sees the critical factor being the pathologically limited "conceptions of social reality" that serve, in effect, to reproduce the class structure from generation to generation. It is not schizophrenia that causes downward mobility but, instead, it is the peculiar conception of reality that, when coupled with the proper genetic predisposition, renders the lower class person unable to deal with stress and, therefore, susceptible to mental illness.

The problem with Kohn's attempt to locate the cause of mental illness in the lower class's "conception of social reality" is that 1) genetic predisposition to schizophrenia has not been demonstrated; and 2) neither the "differential impact" of—nor the "differential exposure" to—stress across the class structure has been empirically verified [21, 42].

The *labeling* or *societal reaction* theory constitutes the third major attempt to account for the higher rate of mental illness among the lower and working classes. Labeling theory, of course, has a long history in the field of deviance that is well known. When applied to the "deviance" of mental illness, the labeling argument emphasizes the difference between physical and mental illness: "Whereas physical illness is seen as an objective deviation from the norms of physical structure and function, 'mental illnesses' are more properly described as infractions of social norms." [43] Mental illness is associated with class, therefore, because of the greater vulnerability of lower class members to the labeling process.

Scheff, the major proponent of this view, has been rightly criticized for the imprecision and ambiguity inherent in his presentation of labeling theory. The genesis of mental illness resides in the breaking of the nameless residual rules of social life. Should the rule-breaker be caught and labeled, he or she then presumably continues in this deviant career because of the rewards that accrue from "playing a role that conforms to the stereotype" of the label [44, p. 387]. The obvious implication from this argument is that the symptoms of mental illness are neither real nor severe but merely part of a learned behavior pattern. It is not surprising, then, that the proponents of a social psychiatric view of mental illness have reacted to Scheff's ideas as strongly as they have. Gove rejects labeling's claims as "overstated and largely incorrect." [45, p. 285] Endleman describes the labeling view as "anti-humane" and "a literally fantastic distortion of the reality of these individuals' situation." [46, p. 373] Furthermore, according to the critics, those who support such a position do so because of "rebelliousness and antinomianism" or "some kind of maverick or rebel orientation toward the world." [46, p. 372]

The strengths of the labeling position lie not, it is certain, in its construction of the etiology of mental illness symptoms. Its strengths, however, do emerge when it becomes necessary to explain why certain actions are considered symptomatic of mental illness while other actions, similar in all relevant respects to the first group, are not so considered. Social and personal resources can operate effectively to insulate the individual from the potentially damaging impact of labeling, including the avoidance of hospitalization or, "failing that, . . . the avoidance of lengthy hospitalization." [34, p. 370]

A POLITICAL ECONOMY APPROACH TO MENTAL ILLNESS AMONG THE AGED

The state of mental health research and practice with older patients is one of confusion and disarray. While there is little, if any, certainty as to the causes of mental illness and lesser still as to the life cycle patterns of incidence characteristic of specific disorders, a social psychiatric understanding of the nature of mental illness continues to affect both research and intervention efforts in this troubled field. Older patients are committed to state hospitals where they receive shock therapy, drug therapy or, perhaps, psychotherapy.[2] While therapies of this sort produce a more compliant patient, it is widely recognized that the major benefit gained from such intervention is *social control*. The symptoms of the aged schizophrenic, for example, are perceived as "intractable," lessened neither with time nor prior treatment [4, p. 250]

In terms of research agenda, the social psychiatric model has produced a concentration of interest in the role of *stress* as a precipitating factor to mental illness. While the evolution of research interest from physical lesions in the brains of the insane to socially-produced stress is certainly a progressive development, the emphasis on stress constitutes a major obstacle to further advances in our understanding of mental illness. The problem with the stress research, not considering the very serious and as yet unresolved difficulties of operationalization

---

[2] Psychotherapy is less likely to be recommended for older patients than either drug or shock therapy in part because of the widely-held view, traceable to Freud himself, that "the mass of material to be dealt with would prolong the duration of the treatment indefinitely." [47, p. 257] For a more sanguine view of the value of psychotherapy for the aged, see Yesavage and Karasu [48].

and measurement, is its deflection of attention away from the social and economic structure of capitalist society and towards an ahistorical preoccupation with individual adaptation to "stressful" life events. Pathology is consequently defined as "the result of failure to adapt to the various crises . . ." of old age [49, p. 650]. Forgotten, apparently, is Neitzsche's contention that "Insanity is a rare thing in individuals but habitual to groups, parties, nations, and ages."

The stress research is a largely positivistic effort to ascertain the strength of correlation between types and amounts of "stress," on the one hand, and symptoms of psychological distress, on the other. Such research insures a place for social science in uncovering the presumed causes of mental illness while at the same time strengthening the already solid niche occupied by psychiatrists in "treating" those who lack the requisite coping skills for successful "adaptation." Of course not all of the research conducted in this area is of one type; difference of perspective does exist although it is more nuanced than irreconcilable. The *humanistic* wing within the social psychiatric movement, while generally in accord with the prevailing assessment of stress as inevitable, ubiquitous, and not necessarily pernicious, sees the discriminations and role losses experienced by old people as exceeding tolerable limits. Society, in fact, is directly implicated through its negative stereotyping of the aged. It is beyond doubt, according to Parsons, that if "it is the broad societal verdict upon older people that they are 'useless,' then the obvious way to legitimize their status is to *be* useless through the incapacitation of illness." [50, p. 253] This is what Bengtson Kuypers describe as the "old age vulnerability cycle" [51] or what others see as "learned helplessness." [52, 53]

The understanding that old people are stigmatized as useless in capitalist societies does take us further along in our understanding of mental illness within this age group. However, the stigma approach fails to probe into the reasons why old people are negativity valued, presuming only that the problem has to do with the fast pace of change inherent in industrialization. The proposed solution to the negative labeling is an individualistic or family solution: family members need to be aware of the problem and mobilize available coping resources to successfully manage it. This argument, while pure in motivation, neglects to understand the following realities;

1. *Stigmatization* is a process conducted not only through the mass media but also more immediately through the personal communications of friends, family members, and associates. The primary group social support system is, in other words, often the major source of negative, stigmatizing information concerning the old person and not necessarily an easily mobilized source of much needed counterinformation.
2. *Negative labels* do not descend as if from nowhere but reflect and legitimate the marginal economic position of old people in modern society. The root of the problem of learned helplessness is not the poor images of old people one sees in television commercials; it is, rather, the inability of old people to compete in labor markets.

3. *The mental health* of the aged is affected by their present economic condition which is itself an outcome of the old person's earlier (pre-retirement) social class position. We know, for example, that those aged diagnosed as paranoid or schizophrenic are significantly more likely to be working- rather than middle-class [13]. We also know that, "Above twenty-five years of age, class status becomes increasingly important . . . in the determination of who is or is not receiving psychiatric care." [54, p. 201]

Our argument is, in brief, that theories and interpretations of mental illness must be specific to social classes and the strata defined by age and gender. In other words, as Schneider has argued, mental illness in a class society has a class character: "the 'mental illness' of the *owner* of the means of production has other causes and forms than the mental illness of those who work on those means." [55, p. 187] Similarly, the mental illness of the aged, that is, the proletarianized aged, has different causes and assumes different forms than the illness of either the non-aged or the middle-class.

The understanding that mental illness in a class society has a class character forms the basis of a political economy approach to the mental health question. It would be absurd to argue, however, on the basis of this understanding, that capitalism and mental illness are parallel historical phenomena, the one being both necessary and sufficient for the production of the other. It may be, as Sipe contends [56, p. 152], that "the demise of capitalism is the precondition to mental health." It would not, however, guarantee mental health just as surely as the historical appearance of capitalism did not *cause* mental illness to first exist. The issue is not whether socialism will create "stable, well organized utopias that immunize their citizens against the development of psychiatric disorders." [57, p. 365] It is, rather, in what ways are the forms and distribution of mental illness affected by the capitalist organization of work. This is the problem that bourgeois theories of illness "assiduously overlook or . . . circumscribe." [55, p. 166] Rather than a consideration of class relations grounded in work, the individualistic theories of positivistic social gerontology look to role loss, or stress, or poorly developed coping skills as the source of mental illness. And, as stress is an inevitable concomitant of the modern world, the solution to the problem is not to eliminate stress—for this would, of course, be impossible—but to teach the individual to adjust or to cope with the stress. Such an approach does not lead even to moderate structural reform but only to a different type of individualistic therapy.

OLD AGE AND SOCIAL CLASS IN CAPITALISTIC SOCIETIES

Class interests are not a constant factor over the life course of a particular birth cohort. They constitute, rather, a presence the salience of which assumes a curvilinear path: the initial entry into labor markets marks the increasing significance of class interests in differentiating members of the cohort, while exit from labor markets at retirement signs their declining salience. Removed at retirement form the "dull compulsion" of economic relations, the aging become a superfluous population. They are no longer necessary for production but become, instead, a dependent population, an economic burden whose continued sustenance requires that routine expectations of profit and reciprocity be superceded by past-oriented sentiments of beneficence.

While beneficient social policy allows the reproduction of their existence, it does not protect the aged from the devaluation necessitated by their transition from economic production to idle superfluity. No longer "required by capital or the agencies of capital," older workers become superannuated and "dismissed in derogatory terms such as 'obsolescent,' 'unproductive,' and 'inefficient.'" [58, p. 88] As a group, the aged realize the *fear* associated with noncompliance to capitalism's norms of economic rationality: the fear of being cast out or "expelled from the social community which has come to encircle us in the place of nature." [19] The aged have been separated from the world of work and consequently are no longer able to continue to actively desire the material goods and commodities that the communications media urge us to buy. The aged are no longer producers; they are no longer consumers. The fear of being cast out was repressed as long as the worker was able to produce and desire the commodities that capitalism turned out. Retirement marks the return of the repressed.

The mental illness of the aged thus shares with the psychiatric disturbances of workers a common source in the economic relations under monopoly capitalism. There are, however, important differences between the two. For the worker, alienation is the form in which mental illness presents itself. Because the worker has control over neither his work nor its products, the *realization* of his work contributes to his alienation. The mental illness of the worker derives not from an "unassimilated past" but "from the ever-present and 'recurring' power of alienating labor." [55, p. 176] Lacking the money for psychotherapy, the worker's alienation may not be diagnosed as mental illness but be present instead as individual maladaptation: "demoralization, alcoholism, or feeling upset, rotten, or over-irritated." [55, p. 193]

For the retired worker, the potential emancipation from the alienating routine of work offered by retirement is rarely realized. Retirement produces confusion and depression. While he may now be at ease, the compulsion to work lingers in his mind: he is idle when he should be at work. Others, still competing in labor markets, view the retiree with *envy*, as strange. These perceptions further contribute to his confusion and disorientation.

A second moment in the production of the aged person's illness is his growing inability to realize in his own life the perverted capitalistic "'pleasure principle' of a totally unfettered mania for buying." [56, p. 214] Because they no longer work, they are useless; because they no longer consume, they are unhappy and depressed. As with the wage earner, the schizophrenia or "psychological disengagement" of the aged retiree indicates his refusal to go on, his refusal "to continue to vegetate under inhuman living . . . conditions." [55, p. 203]

While it is certain that the withdrawal of the aged patient from the world of the mentally "healthy" is caused by the capitalist structure of work, one must recognize that the aged contribute to their own illnesses as well. Retired workers sustain their belief in the middle class norms of production, reciprocity, and youthful vigor. One's intrinsic value under capitalism is determined by the prevailing rates of exchange [37]. We are commodities to be sold on the market; our use-value is determined by our exchange-value. As we view others as commodities (as they view us), so too do we come to view ourselves. Our mental health varies with our success in selling ourselves to others. However, because our success is determined in large part by our sexual attractiveness, the deterioration of beauty with age undermines the aging person's ability to maintain, if not to increase, his value. To compensate for the natural losses in youthful beauty and vitality, the aging person may attempt to disguise the physical signs of deterioration and to undergo what Schneider has termed a "compulsive rejuvenation." The problem, however, is that "those who have been compulsively rejuvenated, . . . become schizophrenic, because they look and are treated like children yet think and feel like old people." [55, p. 235]

Compulsive rejuvenation, regardless of its short-term efficacy, eventually must fail as a strategy. The fear of growing old, that is, the fear of being cast out, eventually is realized as the appearance of age can be no longer disguised. After a lifetime of unconscious internalization of the capitalist ideology of health and value, where to be healthy is to work and to work is to have value, the aged are forced either to accept their devaluation and seek out exchange relationships with others of similar age and worth or to disengage. Like the alienated worker who exhibits symptoms of psychiatric disorder and attempts to "escape to the hospital," the disengaged older person is finally allocated either to a hospital, a nursing home, a rooming house, or an SRO hotel.

THE AGED STRANGER

It is common among human beings to distrust, disparage, or segregate ideas, practices, or people about whom little is known. We distrust, for example, foreigners and strangers. Conversely, the mere familiarity of an object is sufficient to dispose us favorably towards it. Such tendencies, of course, are mutually reinforcing. We like whom we know (or have contact with) and we know whom we like. Barring the disruptive, intrusive and, ultimately, broadening effects that change of various sorts brings, such patterns are often crystallized as institutionalized habits of discrimination.

Behavior that departs from the routinized, expected, role-bounded patterns of normal social intercourse is perceived as strange and, perhaps, threatening. When faced with such a threat, the common response is either to flee (that is, to separate ourselves from the threat) or to displace the threat in some fashion. This has been the prevailing societal reaction to the mentally ill, to the aged and, most especially, to the mentally ill older person. The apprehension of strangeness in the behavior of schizophrenics, for example, influences the manner in which we describe them:

> ... the chronic schizophrenic is intriguing because he negates many criteria which have been used to distinguish men from other animals. The chronic schizophrenic is not Seneca's 'reasoning animal' or Spinoza's 'social animal,' or even a reasonably efficient version of Cassierer's 'symbol using animal.' Since he violates so many functional definitions of man, there is heuristic value in studying him with an approach like that which would be used to study any alien creature [59, p. 67].

Braginsky aptly describes the social psychiatric judgment of schizophrenia with the following words [60, p. 296]:

> The primary axiom that underlies ... [the] psychiatric conception of the schizophrenic is that there is some basic way she differs from the rest of mankind ... she seems to be on another, unnameable continuum altogether. ... It is almost as if she has defected from the human race to join another one. ...

Our historical response to the mentally ill has been consistently to restrict contact between them and us, the upholders of the bourgeois social order. According to Horwitz's analysis, the exclusion of the mentally ill developed in response to the hardening of class boundaries and the cultural atomization and heterogeneity that formed in the wake of monopoly capitalism toward the end of the nineteenth century [61, 62]. Further, those groups most likely to be considered as mentally incompetent and therefore requiring hospitalization were those most marginal and most powerless: the poor, the aged, and the newly arrived. Immigrants, according to Horwitz [61, p. 112] are more likely to be excluded (i.e., institutionalized) when labeled mentally ill because of their "cultural distance from conventional groups." The derogation of the aged as senile began as well during this period. Prior to 1880, Gutmann writes, there was "no concept of senility." [63, p. 437]

The aged as a social category have been similarly displaced due to the economic requirements and policies of late capitalism (e.g., credentialism, the growth of professions, mandatory retirement). In the orgy of Taylorism, IQ testing and other neo-positivistic attempts to quantify human traits and abilities, those beyond the age of sixty-five had come to be thought of as beyond the pale. Gruman's description of this devaluation evokes, mutatis mutandis, the preceding discussion of schizophrenics: "The paradoxical interchange between traditional and modern means that the aged have come to be viewed as something new and strange. Instead of symbolizing the reassuringly familiar, they seem threateningly alien." [70, p. 360]

It may be argued that the aged are strangers everywhere, not only under capitalism. While this is so, it is also true that the same attributes that produce fear and revulsion under capitalism may work to the aged's advantage in other societies (the *Gemeinschaften* of many agrarian and transhumance societies, for example [63, 64]). It is true that there exists the potential for exclusion in all societies to which the aged, because of their special appearance, are especially vulnerable. In some societies, however, the aged are considered to be near the gods and to share in their power. It is "precisely because they are strange," Gutmann argues, that they "are told off to face the ultimate strangers, the gods." [63, p. 440] The awe to which their divine connection entitles them in traditional society diminishes under capitalism. The awe is now only revulsion as the rational workings of the labor market leave the aged "as a stranger in a society that is both his and of his making. Yet he no longer belongs nor can he participate." [65]

I wish to argue that it is the aged's special status as strangers that, under conditions of late capitalism, make them especially vulnerable to mental illness and to social control because of their illness. The strangeness of the aged in traditional societies is largely defined in terms of their appearance and other physical properties (e.g., they are closer to death and to the beyond). They are wrinkled, stooped, and slower (and, perhaps, sicker) than the rest of the community. Under capitalism, however, the aged's strangeness becomes total. It transcends the merely physical and enters the *ideological* sphere as well. By so doing, their strangeness makes them not only different but also suspicious and potentially subversive.

The physical differences between the generations have been well documented and need not be reviewed here. I should point out, however, that these physical differences *have* been found to contribute to the isolation and segregation of the aged [66]. Their reduced physical mobility and sitting posture disable them in social interaction; those who are both old and infirm seem to have lost "some essential properties as human beings." [66, p. 29] The old person constitutes, in Bromley's words, "a strange sort of stimulus person." This perception of the aged is a disincentive to maintaining social contact with them; it is too costly. The resulting isolation, or desolation, further reinforces our perception of the aged as strange, different, and sick. We exclude them; we consequently do not see them. They become unfamiliar to us.

The strangeness of the aged is not contained, however, solely within the physical sphere. By several routes, it crosses the boundary of the ideological domain. The specific ideological sources of the aged's strangeness is the topic of a separate paper [67] and so will not be described in full detail here. Several instances, however, can be offered in support of the argument.

The aged are strangers in the present epoch of "expertise" and "high" technology. When capitalism developed its use of technology to increase profits, a new social type—the "expert"—ascended to displace the entrepreneur in economic importance [68]. Old people, however, were scarcely suited for this new role. The older knowledge of cohorts born before the Great War is irrelevant to technological mastery in the present decade. Old people, in short, are not technically competent. They are not adept at manipulating modern technological devices. Home computers, word processors, video cassette recorders, and electronic arcade games are outside their interest and beyond their ken.

The emphasis on instrumental rationality and technical mastery is not restricted to work requirements but encroaches, indeed suffuses, the primary domain of the family. As with other historical epochs, the period of late capitalism requires the coordination and interdependence of its various institutional spheres, including the economic and familial. The requirement for technical mastery on the shop floor is fulfilled through the family's use of *reason* as its primary means, or device, of socialization [68]. By its reinforcement of instrumental rationality as a dominant characteristic of the favored social character of late capitalism, the family contributes to the reproduction of the existing order. Old people, however, undermine this process. They embody not the self control and instrumental reasonableness of parents but a gentle nurturance and *lack* of machine precision. Rather than insisting upon deferred gratification and calculated reciprocity, the aging grandparent allows the "revolutionary" behaviors of spontaneity, curiosity and *immediate* gratification. Those born and raised before World War II are, as Mead described them, immigrants in time. However, in the context of the modern family, they become more than this. The aged stranger in late capitalism takes on the added quality of subversiveness.

The culture of an earlier period that persists through the dwindling presence of pre-1920 cohorts is gradually displaced as attrition in the aged population guarantees the triumph of rationality. Not content to rely, however, on natural erosion of these extant elements of traditional culture, we attempt to accelerate the modernist transition by restricting old people to the social periphery: retirement villages, senior centers, nursing homes, and city parks. This is the hidden terror of capitalism. The alienation of work can only be traded for the enforced idleness of sickness, unemployment, or retirement. Workers cling to their jobs to allay the fear of being cast out. For old people, however, the fear is no more. The terror has been realized. Their mere presence, then, is unwanted as it causes us to acknowledge our own fear of aloneness and isolation. In seeing old people, we glimpse into our own futures under capitalism.

A major theme of modern character, according to Langman and Kaplan is the "underlying intensification of abandonment and ensuing loneliness." [68, p. 110] In order to repress the fear of our own abandonment, we disregard the present suffering of today's old people. The cultural practices of the aged are perceived as the habits of strangers that suggest disloyalty, if not mental illness. The disengagement of old people is itself seized upon as a sign of subversive disloyalty. We interpret their declining level of social involvement as mental illness: they have ceased to "grow," to be "always 'developing,' and 'maturing'—and manifestly happy." [71, p. 15] Human development and mental health have come to constitute the new loyalty oath of our technological age. To be mentally ill in this rational world of modern living is to give testimony against capitalism's ability to deliver the goods, to provide happiness. This vision of a self in "endless development," a vision that Lears recognizes is "perfectly attuned to an economy based on pointless growth and ceaseless destruction," is belied by the strategy of interiorization selected by many old people [69, p. 30].

The mental illness of the aged, in summary, cannot be understood as an individual problem of adaptation. Further, it will not be resolved as a persistent *social* phenomenon with strategies or therapies of intervention that emphasize individual coping skills or adjustment to the larger society. We may effectively eliminate the symptoms of illness in some mildly regressed patients but, by not treating the structure of social and economic relations under capitalism, mental illness will continue to accumulate on the margins of society where the aged and the poor live out their lives.

REFERENCES

1. R. W. Fox, *So Far Disordered in Mind: Insanity in California, 1870-1930*, University of California Press, Berkeley, 1978.
2. P. Willis, *Learning to Labor*, Columbia University Press, New York, 1981.
3. P. L. Berger, *Invitation to Sociology: A Humanistic Perspective*, Doubleday, Garden City, 1963.
4. S. H. Zarit, *Aging and Mental Disorders*, The Free Press, New York, 1980.
5. C. M. Gaitz and R. V. Varner, Adjustment Disorders of Late Life: Stress Disorders, in *Handbook of Geriatric Psychiatry*, E. W. Busse and D. G. Blazer (eds.), Van Nostrand Rinehold, New York, 1980.
6. L. Lowy, Mental Health Services in the Community, in *Handbook of Mental Health and Aging*, J. E. Birren and R. B. Sloane (eds.), Prentice-Hall, Englewood Cliffs, 1980.
7. G. L. Klerman, Age and Clinical Depression: Today's Youth in the Twenty-First Century, *Journal of Gerontology*, 31, pp. 318-323, May 1976.
8. F. S. Kobata, S. A. Lockery, and S. Y. Moriwaki, Minority Issues in Mental Health and Aging, in *Handbook of Mental Health and Aging*, J. E. Birren and R. B. Sloane (eds.), Prentice-Hall, Englewood Cliffs, pp. 448-467, 1980.
9. M. Meacher, *Taken For a Ride*, Longman, London, 1972.
10. T. S. Szasz, *The Myth of Mental Illness*, Harper and Row/Perennial Library, New York, 1974.
11. W. R. Procci, Schizo-Affective Psychosis: Fact or Fiction?, *Archives of General Psychiatry*, 33, pp. 1167-1178, 1976.
12. D. G. Blazer, Impact of Late-Life Depression on the Social Network, *American Journal of Psychiatry*, 140, pp. 162-166, February 1983.

13. C. Eisdorfer, Paranoia and Schizophrenic Disorders in Later Life, in *Handbook of Geriatric Psychiatry*, E. W. Busse and D. G. Blazer (eds.), Van Nostrand Rinehold, New York, pp. 329-337, 1980.

14. A. Stenback, Depression and Suicidal Behavior in Old Age, in *Handbook of Mental Health and Aging*, J. E. Birren and R. B. Sloane (eds.), Prentice-Hall, Englewood Cliffs, pp. 616-652, 1980.

15. F. Post, Paranoid, Schizophrenia-Like, and Schizophrenic States in the Aged, in *Handbook of Mental Health and Aging*, J. E. Birren and R. B. Sloane (eds.), Prentice-Hall, Englewood Cliffs, pp. 591-615, 1980.

16. R. A. Robinson, The Diagnosis and Prognosis of Dementia, in *Current Achievement in Geriatrics*, W. F. Anderson and B. Isaacs (eds.), Cassell, 1965.

17. W. R. Gove and J. Tudor, Sex Differences in Mental Illness: A Comment on Dohrewend and Dohrenwend, *American Journal of Sociology*, *82*, pp. 1327-1336, May 1977.

18. J. E. Birren and V. J. Renner, Concepts and Issues of Mental Health and Aging, in *Handbook of Mental Health and Aging*, J. E. Birren and R. B. Sloane (eds.), Prentice-Hall, Englewood Cliffs, pp. 3-33, 1980.

19. T. W. Adorno, Sociology and Psychology, *New Left Review*, *46*, pp. 67-80, November-December 1967.

20. _____, Sociology and Psychology, *New Left Review*, *47*, pp. 79-97, January-February 1968.

21. W. A. Rushing and S. T. Ortega, Socioeconomic Status and Mental Disorder: New Evidence and a Sociomedical Formulation, *American Journal of Sociology*, *84*, pp. 1175-1200, March, 1979.

22. S. Kety, Heredity and Environment, in *Schizophrenia*, J. Shershow (ed.), Harvard, Cambridge, pp, 47-68, 1978.

23. C. Ratner, Do the Studies on Identical Twins Prove that Schizophrenia is Genetically Inherited?, *The International Journal of Social Psychiatry*, *28*, pp. 175-178, Autumn, 1982.

24. M. L. Kohn, The Interaction of Social Class and Other Factors in the Etiology of Schizophrenia, *American Journal of Psychiatry*, *133*, pp. 177-185, February 1976.

25. R. Abrams and M. A. Taylor, The Genetics of Schizophrenia: A Reassessment Using Modern Criteria, *American Journal of Psychiatry*, *140*, pp. 171-175, February 1983.

26. W. F. Bodmer and L. L. Cavalli-Sforza, *Genetics, Evolution, and Man*, W. H. Freeman and Company, San Francisco, 1976.

27. H. Brenner, *Mental Illness and the Economy*, Harvard University Press, Cambridge, 1973.

28. B. S. Dohrenwend and B. P. Dohrenwend, *Stressful Life Events: Their Nature and Effects*, Wiley, New York, 1974.

29. L. F. Jarvik, Aging and Depression: Some Unanswered Questions, *Journal of Gerontology*, *31*:3, pp. 324-326, 1976.

30. M. Bressler-Feiner, Narcissism and Role Loss in Older Adults, *Journal of Geriatric Psychiatry*, *14*:1, pp. 91-109, 1981.

31. A. Simon, The Neuroses, Personality Disorders, Alcoholism, Drug Use and Misuse, and Crime in the Aged, in *Handbook of Mental Health and Aging*, J. E. Birren and R. B. Sloane (eds.), Prentice-Hall, Englewood Cliffs, pp. 653-670, 1980.
32. L. I. Pearlin, Life Strains and Psychological Distress Among Adults, in *Themes of Work and Love in Adulthood*, N. J. Smelser and E. H. Erikson (eds.), Harvard University Press, Cambridge, pp. 174-192, 1980.
33. W. W. Eaton, A Formal Theory of Selection for Schizophrenia, *American Journal of Sociology, 86*, pp. 149-158, July 1980.
34. R. J. Turner and J. W. Gartrell, Social Factors in Psychiatric Outcome: Toward the Resolution of Interpretive Controversies, *American Sociological Review, 43*, pp. 368-382, June 1978.
35. L. I. Pearlin and C. Schooler, The Structure of Coping, *Journal of Health and Social Behavior, 19*, pp. 2-21, March 1978.
36. J. J. Dowd, *Stratification Among the Aged*, Brooks/Cole, Monterey, California, 1980.
37. J. J. Dowd, Exchange Rates and Old People, *Journal of Gerontology, 35*, pp. 596-602, July 1980.
38. M. F. Lowenthal, Social Isolation and Mental Illness in Old Age, *American Sociological Review, 29*:1, pp. 54-70, 1964.
39. _____, Antecedents of Isolation and Mental Illness in Old Age, *Archives of General Psychiatry, 12*, pp. 245-254, 1965.
40. M. F. Lowenthal and C. Haven, Interaction and Adaptation: Intimacy as a Critical Variable, *American Sociological Review, 33*, pp. 20-30, February 1968.
41. R. Perrucci and D. B. Targ, Network Structure and Reactions to Primary Deviance of Mental Patients, *Journal of Health and Social Behavior, 23*, pp. 2-17, March 1982.
42. D. Mechanic, Social Class and Schizophrenia: Some Requirements for a Plausible Theory of Social Influence, *Social Forces, 50*, pp. 305-309, March 1972.
43. D. Morgan, Explaining Mental Illness, *Archives Europeans do Sociologie, 26*, pp. 262-280, 1975.
44. M. S. Goldstein, The Sociology of Mental Health and Illness, *Annual Review of Sociology, 5*, pp. 381-409, 1979.
45. W. R. Gove, The Current Status of the Labeling Theory of Mental Illness, in *Deviance and Mental Illness*, W. R. Gove (ed.), Sage, Berkeley, California, pp. 273-300, 1982.
46. R. Endleman, *Psyche and Society: Explorations in Psychoanalytic Sociology*, Columbia University, New York, 1981.
47. S. Freud, On Psychotherapy, in *Collected Papers, Vol. 1*, Hogarth, London, pp. 249-263, 1924.
48. J. A. Yesavage and T. B. Karasu, Psychotherapy with Elderly Patients, *American Journal of Psychotherapy, 36*, pp. 41-55, January, 1982.
49. E. Pfeiffer, Psychopathology and Social Pathology, in *Handbook of the Psychology of Aging*, J. E. Birren and K. W. Schaie (eds.), Van Nostrand Rinehold, New York, pp. 650-671, 1977.

50. T. Parsons, Toward a Healthy Maturity, *Journal of Health and Human Behavior, 1*, pp. 163-173, Fall 1960.
51. V. L. Bengtson and J. A. Kuypers, Psycho-Social Issues in the Aging Family, paper presented at the XIIth International Congress of Gerontology, Hamburg, 1981.
52. E. J. Langer, Old Age: An Artifact, in *Aging: Biology and Behavior*, J. L. McGaugh and S. B. Kresler (eds.), Academic Press, New York, 1981.
53. M. E. P. Seligman, *Helplessness*, Freeman, San Francisco, 1975.
54. A. B. Hollingshead and F. C. Redlich, *Social Class and Mental Illness*, John Wiley and Sons, New York, 1958.
55. M. Schneider, *Neurosis and Civilization: A Marxist/Freudian Synthesis*, (translated by M. Roloff), Seabury, New York, 1975.
56. R. B. Sipe, Late Capitalism and Mental Illness: Toward a Critical Theory of Psychic Crisis, in *The United States in Crisis: Marxist Analyses*, L. Biro and M. J. Cohen (eds.), Marxist Educational Press, Minneapolis, pp. 151-164, 1979.
57. B. P. Dohrenwend, Sociocultural and Social-Psychological Factors in the Genesis of Mental Disorders, *Journal of Health and Social Behavior, 16*, pp. 365-392, December 1975.
58. A. Walker, Towards a Political Economy of Old Age, *Ageing and Society, 1*, pp. 73-94, March 1981.
59. C. Schooler and D. Parkel, The Overt Behavior of Chronic Schizophrenics and Its Relationship to Their Internal State and Personal History, *Psychiatry, 29*, pp. 67-77, 1969.
60. B. Braginsky, On Being Surplus: Its Relationship to Impression Management and Mental Patienthood, in *Impression Management Theory and Social Psychological Research*, J. T. Tedeschi (ed.), Academic Press, New York, 1981.
61. A. Horwitz, *The Social Control of Mental Illness*, Academic Press, New York, 1982.
62. _____, Models, Muddles, and Mental Illness Labeling, *Journal of Health and Social Behavior, 20*, pp. 296-300, September 1979.
63. D. Gutmann, Observations and Culture and Mental Health in Later Life, in *Handbook of Mental Health and Aging*, J. E. Birren and R. B. Sloane (eds.), Prentice-Hall, Englewood Cliffs, New Jersey, pp. 429-447, 1980.
64. D. Gutmann, The Cross-Cultural Perspective: Notes Toward a Comparative Psychology of Aging, in *Handbook of the Psychology of Aging*, J. E. Birren and K. W. Schaie (eds.), Van Nostrand Rinehold Co., New York, 1977.
65. D. Kent, Social and Cultural Factors Influencing the Mental Health of the Aged, *American Journal of Orthopsychiatry, 36*, pp. 680-685, July 1966.
66. D. B. Bromley, Approaches to the Study of Personality Changes in Adult Life and Old Age, in *Studies in Geriatric Psychiatry*, A. D. Isaacs and F. Post (eds.), John Wiley, Chichester, pp. 17-40, 1978.
67. J. J. Dowd, The Old Person as Stranger, in *Becoming Old: A Microsociology of Aging and Later Life*, V. M. Marshall (ed.), Ablex, Norwood, New Jersey, (forthcoming).

68. L. Langman and L. Kaplan, Political Economy and Social Character: Terror, Desire, and Domination, in *Current Perspectives in Social Theory*, Vol. 2, G. McNall and G. N. Howe (eds.), JAI Press, Greenwich, Connecticut, pp. 87-115, 1981.

69. T. J. Lears, *No Place of Grace: Antimodernism and the Transformation of American Culture 1880-1920*, Pantheon, New York, 1981.

70. G. Gruman, Cultural Origins of Present-day "Age-ism": The Modernization of the Life Cycle, in *Aging and the Elderly: Humanistic Perspectives in Gerontology*, S. F. Spicker, K. M. Woodward, and D. D. Van Tassel (eds.), Humanities Press, Atlantic Highlands, New Jersey, pp. 359-387, 1978.

71. J. Seeley, *The Americanization of the Unconscious*, Lippincott, Philadelphia, 1967.

CHAPTER 7

Medicare and Medicaid:
The Process, Value, and Limits
of Health Care Reforms

E. RICHARD BROWN

When President Johnson signed the Medicare and Medicaid legislation into law on July 30, 1965, a great many Americans believed that the elderly would no longer be impoverished by medical care costs and that the poor would get the care they need from essentially the same sources as the middle class. Under the Medicare program, the federal government would pay for most of the costs of hospitalization for the elderly and would insure them for physicians' services and related care—coverage the elderly were unable to obtain at a price they could afford from the private insurance industry. Under the Medicaid program, the federal government would provide grants to the states to greatly expand medical care for the poor, subsidizing those on public assistance and several related categories of low-income persons not receiving public assistance, to enable them to get their care from the private medical market.

These legislative reforms culminated an intermittent half-century of struggle for compulsory health insurance. They represented a substantial compromise of the goal of national health insurance, vigorously pursued in the 1940's. Medicare and Medicaid partially succeeded in fulfilling their more limited objectives of improving the access of the poor and the elderly to medical care and preventing the pauperization of the elderly due to medical expenses. But even these more limited objectives have been compromised by political and fiscal pressures on federal, state, and local governments. The programs proved far more costly than almost anyone imagined, and within a year of their implementation in 1966, cost containment competed with and then replaced the original legislative goal of equity as the dominant concern of state legislatures as well as the Congress.

In this chapter we will examine the background of the landmark reform legislation establishing the Medicare and Medicaid programs. What problems generated interest in public health insurance and subsidy programs? What political, social, and economic forces shaped the struggle for such programs in the decades up to the 1960's? What political process resulted in the specific Medicare and Medicaid legislation, particularly those parts that came to have important consequences for the programs?

We will next consider the implementation of the programs. How do they work? Whom do they cover? How much do they cost? Who provides care for Medicare and Medicaid beneficiaries? How have the programs changed in the decade and a half of their existence?

Finally, we will draw some lessons from the experience with Medicare and Medicaid. What has been the value of these programs to the people they were intended to benefit? What have been their limitations? Can the problems be remedied or must these programs be replaced with entirely new ones? What lessons from Medicare and Medicaid can be applied to future health program legislation?

BACKGROUND: 1930–1965

Inequities and Instability

Half a century ago the Committee on the Costs of Medical Care[1] documented the great disparities in access to health services due to the unequal distribution of income in our society. In a study conducted between 1928 and 1931 the committee found that persons in upper-income families averaged one and a half times as many hospital admissions and twice as many physician visits each year as members of low- and moderate-income families [1, p. 599] The lesson from these research findings and ordinary experience was simple: when medical care is produced and sold in a market system, its distribution parallels the class structure of society. Economic demand becomes the basis for use, creating inequities in access to health care, whereas equity would require that health need be the primary determinant of use.

Adding to such inequalities, many working-class and middle-class persons who could afford ordinary medical expenses—physicians' fees, prescription drugs, simple laboratory tests—were either totally impoverished by extraordinary expenses related to hospitalization or were forced to forego such care when it was really needed. These financial and medical problems added to the personal and social burdens of illness and were borne individually by those afflicted unless relieved by charity, a partial solution that always carried with it a humiliating means test.

In addition to the deprivations suffered by the public, hospitals and physicians felt the pinch of frequent downward business cycles. Unstable and declining incomes, particularly during the Great Depression, were a source of bitterness for

---

[1] The Committee on the Costs of Medical Care was a foundation-funded project created to conduct policy-oriented research on problems in the organization and financing of medical care and to recommend solutions to those problems. Between 1927 and 1933 it produced twenty-six research studies, summarized in references [1, 2].

doctors. Some hospitals were forced to close their doors. These problems of inequities in access, impoverishment due to large medical expenses, and unstable hospital and physician revenues called forth two distinctly different strategies, one focused on public health insurance and the other on private insurance.

Public Insurance: Defeats

For decades American social reformers, socialists, and even a worried medical profession had been watching the development of compulsory public health insurance in Europe. In 1883, Bismarck established the Sickness Insurance Act to help stem growing support for socialism among the German working class. In 1911, Lloyd George and the Liberal party enacted the National Health Insurance Act to win English workers' votes from the socialistic Labor party.

Efforts to establish some kind of public health insurance system in the United States date back to the 1915-18 campaign of the American Association for Labor Legislation, but it was the effort to link health insurance to the 1935 Social Security Act that was the most important antecedent of the Medicare and Medicaid bill passed three decades later. Although the original bill to create a system of social insurance for the aged, the unemployed, the blind, the widowed, and their children included only a suggestion that the new Social Security Board study the need for a government health insurance program, opposition from the powerful medical profession was so swift and formidable that President Roosevelt abandoned the issue, fearing it might sink the whole Social Security bill [3, pp. 7-9; 4, pp. 185-204].

In the 1940's, bills to establish a compulsory national health insurance program were regularly introduced into the Congress, and just as regularly defeated by the American Medical Association's well-funded political campaigns. The annual battles over the Wagner-Murray-Dingell national health insurance bills culminated in President Truman's strong personal endorsement of the 1949 version of the bill. The bill would have covered all medical, dental, hospital, and nursing services; been financed by a payroll tax; included all contributors and their dependents and subsidized the poor; been administered by a federal agency; and included freedom of participation by doctors and hospitals and freedom of choice for patients and doctors alike. The Wagner-Murray-Dingell bills embodied the view—supported by Truman's advisors, the labor movement, and public opinion polls—that financial means should not determine a person's access to health care. But the AMA's massive public relations and lobbying campaign, caricaturing the proposal as one step away from a socialist America, stopped the proposal at its Congressional starting gate. With this defeat, proponents of national health insurance gave up any serious prospects of enacting a proposal, although bills were ritualistically introduced through 1952 [3, pp. 9-14; 4, pp. 205-227, 293-301, 340-377].

Private Insurance: Success and Limitations

Partly in response to the "threat" of government health insurance and more fundamentally in response to hospitals' needs for greater financial stability, the American Hospital Association actively expanded its Blue Cross hospital insurance plans, first introduced in 1929 by Baylor University Hospital in Dallas, Texas. Medical societies followed suit with Blue Shield plans covering mainly physicians' fees for surgical and obstetrical services in the hospital. After the threat of compulsory national health insurance the AMA found voluntary private insurance an attractive alternative and praised it as "the American way." [4, pp. 228-251; 5] By 1940, 12 million people (less than 10% of the population) were insured for hospital expenses and far fewer for surgical or other physicians' fees [6, pp. 184-185].

But private health insurance proved very popular. The risk of medical misfortune was spread among many individuals and families, enabling them to obtain more expensive kinds of care without necessarily devastating their finances. The demands of labor unions for greater economic security and more benefits encouraged the spread of work-related group plans. In 1945, after several years of cost-plus government war contracts and labor pressure on employers, enrollment in hospital insurance plans provided coverage for 32 million persons, 24 percent of the population [7]. After the war commercial insurance companies, following the Blue Cross lead, pushed energetically into the health insurance market they had previously considered unprofitable.

Although private health insurance coverage was growing rapidly, it left out many services and important population sectors. In 1950 private health insurance paid for only 37 percent of total hospital costs and only 12 percent of physicians' services [7]. Perhaps more important, private health insurance was available mainly to the middle and upper-working classes—that is, those covered by union- or employer-sponsored plans and those affluent enough to buy individual insurance policies. It was becoming apparent that private health insurance would not meet the needs of the poorly paid, nonunionized working population or their families, or those who were very poor and unable to work—single-parent households with very young children, the blind and disabled, and the aged.

The Legacy of Social Security

The Social Security Act of 1935 and the defeat of the Wagner–Murray–Dingell bills throughout the 1940's reinforced and codified in federal law two levels of distinctions in social welfare programs. The Social Security Act comprised a group of programs that would provide federal support only for the "deserving poor," those who are poor through some misfortune that is beyond their control—persons who are too old to work, the blind and disabled who are unable to work, dependent widows and children, and those who truly could not find work. All others who might be indigent, including the working poor and persons who do not work for reasons other than those included in the act, were considered "undeserving" of federal relief and were left to the resources and charity of the states, local governments, and private agencies. This distinction had a long tradition in Anglo-American social philosophy. Cotton Mather, for example, had urged colonial Boston merchants to provide charity only to the "poor that can't work." And the founders of a Philadelphia charity group in the 1870's sought to develop "a method by which idleness and begging, now so encouraged, may be suppressed and worthy self-respecting poverty be discovered and relieved at the smallest cost to the benevolent." [8, pp. 12-15, 98]

But the Social Security Act added another important distinction *among* the "deserving" poor—the distinction between social insurance and public assistance. As Robert and Rosemary Stevens have noted [9, p. 11], "Benefits made available under social insurance were contributory, work-related, available to beneficiaries as a right, and determined by Congress. Public assistance, on the other hand, was a matter for administrative discretion at the lowest levels of government." [10, pp. 193-200, 219-227]

Workers *earn* their rights to benefits from social insurance programs by their contributions. Public assistance involves no direct contributions by individuals into programs from which they might later draw benefits. The Social Security Act provided contributory social insurance programs for the aged, and grants to the states for "categorical" public assistance to the elderly, to dependent children, and to the blind. In addition, it created a hybrid program of unemployment compensation that was not contributory on the part of workers but in other respects was very much like social insurance. As the Stevenses observe, the distinction between social insurance and public assistance, codified in the Social Security Act, has dominated social welfare legislation in the United States ever since, including the strategies leading up to the enactment of Medicare (a social insurance program), and Medicaid (a public assistance program), and their history since 1965.

Three Steps Back, Two Steps Forward

The defeat of the Wagner-Murray-Dingell bills to create a compulsory national health insurance system for all Americans was a major setback in efforts to develop health insurance along social insurance lines. Following the defeat of Truman's national health insurance proposal in 1949, his chief advisers on social security proposed a federal plan that would limit health insurance to the beneficiaries of the Old Age and Survivors Insurance program, the social insurance part of the Social Security Act. Tying the plan to the social security program would avoid the stigma of welfare, and it would let the plan bask in the legitimacy and popularity achieved by social security. Backing away from any general insurance plan for the entire population, Truman's advisers believed they could sidestep the opposition of the AMA and its allies by restricting the program to social security beneficiaries, excluding physician services, and limiting benefits to sixty days of hospital care [3, pp. 13-23].

Indeed there seemed to be political merit to their plan. By 1950, private hospital insurance plans covered 51 percent of the population, more than double the proportion covered just five years earlier [7]. The spread of private health insurance, especially to workers in unionized industries, undercut the labor movement's political support for national health insurance. Liberal political programs that seemed to have a broad base of popular support a few years earlier were under attack in 1951, undermined by the Korean War and the rise of McCarthyism.

Furthermore, the Social Security Amendments of 1950 also undercut the demands for national health insurance. The amendments expanded categorical public assistance programs to include federal cost-sharing grants to the states to cover hospital and other medical care for public assistance recipients paid for directly by welfare agencies through "vendor payments." Despite its meager funding, this program provided opponents of national health insurance with the hope that medical care for the poor could be kept isolated from the health care needs of the rest of the population and kept narrow in its impact. Even by 1960, medical vendor payments under all public assistance programs totaled only $514 million nationally, with more than half the amount going for hospital and nursing home care [9, p. 23].

The Eisenhower years drained any remaining vitality from efforts to pass even more limited insurance plans. Eisenhower had campaigned for the presidency in 1952 against "socialized medicine," a rubric under which he included both the Truman general health insurance proposal and the limited social security-based hospital insurance plan for the aged. Hearings on the latter plan were held in 1958 on Representative Aime Forand's bill that would provide up to 120 days of hospital and skilled nursing home care and necessary surgery for persons receiving social security benefits. The AMA spent a quarter of a million dollars lobbying against the bill, which was defeated in 1959 in the Ways and Means Committee, chaired by Representative Wilbur Mills.

Despite the apparent demise of the Forand bill, the hearings and the AMA's campaign against it dramatized the medical-financial needs of a large segment of the elderly and vividly reflected the dichotomized approach to social welfare legislation in the United States. The proponents of the Forand bill pointed out that among persons sixty-five years old and over, about three-fifths had annual incomes less than $1000, more than half had no hospital insurance, and even those with insurance found it inadequate. Moreover, the elderly were more than twice as likely as those under sixty-five to need medical care. The bill's opponents had to concede the great need of many of the aged—though they disputed many of the statistics—but they favored a welfare approach over the Forand bill's social insurance approach. They argued that a welfare program, which would include a means test and be administered by the states and local governments, would be directed only to those who are really in need and that it should provide for meeting a broader range of medical needs than the Forand bill's hospitalization benefits. Theodore Marmor notes the irony of the conflict: the more liberal supporters of the social insurance-based Forand bill proposing a limited hospital-surgical insurance bill for all the aged to be financed by the inherently regressive social security taxes; the more conservative opponents of the bill favoring broader benefits for only the destitute aged to be financed from the more progressive federal tax revenues through a welfare-based program [3, pp. 29-54].

Kerr–Mills

By 1960 it was widely accepted, in and out of the Congress, that some federal program was necessary to help the elderly meet the high cost of getting sick. Although the House Ways and Means Committee again defeated the Forand proposal, public sentiment continued so strongly in favor of it that the committee had to come up with an alternative. That political necessity opened the door to the basic welfare approach favored by the opponents of the original Forand bill. Sponsored by Representative Mills and Senator Robert Kerr and enacted in 1960, the Kerr-Mills Act expanded the existing system of federal grants to states for vendor payments for medical care provided to welfare recipients under old-age assistance. The program provided more generous federal matching grants to the states in the hope that every state would develop its own program of adequate care, and it added a new category of vendor payments to cover elderly persons (in 1962, the blind were included) who were not receiving cash assistance but were too poor to pay their own medical bills. This group was labeled "medically needy," and the concept of "medical indigency" was carried over into the Medicaid program [9, pp. 26-30].

As was predicted by Forand and supporters of his bill, the states moved slowly in implementing Kerr-Mills. The more affluent states that already had substantial vendor payment programs expanded their benefits and coverage while the poorer states participated only marginally, if at all. By the end of 1962 only twenty-eight states had Kerr-Mills programs. By 1965, forty-four of the fifty-four states and territories had some program in effect, but five large and relatively affluent states—New York, California, Massachusetts, Minnesota, and Pennsylvania—which together included 31 percent of the aged in the country, were receiving 62 percent of the federal funds for the "medically needy" program. The program increased the flow of funds to hospitals and nursing homes, encouraging the rapid expansion of the latter industry. Of total vendor payments of $1.4 billion in fiscal year 1965-66, two-thirds went to hospitals and nursing homes [9, pp. 31-36].

Kerr-Mills satisfied few interest groups. Senior citizens groups continued to campaign for social security-based health insurance to meet the ever rising costs of medical care without the indignities of a means test. The rising costs of welfare medical care remained a burden on the states, even with the additional federal aid.

The Momentum for Medicare

In his first few weeks in office in 1961, President Kennedy sent a proposal to Congress calling for the extension of social security benefits to cover hospital and nursing home care, but not including surgical benefits that had been a part of the Forand bill. The administration back-stepped from the Forand and earlier proposals in order to widen the base of support for its bill, anticipating an uphill struggle despite the Democratic majority in both houses and the two-to-one public opinion support for the idea. The bill, introduced by Senator Clinton Anderson and Representative Cecil King, was a competitor of the Kerr-Mills program, a severe disadvantage since Mills chaired the powerful House Ways and Means Committee which had to approve the bill. As a result of Mills' commitment to the program which bore his name, the political opposition of Republicans and Southern Democrats (including Mills), and vocal opposition of the AMA and the Health Insurance Institute (representing the private insurance industry), the bill was firmly defeated in the House Ways and Means Committee. A similar proposal by Senator Anderson in 1962 also met its demise [3, pp. 39-54; 9, p. 46].

But pressure continued to build as medical costs for the elderly continued to rise, as senior citizens groups and the AFL-CIO grew more vocal in their support, as the civil rights movement grew larger and more insistent, and as the Kerr-Mills program remained ineffective. In 1963, Kennedy again urged the Congress to approve his proposals for hospital insurance, the King-Anderson bill was reintroduced, and the House Ways and Means Committee once again held hearings. The next year, the Senate for the first time approved a proposal for hospital insurance as an amendment to the Social Security Bill, and Mills' committee was within one vote of a pro-health insurance majority. But in October 1964, Mills was able to kill the bill in a House-Senate conference committee [3, pp. 54-57; 9, p. 46].

The Democratic sweep of the November 1964 elections assured that health insurance would finally be enacted. The defeat of the Goldwater Republican platform of opposition to social programs was taken as a popular mandate. The Democrats gained a two-to-one majority in the House, and the composition of the Ways and Means Committee was altered in favor of compulsory hospital insurance. President Johnson called for immediate action on the King-Anderson "Medicare" bill. However, while Congress was certain to pass some health insurance bill, its substance was not so certain.

Republicans and AMA spokespersons shifted from simple opposition to Medicare, to what one AMA official called "more positive programs." Raising their now familiar criticisms that the King-Anderson bill provided too narrow a set of benefits, would be too expensive, and made no distinction between the indigent elderly and those better off, the AMA proposed its own "Eldercare" program that included physician and other outpatient care as well as hospital and nursing home benefits, and would be administered by the states as a welfare program. The AMA proposal was introduced in the House by Ways and Means Committee members Thomas Curtis and Sydney Herlong. Another committee member, Republican John Byrnes, introduced his own bill that was similar to the AMA bill and had support from the House Republican leadership [3, pp. 61-62; 9, pp. 46-47; 10, pp. 157-294].

As the Ways and Means Committee began its work under Mills' firm hand, it had before it several different proposals, all of which were regarded by their proponents as mutually exclusive. Unexpectedly, however, Mills suggested a compromise incorporating elements of all three bills. The Administration's King–Anderson proposal would be included as hospital insurance financed through additional social security taxes, providing inpatient hospital and nursing home care benefits to all persons eligible for social security retirement benefits. (The hospital insurance plan became part A of the Medicare program.) The essence of the Byrnes proposal was incorporated as a separate voluntary insurance plan covering physicians' services for the elderly, paid for by premiums from those who choose to enroll and by federal subsidies, and administered by private insurance carriers. (The physicians insurance became part B, or Supplemental Medical Insurance.) The committee also added an expanded and liberalized program of federal assistance to the states for the medically indigent and needy, which the AMA had supported as a substitute for the other proposals. (This expansion of the Kerr–Mills concept became known as Medicaid.)

Mills' compromise undermined AMA opposition, played to the Republicans, and gave the Administration more than it ever hoped to get in one legislative session. Wilbur Cohen, then HEW Assistant Secretary for Legislation, called it "the most brilliant legislative move I'd seen in thirty years." [11, p. 187] For Mills the compromise proposal apparently represented his desire to be the "architect of victory" rather than a defeated obstructionist. Mills also explained that including the voluntary premium-supported physicians insurance program would "build a fence around the Medicare program" and undermine later demands for liberalization, including inclusion of physician coverage under social security, that "might be a burden on the economy and the social security program." [3, p. 69]

Once the Administration was convinced that Mills was not trying just to scuttle the King-Anderson bill, they delightedly endorsed the compromise. The new bill passed the House and was approved with some changes by the Senate. It was finally approved by both houses as Public Law 89-97, including Medicare as Title 18 and Medicaid as Title 19 of the Social Security Amendments of 1965. On July 30, 1965, President Johnson flew to Independence, Missouri and signed the bill into law in the presence of Harry Truman, who had vigorously supported a broader, compulsory health insurance plan for the entire population some sixteen years earlier. Johnson observed that the marvel was not "the passage of this bill but . . . that it took so many years to pass it." [3, 63-74; 9, pp. 47-48; 11, p. 4]

FROM VICTORY TO IMPLEMENTATION

The flourish with which Johnson signed the Medicare and Medicaid legislation into law marked the end of victory and the beginning of implementation. The programs quickly involved many millions of people, required massive administrative machinery and enormous amounts of federal funds, and met drastically different political responses.

Medicare

Part A, the hospital insurance (HI) portion of the Medicare program, covers the major portion of inpatient hospital care, 100 days of nursing home care following hospitalization, and 100 home health care visits, also following hospitalization. This part of the program is financed by an increase in the social security tax paid into a special trust fund; anyone who is eligible for social security retirement benefits is also covered by HI benefits. Because it is paid for by all working persons in the country, it is considered "compulsory."

Part B, the supplementary medical insurance (SMI), covers physicians' and surgeons' services (whether in the hospital, office, clinic, or home), home health services not necessarily following hospitalization, diagnostic tests and procedures, and the like. Unlike part A, SMI is a voluntary program in which anyone eligible for part A benefits may enroll. It is supported by monthly premiums paid by enrollees into another special trust fund and matched by federal general tax revenues.

Medicare began in 1966 with an enrollment of 19 million aged persons in part A and nearly 18 million in part B, a testament to the successful campaign conducted by the Social Security Administration to inform the nation's elderly about the program. By 1978 enrollment in both HI and SMI had surpassed 26 million, including nearly 24 million persons sixty-five and over; the remainder are disabled persons under sixty-five and kidney disease patients who qualify for the End-Stage Renal Disease program, both added to Medicare in 1973 [12, p. 3]. Thus, very nearly all persons over sixty-five in the United States, with the exception mainly of undocumented immigrants, were covered by Medicare.

Following the pattern in private insurance programs, Congress included substantial "deductibles" (paid by the patient before the plan pays anything) and "co-insurance" (a portion of the remaining charges for which the patient is responsible). Under part A the patient had to pay, as a deductible, the first $40 of a hospital bill (increased to $264 by 1982) and, as co-payments, $10 a day for the sixty-first through the ninetieth day of hospitalization (raised to $75 a day by 1982). Part B, the SMI, required a monthly premium from each enrollee of $3 per month (up to $12 in 1982), a deductible of $50 (raised to $75 by 1981), and co-payments equal to 20 percent of the remaining bill.

Elderly patients would have to keep proper records and submit their bills to Medicare so they could be credited with the deductible and begin obtaining their benefits. In addition, physicians could bill Medicare patients more than the "reasonable charges" set and reimbursed by Medicare, with the patient paying the difference [9, pp. 48-51]. For most elderly persons these deductibles, co-insurance, and added charges could quickly climb beyond their financial resources. They would then have to turn to supplementary private insurance or Medicaid.

Medicaid

Medicaid was intended to "pick up the pieces" left over by Medicare—to cover the deductibles and co-insurance for indigent Medicare patients, pay for services not covered or covered only inadequately by Medicare (that is, outpatient and nursing home care), and pay the costs of medical care for indigent persons other than the elderly. Unlike Medicare, which is primarily a social insurance program administered by the federal government as an earned right to "entitled" persons, Medicaid is a public assistance program following the well-established pattern of other welfare measures.

Medicaid provides federal contributions to the states' approved programs of medical assistance, with the federal share ranging from 50 percent for states with higher per capita incomes up to 83 percent for the poorer states. The generous matching formula was intended to encourage all states, including the poorest, to develop Medicaid programs. Alabama, Arkansas, and Mississippi finally began their programs in 1970. Both Alaska and Arizona complained that, because nearly all Eskimos and Indians would be eligible, the costs would be more than they could bear. Nevertheless, Alaska implemented a Medicaid program in 1972; Arizona remained the only state without one until it adopted a very restricted one in 1982 [9, p. 58-61].

By 1972, with all current state Medicaid programs (except Arizona's) operating, 17.6 million poor people in the United States were enrolled in Medicaid. Enrollment reached nearly 23 million in 1977 and has been gradually declining since [13, p. 13]. Although the size of the Medicaid program may seem impressive, restrictions on eligibility have kept many of the nation's poor off the Medicaid rolls.

Title 19 required state Medicaid programs to include all "categorically needy" persons—those receiving cash grants under Old Age Assistance, Aid to the Blind, Aid to Families with Dependent Children (AFDC), and Aid to the Permanently and Totally Disabled. In addition, the states were also required to cover the "categorically related needy," persons not receiving cash grants because of certain eligibility restrictions imposed by the states. Besides these mandated groups, states could opt to include additional "categorically related needy" groups and the "categorically related *medically* needy"—that is, persons who would be eligible for public assistance (children, the aged, blind, and disabled) but whose incomes are above the state's standard set for cash grants.

California and New York quickly established the most liberal eligibility standards and most generous benefits of all state Medicaid programs. In 1977 they each spent more than $1.5 billion in state and local funds (in addition to the federal contributions) on their Medicaid programs [14, p. 41]. California's program, known as Medi-Cal, in 1971 even added coverage for "medically indigent adults," a category which, unlike "medically indigent children," is not matched with any federal contribution and absorbed 41 percent of the state's Medi-Cal costs [15, pp. 550-561]. California and New York together account for 27 percent of all Medicaid recipients in the U.S. [14, p. 57]. Although California and New York were very generous in setting eligibility levels, many states were very restrictive. In 1977, twenty state programs excluded the medically needy or indigent [14, p. 6]. And the states are free to set income levels for public assistance cash grants, and therefore Medicaid eligibility, far above or far below the federal government's official poverty level.

The confusing array of "categorical" groups and income levels that had to be or could be included in state Medicaid programs suggests that many categories and numbers of persons, although poor, were excluded from the programs. Somewhere between 40 and 67 percent of all poor persons in the United States are ineligible for Medicaid because of categorical or income requirements [14, pp. 62-63; 16, pp. 159-182]! In eight states, Medicaid recipients totaled less than 20 percent of the poverty population in 1970 [14, pp. 62-63]. To be eligible for Medicaid, "one had to wear the appropriate label," as Robert and Rosemary Stevens observe. "To be just 'poor' was not sufficient." [9, p. 2]

Impact on Access and Equity

The poor have greatly increased their use of health services, though not commensurate with their needs, since the large disparities found by the Committee on the Costs of Medical Care half a century ago. Whereas the Committee found that upper-income groups had far more physician visits and hospital admissions than low-income groups, the National Health Interview surveys in the late 1970s found that poor adults actually had more physician visits, and poor persons of all ages averaged more hospitalizations than the nonpoor [16; 17, p. 132].

These very substantial improvements are clearly attributable to the combined effects of Medicare, Medicaid, community health centers for the poor, and public hospitals and clinics. For example, in 1976 poor children averaged 65 percent more physician visits than in 1964, poor adults averaged between 27 and 33 percent more visits, and the elderly poor, 18 percent more visits. In each age group, the poor registered a much greater increase over this period than did the nonpoor [18, p. 61].

However, some very important gaps remain. Children in upper-income families still average considerably more visits to physicians than children below the poverty line. And the nonpoor of all ages are far more likely than the poor to receive dental care or preventive medical care [16; 18, pp. 59, 61].

In addition, when people are grouped according to their health status, the nonpoor use health services much more than the poor do. Among those who report they are in fair or poor health, a measure of health status that correlates well with clinical symptoms and other indicators, persons with incomes twice the poverty level make 24 percent more physician visits than those with incomes below the poverty line. The differences are especially marked for children. When people are grouped according to number of days of bed disability, upper-income groups make three-fourths more physician visits each year than lower-income groups of comparable health status [16; 19, pp. 4-27].

The differences noted between income groups are also found between nonelderly blacks and whites. Even when controlling for income, blacks tend to be in poorer health and have less access to physician and dental care and preventive medical care of all kinds [16; 19, pp. 43-51].

Despite the large inequities that remain between the poor and nonpoor, Medicaid has demonstrably contributed to the improvements that have occurred since its inception. Poor persons with Medicaid make substantially more physician visits than the poor who have no insurance coverage [16]. The poor who don't wear a "label" that qualifies them for Medicaid are left far behind the Medicaid-eligible poor.

Medicare—which, together with supplementary Medicaid or private health insurance, provides more universal coverage and more financial incentives for provider participation than Medicaid alone does—has effectively reduced the gap in use of health services between the poor and nonpoor elderly population. In 1964 nonpoor elderly persons averaged substantially more physician visits. By 1978 the gap had been reduced by half, from 22 percent down to 10 percent. It also appears that income differences in usage have virtually disappeared among elderly persons who have chronic health problems. Even utilization differences between elderly blacks and elderly whites have been greatly reduced and, in many areas, essentially eliminated [16; 20, pp. 55-83].

Thus, there is considerable evidence that Medicaid and Medicare have greatly improved the use of health services by the poor, but these improvements are not so dazzling as to blind us to their limitations. Rates of usage are still not equal across all age groups or for all types of care, and more significantly, they still fall well behind need, which the poor have in greater measure than other groups and which would be the criterion for a truly equitable health care system.

Who Cares for the Poor?

Medicaid and Medicare were intended not only to increase the use of health services by the elderly and nonelderly poor. They were also intended to enable the poor to obtain their care from "mainstream" medicine—that is, from the same sources that upper-working-class and middle-class people use. How well have they succeeded?

Most people, regardless of income or insurance status, report having a regular source of medical care, an important condition for having access to health services. However, one in four low-income persons does not have a regular physician or other regular source of care compared to fewer than one in five upper-income persons. Low-income persons *with* a regular source are far more likely than upper-income groups to rely on hospitals and clinics as that source, and to travel longer and wait longer to see a physician [16; 18, pp. 68-70; 19; 21, pp. 201-206; 22, pp. 567-582]. These inequities apply to low-income persons with Medicaid as well as to the poor who have no insurance coverage [16]. There even is evidence that although low-income children have increased their overall use of medical care, they now get a smaller proportion of that care from private practitioners, and thus more of it from hospitals and public clinics, than they did before Medicaid [23, pp. 583-590]. While hospital- and clinic-based care is generally technically competent, it tends to be more episodic, to be related to immediate medical problems, and to provide less continuity and follow-up.

One reason why even people with Medicaid are less likely to have a private physician is that most doctors treat few, if any, Medicaid patients. One-fifth of all physicians see no Medicaid patients at all. Just 6 percent of all physicians care for one-third of all Medicaid patients [24, pp. 37-49; 25, pp. 2433-2437; 26, pp. 225-233].

Physicians do not discriminate against Medicare patients in the same way. There are two financial reasons why they don't, both related to reimbursement policies designed to encourage doctors to participate in the Medicare program. First, Medicare pays physicians about the same fees for physician care as does Blue Shield, the medical society plans. A study of fees paid to physicians in 1975 found that for a number of common visits and procedures, Medicare paid only 5 to 8 percent less than the *highest* fees paid by the Blue Shield plans surveyed. Medicaid fees, on the other hand, averaged 20 to 25 percent less than Medicare and Blue Shield fees [27, pp. 62-78]. The chief complaint of physicians against Medicaid is what they regard as inadequate reimbursement [28, pp. 43-58].

Second, the Medicare program permits physicians to bill their Medicare patients their "usual, customary, and reasonable" charge, which is usually somewhat higher than Medicare's fees. Medicaid requires physicians to accept the "assigned" fee because Medicaid patients are considered too poor to pay extra charges. (We will shortly see how this rationale has been increasingly discarded.) In order to meet all of these deductibles, co-payments, "unassigned" charges (in excess of those reimbursed by Medicare), and care not covered by Medicare benefits, the elderly have had to buy supplementary private insurance or be eligible for Medicaid supplementary coverage.

The added costs have remained a burden to the elderly whose financial plight Medicare was supposed to relieve. In 1977, Medicare paid for 44 percent of all health care costs for the aged; another 14 percent were met by Medicaid and 7 percent by private insurance. Direct out-of-pocket payments still amounted to 29 percent of the elderly's total health costs [29, pp. 65-90]. Medicare and Medicaid have not reduced out-of-pocket costs to the elderly as much as they have increased the total amount of money spent on health care per elderly person. Between 1966 and 1977, total health care spending per person sixty-five and over increased nearly four times while these patients' direct payments increased only two times. Nevertheless, these out-of-pocket costs—including deductibles, co-payments, "unassigned" charges, and care not covered by any third-party benefits—continue to be a significant factor in the living expenses of the elderly, amounting to more than 16 percent of family income for elderly persons with family incomes below $10,000 in 1981 [30, p. 23].

Financing: The Leviathan Awakes

It is not simply the fact that fees are absolutely low that discourages provider participation in Medicaid. It is rather that Medicaid fees are low *compared* to doctors' higher private charges [31, pp. 266-280]. In other words, in the market for physician services, and consistent with general market dynamics, fees set below the prevailing market price attract few physicians. Ironically, it was the availability of public funds that enabled and encouraged physicians and hospitals to increase their fees.

The injection of public monies into the largely private medical market provided what seemed like unlimited revenues for physicians and private hospitals to order more services and products for their patients, to finance new capital investment, and to raise their prices. Government payments for physicians' services leaped from 7 percent of total expenditures on physicians in 1965 to 20 percent in 1967 and have remained at 25 percent or higher since 1974. From 1965 to 1967 government payments for hospital care jumped from 39 to 55 percent of total hospital costs and have stayed at or near that level since then [32, pp. 1-54].

Added to the large and growing private insurance coverage of hospital and physician care, increased public spending encouraged a consequent jump in medical prices. In the five years after the introduction of Medicare and Medicaid, hospitals and physicians raised their charges at more than twice the annual rate of increase in the years before the programs [33, pp. 3-22]. The "reasonable cost" basis of reimbursing hospitals, which Congress included in the Medicare and Medicaid legislation to appease the hospital industry, created an astoundingly inflationary program [34, pp. 1-47]. Medicare's "usual, customary, and reasonable" fees which it paid to physicians enabled them to continuously push up prices for their services and to increase their total incomes by ordering more services for their patients. These inflationary spirals reverberated throughout the medical system, with price increases contributing substantially more than utilization increases to overall rises in health care expenditures since Medicare and Medicaid began [35, pp. 136-144].

The market system in health care works effectively to absorb every additional dollar of public and private funds into increased prices, capital investment, and profits and high incomes. The market system permits each health care unit—whether physician, hospital, nursing home chain, drug company, or other provider—to develop roles based on economic demand and expected profitability rather than on any politically or technically determined assessment of the community's health needs. Market competition among hospitals to attract physicians and their well-insured patients encourages hospital directors to provide the most advanced medical technology and the most modern facilities and services available. Medical technology companies promote their products to doctors and hospitals regardless of the medical effectiveness or safety of their wares.

Physicians also play a central role in generating demand for hospital care as well as for their own services. Their training, the threat of malpractice suits, and especially the financial incentives in the fee-for-service system encourage physicians to order ever larger quantities of diagnostic and therapeutic procedures.

Although Medicaid pays less than private insurance for many procedures, Medicaid patients have been a lucrative practice for many surgeons, with Medicaid recipients receiving nearly twice the rate of surgery as the general population [36, pp. 1, 15; 37], a doubtful advantage given the high and probably excessive surgery rates in the U.S. [38, pp. 135-144; 39, pp. 883-891; 40].

Hospitals used the new programs to their maximum advantage. The cost-plus method of Medicare and Medicaid reimbursement for inpatient care encouraged hospitals to finance modernization and expansion through debt financing, which increased from 40 percent of total construction costs in 1968 to 68 percent in 1976 [41, pp. 8-10]. With the increased revenues from Medicare and Medicaid, as well as from expanding private insurance, private hospitals' assets per bed increased 124 percent between 1965 and 1975, compared to an increase of only 80 percent in the preceding decade [42, p. 4].

Thus, the beneficiaries of Medicare and Medicaid have included more than the elderly and the poor. In 1980 hospitals collected $36 billion, out of their total revenues of $100 billion, from Medicare and Medicaid. Nursing homes collected nearly $11 billion, over half their total revenues, from these programs. Indeed, 41 percent of all state and local contributions to the Medicaid program go directly into the coffers of the largely for-profit nursing home industry. Physicians collected $10 billion from Medicare and Medicaid, more than 21 percent of doctors' total revenues. The drug industry also takes its share, $1.3 billion in 1980. Altogether Medicare and Medicaid pumped $63 billion into the medical care system in 1980 [32].

Fiscal Pressures on the States and Local Governments

These expenditures naturally reflected major commitments of federal and state tax resources. Federal spending for all types of health services grew from $4 billion in 1965 (just before Medicare and Medicaid began) to $15.7 billion in 1970, $33.8 billion in 1975, and $65.7 billion in 1980. State and local spending grew less rapidly—from $4.8 billion in 1965 to $31.3 billion in 1980—but represented an even greater burden on the more limited taxable resources at these levels of government [32].

In California, for example, the state's own expenditures on Medi-Cal totaled $252 million in 1966-67, the program's first year, absorbing 8.4 percent of the state's general tax funds. Ronald Reagan, then in his first year as governor, pounced on the program's liberal benefits, eliminating certain optional services, freezing physicians' fees, and requiring prior authorization for certain kinds of hospital care. Nevertheless, the program's costs to the state continued to rise, in 1971 reaching half a billion dollars in state revenues and consuming 10 percent of the state's general tax funds [43]. By then Reagan had broader political support from Washington as well as within the state for imposing more stringent cutbacks. His 1971 Medi-Cal Reform Act actually added new groups to the Medi-Cal rolls, but it instituted a stronger prior authorization requirement for inpatient hospital care, imposed restrictions on reimbursement to providers, and shifted more of the costs of health care for the poor from the state to the counties.

The results were typical of many states' efforts to restrain their own Medicaid costs. In the three years preceding this "reform," from 1968 to 1971, the counties' total Medi-Cal share had risen less than 3 percent despite an increase of 54 percent in the number of Medi-Cal recipients; but in the next three years, to 1974, the counties' share rose 25 percent compared with an increase of only 4 percent in Medi-Cal beneficiaries [44, pp. 19-20; 45, p. 7]. By 1974, Medi-Cal was a major burden on California counties, accounting for four out of every ten dollars they spent on health services. Meanwhile, they had to run an increasingly expensive public hospital and medical care system for all the poor who were either not covered by even California's generous Medicaid program, or were Medi-Cal eligible persons who could not obtain care in the private sector. Under these burdens, the costs to the counties for public medical care programs, including the local contribution to Medi-Cal and unreimbursed costs for county-run public hospitals and other health services, more than doubled between 1967 and 1974. County health costs took a bigger bite of county property taxes, increasing from 30 percent of total property tax revenues in 1967 to 36 percent in 1974 [44, pp. 14-15]. A substantial portion of rising county property taxes is attributable to these increased health costs.

The consequences of these rising local costs have been significant. Because welfare, Medicaid, and other programs intended to sustain the poor are supported at the local level mainly by regressive property taxes and at the state level by even more regressive sales taxes and somewhat progressive income taxes, they tend to redistribute income from the working class and lower middle class to the poor [46, pp. 1-23]. The unpopular tax base of these programs and services, added to the fact that they serve mainly the poor and not those who disproportionately pay for them, has made Medicaid, other welfare programs, and public hospitals politically vulnerable. Given the rising local costs of public medical care programs and economic and political conditions that impose fiscal constraints, it is not surprising that many California counties have closed their public hospitals. California's once extensive county hospital system has shrunk from sixty-five hospitals operated by forty-nine of the state's fifty-eight counties in 1964, to thirty-seven hospitals in twenty-nine counties in 1981 [47]. It is, of course, the poor—Medi-Cal patients and those who do not qualify for the program—who suffer most from all of these cutbacks.

California is certainly not alone in this situation. Illinois' Medicaid program cost the state 280 percent more in 1973 than it did five years earlier [9, p. 293]. Governor Richard Ogilvie in 1971 announced cutbacks, cost-sharing by patients, and restrictions intended to make providers of care "account for the services they deliver to Medicaid recipients," but also forcing recipients themselves "to have more responsibility for their actions in obtaining health services." [9] One of Illinois' tools for cutting the costs of welfare programs, like Aid to Families with Dependent Children and Medicaid, is simply not to increase income eligibility levels to keep up with inflation. From 1975 to 1981, Illinois increased its AFDC and Medicaid income standards by 16 percent [48], a period when the consumer price index increased 53 percent! Illinois' failure to increase its income eligibility levels has not only kept many of its poor residents off the Medicaid rolls, it has also shifted more of the burden of indigent medical care to the local level. The proportion of Chicago's Cook County Hospital patients who are covered by Medicaid dropped from 65 percent in 1973 to only 27 percent in 1979, adding more patients, and thus more expense, to the county's own tax resources, thereby compounding its fiscal problems.

The Politics of Cost Containment

Throughout the country the litany of state cutbacks and cost-containment devices was familiar. Many of them were encouraged or permitted by the Social Security Amendments of 1967, 1971, 1972, and 1981, intended to give the states and the federal government more options and power to control and reduce Medicaid and Medicare costs. The cost-containment strategies included restricting eligibility by reducing maximum income levels or dropping optional groups from Medicaid; elimination of optional medical services; the imposition of cost-sharing by the patient to discourage the use of services and the purchase of prescription drugs; programs to control provider fraud and abuse; restrictive reimbursement practices (to counter the expensive "reasonable costs" reimbursement to hospitals and "reasonable fee" payments to doctors); review of utilization in hospitals and nursing homes; and regulation of capital investment in health facilities [15; 49, pp. 10-16].

The entry of the government into financing health care on such a grand scale assured that it would have to intervene politically to control the system in which it had developed such a large stake. However, each of the cost-containment methods tries to compensate for or reduce the irrationalities of the private market, but without challenging essential private control or the market system. Such a challenge is viewed by the economically and politically powerful health industry as intolerable. Even if individual members of Congress, state legislatures, or governmental agencies are ideologically disposed to eliminate private control of these public resources now channeled into the health industry, the political costs would be very high and essentially unacceptable [50, pp. 69-84].

So less effective, but politically more acceptable, cost constraints are imposed. In addition to the lower reimbursement rates paid to physicians, Medicare and Medicaid reimburse hospitals at lower levels than private insurers. In California in 1979, for example, Blue Cross and commercial insurance companies reimbursed hospitals 12 percent more than their "full financial requirements" (which includes the actual costs of providing care, working capital, and capital replacement costs). In the same year Medicare reimbursed hospitals 4 percent less than their full financial requirements, and Medi-Cal paid them 18 percent less [51, p. 56]. This differential penalizes public hospitals, as well as private hospitals that serve a large number of poor persons, because of their dependence on Medicare and Medicaid for patient care revenues. Most private hospitals that serve relatively few Medicaid and Medicare patients, however, shift this unreimbursed portion of their care onto charges for privately insured patients, resulting in an indirect (and regressive) tax paid through hospital insurance premiums.

Maintaining low reimbursement rates discourages physicians and hospitals from caring for Medicaid patients. That practice, as well as restricting eligibility of low-income persons, tends to shift the financial burdens onto local governments—in those communities which still have public hospitals and clinics. Both practices, as well as curtailment of optional services and the imposition of cost-sharing by the patient, also shift the burden of containing costs (in the form of out-of-pocket payments and the foregoing of care) onto the poor themselves, undoubtedly the group least able to bear the burden but also the least able to oppose such measures. The earlier California experience with co-payments suggests that they may even result in higher overall costs to the Medicaid program because more expensive services, such as hospitalization, requiring no co-payment, tend to be substituted for less expensive care, such as ambulatory services, which have been deferred because of co-payment [52, pp. 457-466].

Until 1981 major cutbacks were imposed only in Medicaid programs and not against Medicare beneficiaries because the Medicare population includes large numbers of voters from all social classes while Medicaid is limited to the poorer and politically less powerful groups. In 1981, in order to increase the military budget and reduce taxes, the Reagan Administration and a more conservative Congress cut massive amounts of federal funds from public assistance programs, like Medicaid, with greater ease than from Social Security or Medicare. The Omnibus Reconciliation Act of 1981 reduced the federal match for Medicaid by 3 percent in fiscal year 1982, 4 percent in 1983, and 4.5 percent in 1984, although states may offset at least some of these reductions by a variety of fiscal and policy programs or by having an unemployment rate 50 percent greater than the national average. States were also permitted even greater latitude to reduce benefits and eligibility. In addition, the Administration began an attack on Medicare spending that accelerated the next year. In 1981 the Congress voted to eliminate or reduce some Medicare benefits, increase Medicare co-payments and deductibles, and reduce reimbursement rates to hospitals. The further reductions in Medicaid and Medicare adopted in 1982 are likely to accelerate the shift of costs from the federal government to local governments, the elderly and poor themselves, and privately insured patients.

The states are unlikely to shoulder the burden being dropped by the federal government. In 1982 California, for example, eliminated its state-funded "medically indigent adult" portion of the Medi-Cal program, turning over responsibility for its 280,000 recipients to the counties along with less than 70 percent of the $750 million the state had been spending on the program. The state also formally abandoned its goal of providing "mainstream" medicine for the poor by adopting a policy of contracting with high-volume, low-cost doctors and hospitals to care for all remaining Medi-Cal patients, a major change from the "freedom of choice" principle on which the program had been based since its inception. These actions, which other states are likely to follow, illustrate that government will protect itself from impending fiscal disaster by imposing severe constraints on program expenditures and the demand side of the medical marketplace.

Both Medicare and Medicaid also attempt to regulate the market by influencing provider behavior. Campaigns against provider fraud and abuse are marginally effective in their financial impact on Medicaid programs, but the high visibility of individual cases of fraud exposed by investigations makes this mode popular with officials and politicians. More significantly, utilization review programs provide for professional peer review of physician decisions to order some kinds of expensive hospital care. Experiences in a number of states indicate that mandatory review programs tend to retard the growth of Medicaid costs, at least for some kinds of care, although other experiences, particularly with voluntary programs, found no savings [53, pp. 113-128; 54, pp. 1-76; 55, pp. 574-580; 56, pp. 253-265]. In recent years, state Medicaid programs and Medicare have begun to scrutinize hospital costs and evaluate the reasonableness of costs that were formerly simply reimbursed [34]. In addition, a number of states have instituted rate-setting mechanisms, some of which reimburse hospitals prospectively rather than on the prevailing fee-for-service basis, forcing hospitals to live within relatively fixed budgets instead of generating as much revenue as possible [51, pp. 10-41; 57, pp. 1-40; 58, pp. 67-88]. All of these methods, together with state-run certification of need for hospital expansion or purchase of expensive equipment, have the potential of slowing the rate of increase in hospital costs [59]. Although these methods have gained political popularity among the states because of the danger of Medicaid budgets dragging state treasuries into fiscal collapse, Reagan Administration officials opposed such infringements on market prerogatives until their own efforts to control Medicare and Medicaid spending were endangered by the present relatively "free market" state.

LESSONS FOR THE FUTURE

The experience with Medicare and Medicaid can improve our understanding of the potential value and limits of reform in the health system.

Value of the Reforms

Without question Medicaid and Medicare have improved the access of the elderly and the poor to medical services. This conclusion is supported by the increased use of services by the elderly and the poor since the programs began. It is also clear that the poor with Medicaid make greater use of services than the poor who have no insurance coverage.

Nevertheless, these benefits have not been sufficient to eliminate inequities. Poor children make fewer visits to physicians than children from nonpoor families. The poor of all ages receive less dental and preventive medical care than the nonpoor. Most significantly, when people's health status is taken into account, use of health services is still related to income, with those better off receiving more care than poorer persons in comparable states of health. Similarly, the white population still makes greater use of health services than blacks although this difference has also been reduced over the past decade and a half, particularly for the elderly.

Despite these limitations, we should not ignore the very important improvements Medicare and Medicaid have generated. The effects of these increased rates of use on health status are more difficult to determine because most types of medical care have not been proven to lead to better health. Some types of preventive care, such as immunizations and prenatal care, have been shown to reduce the incidence of illness and death. Unfortunately, these are the very kinds of services that remain less accessible to the poor. However, diagnostic and curative types of care are important to all people. They reduce the burden of disease by limiting it, speeding recovery, preventing or limiting disability due to illness or injury, and providing comfort and palliation. These are important benefits of improved access to and utilization of medical services, benefits that the elderly and the poor now receive in greater measure than before Medicare and Medicaid.

Limitations of the Reforms

One of the greatest limitations in the Medicare and Medicaid legislation was the separation of medical care for the poor from the program for the elderly. As a social insurance program, Medicare is paid for by everyone and ultimately benefits everyone as they reach retirement age. Medicaid, a welfare-linked public assistance program, is paid for by everyone but benefits only those in the bottom classes of society. Thus, Medicare has a broad base of political support while Medicaid's base is narrowed. The importance of this difference in political base and support was reflected in the ease with which the Reagan Administration cut funds from the Medicaid program and the overwhelming opposition they faced when cuts were first proposed for Medicare. Broad-based social insurance programs generate powerful support when threatened, while the dividing line between "deserving" and "undeserving" poor, inherent in welfare programs, shifts almost continuously with changes in economic and political conditions. A single social insurance program for the elderly and the poor would have made health care for the poor less vulnerable.

Medicaid was further limited by making it a state-run program with the federal role limited to contributions and a set of very minimal program guidelines and requirements. State control resulted in wide variations among Medicaid programs, with some states providing relatively generously for a comparatively substantial portion of their low-income residents and other states creating very stingy programs. A single federal program would have assured at least a uniform base of coverage and benefits. The experience with Medicaid suggests the disaster that awaits health programs under the Reagan Administration's block grants to the states that have replaced many categorical programs funded and monitored by the federal government.

A third limitation to both programs is their regressive financing. Social security taxes are inherently regressive since they tax income at a uniform rate at all levels of income up to the income limit, after which additional income is exempt. Even though Medicare's financing is regressive, its benefits are available to everyone, although they are largely deferred until retirement age. The Medicaid program is less regressively financed, but its welfare-related benefits represent a transfer of income from the upper working class and middle class to the poor. If taxes were drawn more progressively, there would be greater equity in the society and less demand for reducing government spending and less vulnerability for either program.

Another fundamental limitation was the integration of both programs into the present market system. Because each unit in the system has the autonomy to stake out its market and seek to maximize revenues and profits, the market system inherently drives up prices and total expenditures. All of these problems are exacerbated, as we have seen, in a fee-for-service context with providers' incomes based on the number of services they perform, and with reimbursements geared to charges and costs for providing each service. And many of the poor and the elderly have become, like other well-insured patients in the fee-for-service system, the victims of unnecessary and excessive surgery and other medical procedures. In this way, Medicare and Medicaid have turned public funds into subsidies to the privately controlled market. Although the government has in the last decade moved increasingly to regulate the market in order to rationalize it and reduce the growth of expenditures, it has not attempted to replace private control of each market unit with public ownership or control. Public accountability through public ownership and control would greatly increase the likelihood that Medicare and Medicaid would serve the population's health needs without those needs having to compete with each unit's desire for profits.

Finally, because they did improve medical care conditions for the elderly and the poor, Medicare and Medicaid have undoubtedly reduced the most pressing needs, and therefore the political demand, for national health insurance. That is, of course, the danger with any reform. Nevertheless, the very existence of Medicare in particular has undermined opposition to national health insurance. After all, Medicare has not made the U.S. a socialist country, nor has the medical system collapsed, both dire predictions of the medical profession. Medicare's existence and its obvious benefits have actually legitimized the demand for national health insurance.

Strategy for the Future

The lessons we have learned from the Medicare/Medicaid experience can be translated into several policy guidelines and principles.

First, to improve equity, we should avoid isolating programs for the poor and should broaden the base of support of public health care for all constituencies. Future programs (especially national health insurance) should consist of a single program for all the people—the poor and the nonpoor; the employed, unemployed, self-employed, and retired; primary enrollees and dependents. There must be no distinctions in benefits or coverage because these will inevitably result in inequities.

Second, to distribute the financial support for health programs more equitably and avoid the backlash experienced by Medicaid and public hospitals from low- and moderate-income taxpayers, health programs should be progressively financed. In the tradition of social insurance programs, some of the financing may come from payroll taxes. These should be scaled progressively. The majority of support for the entire system, and not only for the subsidies for the poor, should be derived from general tax revenues, and these taxes should be made more progressive than they are.

Third, to assure a stronger uniform base of coverage and benefits throughout the country, the scope of benefits and coverage should not be left to the states to decide. Local control and administration of national health programs is desirable because it makes the programs more responsive to communities' needs, but local and state administration should be carried out within firm and generous program requirements that apply to every state and locality.

Finally, a national health service is preferable to national health insurance to eliminate the fiscal, organizational, and programmatic irrationalities in the present market organization of medical care. An insurance program would leave each unit in the system independent of all other units, free to exploit the medical market to its advantage. A national health service would take health care out of the marketplace and make it a genuine public service. There would still remain forces that would tend to distort the provision of care from simply meeting the population's health needs: professional groups and institutions undoubtedly would still try to maximize their returns, even at the expense of the system's intended beneficiaries; and communities would be likely to compete with one another in seeking resources from a necessarily limited resource base. But a national health service would permit a degree of public accountability unavailable in any other system, and it would greatly increase the likelihood that the health care system will be matched to the population's health needs. The bill introduced into the Congress by Representative Ronald Dellums would create just such a national health service—a universal and uniform system of benefits and care, progressively financed, and locally controlled.

If political conditions do not permit enactment of a national health service, at least a responsive, accountable, and efficient national health insurance system may control some of the worst features of the market system. A national health insurance program should be uniform in its coverage and benefits, progressively financed, have to live within a fixed national budget each year, include a large role for public planning and regulation, and be administered by public bodies at national, state, and local levels.

A national health plan based on these principles would maximize the opportunity of meeting the health needs of the population, building on the successes of Medicare and Medicaid, but avoiding many of the most severe limitations of these reforms.

ACKNOWLEDGMENT

A somewhat different version of this chapter will be published in the forthcoming book *Reforming Medicine: Lessons of the Last Quarter Century*, edited by Victor Sidel and Ruth Sidel, and published by Pantheon Books, a division of Random House, Inc.

REFERENCES

1. I. S. Falk, C. R. Rorem, and M. D. Ring, *The Costs of Medical Care*, University of Chicago Press, Chicago, 1933.
2. *Medical Care for the American People*, University of Chicago Press, Chicago, 1932.
3. T. R. Marmor, *The Politics of Medicare*, Aldine Publishing Company, 1973.
4. J. G. Burrow, *AMA: Voice of American Medicine*, Johns Hopkins University Press, Baltimore, 1963.
5. E. Rayack, *Professional Power and American Medicine: The Economics of the American Medical Association*, World Publishing Company, Cleveland, Chapter 5, 1967.
6. Cambridge Research Institute, *Trends Affecting the U.S. Health Care System*, Health Resources Administration, Washington, D.C., pp. 184-185, 1976.
7. M. S. Mueller, Private Health Insurance in 1973: A Review of Coverage, Enrollment, and Financial Experience, *Social Security Bulletin*, *38*, pp. 21-40, Feburary 1975.
8. R. H. Bremner, *American Philanthrophy*, University of Chicago Press, Chicago, 1960.
9. R. Stevens and R. Stevens, *Welfare Medicine in America: A Case Study of Medicaid*, The Free Press, New York, 1974.
10. E. Feingold, *Medicare: Policy and Politics*, Chandler Publishing Company, San Francisco, 1966.
11. R. Harris, *A Sacred Trust*, New American Library, New York, 1966.
12. Medicare: Persons Enrolled, 1979, *Health Care Financing Notes*, Health Care Financing Administration, Baltimore, January 1981.

13. *The Medicare and Medicaid Data Book, 1981*, Health Care Financing Administration, Baltimore, April 1982.
14. Medicaid/Medicare Management Institute, *Data on the Medicaid Program: Eligibility, Services, Expenditures*, 1979 edition (revised), Health Care Financing Administration, Baltimore, 1979, p. 41.
15. B. A. Myers and R. Leighton, Medicaid and the Mainstream: Reassessment in the Context of the Taxpayer Revolt, *Western Journal of Medicine, 132*, pp. 550-561, 1980.
16. K. Davis, M. Gold, and D. Makuc, Access to Health Care for the Poor: Does the Gap Remain?, *Annual Review of Public Health, 2*, 1981.
17. *Health, United States, 1979*, Department of Health Education and Welfare, Hyattsville, Maryland, 1980.
18. *Health of the Disadvantaged*, Department of Health and Human Services, Hyattsville, Maryland, 1980.
19. L. A. Aday and R. M. Andersen, Equity of Access to Medical Care: A Conceptual and Empirical Overview, *Medical Care, 19*, December 1981 (suppl.)
20. M. Ruther and A. Dobson, Equal Treatment and Unequal Benefits: A Reexamination of the Use of Medicare Services by Race, 1967-1976, *Health Care Financing Review, 2*, Winter 1983.
21. M. C. Olendzki, R. P. Grann, and C. H. Goodrich, The Impact of Medicaid on Private Care for the Urban Poor, *Medical Care, 10*, 1972.
22. S. L. Gortmaker, Medicaid and the Health Care of Children in Poverty and Near Poverty: Some Successes and Failures, *Medical Care, 19*, 1981.
23. S. T. Orr and C. A. Miller, Utilization of Health Service by Poor Children Since Advent of Medicaid, *Medical Care, 19*, 1981.
24. J. Mitchell and J. Cromwell, Medicaid Mills: Fact or Fiction?, *Health Care Financing Review, 2*, Summer 1980.
25. _____, Large Medicaid Practices and Medicaid Mills, *Journal of the American Medical Association, 244*, 1980.
26. J. E. Kushman, Participation of Private Practice Dentists in Medicaid, *Inquiry, 15*, 1978.
27. I. L. Burney, G. J. Schieber, M. O. Blaxall, and J. R. Gabel, Medicare and Medicaid Physician Payment Incentives, *Health Care Financing Review, 1*, Summer 1979.
28. D. D. Garner, W. C. Liao, and T. R. Sharpe, Factors Affecting Physician Participation in a State Medicaid Program, *Medical Care, 17*, 1979.
29. C. R. Fisher, Differences by Age Groups in Health Care Spending, *Health Care Financing Review, 1*, Spring 1980.
30. *Changing the Structure of Medicare Benefits: Issues and Options*, Congressional Budget Office, Washington, D.C., March 1983.
31. J. Hadley, Physician Participation in Medicaid: Evidence from California, *Health Services Research, 14*, 1979.
32. R. M. Gibson and D. R. Waldo, National Health Expenditures, 1980, *Health Care Financing Review, 3*, September 1981.
33. R. M. Gibson and M. S. Mueller, National Health Expenditures, Fiscal Year 1976, *Social Security Bulletin, 40*, April 1977.

34. S. M. Weiner, "Reasonable Cost" Reimbursement for Inpatient Hospital Service Under Medicare and Medicaid: The Emergence of Public Control, *American Journal of Law and Medicine, 3*, 1977.

35. R. Andersen, R. Foster, and P. Weil, Rates and Correlates of Expenditure Increases for Personal Health Services: Pre- and Post-Medicare and Medicaid, *Inquiry, 13*, 1976.

36. R. D. Lyons, Surgery on Poor Is Found Higher, *New York Times*, September 1, 1977.

37. House Committee on Interstate and Foreign Commerce, *Cost and Quality of Health Care: Unnecessary Surgery*, Government Printing Office, Washington, D.C., 1976.

38. J. P. Bunker, Surgical Manpower: A Comparison of Operations and Surgeons in the United States and in England and Wales, *New England Journal of Medicine, 282*, 1970.

39. E. G. McCarthy and M. L. Finkel, Surgical Utilization in the U.S.A., *Medical Care, 18*, 1980.

40. L. Frederick, How Much Unnecessary Surgery?, *Medical World News*, May 3, 1976.

41. *Capital Formation in Health Care Facilities*, Health Resources Administration, Washington, D.C., 1979.

42. *Hospital Statistics*, 1977 edition, American Hospital Association, Chicago, 1977.

43. R. A. Derzon and C. L. Celum, The Medi-Cal Program: Strategies for Constraining Costs in the Largest Single Expenditure in the State Budget, Health Policy Program, University of California, San Francisco, December 1979.

44. *Health Care Costs and Services in California Counties*, California Department of Health, Sacramento, February 1978.

45. *California's Medical Assistance Program Annual Statistical Report, Medi-Cal Program 1978*, Center for Health Statistics, Department of Health Services, Sacramento, July 1979.

46. E. Sparer, Gordian Knots: The Situation of Health Care Advocacy for the Poor Today, *Clearinghouse Review, 15*, May 1981.

47. E. R. Brown, *Public Medicine in Crisis: Public Hospitals in California*, California Policy Seminar Monograph Number 11, Institute of Governmental Studies, University of California, Berkeley, 1981.

48. Personal communication from William V. Opper, Illinois Department of Public Aid, to Ronni Scheier, *Chicago Reporter*, May 8, 1981.

49. S. F. Loebs, Medicaid—A Survey of Indicators and Issues, in *The Medical Experience*, A. D. Spiegel (ed.), Aspen Systems Corporation, Germantown, Maryland, 1970.

50. T. R. Marmor, D. A. Wittman, and T. C. Heagy, The Politics of Medical Inflation, *Journal of Health Politics, Policy and Law, 1*, 1976.

51. J. H. Hafkenschiel, et al., *Mandatory Prospective Reimbursement Systems for Hospitals*, California Health Facilities Commission, Sacramento, April 2, 1982.

52. M. I. Roemer, et al., Copayments for Ambulatory Care: Penny-Wise and Pound-Foolish, *Medical Care, 13*, 1975.

53. A. Dobson, et al., PSROs: Their Current Status and Their Impact to Date, *Inquiry*, *15*, June 1978.
54. R. H. Brook, K. N. Williams, and J. E. Rolph, Controlling the Use and Cost of Medical Services: The New Mexico Experimental Medical Care Review Organization—A Four-Year Case Study, *Medical Care*, *16*, September 1978 (suppl).
55. A. Fulchiero, et al., Can the PSROs Be Cost Effective?, *New England Journal of Medicine*, *299*, 1978.
56. M. Westphal, E. Frazier, and M. C. Miller, Changes in Average Length of Stay and Average Charges Generated Following Institution of PSRO Review, *Health Services Research*, *14*, 1979.
57. G. Coelen and D. Sullivan, An Analysis of the Effects of Prospective Reimbursement Programs on Hospital Expenditures, *Health Care Financing Review*, *2*, Winter 1981.
58. J. Cromwell and J. R. Kanak, The Effects of Prospective Reimbursement Programs on Hospital Adoption and Service Sharing, *Health Care Financing Review*, *4*, December 1982.
59. J. R. Howell, *Regulating Hospital Capital Investment: The Experience in Massachusetts*, National Center for Health Services Research, Hyattsville, Maryland, March 1981.

Reprinted with permission of Pantheon Books, a division of Random House, Inc From *Reforming Medicine: Lessons of the Last Quarter Century*, Victor and Ruth Sidel (eds), Pantheon, New York, 1984.

CHAPTER 8
Public Policy and the Nursing Home Industry
CHARLENE HARRINGTON

The nursing home industry is a multibillion dollar business in the United States, characterized by rapid growth in profits and large chain-owned corporations. Nursing homes were a cottage industry until the early 1960's when they began to expand with the infusion of public funds from Medicaid and Medicare. By 1980, there were 23,000 nursing homes in the U.S. serving 1.4 million residents, mostly old and disabled [1].

This chapter describes the current nursing home industry as it has evolved with its high growth and profits rates. The industry, while private in nature, is effectively a public program defined by public policies, particularly by the Medicaid program. Demand for services is artificially generated because of a lack of public program alternatives and favorable reimbursement public policies which benefit the nursing home industry. While state and federal government regulate the industry, the effectiveness of regulatory activities in protecting the consumer is questionable, where poor quality of care is commonly found. Older persons are forced into such facilities against their will, where the facilities serve as agents of social control over those who are frail, poor, without family supports, and unwanted. While some observers argue that the entire structure of the nursing home industry requires radical change, the politics and economics of the current situation reinforce continued expansion of the industry and the use of institutionalization as a primary modality of treatment for the frail aged.

QUALITY OF CARE

Serious questions must be raised about the appropriateness of institutional care as a treatment for many aged. In nursing homes, the residents tend to lose control of decisions about their treatment and their daily living activities. Institutionalization makes it more difficult to sustain family ties and social relationships. The morale, health status, and functional capacity of individuals placed in institutions frequently deteriorate. And many older people spend their

144

last years in such facilities against their will. The aged have a general fear and loathing of institutional placement.

The fears of institutional placement are in part related to the poor quality of care and undesirable conditions in many institutions. The quality issues have been investigated by many different groups [2, 3]. Criticism of nursing homes include a long litany of abuses: negligence leading to death and injury, unsanitary conditions, poor nutrition and inadequate amounts of food, hazards to life and safety including lack of fire protection, lack of dental care, eye care, and podiatry, lack of social services, and inadequate control of drugs and overmedication. The themes of neglect by facilities, physicians and nurses are all too common.

Nursing homes are severely short on staff, especially registered nurses, so they rely on untrained and unlicensed personnel [2-4]. Increasing the state nursing standards to a level considered adequate by professional standards would cost the public programs millions of additional dollars which they are not willing to spend during times of financial distress. These problems along with the general conditions of institutional life with its lack of privacy, impersonal atmosphere, and rigid, arbitrary schedules make basic institutional living unacceptable and undesirable except in those cases where clients are severely disabled [5].

Nursing homes play a role in caring for those aged and disabled who are least desirable in the society. Such individuals are removed from the social environment and isolated into institutions. At the same time, institutions are agents of social control over the residents, who must live according to institutional standards. The legal and ethical issues in terms of abridgement of civil rights for patients have not been well established for the aged in nursing homes. The rights to refuse drug and other treatments in nursing homes are also not established, even though such rights have been established for mental patients in mental institutions. The right to refuse institutionalization in cases where individuals have not been legally declared incompetent to make decisions and not been placed under conservatorship is also not protected.

The causes of the poor quality of care in some nursing homes are issues for debate. Some have attributed the problems to excessive profit-taking by proprietary facilities. Although research studies have not shown conclusive differences with lower quality of care in proprietary facilities than in public or non-profit facilities, this is probably more due to inadequate research measurement than to lack of differences. Vladeck [3] and others have concluded that profit nursing homes are more associated with poor quality of care in general than non-profits. Many other reasons are associated with poor quality of care. In some cases, fraud and abuses have led to the undesirable conditions.

The families and patients are dependent upon the facilities and find it difficult to complain about the quality of care because of fear of eviction or retaliation in situations where there are few other options or alternative facilities. In other situations, the patients have no advocates from outside the institution.

Quality of care is not assured even when facilities are charging high rates and are making profits and could thus afford to make improvements in care. On the other hand, incentives or regulations which ensure that resources will be utilized for patient care are difficult to develop.

REGULATORY ACTIVITIES

While nursing homes are required to meet state and federal licensing standards, the public regulatory efforts have been considered to be seriously lacking by most observers [3, 6-8]. State and federal regulations themselves are frequently too vague to be enforceable. In other situations, the public sanctions for noncompliance are ineffective, due to the complexity of preparing legal actions and length of time required to enforce such actions. In other situations, the administrative enforcement practices are inadequate due to lack of personnel and resources, weak procedures for enforcement, and the reluctance of staff to institute sanctions on the facilities. In some areas, where a shortage of available nursing home beds exists, the licensing and certification staff are reluctant to bring legal action and/or to close noncomplying facilities because there are no alternative placements for the residents.

Certainly, the nursing home industry is effective in influencing recent policies for deregulation. This has taken the form of federal program budget cuts and proposed weakening of federal certification standards. During the last two years, public protests over proposed regulatory changes to reduce standards have been effective in preventing the adoption of many of these changes. On the other hand, the federal, and in many cases, state budget cuts in licensing have reduced the licensing activities even though the regulations have been retained. Many senior advocate organizations believe that deregulation will bring about reductions in quality of care. The key question is whether the reduction in regulatory activities will have a measurable or visible effect on quality of care in nursing homes. And if so, will public policymakers, researchers, and consumer advocates be observing and evaluating such effects.

DEMAND FOR AND UTILIZATION OF NURSING HOME SERVICES

Nursing home industry viability is contingent upon a high demand for services. The market for nursing homes is complex because demand is dependent upon a number of factors that are not necessarily correlated with need for services (based upon physical or psychological factors). Utilization refers to those days that services are actually delivered.

In order to maximize profits, nursing homes generally attempt to control two factors. First, nursing homes prefer to select private paying patients because they can generally obtain higher rates of payment for such patients than what is paid by Medicaid [9]. Second, nursing homes may seek those patients that have the lower level of nursing care needs to reduce their costs of delivering the services. Such a practice called "skimming" refers to selecting those patients who are the lowest cost and need the least care. The longer the waiting lists, the more likely nursing homes are able to be selective in choosing their patient population.

The demand for nursing home services as measured by waiting lists and occupancy rates continues to be high in almost all states (an average of 89 percent in 1980 [1]. The fact that nursing home occupancy rates are uniformly high regardless of the ratio of beds to the aged population in the states suggests that utilization is based upon other factors than need for services. In other words, the supply of nursing home beds stimulates demand to fill available beds because of a variety of complex factors.

Further evidence that demand and supply are artificially inflated can be shown by examining the rate of inappropriate placement. Inappropriate placement refers to those residents whose functional status is capable of functioning in a more independent manner outside of an institutional setting. The extent of inappropriate utilization is estimated to range from 5 to 75 percent depending upon the criteria used [10]. The high estimates are supported by data from the National Survey of Institutionalized Persons which showed that only 30 percent of the residents were consistently or extremely dependent in self-care activities [11]. The National Nursing Home Survey, using self-reported data from nursing homes, also showed only 39 percent of residents to be extremely dependent in self-care [12].

Probably the primary reason for high demand for and utilization of nursing home rates, even when such services are inappropriate, is failure of the state to provide alternative services to institutional care. The majority of Medicaid dollars are spent on institutional care (nursing homes and hospitals) and professional services (physicians, dentists, drugs, glasses, and others) with only 5 percent of Medicaid dollars spent on other services [13]. States have recently been developing new community based alternatives in demonstration and waiver projects, but these still remain small in comparison to nursing home services.

Many other barriers prevent use of alternatives to institutional care. The current long term care system is incomplete, fragmented, and inadequately financed. Recently the social service programs for in-home support services have been reduced because of federal budget cuts, when such programs were not able to meet the demand before budget cuts. In other situations, the lack of information about alternative services is a factor in inappropriate placement.

In many instances, older people do not have family supports and friends that can provide assistance to keep them from being placed in institutions, even when their physical needs may not require institutional services. In other situations, the aged are unable to afford to purchase alternative services because of low incomes and high medical costs. Medicaid has restrictive eligibility policies in some states which forces the aged to become indigent to qualify for medical care.

Medicare pays for very little home and hospice care, and does not pay for drugs and eyeglasses and other such services outside of institutions. Because some aged find it difficult to qualify for appropriate community based services, they are sometimes forced into institutions as their only alternative when they become eligible for Medicaid.

NURSING HOME OWNERSHIP

Nursing homes have moved rapidly toward ownership by large nursing home chains. Proprietary facilities operate 75 percent of the nursing homes in the U.S. [1] and a growing number of these chains are publicly-held corporations. The nursing home industry is consolidating fast. Forbes reported that the ten largest chains accounted for 10 percent of the total number of beds in the country [14], and in 1983, thirty-two corporations controlled 17 percent of the beds [15]. These largest chains included Beverly Enterprises, ARA Services, National Medical Enterprises (which bought National Health Enterprises) and Cenco Inc. The top corporations are listed on the New York Stock Exchange and the American Stock Exchange.

In 1983, the chain ownership of beds increased by 30.4 percent over the previous year, but most of this growth was through acquisition of existing homes, and not new construction [15]. This trend, called horizontal growth, is expected to continue to the point where five to ten nursing home corporations will own 50 percent of all the beds in the U.S. by 1990.

The chain operated corporations are able to develop sophisticated management techniques for reducing costs such as centralized planning, bulk purchasing, sharing of costly equipment, prototype construction and standardized space design [16]. Chain facilities tend to make intensive use of high margin, capital intensive services such as laboratories and supplies. And chains are generally highly leveraged with about 60 percent of their capitalization in long-term debt. The success of such activities in generating growth and profits suggests that the trends will continue toward such operations which are becoming part of larger corporations that also own hospitals and other types of health services.

Nursing home corporations are moving quickly to diversify investments. Most nursing home chains control other types of businesses such as pharmaceutical suppliers and respiratory therapy companies in what is termed vertical integration. Unicare Services, for example, a chain in Milwaukee, owned figure salons, a drugstore chain, a car wash, a restaurant chain and other businesses [3]. The latest activities of nursing homes have been to develop other long-term care businesses, because of the recent problems in building new nursing homes due to high interest rates. These activities have involved operating home health care corporations.

In California in 1983, the proprietary nursing home industry sponsored legislation that would allow for the operation of proprietary adult day health care centers (where only nonprofit adult day health care programs were allowed).

The expansion into all areas of the long-term care gives the nursing home industry control and influence over the entire long-term care delivery system. The change of noninstitutional care organizations from largely nonprofit community-based agencies to proprietary and large corporate or chain-owned organizations will most likely have the same negative impact as it has for nursing homes.

Vladeck points out that the real owners of the nursing home industry are the banks [3]. Most owners have little equity in their facilities with the banks holding large mortgages. The banks and investment corporations are promoting the move toward consolidation of the nursing home industry and also have promoted the growth of institutions over that of smaller community-based noninstitutional programs which generally have greater financial risks.

PROFITS

The health care business is healthy. The price earnings ratios in the nursing home industry are commonly between 14 and 18 percent. Beverly Enterprises with $450 million in business in 1982, reported a growth of 700 percent since 1978. National Health Enterprises reported 900 percent growth since 1978. Beverly Enterprises added over 10,000 beds and increased its size by 25 percent in 1982 [14, 16]. Moskowitz reported that an investment of $10,000 at the start of 1982 in the four top health care corporations (including hospitals and nursing homes) was worth $18,000 at the end of the year [17]. An investment of $10,000 five years ago would have been worth over $100,000 in 1983.

The investment forecasts for the nursing home industry are strong because of several factors. One is what Forbes called "gray gold" because of the rapid growth of the aged population from 25 to 30 million by 1990 assuring the demand for nursing home care [14]. The demand for nursing home beds continues to be strong for a variety of other reasons centered around lack of other community based program options, discussed in the preceding section. If demand were to continue at its present rate, there would be a need for 2.5 million nursing home beds by 1985 (an increase of 90% between 1976 and 1985) [18].

Price increases have continued each year for nursing homes, primarily supported by public dollars (56%). Private insurance and philanthropy pays for about 1 percent of the total care, and patients pay for 43 percent directly out-of-pocket. Medicaid pays for 50 percent of the total nursing home bills while Medicare only pays for about 2 percent and other public programs pay for the remainder [13]. Because Medicaid pays for half of all nursing home costs, Medicaid policies established by the states are critical in shaping the industry.

NURSING HOME REIMBURSEMENT

Medicaid reimbursement policies are a powerful device for influencing the nursing home industry [19, 20]. States have recently been focusing on controlling nursing home reimbursement costs to lower the rapid growth rates in the program, which were occurring at about 16 percent per year. Nursing home reimbursement policies are complex and usually take into account inflation, cost of services, size, hospital affiliation, nursing hours, and other factors [21-23].

Most states pay nursing homes on a prospective basis by setting ceilings on total facility costs and sometimes on specific cost centers. Other states still use a retrospective per diem payment system which generally is higher in costs [20].

While proprietary nursing home chains widely describe their profits and growth in order to attract investors, when the industry presents its cost data to states, they generally argue that higher reimbursement rates are needed. The industry has been successful in obtaining favorable reimbursement rates from state Medicaid agencies until the last two years when many states were facing budget crises and pressures to control overall program costs and reimbursement rates.

Some states such as California found that the average nursing home facility made a profit of 41 percent on net equity in 1978-79 [24]. A similar study in Texas showed an average profit on net equity of 34 percent for 1978 [25]. Since many states do not limit the amount of profits facilities can make, nursing homes are able to reduce expenditures to maximize profits.

Nursing homes have made money from their real estate and capital investments through frequent sales arrangements and also use management lease arrangements to increase revenues [2-3]. As Vladeck points out, nursing homes have used the accelerated depreciation policies under Medicare and Medicaid to pay for the capital investments plus their return on equity investments [3]. The complex mechanisms used by nursing homes to increase their profits are difficult to track and to understand for those not in the financial arena. And even non-profit nursing homes operate with a growth imperative with similar pressures to maximize revenues and control costs. The differences between nonprofit and profit facilities are often blurred, and are based on management and distribution of profits rather than other corporate behavior.

NURSING HOME POWER AND POLITICS

The nursing home industry is the third most powerful health association in most states, after hospitals and physicians. In terms of power, nursing home associations are highly organized collecting large contributions for political campaigns and political lobbying activities. The associations direct major efforts toward influencing the development of administrative regulations, rates, and licensing activities, and also focus on legislators and their legislative activities. Nationally, the American Health Care Association, a proprietary trade organization, is the largest and most influential organization while the smaller American Association of Homes for the Aging represents voluntary institutions [3].

In a recent study of eight states, data showed that the industry has been particularly effective with legislative and administrative bodies [26]. Such lobbying activities have promoted weak regulation of the industry and favorable rates for the most part within certain recent limitations due to state financial constraints. Litigation has also been used as an effective tool by the nursing home industry to promote favorable public policies. The industry is able to invest substantial sums into such activities and hire talented individuals for legislative, administrative, and legal actions.

Nursing home residents and their families are seldom organized and have few recourses in influencing both public policies and the activities and quality of care in individual nursing homes. While most states have mechanisms for ombudsman programs, complaints are frequently difficult to substantiate and seldom result in corrections. In some communities, citizen groups have been organized to reform nursing homes and serve as public watchdogs for the residents in certain areas. But such groups have not developed a strong power base for effective political action. Without political contributions, citizen groups are not able to compete very effectively in most areas where they exist. Until consumers are better represented with consumer lobbyists and able to influence public policies and political decisions, the balance of power will remain in the hands of the nursing home industry.

One feature frequently overlooked is the political impact of the growth in large chain-owned corporations. Not only are such corporations able to build effective economies of scale and to maximize profits, the corporations are effective in using their resources to influence political decision-making at both federal and state levels. The corporations are also immune to a great extent from local political processes, unlike the small locally-owned nursing homes. Local community organizations have less influence in bringing about changes in quality, costs, or management when nursing homes are owned and operated by large corporations with management based out of the local area or even out of the state.

Even more important, professionals working with nursing homes, whether nurses, physicians, or health facility administrators, also have less influence on the policies and practices of large corporations than they do on locally owned and operated facilities. The slow erosion of power and influence by health professionals over their practice within large corporate health institutions is insideous. To reverse this trend, communities and professionals could oppose corporate management and ownership of health facilities in their communities. When given the opportunity to make decisions on certificate of need (review and approval for building or remodeling of facilities under health planning), local zoning, facility bond approvals, operating and use permits, and other approvals, individuals and groups could take steps to reverse the take-over by corporations and make decisions that promote local ownership and local control.

POLICY OPTIONS

Given the current situation in nursing homes, there are a variety of public policy options. Ruchlin identified the following options: 1) rescind the regulatory programs substituting marketplace forces, 2) accept the current situations, 3) extend the current regulatory programs, 4) strengthen existing regulatory mechanisms, and 5) refocus the regulatory program from current emphasis on structure process to outcome orientations [8]. There are other options such as changing the public financing of long-term care, and diverting individuals from nursing homes into community-based care programs.

In reviewing the range of policy options, clearly there is no evidence to support the idea that marketplace forces are appropriate or effective in the nursing home industry. All evidence suggests that demand for nursing home services exceeds supply and qualitative differences among facilities are difficult for consumers to detect. Traditional factors such as quality of care, costs, and environment do not play a significant role in nursing home selection and placement decisions. Increasing the supply of beds will most likely result in greater utilization of nursing homes and not make the facilities more competitive or bring about improvements in quality, costs, or environment.

Regulatory activities are too weak and ineffective and should be strengthened. But many reviewers question whether a regulatory system can ever truly protect the consumer in a situation where large proprietary chains and facilities dominate the market with their efforts oriented toward profit making and growth. As nursing homes have grown in political influence, efforts to regulate the faciliities at both the federal and state levels have become more difficult. At a time when the evidence suggests greater need for consumer protection, the politics have brought about the deregulation movement.

Clearly, unless efforts are made to reduce demand for nursing home services, the situation of disequilibrium in the marketplace for nursing home services will continue. When occupancy rates are high and waiting lists for facilities are long, it is difficult to make regulation effective. And facilities will continue to seek the private paying and least disabled individuals. Demand for services can only be reduced if alternative community-based services are available and public and private financing of such services is provided.

In an environment where the nursing home industry is powerful and persuasive in maintaining its current share of public dollars and maintaining its reimbursement growth rates, through administrative and legislative influence, it appears extremely difficult to predict positive changes. Not only does the political power of the industry continue to grow but many states are experiencing financial crises that preclude any expansion in alternatives to institutional care.

While many would advocate legislation to prohibit proprietary nursing homes, nonprofit requirements are easy to circumvent [3]. And it is not politically realistic to believe that public policymakers or even the public would support the abolishment of proprietary ownership of nursing homes in the U.S. If the ownership patterns are continued, other strategies for forcing responsible management of nursing homes are necessary.

One alternative approach is to change the financing of long-term care services away from fee-for-service reimbursement which tends to encourage expanded utilization and costs. Health maintenance organizations with prepaid capitated financing have been designed as alternatives to traditional financing to give providers incentives to keep people healthy and prevent illness. The same approaches could also be used for long term care services to give providers incentives to keep people more independent and healthy. While such an approach has not been given a great deal of consideration, the Senate now has proposed legislation which would expand the development of long-term prepaid plans.

In the long run, the only way to solve the problems created by the long-term care industry is to reduce the demand for and utilization of nursing home services. Even this change is threatened by the movement of nursing home chains into the ownership and management of noninstitutional programs. Efforts to restructure the nursing home industry and the whole long-term care system will require new vision and concentrated energy on the part of many groups, families, friends, physicians and health professionals, legislators and public policy makers.

REFERENCES

1. U.S. Department of Health and Human Services, National Center for Health Statistics, *Master Facility Inventory, 1978*, unpublished tables, U.S. Department of Health and Human Services, Washington, D.C., 1980.
2. U.S. Congress Senate Special Committee on Aging, *Nursing Home Care in the U.S.: Failure in Public Policy*, an Introductory Report and Supporting Papers N.1-7, U.S. Government Printing Office, Washington, D.C., 1974-1976.
3. B. C. Vladeck, *Unloving Care: The Nursing Home Tragedy*, Basic Books, New York, 1980.
4. U.S. General Accounting Office, *Entering A Nursing Home—Costly Implications for Medicaid and the Elderly*, U.S. Comptroller General of the United States, General Accounting Office, Washington, D.C., 1979.
5. U.S. Department of Health and Human Services, Health Care Financing Administration, *Long Term Care: Background and Future Directions*, U.S. Government Printing Office, Washington, D.C., 1981.
6. R. N. Brown, An Appraisal of the Nursing Home Enforcement Process, *Arizona Law Review, 17*:2, 1975.
7. American Bar Association, *Model Recommendations: Intermediate Sanctions for Enforcement of Quality of Care in Nursing Homes*, Commission on Legal Problems of the Elderly, Washington, D.C., 1981.
8. H. S. Ruchlin, An Analysis of Regulatory Issues and Options in Long-Term Care, in *Reform and Regulation in Long-Term Care*, V. LaPorte and J. Rubin (eds.), Praeger, New York, 1979.
9. W. J. Scanlon, Theory of the Nursing Home Market, *Inquiry, 17*:2, pp. 25-41, 1980.
10. U.S. Congress Senate Special Committee on Aging, *Health Care For Older Americans: The "Alternatives" Issue*, Parts 1-7, U.S. Government Printing Office, Washington, D.C., 1977-78.

154 / POLITICAL ECONOMY OF AGING

11. U.S. Department of Commerce Bureau of the Census, *1976 Survey of Institutionalized Persons: Study of Persons Receiving Long Term Care*, Current Population Reports, Special Studies, Series No. 69, U.S. Government Printing Office, Washington, D.C., 1978.

12. U.S. Department of Health and Human Services, National Center for Health Statistics, *The National Nursing Home Survey: 1977 Summary for the United States*, Publication No. (PHS) 79-1974, U.S. National Center for Health Statistics, Washington, D.C., 1979.

13. D. R. Waldo and R. M. Gibson, National Health Expenditures, 1981., *Health Care Financing Review*, 4:1, pp. 1-35, Summer 1982.

14. J. Blyskal, Gray Gold, *Forbes*, pp. 80-81, November 23, 1981.

15. S. LaViolette, Nursing Home Chains Scramble for More Private-Paying Patients, *Modern Healthcare*, pp. 130-138, May, 1983.

16. B. Keppel, Multihospital Affiliation in Hand, Beverly Aims to Double Its Size, *Modern Healthcare*, pp. 70-72, June, 1982.

17. M. Moskowtiz, The Health Care Business is Healthy, The Money Tree, *San Francisco Chronicle*, p. 50, March 28, 1983.

18. U.S. Congress, Congressional Budget Office, *Long Term Care: Actuarial Cost Estimates*, A CBO Technical Analysis Paper, U.S. Government Printing Office, Washington, D.C., 1977.

19. B. Spitz, *State Guide to Medicaid Cost Containment*, Intergovernmental Health Policy Project, Center for Policy Research, National Governor's Association, Washington, D.C., 1981.

20. C. Harrington and J. Swan, Medicaid Nursing Home Reimbursement Policies, Rates and Expenditures, working paper, Aging Health Policy Center, San Francisco, California, 1983.

21. C. E. Bishop, Nursing Home Cost Studies and Reimbursement Issues, *Health Care Financing Review*, 1:4, pp. 47-64, 1980.

22. R. Schlenker and P. Shaughnessy, *A Framework for Analyzing Nursing Home Cost, Case Mix and Quality Interrelationships*, Working paper No. 7, Center for Health Services Research, University of Colorado, Health Sciences Center, 1981.

23. P. L. Grimaldi, *Medicaid Reimbursement of Nursing-Home Care*, American Enterprise Institute for Public Policy Research, Washington, D.C., 1982.

24. California Health Facilities Commission, *Economic Criteria for Health Planning Report, FY 1981-82/FY 1982-83, Volume II*, Draft Report, Health Facilities Commission, Sacramento, California, December 30, 1981.

25. C. Harrington, J. Wood, G. La Londa Berg, and M. Bogart, *Texas Case Study: Medicaid, Title XX, and SSI Programs*, Aging Health Policy Center, San Francisco, 1983.

26. C. Harrington and R. J. Newcomer, *Medicaid Programs in Eight States: A Study of Policy Changes*, Aging Health Policy Center, San Francisco, 1983.

PART III: INSTITUTIONS AND STRUCTURED DEPENDENCY: INCOME, LABOR AND CONTROL OF CAPITAL

While the welfare state in advanced capitalist societies is organized primarily for the elderly, such organization came about precisely because it was in the best interests of corporate capital to forceably unemploy chronologically older members of society in exchange for pensions and related benefits.

In this section, the issues of income, work and retirement among the elderly are explored from a range of political economic perspectives. We begin with Robert Binstock's analysis of the changing stereotypes of the aged in the United States, from the "poor, frail and deserving" folk of earlier times to the "politically potent, relatively well off and costly burden" which they are seen as constituting today. The scapegoating of the elderly is seen as diverting attention from more fundamental problems such as unemployment, inflation and declining economic productivity, and as further allowing us to ignore the problematic aspects of existing public policies for the aged.

One critical outcome and reflection of this scapegoating is recent concern over the "crisis" of old age security. In Chapter 10 Myles locates the roots of that perceived crisis in a larger conflict over the "proper role of the democractic state in a market economy."

While that role was seen as an expansive welfare-promoting one from the post war period to the early 1970's, a protracted economic recession led to a "welfare backlash" in many advanced capitalist societies by the mid 1970's. As the largest single item in the welfare budget, social security came under particular attack with the graying of the population inaccurately sited as causing the perceived crisis.

To "blame" the aged and their growing numbers for the crisis of the welfare state is to forget, however, the social creation of a large unemployed category of persons well in advance of physiological decline. In Chapter 11 Graebner traces the history of retirement in the United States and the manner in which it became institutionalized as a means of enabling employers to simply and legally rid themselves of their most expensive workers.

Age discrimination is seen as having developed as a logical response to the dominant economic needs of a capitalist society—needs which were exacerbated during periods of economic depression. Economic theorists, medical researchers, and the scientific management school of business and industry are seen in this chapter to have together provided an "empirical" rationale for discrimination against older workers. While the chapter forcuses on the period from the late 1800's to the mid 1920's, it provides a critical historical context for understanding the subsequent growth and institutionalization of forced retirement in American society.

CHAPTER 9

Reframing the Agenda of Policies on Aging

ROBERT H. BINSTOCK

Policy issues concerning older Americans have been framed for a long time by an underlying *ageism*—the attribution of the same characteristics, status, and just deserts—to a group that is artificially labeled "the aged."

From the Townsend Movement of the 1930's until about four or five years ago, several categorical stereotypes concerning the aged were axioms of public rhetoric in America. Simply put, they were:

1. The aged are poor, frail, and perceived in negative terms; hence, they are in need of collective assistance and require some positive image-building.
2. The aged are relatively impotent as a political force; so their advocates should help to develop "senior power."
3. The aged are "the deserving poor," because their disadvantaged plight is forced upon them by mandatory retirement, the frailties and disabilities of old age, and the prejudices of a youth-oriented society. Consequently, with this rationale satisfying the Protestant ethic within American political ideology, there is no reason why a wealthy American society should not do more for them.

Since 1978, however, beginning in the middle of President Carter's Administration, these ageist axioms have become virtually reversed. We now find—in the media, political speeches, public policy studies, and in the writings of so-called scholars—a new set of axioms.

1. The aged are relatively well-off; not poor, but in great shape.
2. The aged are a potent political force because there are so many of them, and they all vote in their self-interest; this "senior power" explains why more than one quarter of the annual federal budget is expended on benefits to the aged.
3. Because of demographic changes, the aged are becoming more numerous and politically powerful, and will be entitled to even more benefits and substantially larger proportions of the Federal budget. They are already costing too much, and in the future will pose an undeserved, unwarranted, and unsustainable burden on the American economy.

If you have not been observing these pronouncements in scholarly journals, you have certainly seen them in: *The National Journal, The Washington Post, The New York Times,* and *The Wall Street Journal.* Perhaps the "new wisdom" was captured most succinctly and effectively by *Forbes* magazine: "The myth is that they're sunk in poverty. The reality is that they're living well. The trouble is there are too many of them—God bless 'em." [1, p. 51] .

Even as the discarded axioms concerning the aged were obviously faulty, so too, are the new ones. Let us briefly examine these three new axioms.

AXIOM NUMBER 1

The Aged Are Well Off:
They Have Been Lifted Out of Poverty

A relatively small number of aged are very well-off; many are moderately comfortable; many are extraordinarily poor. How poor is extraordinarily poor?

As we know, there are many approaches to measuring the income adequacy of older persons. And each approach can involve a variety of specific measures. One approach is to use absolute standards such as the "poverty line," the "near poor line," or the hypothetical budgets for an elderly couple that are constructed by the Bureau of Labor Statistics (BLS). Another approach is to compare the income status of older persons to that of the population in general, using medians or averages. Or, one can measure income adequacy by employing various replacement ratios which are constructed on assumptions regarding what a retiree needs as income in order to maintain the same standard of living that he or she had in the years just before retirement. Each of these approaches, and even the specific measures used to implement them, can yield a result that is substantially different from the others.

Consider some of the wide discrepancies in reports on income adequacy that have been produced through the use of absolute measures. In 1977, for example, the official poverty line indices used by the Federal government led to a determination that 14 percent of persons sixty-five and older were in poverty even after they had received cash transfers from government programs [2, p. 1576] . A different analysis for 1977, undertaken by the Congressional Budget Office (CBO) reduced the proportion of elderly poor to 6 percent by taking into account the value of non-cash or in-kind government benefits which older persons received [3] . Still another estimate of poverty among the elderly in 1976, undertaken by Molly Orshansky (the creator of the initial poverty line indices), yielded an estimate that 36 percent of older Americans "have too little income of their own to live by themselves." [4, p. 203] . Each of these widely divergent estimates was technically correct, and the discrepancies among them can be reconciled with sufficient background interpretation. But any one of them could be substantially misleading if used irresponsibly and out of context.

Perhaps the best way to gain an understanding of the economic status of older Americans is to consider a specific budget. Let us examine for a moment an example of a "poverty line budget"—a budget that is constructed on the assumption that it is adequate for sustaining a "temporary emergency diet." In 1981 the poverty line (or "threshold") for an elderly couple was $5,498 [5]; if the couple had this much income it was not counted as "in poverty." According to the budgetary assumptions used in constructing the poverty line, this couple would have $153 per month for shelter (either for rent or for mortgage, property tax, and home maintenance costs), and $17.62 a week, per person, for food. The remaining $76 a month, per person, would be available for clothing, transportation, utilities, taxes, personal and property insurance, recreation, and medical and dental care. The average expenditures for medical and dental care are clearly assumed to be minimal. Yet, in the same year, out-of-pocket medical and dental expenses, alone, averaged over $76 a month for each elderly person. So even with extensive Medicare and Medicaid benefits, which account for 98 percent of the in-kind benefits attributed to older persons [6, pp. 1821-1825], many couples that had made it up to the poverty line, or even exceeded it, would have had little or nothing left for clothing, transportation, utilities, and all the other items, after paying their out-of-pocket health care expenses. In short, receiving in-kind benefits from the government may change the category in which one is officially classified by CBO economists, but it does not necessarily lift one out of poverty in a functional sense.

This example should provide some perspective on the exceedingly harsh statistical measure of income adequacy that is imposed by the poverty line. We have just examined the budget of a couple that has made it up to the poverty line. Over four million older persons are below this line, and several million more are clustered just above it. With this perspective in mind, we can better interpret the current axiom of public rhetoric which glibly states that older Americans are now relatively well off.

Some will argue that this portrayal of the economic status of the elderly ignores two important sources of income that are not included in poverty line statistics or in analyses of in-kind transfers through government programs. What about intra-family transfers, the income that older persons may receive from their children and other kin? And what about the income that older persons could obtain from their assets such as home equity? After all, a great many older Americans own their own homes and have fully paid off their mortgages.

To date, very little is known about the impact of intra-family transfers. One study found that they altered the well-being of about 28 percent of aged families [7]. But relatively large transfers flow *both* ways, with slightly more aged families receiving assistance than giving assistance to younger children. The net result is unclear from data currently available.

The equity that many older persons have in their homes represents a potential source of additional money income for them. But converting this asset into a liquid stream of income is not as simple as it would seem. Substantial changes would be needed in financial and marketing practices, and in statutory law, in order to unlock home equity; and even if such changes are advisable, they could take many years to effect in a responsible fashion. Unlocking home equity is a good idea, but a great deal will need to be done to bring it to fruition in a fashion that will substantially help older persons.

AXIOM NUMBER 2

The Aged Are a Potent, Self-Interested Political Force

The aged do constitute a large block of participating voters. They comprise from 15 to 16 percent of those who vote in national elections. But older persons do not vote in a monolithic bloc, any more than middle-aged persons or younger persons. For instance, the *New York Times/CBS News* "exit poll" during the 1980 Presidential election reported that 54 percent of voters sixty years of age and older voted for President Reagan; among voters thirty to forty-four years old, 54 percent voted for President Reagan; and among voters in the middle, forty-five to fifty-nine years old, 55 percent voted for the President [8, p. 28].

Candidates, not issues, run for office. A voter's response to any one issue is part of an overall response to a variety of issues in a campaign, and to still many other campaign stimuli that have little to do with issues at all. Moreover, within a heterogeneous group such as older Americans, responses to any single issue are likely to vary substantially. Human beings do not suddenly become homogenized with respect to their political behavior when they reach a particular birthday.

But don't politicians behave as if older persons vote as a bloc because of issues? Aren't they terrorized by so-called "senior power?"

The answer if not so clear. It certainly is evident that no politician wants to offend the aged if he or she can avoid doing so. On the other hand, the Omnibus Reconciliation Act of 1981 legislated nine provisions narrowing benefits and eligibility under OASDI, of which at least five can be interpreted as directly affecting Old Age Insurance benefits. Or consider that Congress enacted automatic cost-of-living adjustments for social security benefits in 1972. The introduction and passage of that legislation confounded long-standing conventional wisdom regarding the stimulus-response mechanisms of the politics of aging and of other broad constituency groups. The conventional wisdom had it that Congress was very well-served politically by enacting ad hoc social security benefit increases every few years, thereby receiving periodic fresh credits from constituents which were translated into subsequent rewards through election returns. Then why enact an automatic mechanism that evokes no recurring credits and electoral rewards?

Without opening up this topic any further in the scope of this presentation, let me say that the politics of aging are much more subtle and complex than conventionally perceived. I will simply state, in summary, that the axiom of public rhetoric regarding the potency of senior power is unsophisticated and inaccurate.

AXIOM NUMBER 3

Demographic Changes Mean That the Aged Will Pose an Unsustainable Burden on the American Economy

In 1978, at the same time that the stereotype of poverty among the aged was being transformed, journalists, scholars, and public officials began to recognize the economic implications of an aging population. Attention was directed to the "graying of the budget"—the demographic age changes and public program benefit structures which have led to a situation in which the Federal government currently expends more on aging than on national defense. Moreover, on the basis of reliable predictions of increases in the number of older Americans, and assumed continuity in present program benefit structures, projections were made that the 27 percent of the Federal budget expended on the aging in 1982 [9, p. 45] will reach 40 percent early in the next century [10, p. 1576] and 63 percent by the year 2025 [11]. On the basis of such dramatic projections, some journalists began to suggest that American society could not afford to maintain collective public efforts to sustain the economic burden of an aging population [12, pp. 1712-1717].

Numbers that express the percentage of Federal expenditures devoted to a single function such as "benefits to the aged" or "defense" may be important political symbols. But they do not necessarily represent unsustainable economic burdens. The pertinent question to be addressed is: Can the American *economy* afford to continue, well into the next century, the current policies through which it provides benefits to the elderly? Or, put another way: What proportion of the Gross National Product (GNP) will be required to sustain public benefits to the aged at various points in the future, and how do those proportions compare with the current proportion of GNP spent on the aged?

A recent analysis by economists Robert Clark and John Menefee sheds some interesting light on this issue [13, pp. 132-137]. They have projected to the year 2025 the proportion of GNP required to maintain current benefits per older person in real dollar terms (1978 dollars), using alternative assumptions.

One projection rests on the assumption that increases in the level of benefits per person will be tied to the Consumer Price Index (CPI). With this assumption they find that the proportion of GNP needed to finance benefits to the aged in the years ahead is smaller than at present. The proportion of GNP expended on Federal benefits to older Americans in 1978 was 5.3 percent. Maintenance of these benefits per person in real 1978 dollars, according to Clark and Menefee, would require 3.8 percent of GNP in the year 2000; 3.3 percent in 2010; and 3.8 percent in 2025. Under this scenario, it would seem that the costs of an aging population will not be at all difficult to sustain.

But an alternative projection, based on the current rate of inflation for health care costs, yields a substantially different picture. In recent years, health care costs have been inflating at nearly double the rate of the CPI. When Clark and Menefee undertook a projection which used the true contemporary rate of inflation in health care costs, rather than a rate tied to the CPI, they found a consistent trend of increase in the proportion of GNP required to sustain present per person levels of Federal benefits to the aged. The 1978 percentage of 5.3 rises to 6.7 percent in the year 2000; 7.28 percent in 2010; and 10.15 percent of GNP in 2025.

Judging from this study, the challenge of sustaining the costs of an aging population will lie in our willingness and ability to confront and control the causes of runaway health care costs. The problem is not, as many would have us believe, one of sustaining social security and other cash income transfers to older Americans.

This conclusion is buttressed by another analysis which was undertaken by the Technical Committee for the 1981 White House Conference on Aging (WHCOA) which addressed the "Implications for the Economy" of population aging. In the context of an overall study of *Economic Policy in an Aging Society* it examined the probable aggregate economic effects of an *expanded* public income transfer program that would be used as a direct measure for addressing income adequacy problems of the elderly through the year 2025.

In analyzing the economic impact of increased transfers that would guarantee adequate income for all older persons over the next twenty-five years, the Committee chose a relatively high absolute standard of adequacy, an income consistent with the BLS Intermediate Budget for Retired Couples. In addition, it posited that such transfers would only be made to those below the BLS standard and would be financed by increased taxes rather than by a redistribution of tax revenues.

The WHCOA Committee's analysis led to the finding that such a program of increased income transfer and taxation "would not have a significant effect on the overall economy." [14, p. 29] To be sure, such a program would add to Federal expenditures; the analysis indicated that $19 billion would be required to fund the program in 1981, but the amount needed would decline to $12 billion (in current dollars) by 2025. Nonetheless, the Technical Committee found that an immediate and ongoing direct guarantee of an adequate income to all older persons for the next twenty-five years would have no harmful effects on the American economy.

No definitive judgments can be made on the basis of either this WHCOA Committee report or the analysis conducted by Clark and Menefee. They are among the first in what will undoubtedly be a spate of serious technical studies examining the implications of an aging population for the American economy. But they do provide an early indication that the axiom concerning the unsustainable costs of an aging population is off target. What seems to be unsustainable is the spiraling costs of health care. The most critical economic implications of an aging population appear to lie in our approaches to the costs and financing mechanisms of health care.

THE NEED TO REFRAME OUR POLICY AGENDA

What I have tried to suggest in briefly discussing these new axioms of public rhetoric is that the challenges of dealing with what we perceive as a crisis in policies toward aging need to be met by reframing the issues which we consider, and the assumptions we make. Neither the old axioms nor the new axioms are very useful for confronting the policy dilemmas we face.

We need to reframe our public policy agenda in a fashion that:

- recognizes the heterogeneity or diversity of older Americans, with respect to their economic and other needs;
- recognizes that so-called "senior power" is not a formidable obstacle to sensible and humane reforms;
- and recognizes that the financial costs of sustaining collective benefits to older Americans rest largely with our willingness to deal with the factors that underlie the exponential increases in the expenses of health care.

The current crisis mentality concerning policies toward older Americans provides us with a rare opportunity to reframe our public policy agenda in terms of fundamental issues regarding the nature and extent of governmental responsibility for older persons. But the opportunity is not being seized. Let me put it in brief, outline fashion:

1. As we know, agenda-setting—the capacity to frame and reframe the issues of public policy—is a major source of power in our political system, probably a more important source of power than votes.
2. *Substantial* reframing is a slow process unless you undertake it from a very powerful position.
3. But if you are in a very powerful position you are unlikely to reframe the agenda except in a relatively *incremental* fashion, for you have a large political, and/or economic, and/or social stake in the status quo.
4. More fundamental reshapings are likely to be initiated by intellectuals, and to take a substantial time to percolate through different strata of society, and to filter through the media, in order to have impact.
5. The intellectuals and other self-styled sources of expertise, however, are currently failing us. They are engaging in irresponsible demogoguery, lining up with the new axioms of public rhetoric regarding older Americans—in a knee-jerk fashion—even as they used to line up with the three previous axioms that pervaded our public dialogue for four decades.

Consider three recent types of irresponsible demogoguery through which scholars and experts are failing us.

The first type we might term "The Dangling Innuendo." The currently celebrated MIT economist, Lester Thurow, author of the best selling *"The Zero Sum Society,"* argues vehemently against President Reagan's proposed cuts in social welfare spending. In a 1981 article in the *New York Times Magazine* he vigorously defended a variety of social welfare programs, but went on to say:

> When it comes to elderly veterans, however, the United States spends like a drunken sailor. . . . Veterans over 65 receive three times as much health care as those under 65. . . . Given the general availability of Medicare for the elderly, the V.A. should stop paying health-care costs for elderly veterans [15, p. 56].

Thurow never explicitly says that older veterans can be "double dippers" in the VA and Medicare—getting reimbursed twice for the same operation (or perhaps getting two heart transplants, one through the VA and one through Medicare). But an uninformed person on these matters, as many persons are, could certainly not be blamed for inferring that there is something going on that enables an older veteran to obtain two government transfers that can be used in additive fashion.

A second type of irresponsibility might be called "Let the Most Useful Case Stand for All Cases." Another distinguished economist, Martin Feldstein, Professor at Harvard, and President of the National Bureau of Economic Research, argues vigorously and often for major cuts in social security. Among his favorite weapons is a routine through which he implies that all older persons are sitting around getting just about as much money from social security benefits in retirement as they earned while working. In a recent article he and his wife, economist Kathleen Feldstein, informed us:

> ... A married man who retired in 1980 at age sixty-five after earning average wages all his working life found his benefits would replace 77 percent of his peak earnings. Since these benefits are untaxed, they replace more than 90 percent of his after-tax peak earnings. And for lower income workers, the replacement rate was even higher [16, p. 46].

Feldstein uses this argument frequently, and sometimes manages to contrive his hypothetical case so as to yield even more dramatic results. In an essay written a month earlier than the one just quoted the hypothetical man was receiving "benefits for himself and his wife that exceed 90 percent of his peak earnings," and Feldstein suggested that "many retirees find that their Social Security benefits replace more than 100 percent of their peak after-tax earnings." [17, p. 46] In neither instance does Feldstein tell the reader that the *man* who earned average wages all his life and retired at age sixty-five is a very atypical case. He does not tell us that over two thirds of social security beneficiaries retire before age sixty-five, and thereby receive reduced benefits. He does not tell us what widows benefits are like. He does not tell us a lot of things. But he does imply that virtually all social security beneficiaries have replacement rates that are extraordinarily high—approaching or exceeding 100 percent of peak earnings.

A third type of irresponsibility might be labeled "'Man Bites Dog' Makes a Better Story." Just prior to the 1981 White House Conference on Aging the National Council on the Aging (NCOA) held a press conference to report on its latest Harris poll of the elderly. An ensuing story in *The New York Times* carried the headline, "POLLSTER DETECTS 'MYTHS' ON PROBLEMS OF AGED," and reported: "'On ever single issue tested,' said Mr. Harris, 'the elderly are perceived as being in much more desperate shape than they actually are.'" [18, p. A18] Both NCOA's press release and the *Times* story went on in this vein. Then, in the last paragraph, we find, as only an aside: "'But within the over 65 population,' he said, 'were four groups who in the aggregate report living a *miserable*, dismal existence: Blacks, Hispanics, those with incomes under $10,000, and women.'" [18, p. A18] Strange, neither the *Times* story, nor the NCOA press release mentioned that, in the aggregate, women constitute more than half of the population in question. It would be interesting to know the additive findings from those four sub-groups, without even double counting.

I am tempted to go on and on with examples of other types of irresponsibility. But the main point is that American society, both younger and older Americans, deserve better than this level of public policy discussion. Even as the long-standing ageist axioms of public rhetoric regarding "the aged" have served us poorly in the long run so, too, I suspect, will the new ones.

We have experienced a long period in which three themes reflecting the characteristics of ageism have provided the foundations of public policy toward older persons. The first has been that older persons are homogeneous; they're all the same. The second has been the corollary; since they're all the same, we should have age-categorical programs. And the third underlying theme has been a presumption that any (and all) problems that can be identified with respect to conditions of aging should have a governmental program developed to solve them. This general presumption regarding social problems has brought us to a point where we have some 500 Federal grant-in-aid programs.

The central contemporary policy challenge, I believe, is to refashion these underlying premises by asking fundamental questions about the nature and extent of collective responsibility toward older persons.

Do we, for instance, wish to provide cash income transfers to older persons on the basis of their work histories? Or, on the basis of their existential needs so that they can survive with some modicum of human dignity?

Do we want to provide tax free in-kind transfers and tax and price subsidies to people because of their age, without regard to financial need? If so, why?

If we begin to frame such issues, I suspect our premises will begin to change. We may discard the three former themes for three new themes to undergird our policy debates. A first would be to recognize that older Americans are heterogeneous in nature; this implies more of a need-targeting approach than we have at present. A second theme would be an acknowledgment that not all problems and issues that we can identify with respect to aging are necessarily the responsibility of government to solve. And a third underlying theme would be an effort, within those areas that are appropriately the responsibility of government, to make sharp priority decisions about how to expend scarce public resources.

My own view is that these foundation themes for public policy make more sense than those to which we have grown accustomed. If we fight our public battles along these lines, I suspect that we will improve our prospects for aging together and for avoiding the intergenerational conflict which some of our irresponsible experts and the media seem to be trying to encourage.

My main message to you is that the challenge of meeting appropriate public responsibilities to older persons is not economic, but a challenge of courageous and responsible political leadership. And that means that the issues of value conflict on our public policy agenda need to be substantially reframed, away from the ageist mold in which we have cast them up to now.

It is not sufficient to defend the programs that are on the books, because they are not substantially alleviating the problems of those within the older population who are most seriously disadvantaged and vulnerable. It is not sufficient to pretend that the demographics of aging pose an unsustainable economic burden, or that the politics of senior power ties our hands. If we ask ourselves what we are about, feasible policy options for long-term reform will follow readily enough.

REFERENCES

1. *Forbes*, The Old Folks, February 18, 1980.
2. H. H. Brotman, The Aging of America: A Demographic Profile, *National Journal, 10*, 1978.
3. Congressional Budget Office, *Poverty Study of Families Under Alternative Definitions of Income*, Background Paper No. 17, revised, U.S. Government Printing Office, Washington, D.C., June, 1977.
4. U.S. House of Representatives Select Committee on Aging, *Poverty Among America's Aged*, U.S. Government Printing Office, Washington, D.C., 1978.
5. U.S. Bureau of the Census, *Current Population Reports, Series P-60, No. 134*, Money Income and Poverty Status of Families and Persons in the United States, 1981, U.S. Government Printing Office, Washington, D.C., July, 1982.
6. T. C. Borzilleri, In-Kind Benefit Programs and Retirement Income Adequacy, *National Journal, 12*, October 25, 1980.
7. M. Moon, *The Measurement of Economic Welfare—Its Application to the Aged Poor*, Academic Press, New York, 1977.
8. The New York Times/CBS News Poll, How Different Groups Voted for President, *New York Times*, November 9, 1980.
9. U.S. Senate Special Committee on Aging, *Developments in Aging: 1981*, Vol. I, U.S. Government Printing Office, Washington, D.C. 1982.
10. J. A. Califano, Jr., U.S. Policy for the Aging—A Commitment to Ourselves, *National Journal, 10*, 1978.
11. U.S. Senate Special Committee on Aging, *Emerging Options for Work and Retirement Policy*, U.S. Government Printing Office, Washington, D.C. 1980.
12. R. J. Samuelson, Aging America—Who Will Shoulder the Growing Burden?, *National Journal, 10*, 1978.
13. R. L. Clark and J. A. Menefee, Federal Expenditures for the Elderly: Past and Future, *The Gerontologist, 21*, 1981.
14. Technical Committee on an Age-Integrated Society—Implications for the Economy, 1981 White House Conference on Aging, *Economic Policy in an Aging Society*, 1981 White House Conference on Aging, Washington, D.C. 1981.

15. L. C. Thurow, Undamming the American Economy, *New York Times Magazine*, May 3, 1981.
16. M. Feldstein and K. Feldstein, Social Security Changes Near, *The Boston Globe*, March 30, 1982.
17. _____, It's Time to Do Something about Social Security Costs, *The Boston Globe*, February 2, 1982.
18. W. Weaver, Jr., Pollster Detects "Myths" on Problems of Aged, *The New York Times*, November 19, 1981.

Reprinted from, *Proceedings of a Symposium on Income Maintenance*, May 17, 1982, Washington, D.C., partially supported by Administration on Aging grant #90AP0005/02; the views expressed are those of the author and are not attributable to the Administration on Aging.

CHAPTER 10

Conflict, Crisis, and the Future of Old Age Security

JOHN F. MYLES

During the decades following World War II the rapid growth in old age security entitlements in all capitalist democracies was widely hailed as a necessary, indeed inevitable, consequence of industrialization and economic growth. Industrialization, it was thought, had simultaneously rendered the labor of older workers redundant [1] and provided the wealth to make it unnecessary [2]. A retirement wage sufficient to permit or induce withdrawal from the labor force in advance of physiological decline could, and should, be made available to all.

In the mid-1970's, however, a contrary view began to take form. Rather than being natural or inevitable, it was argued that the combination of rising entitlements and an increasing number of retirees was part of a long-term process bound to self-destruct. In the long term, the old age security systems that were the pride of the post-war welfare state were doomed to collapse under the weight of changing demographic and fiscal realities. The "crisis" of old age security had been discovered.

In the usual formulation, the roots of the crisis are attributed to demography; the system of old age security entitlements currently in place in the capitalist democracies simply cannot withstand the rise in the number of old people projected for the decades ahead. Just as Wilensky argued that changing demographic realities gave rise to the modern welfare state, so too, it is now argued, demography will bring about its demise [2].

But what is the nature of this demographic imperative? In the pages that follow, I shall argue that the usual formulation of the demographic argument is, at best, highly misleading. This is not to say that demography is irrelevant to our understanding of the current situation. The size and composition of populations represent real constraints on any national political effort, whether for warfare or welfare. What is required, however, is to correctly identify the forms of social organization and institutional arrangements that make a particular demographic formation into a "problem." To understand the current situation, I will suggest, it is necessary to situate it within the broader context of the postwar welfare state and the political and economic foundations upon which it was constructed. The current conflict over the future of old age security is a symptom of a larger conflict over the proper role of the democratic state in a market economy. The postwar Keynesian consensus upon which the welfare state was constructed has broken down with the result that the various social institutions it spawned, including retirement benefits for the elderly, have now become the focus of renewed debate and political confrontation. The implication of this is that the long-term future of old age security—and, hence, of old age as we now know it—depends less on innovative fiscal management practices than on the eventual political realignments of a post-Keynesian political economy.

POPULATION AGING AND THE CRISIS IN OLD AGE SECURITY

In the conventional formulation, the crisis of old age security is explained by a rather straightforward exercise in demographic accounting. As Keyfitz has argued, the current generation of adults is simply not producing enough children to support it in its old age [3]. Due to declining fertility, the size of the elderly population will grow to a point where the economic burden on the young will become intolerable. Eventually, the demographic bubble will burst, old age security programs will go broke, and an intergenerational class struggle will ensue [4]. To avoid this eventuality, it is necessary to show restraint now [5]. Promises should not be made to the current generation of workers which future generations will be unwilling or unable to keep [6].

To evaluate this argument, it is necessary to identify its core assumptions. Old age pensions, in this view, are the product of an implicit social contract made between sequential age cohorts [7]. Each cohort, as it were, agrees to support the cohort it precedes, under the assumption that it will receive similar treatment from the cohorts that follow. But since age cohorts vary in size, the contract is inherently unstable. While it is relatively easy to provide generous benefits to a small retired population, to provide the same benefits to a very large cohort of retirees may become an intolerable burden [3]. The result is a conflict between cohorts leading to dissolution of the contract.

The notion of social contract between age cohorts is clearly intended as a metaphor that will enable us to understand and predict changes in popular support for old age entitlement programs. The question to be answered is whether the empirical evidence gives any indication that the metaphor captures reality. Where the conditions specified by the model have been met, it would seem reasonable to expect some evidence of the intergenerational conflict and resistance to public spending on the elderly that it predicts.

Several western nations are already quite old by demographic standards. The elderly constitute more than 16 percent of the populations of West Germany, Austria, and Sweden, a figure which is not far from the 18 to 20 percent level at which the North American population is expected to peak in the next century. As Heinz and Chiles observe [8, p. iii] :

> Western European social security systems have already experienced the impact of population aging for some time now. The Federal Republic of Germany, for example, currently has a ratio of social security contributors to beneficiaries of less than 2:1, which is the level not projected to be reached in the United States until the year 2030, when the postwar baby boom generation reaches old age.

Moreover, the tax burden necessary to finance old age security in these countries has already reached levels that exceed those projected for the United States in the next century. Prior to the recent amendments to the Social Security Act, the United States Social Security tax rate was expected to peak at 20.1 percent in the year 2035 [9]. But by 1978, the effective tax rate to support old age security was already 18 percent in Germany, 20 percent in Sweden, 23 percent in Italy, and 25 percent in the Netherlands [10, p. 43]. The experience of these nations, however, provides little evidence of the growing backlash and intergenerational hostility anticipated by the proponents of the conventional law.

Although a number of countries experienced a "welfare backlash" in the late 1970's, Wilensky has shown that this pattern was unrelated either to the size of the elderly population or to levels of public spending and taxation [11,12]. Indeed, according to Wilensky's estimates, the very oldest of the capitalist democracies—Germany, Austria, Sweden—were among the countries that experienced the least amount of popular resistance to rising welfare expenditures. And informed observers generally agree that, despite official concern over rising costs, public support of old age security systems remains high in these countries [13,14].

There are some obvious reasons for such widespread support of old age security, even in the face of rising costs. First, familial bonds provide a strong basis for solidarity between generations. In the absence of suitable public provision for the elderly, adults of working age would be required to provide for their aging parents directly. For these individuals, a generous old age security system is experienced not as a burden but as relief from a burden. Should recent efforts by the Reagan administration to revive the tradition of filial support laws be successful, Americans will have the opportunity to rediscover this fact. In a new reading of the Medicaid law the administration has affirmed the right of state officials to require children to help pay for their parents in nursing homes. This return to the Elizabethan Poor Law tradition of family responsibility does not do away with intergenerational transfers; instead, it restores the uncertainties and increases the financial disruption within working-age families that are eliminated when risks are pooled in a public transfer system.

Less obvious, but more important perhaps, is the fact that the key claim of the demographic model—that population aging increases the burden of dependency on the working population—is incorrect. Throughout the postwar years, population aging was not generally associated with a rise in either total or age-based dependency in Western Europe but, rather, with a decline [15,16]. This was due to a decline in the size of the very young population and an increase in female labor force participation. Canadian and American projections indicate a similar trend for the future. While the size of the elderly population will continue to grow, total age-dependency ratios will first decline and then rise slowly back to current levels [17, p. 25; 18, p. 17]. At no point are they projected to reach the levels achieved during the early 1960's, the peak of the baby boom period.

The issue for the future then is not the size of the dependent population but rather its changing composition—fewer children and more retirees. The usual strategy in evaluating this change is to compare public expenditures on the old with public expenditures on the young. Since public expenditures on the old are, on average, three times public expenditures on the young, it is clear that total public expenditures on the nonworking population must increase as the population ages. But to assess the true economic impact on the working population, it is necessary to establish total expenditures on the young and old, not just that portion passing through the public purse. Wander concludes that the total cost of raising a child to age 20 is one-fourth to one-third higher than that necessary to support an elderly person from age sixty to death, indicating that total intergenerational transfers (public plus private) may well decline as the population ages [19].

It is necessary to be precise about the point of the preceding arguments. It would be naive to assume that the dramatic transformation of the American age structure projected for the decades ahead will be without effect. Any major social transformation is likely to generate conflict between those who stand to lose and those who stand to gain from such change. The trick is to correctly identify the likely winners and losers. In the conventional formulation, the political fault line produced by population aging is a new cleavage between old and young, a claim for which the historical record provides precious little empirical support. Among the reasons for this is a less than complete reading of the demographic accounts upon which the conventional analysis is based. The main result of population aging is to alter the composition of the nonworking population, not its size. To correctly identify the origins of the crisis, therefore, it is necessary to locate those actors and institutions for whom this demographic reality represents a problem.

THE ANATOMY OF THE CRISIS

As Marshall pointed out in his now justly famous essay, the postwar period was a time of remarkable optimism that the traditional problems and conflicts of the capitalist democracies could be resolved and reconciled [20]. In the developed countries of western Europe and North America, it appeared that a truce had been called in the ongoing war between the principles of citizenship and those of class. With an appropriate blend of Keynes and Beveridge, the rights of persons and the rights of property could be reconciled to the advantage of both. Welfare expenditures were construed as an investment in human capital, that would improve the quality of the work force and reduce the waste of human resources produced by inadequate diet, health care, and education. Public pension systems would help regulate unemployment and allow employers to replace older workers with more efficient, and less costly, younger workers. Most importantly, redistributive policies would provide the means to regulate the traditional boom and bust cycle characteristic of the capitalist economies.

Such optimism about the compatibility of a welfare state and a market economy was not without foundation. Throughout the 1950's and 1960's both experienced unprecedented levels of real growth. As the economies of the capitalist democracies grew, expenditures on social welfare grew even more rapidly. Even among the so-called welfare laggards, the rate of growth was impressive. In the United States, income maintenance expenditures alone grew from 5 percent of the gross national product (GNP) in 1957 to 14 percent of the GNP in 1977. One could, it seemed, socialize consumption while retaining private ownership of the means of production to the mutual advantage of both.

By the mid-1970's, however, this optimism was beginning to wane. A protracted economic slump, characterized by declining output, rising unemployment and inflation, and a shift in the international division of labor brought about a radical reassessment of the postwar welfare state. Rather than a means to reinvigorate capitalism, the welfare state came to be construed as a fetter on capital accumulation. As Heclo observes [21, p. 32]: "What came to be labeled as the welfare state was an arrangement for living with mutually inconsistent priorities, a system of tolerated contradictions." Or as Geiger and Geiger pointed out, meeting human needs and maximizing economic efficiency had become mutually incompatible goals [22].

The problem was not due to state intervention in the economy as such (it is always possible for the state to intervene in a manner that is market-conforming) but, rather, to the fact that the state which was intervening was a democratic state—one in which workers in their capacity as citizens can lay claim to a share of the social product over and above any claims they possess in their capacity as wage earners. While a democratic polity may choose to respect the norms of the market—that is, to link benefits to contributions—it is by no means constrained to do so and, in general, has not done so. All national pension systems, as they have evolved in the western capitalist democracies, have incorporated democratic principles of equality, need, and adequacy into their distributional practices: all redistribute income, to a greater or lesser degree, from high wage earners to low wage earners; the majority make allowance for need in the form of supplements for dependent spouses and survivors; and, historically, the majority of countries have legislated increases for the elderly to provide them with a larger share of a growing economic pie. Throughout the postwar period, labor discovered that wage gains that could not be won at the bargaining table could be won through legislation. Among the more politically acceptable ways to achieve this was to legislate an increase in the value of the wage to be received after retirement. As labor strategy, this practice has been more overt in Europe but its effects have been no less real on this side of the Atlantic.

The result was a rapid growth of income entitlements as well as health care and social service entitlements which were quite independent of market capacity or performance. On the distributional side, the market was being made increasingly irrelevant. For progressives, this was the achievement of long sought after objectives; for conservatives, it was democracy run amok.

Given this context, it is not surprising that old age security programs should come in for particular scrutiny. By the mid-1970's, old age and disability pensions averaged 62 percent of all income maintenance expenditures in the Organization for Economic Cooperation and Development area [23, p. 20]. In the United States, the figure was 73 percent. And this does not take into account the in-kind and social service expenditures, including health care, which go to the elderly. In the areas of health care and income transfers, the modern welfare state has in large measure become a welfare state for the elderly. As the Reagan administration recognizes, it is exceedingly difficult to dismantle the one without also dismantling the other.

It is also apparent why population aging is perceived as a problem in this situation. Although more old people do not necessarily mean more transfers from the working to the nonworking population, population aging does change the composition of these transfers. A larger percentage of transfers will pass through the public purse, giving government an even greater role in distributing the nation's income. Accordingly, old age security has become the object of attack, particularly in the United States where it is the most important nonmarket mechanism for the allocation of income in the national economy. To an outsider, the scale and intensity of this attack appear quite remarkable but it is hardly surprising that the system is now in crisis, a consequence of the severe trauma induced by this attack.

What of the future? I can foresee three possible scenarios. First, it may well be that the system will right itself again; the current economic crisis will pass; the wind will be taken out of the neoconservative sails; and we shall continue much as we have in the past. Neo-Keynesian demand management strategies will again hold sway; the welfare state will return to favor; and people will grow old in the future much as they have in the recent past. This seems to be the hope of the traditional postwar liberals, a hope, however, which is hard pressed in the face of current economic realities.

The second is that history will be rolled back: the gains in social citizenship achieved during the past several decades will be dismantled or, more likely, allowed to slowly suffocate, while the market is restored to a position of preeminence. Old age pensions would not necessarily disappear, merely made market conforming: distributional practices based on need, adequacy, or equality would be abandoned; accessibility to entitlements made more difficult (e.g., by raising the retirement age), and a larger share of the pension industry returned to the private sector where benefits are calculated according to strict market criteria. Tax incentives to encourage private pension saving (IRA's) and the recent adoption of the recommendations of the bipartisan committee on Social Security are indicative of this trend in the United States.

The third solution being advanced, particularly among some European social democrats, is the one proposed long ago by Al Smith when he remarked that the "only cure for the evils of democracy is more democracy." If democratic control over distribution is incompatible with the efficient functioning of the market, then one might conceivably restrict the latter rather than the former. Rather than contract democratic control of the economy, one should expand it; rather than abandon the principles of social citizenship, the rights of citizenship should be extended to include economic citizenship. We can anticipate seeing some interesting experiments in this direction in Sweden in the next few years.

Whether in the long run the current crisis produces a restoration of the rights of property, further expansion of the citizenship principle, or a restabilization of the status quo, in the short and medium term old age policies will reflect the halting and contradictory attempts at reform characteristic of all public policy formation. But the "muddling through" that frequently seems to characterize the policy process should not blind us to the fact that now, as in the past, old age policies are not produced randomly nor in a political-economic vacuum. Old age policies, whether in the field of pensions, health care, or social services, are ultimately distributional policies. And in an era when the politics of distribution have intensified—marked by increasing conflict—it is not surprising that they have become subject to special attention. As with all distributional policies, social programs for the elderly reflect current arrangements for managing the contradictions of a democratic state in a market economy. If there is now a crisis in old age security it is because the existing arrangements for managing this relationship have been brought into question. As Marshall anticipated, the principles of citizenship and social class are once again at war [20].

Whatever the outcome of this confrontation, the future of old age is uniquely tied to the future history of the welfare state. This is hardly surprising since the social character of old age in the contemporary period is very much the product of the welfare state. After World War II, as Xavier Gaullier has remarked [24], "old age became retirement." The cause, at least the proximate cause, of this development was the advent of the retirement wage, an income entitlement sufficient to allow or induce the elderly worker to withdraw from productive activity in advance of physiological decline. And for a variety of reasons, it is the state that has assumed primary responsibility for the administration of this wage. Both the right to retire—and hence to become old—and the rights of retirement are today the product of national legislation. Politics, not demography, now determines the size of the elderly population and the material conditions of its existence.

REFERENCES

1. W. Graebner, *A History of Retirement*, Yale University Press, New Haven, 1980.
2. H. Wilensky, *The Welfare State and Equality*, University of California Press, Berkeley, 1975.
3. N. Keyfitz, Why Social Security Is In Trouble, *Public Interest, 58*:102, p. 19, 1980.
4. K. Davis and P. van der Oever, Age Relations and Public Policy in Advanced Industrial Societies, in *Population and Development Review, 7*, pp. 1-18, March 1981.
5. R. Clark and D. Barker, *Reversing the Trend Toward Early Retirement*, American Enterprise Institute, Washington, 1981.
6. A. Laffer and D. Ranson, A Proposal for Reforming Social Security, in *Income Support for the Aged*, G. S. Tolley and R. V. Burrhauser (eds.), Ballinger, Cambridge, Massachusetts, pp. 133-150, 1977.
7. M. Friedman, Payroll Taxes No; General Revenues Yes, in *Financing Social Security*, C. Campbell (ed.), Institute for Contemporary Studies, San Francisco, pp. 25-30, 1978.
8. J. Heinz and L. Chiles, Preface in *United States Senate Committee on Aging, Social Security in Europe: The Impact of an Aging Population*, Washington, 1981.
9. D. Leimer, Projected Rates of Return to Future Social Security Retirees under Alternative Benefit Structures, in *Policy Analysis With Social Security Files*, Social Security Administration Research Report No. 52, Washington, pp. 235-257, 1979.
10. B. Torrey and C. Thompson, *An International Comparison of Pension Systems*, President's Commission on Pension Policy, Washington, 1980.
11. H. Wilensky, *The 'New Corporatism', Centralization, and the Welfare State*, Sage, Beverly Hills, 1976.
12. H. Wilensky, Leftism, Catholicism and Democratic Corporatism: The Role of Political Parties in Recent Welfare State Development, in *The Development of Welfare States in Europe and America*, P. Flora and A. Heidenheimer (eds.), Transaction Books, New Brunswick, New Jersey, pp. 345-382, 1981.
13. S. G. Ross, Social Security: A World-Wide Issue, *Social Security Bulletin, 42*:8, pp. 3-10, 1979.
14. R. F. Tomasson, Government Old Age Pensions under Affluence and Austerity: West Germany, Sweden, the Netherlands, and the United States, paper presented at the meetings of the 10th World Congress of the International Sociological Association, Mexico City, August, 1982.

15. Organization for Economic Cooperation and Development, *Labour Force Statistics, 1959-1970*, Paris, 1972.
16. Organization for Economic Cooperation and Development, *Labour Force Statistics, 1968-1979*, Paris, 1981.
17. R. Clark and J. Spengler, *The Economics of Individual and Population Aging*, Cambridge University Press, Cambridge, 1980.
18. Health and Welfare Canada, *Retirement Age*, Ministry of National Health and Welfare, Ottawa, 1978.
19. H. Wander, ZPG Now: The Lesson from Europe, in *The Economic Consequences of Slowing Population Growth*, Thomas Espenshade and William Derow (eds.), Academic Press, New York, 1978.
20. T. H. Marshall, *Class, Citizenship, and Social Development*, University of Chicago Press, Chicago, 1964.
21. H. Heclo, Toward a New Welfare State?, in *The Development of Welfare States in Europe and America*, P. Flora and A. Heidenheimer (eds.), Transaction Books, New Brunswick, pp. 383-406, 1981.
22. T. Geiger and F. M. Geiger, *Welfare and Efficiency: Their Interactions in Western Europe and Implications for International Economic Relations*, Macmillan, London, 1978.
23. Organization for Economic Cooperation and Development, *Public Expenditure on Income Maintenance Programs*, Paris, 1976.
24. X. Gaullier, Economic Crisis and Old Age, *Aging and Society*, 2:2, pp. 165-182, 1982.

Reprinted with permission from *Milbank Memorial Fund Quarterly/Health and Society*, *61*:4, pp. 462-472, Fall 1983.

CHAPTER 11
Retirement and the Origins of Age Discrimination
WILLIAM GRAEBNER

Age discrimination, of which retirement is a particular variant, dates from the last quarter of the eighteenth century. Not until a century later, however, did either the larger phenomenon of age discrimination or the specific mechanism of retirement come to affect large numbers of persons. In the two decades before 1900, age discrimination grew virulently, as the owners and managers who made personnel decisions for American corporations redefined the work force to achieve increased efficiency.

Between 1885 and 1940, age discrimination went through two major historical stages. Before 1915, age discrimination was born and nurtured at the hands of a capitalist economy that, relative to its twentieth-century counterpart, was very competitive and committed to a high level of productive efficiency in the pursuit of short-term profit. The competitive structure of the economy was primarily a product of the rise of national markets caused by the growth in the rail system and urbanization, but competitive conditions were exacerbated, in a visible way that led directly to age discrimination, by the increasing popularity of the shorter workday. Economists and physicians constructed an ideology that reinforced and rationalized this discrimination; scientific managers carried it out in shop, factory, and office.

Employers sought to recover the costs attendant on a shorter workday by utilizing available technology to obtain more product from each worker. The preponderance of evidence indicates, however, that it was not the technology itself, but rather the speed at which it was operated, which brought grief to older workers. Employers apparently felt that the high capital costs of new machinery could be justified only if that machinery were operated at speeds that led inevitably to the obsolescence of workers too old to maintain required levels of

The references cited in this chapter are exemplary rather than exhaustive. The reader is directed to Graeber, W., *A History of Retirement: The Meaning and Function of an American Institution, 1885-1978*, Yale University Press, New Haven, 1980, for the unabridged chapter and complete references and notes.

productivity. In the printing industry (the data base for many of my conclusions), this entire process was the subject of negotiations between labor and management. As labor lost control of the work process, trade unions succumbed to the temptation to bargain away the rights of older workers.

It is also possible that employers introduced new technology and insisted on high-speed operation in order to force older workers out of the labor force. In the late nineteenth century, the effort to develop a more stable, more tractable, and more disciplined working class was sometimes defined in terms of eliminating older workers with seniority, influence in the union, or preindustrial work habits. Certainly there is evidence for the general case that technology was often introduced for some other purpose than increased efficiency, narrowly defined.

In the two decades after 1915, age discrimination worsened absolutely because of continued technological change, an intensification of the youth cult during the 1920's, and the unemployment of the Depression. By 1930, it had become a subject of study by social workers, fraternal organizations, labor unions, business trade groups, and committees of the House and Senate. In a political sense, the issue had arrived.

At the same time, however, age discrimination had begun to change with the changing face of American capitalism. As business increasingly sought to trade immediate profit for future security (economic efficiency for social efficiency, in other words), older workers became valuable for their stability and conservatism. Some capitalists discovered that older workers could meet traditional demands for efficiency by contributing to reduced rates of work-force turnover and by servicing particular product markets. Having succeeded before 1920 in creating a less tradition-bound industrial working class, post-1920 employers often experienced the most difficulty with younger workers. The older worker of 1930 (say, thirty-five years old in 1900) belonged to the first generation of workers to reach old age under the full-blown pressures of ageism. Made cautious and cooperative through pension plans and threats of job loss, this older worker had become a reasonable ally for certain employers.

By the late 1920's, technology was one of the most common explanations of the employment problems of older workers. Herbert Hoover's Committee on Recent Economic Changes found the essence of the problem in a new job mix that placed a premium on youthful vigor. Labor-saving machinery, commented the *Commercial and Financial Chronicle*, had displaced men and reduced opportunity. Even in the midst of the Great Depression, when one would expect such an analysis of unemployment to have been overthrown by the sheer numbers of those without jobs and the collapse of the world economy, the technological argument remained influential, prompting a 1936 investigation of unemployment and technology by the House of Representatives. By 1960 the centrality of technology had emerged as an article of faith among social gerontologists [1, p. 136].

The only legitimate early study of the problem, by English economist William Beveridge in 1909, took a diametrically opposed point of view [2, pp. 12, 116-117,

120]. Machinery, Beveridge said, did not cause unemployment, for if machinery had been making labor superfluous, the price of labor would have fallen with the advance of technology. In fact, the opposite had happened. Although Beveridge reduced unemployment to "specific imperfections of adjustment," including regular changes in industry, fluctuations in industrial activity, and the need for reserves of labor to meet incidental fluctuations in trade, he was well aware that older workers were not absorbed as easily as younger workers. Since technology was not involved, the problem must reside in some characteristic of the older worker which served to inhibit his employment. Older workers, Beveridge reasoned, lacked a quality essential in a rapidly changing society—adaptability. Beveridge had, in effect, reversed the technological argument, moving from an inflexible technology to the inflexible worker.

The printing industry offers some opportunity to test the technological theory in an historical context. As late as 1885 there was apparently no discrimination in the printing industry, a classic craft in which type was set by hand in thousands of small shops. Ottmar Mergenthaler built his first direct-linecasting machine in 1884. When the problem of correcting errors was solved the next year, the success of his machine was assured. By 1892 the inevitability of the Mergenthaler, or Linotype, had been conceded by the few remaining skeptics [3, pp. 100-103].

This was one view: that the Linotype had resulted in the replacement of the older, slower workers, as well as the traveling, or "tramp," printers, as they were called. Other sources confirm the coincidence of the Mergenthaler and age discrimination. Between 1895 and 1915, older workers were phased out for younger men with better eyesight, more speed, and more endurance. Age limits in hiring became commonplace in the industry, and some firms were willing to take the more unusual and unpopular action of releasing older employees [4, p. 155; 5, p. 258]. Mike Bachman, a seventy-eight-year-old traveling printer, was a figure of some fame precisely because he had managed to grow old and remain independent while operating the Linotype. His arrival in Urbana, Illinois in 1922 for a "sit" on the campus newspaper, the *Daily Illini*, was a major event.

For reasons on which masters and journeymen disagreed, Mike Bachman and his kind had become rare. The *Inland Printer*, voice of the employers, was torn between what it saw as the absurdity of superannuation in an industry in which brains, skill, and experience played such a major role and strength and endurance such a minor one, and the inevitability and rationality of the whole process. The latter viewpoint was dominant. Acknowledging that labor had been intensified and that intensification was in some measure responsible for the problems of the older worker, owners located the source of this intensification in two factors: first, technology, which they labeled at once as benign and a mark of the "advance of civilization"; second, the reduction in working hours, for which, of course, the workers were responsible. Technology produced superannuated workers because "the daily task is more exacting." [6, 691-692].

The victims of this reorganization shared with the owners a sense of the inevitability of what was happening to them, but their resignation emerged from an analysis of capitalist modes of production rather than technology itself. They understood that not the machine but the demands placed on its operator by the shop owner were behind "the 'grind' the 'old boy' has to undergo today in order to hold his job." [7, p. 429] Although printers agreed that good eyesight and supple fingers were requisites of Linotype operation, they would not accept the master's argument that the mere operation of typesetting machines damaged the nervous systems and general health of the worker. It was, wrote one typesetter, "the unnatural pace that kills." [8, p. 2] Employees did, however, acknowledge the claim of their employers that the capital requirements imposed on the industry by typesetting machinery entailed certain operating requirements. A $3,500 piece of machinery, the Mergenthaler had to be operated efficiently (extensively and intensively) to be economical [4, pp. 155-157].

By the early 1920's the system that had ousted the older workers was beginning to produce concern among their more youthful replacements. A Memphis machine operator predicted that the "'speeding-up' system is going to put a whole lot of us on the bench at a much younger age than the limits of the pension now allows and we had each better be preparing for that time." [6, p. 430]

Aging machinists faced the same problems as their counterparts in printing and arrived at similar conclusions. Faced with the competition of younger men and liable to dismissal at the first sign of age, machinists who had not yet reached middle age felt compelled to deceive their employers by dyeing their hair. As employers demanded more from their workers and increased the speed of their tools, the older machinists who could not keep pace were replaced by boys. Like the junior printers, these younger employees were often trained outside the apprenticeship system, in part because the increased division of labor made broad-based training unnecessary; and in part because veteran employees would no longer tolerate an institution that produced their competitors and accelerated their superannuation [9, pp. 409-411].

IMPERATIVES OF THE WORKDAY

Technological imperatives and labor-force modification are part of an answer to the conundrum of age discrimination. But why the speedup? Why in the last years of the nineteenth century and the first decade of the twentieth were American employers so interested in squeezing the most from their labor?

Behind the speedup was a set of interrelationships that revolved around the shorter working day. Historians who have studied the politics of the working day have centered their inquiries on the Haymarket Riot of 1886 and questions of social order. For most employers and workers, however, the shorter working day was important largely for its economic implications.

The modern phase of the agitation for a shorter working day began in 1886, when the ten-hour day and the six-day week were the common experience of American labor. A national strike in that year failed, but agitation continued, pushed by national unions [10, p. 160]. In the printing industry, working-day politics had their beginnings in 1887, and within four years the International Typographical Union (ITU) had secured agreements covering limited numbers of the nation's newspaper workers. At the 1898 Syracuse conference, representatives of management and labor agreed to extend the nine-and-a-half-hour day to most of the industry as of November 21, 1898, and the nine-hour day a year later. Through a strike initiated in 1905, the ITU and its companion unions reduced the working day to eight hours in some areas of the industry [11]. Aggregate data for other industries indicates that the printing experience was typical. Nationally, the decline in the working day was gradual from 1892 through about 1915. For eleven selected industries, a major decline of .6 percent occurred in 1892-93, and another, of .9 percent, in 1901-02 [12, pp. 32-48].

In presenting its case for the shorter working day, labor offered a number of rationales: shorter hours would mean more time for recreation, leisure, and education as well as less toil before the machine. For the most part, however, these considerations were peripheral. The shorter working day was a work-sharing program that the printers (capital and labor) believed would help solve the threatening problem of technologically induced unemployment. This analysis was shared at least by cigar makers, painters, engineers, blacksmiths, machinists, iron molders, and silk weavers [10, p. 160]. Work sharing was a goal of the major unions of typesetters and printing pressmen in 1898.

No matter how benign the intent of the labor organizations, the major impact of the shorter working day was to intensify the pressures on older workers. The Syracuse agreement inaugurated a decade of industry interest in cost cutting. Employers who could neither pass their costs on to consumers nor reduce wages sought to lower operating expenditures by eliminating less efficient older employees.

The union printers must share responsibility for the speedup and its consequences for older workers. Pressed by owners at their 1898 convention about potential increases in labor costs, union spokesmen *offered* the speed-up. An organizer for the ITU said he was "satisfied that so far as the compositors are concerned that a man can do in nine hours what he can do in ten. . . . I know I can do in eight hours what I can do in ten." [13] Railroad workers pressing for the eight-hour day made the same argument in 1916 [14, pp. 384-385]. Employers would discover that this was not simply talk, that output could be maintained during a shortened workday. When the steel industry switched to the eight-hour day from the twelve-hour day in 1922, for example, the jump in productivity was prodigious [15, pp. 537-538]. By inviting the speedup in return for the shorter working day, labor organizations bargained away the job rights of older workers who could not produce at higher speeds and of the unemployed, who could be absorbed only if output levels remained stable.

AN ECONOMIC RATIONALE

During the late nineteenth century, economists labored to develop a theoretical framework that would tie the seemingly harmful industrial realities of the shorter working day and higher wages to the desirable goal of increased productivity. Where capitalism had experienced these phenomena at an early date, as in England and Germany, the economic rationale was most developed. Gerhart von Schulze-Gävernitz used the classic case of the English cotton textile industry as evidence that high wages and falling work hours could be reconciled with productivity, through the mechanism of age discrimination [16, p. 17]. In an 1871 work on factory legislation, Ernest von Plener for the first time raised the issue of the age of the work force. Following the introduction of shorter hours, he wrote, "the operatives, *especially the younger ones*, no longer exhausted by excessive bodily effort, produced the same amount, and frequently even turned out more in the shorter time, having, owing to the almost universal system of payment by the piece, a special interest in doing so." [17]

The conviction that the modern workman must be a superior being was especially strong in the classic work of Lujo Brentano, a German economist whose *Hours and Wages in Relation to Production* was published in 1894 [16, p. 17]. Brentano grounded this belief (which one also finds in the work of Frederick W. Taylor) in the liberal classicism of Adam Smith, who had emphasized that the well-fed worker, hopeful of a secure future, would "exert [his] strength to the utmost." [16, p. 17] But Brentano went well beyond Smith in articulating a theoretical relationship between high wages, shorter hours (which together formed the standard of living), and productivity. A higher standard of living, Brentano suggested, changed the outlook of the workman, who under its influence renounced his home and his "accustomed surroundings." His energy awakened, this new worker was capable of more intensive labor. Meals and rest periods could be eliminated. Employers, now possessed of "superior workmen, well paid, well fed, intelligent, strenuous, and eager," would install "faster, more delicate machines," as the English had done in their cotton mills. More than any other single work published in the late nineteenth century, Brentano's *Hours and Wages* provided the capitalist class with a powerful rationale for eliminating older workers who were inefficient and tradition-bound, and for hiring younger workers with more muscle, more energy, and fewer ties to the past [16, p. 17].

Several American economists contributed to this flowering ideology. Three years into the severe depression of the 1870's, Francis Walker suggested relieving the pressure on labor markets through legislation "prohibiting labor for all classes beyond the term which physiological science accepts as consistent with soundness and vigor." [18, p. 78] An interest in productivity rather than unemployment informed Jacob Schoenhof's *Economy of High Wages*, published in 1892. A laissez faire economist and low-tariff Democrat, Scheinhof traveled the world for the Department of State, comparing wage rates and productivity and concluding that productivity increases depended upon rising living standards. As an example of the relationship between low wages and low productivity, Schoenhof pointed to the English nail industry, where "old and young, husbands, wives, and daughters, all work at nail making from four or five in the morning until late at night." [19, pp. 6, 10-11, 225] An economy that offered labor to inefficient workers was not functioning properly.

It remained only for the theory to be incorporated into the mainstream of American economics. That task fell to Alfred Marshall, dean of turn-of-the-century economists and author of a number of popular textbooks. In *Principles of Economics*, Marshall tied elemental physical characteristics to profit [20, pp. 193-203]. Health and strength were the basics of industrial efficiency. Discussing Marshall's physical emphasis in an article written in 1906, well-known statistician Frederick Hoffman concluded that for the nation to maximize its productive potential, given the present capacities of its population, work should normally begin at age fifteen and cease at sixty-five. Economic theory was linked to the workplace in an alliance detrimental to older workers and mandating retirement [21, p. 3].

SUPPORT FROM SCIENCE AND MEDICINE

Science came to the support of capitalist economics in late-nineteenth-century studies of work and fatigue. Prevailing theories originated in the work of George Beard, a physician who in the 1870's popularized the idea of "neurasthenia," a catchall illness with an endless list of symptoms, including anxiety and fatigue. The disease was hereditary and cumulative. "No two persons," writes historian Charles Rosenberg, "would be born with the same amount of nervous force; no two persons would be subjected to the same external pressures. Only those individuals whose endowment of nervous force was inadequate to the demands of daily life succumbed to neurasthenia." [22, p. 249] The closer one's contact with the new technology of the nineteenth century—the steam engine, the Linotype, the sewing machine, even the telegraph—the faster one's supply of nervous force would be consumed, never to be replenished.

In their various forms, these work-related ideas encouraged employers in their proclivity to select younger workers, whose contact with the technological sources of nervous tension had heretofore been limited; they led logically to the notion of a "work life," which naturally ended well before death, perhaps even in middle age; and they defined the older worker as one who had used up a considerable portion of his allotted nervous force.

LINKS TO THE WORKPLACE: SCIENTIFIC MANAGEMENT

The crucial figure linking the theoretical and empirical constructs of the economists and the physicians to the workplace was the corporate manager—and, increasingly after 1885, the "scientific" manager. Here the economist found a resolute ally. Forged in the same competitive and technological environment that had produced the work of Brentano and Marshall, scientific management shared with economics a variety of assumptions and attitudes concerning the relationship between labor and industrial efficiency. Applied to the workplace, scientific management contributed to the displacement of older workers.

From the very first, Frederick W. Taylor and his fellow managers had as their central aim an increase in labor productivity, whatever the state of technology. As the working day decreased during the late nineteenth century, Taylor's phrase "an honest day's work" took on new meaning, and his lifelong interest in "soldiering"[1] was heightened [23, p. 6]. Searching for methods to increase the intensity of labor, scientific managers concentrated on two areas: wage incentives and work-force selection. While the second is often ignored or misunderstood, it was central to Taylor's outlook. In "Shop Management," written in 1903 and one of his most influential papers, Taylor noted that the system owed its success to the rejection of ordinary workmen and the employment only of unusual ones [24, p. 66]. Eight years later, in *The Principles of Scientific Management*, Taylor reemphasized the point in his famous example of Schmidt, a laborer selected for intensive effort in large part because of his superior strength [25, pp. 1-134].

Scientific management demanded more of its workers than a heightened level of intensity; it also required a certain kind of flexibility. If not exactly scientists, these managers and those to follow were experimenters, with the factory as their laboratory. Labor must be willing to cooperate, first in the process of experimentation, then in a reconstruction of its work habits. In the early nineteenth century, capitalists staffed their factories with children, in part because, as Englishman Andrew Ure wrote,

> . . . it is found nearly impossible to convert persons past the age of puberty, whether drawn from rural or from handicraft occupations, into useful factory hands. After struggling for a while to conquer their listless or restive habits, they either renounce the employment spontaneously, or are dismissed by the overlookers on account of inattention [26, p. 100].

A similar obstacle confronted the aggressive management movement and, to a lesser extent, most late-nineteenth and twentieth-century capitalists. They used the same solution as their predecessors: recruit a young, flexible labor force, willing to play the guinea pig, unfettered by craft traditions and dysfunctional work routines.

The Blackford system of character analysis was something of a second cousin to scientific management, having no interest in how work was carried on, but sharing with the larger movement a fascination with objective standards and the

---

[1] "Soldiering" described workers who presumably would consciously work at less than optimum levels of effort.

belief that just as there was one right way to do every job, so also was there for every job one right type of worker. Ostensibly, Katherine Blackford had little to say about older workers [27, p. 29]. Her work contains only one extended reference to age, and that a warning to employers to avoid rigid age regulations: "Years, as we have seen, are not always the test of a man's age. Youthfulness is of the spirit and is not measured by calendars and birthdays. The man who looks young for his years is usually advancing. He who looks older than he should be is slipping backward." [27, p. 29] As the statement indicates, however, physical appearance was fundamental to the Blackford system, the exterior a sound measure of inner qualities.

In spite of Blackford's caveat about age restrictions, her work was saturated with a youth bias. Industrial disturbances, she claimed, occurred when workers were imperfectly suited to their jobs because employers selected men unfitted for their tasks. This was rhetoric, of course, designed to sell the system; but for older workers it was rhetoric with a vengeance, for it implied that the existing, older (as opposed to the potential, younger) work force was composed of misfits. When Blackford suggested the need for society to begin early in youth to develop and determine attitudes and abilities, when she discussed the "young person's" inclinations and preferences, the point was clear: concentrate on the young, for the old are beyond redemption [28, pp. 9-10, 36-37].

This focus on matching worker and job was also present in the industrial health and safety movements. Although these movements originated in part in Progressivism's concern for social justice, each was also generated by several notions of efficiency. Insofar as this was true, older workers did not fare well. Employers in the railroad industry found in the rapidly developing system of seniority a convenient explanation for the shameful accident situation in the first decade of the century [29, p. 907]. Older workers were also held responsible for higher accident rates in industries in which the installation of piecework systems had resulted in a premium on speed [30, pp. 7, 10]. In each case there was just enough truth to the charge for it to have some impact.

POST-1915: THE VALUE
OF THE OLDER WORKER

Before 1915 managerial activity had been dominated by efficiency motivation, and older workers were seen largely as inefficient burdens; after 1915, although age discrimination in hiring continued to worsen, a number of firms, supported by scientific managers and industrial psychologists of the twenties, came to see older employees as valuable for their potential contributions to reduced labor turnover, work-force control, and social conservatism.

Turnover, a factor of some importance in the relationship between age and work, first became a serious problem on Detroit assembly lines in the years after 1914 and for a large proportion of American industry during the First World

War, when firms had to train large numbers of new workers [31, p. 424]. Corporate planning departments (the counterpart of government efficiency commissions) usually recommended transferring older employees to new jobs rather than discharging them when they became relatively inefficient; superannuated employees were to be transferred to a "reserve department," where they would be employed in work of a "fill-in" character [31, p. 424; 32].

As studies of turnover began to reveal that workers over twenty-five were more likely to stay with their employers, the older worker became, for a limited number of companies, a money-making proposition. To some extent, the new interest in turnover was a function of advances in cost accounting, for it was now much easier to isolate any particular cost and its relationship to the total cost of the product. An older, less efficient worker might be tolerated and kept on if, in an accounting sense, his work, relative to that of a hypothetical replacement, was efficient. But decreased labor turnover was also conceived as a method of building conservative values into one's work force, an exercise that assumed special importance in the years immediately following World War I and in the late 1930's. Employers knew that a strike posed a whole range of different questions for older workers than for younger ones, and that their responses to those questions were more likely to be conservative.

Management must have learned a great deal from the 1915 Hartford strike, where Pratt and Whitney employees went out for the eight-hour day without a reduction in wages. Of 3,000 employees, only 1,152 struck, and a substantial proportion of those who remained at work were older [34, pp. 850-851]. Although it is possible that in this case, the issue, the eight-hour day, did not have much appeal for older workers, other evidence suggests another explanation. Older workers *had* taken part in much of the shorter-hour agitation; for many of them, the result was an inability to secure employment when the strikes were over. They remained on the strike rolls of their locals, drawing whatever benefits fellow workers could provide [35, p. 84]. For some, the frustration of unemployment became so great that they were tempted to break with the union.

According to Peter Friedlander's recent study of class and culture in a United Automobile Workers' local in the late 1930's, the conservatism of the older workers was a product not of fears of unemployment but of their continuing ties to European peasant culture [36]. These first-generation immigrants were fearful, submissive, and therefore laggards in the union movement, because of their reluctance to challenge constituted authority—in this case, management.

A version of Friedlander's generational explanation was a part of business ideology. Employers realized that older workers had a different set of values than younger workers, and that social stability could be enhanced by maintaining, or reestablishing, links for the transmission of the older generation's social conservatism. Testifying before a Senate committee investigating unemployment in the late 1920's, James T. Loree, general manager of the Delaware and Hudson

Company, emphasized how his railroad often employed three generations of the same family because the older generations, though less efficient, had a positive influence on the younger men. An Indiana mine superintendent found that by maintaining a reasonable quota of workers over forty-five he had improved the morale of the entire work force and eliminated wildcat strikes [32].

During the 1930's, anxiety over social upheaval brought increased attention to potential sources of stability. Excessive radicalism, associated in the public mind with youth and immaturity, could be countered with age. Research, none of it of lasting scientific validity, supported the perception of old age as a period of conservatism [37, pp. 331, 335].

For employers this meant that older workers would be more likely to resist "outside influences and agitation," a prospect of considerable importance, especially after the economy turned downward in 1937 [38, p. 104]. This analysis had its analogue even among New Deal liberals like Secretary of Labor Frances Perkins, who in late February 1938 announced that American industry had an "overabundance of youth. They have the courage and energy of youth in their dealings with industry and none of the wisdom and practical common sense of those older men with families to support, homes to keep up and children to send to school." A number of industries, Perkins said, would be better off negotiating with older workers. "More could be accomplished," she said, "through the stability of people who have gone by youth and can think in terms of their whole range of experience." [39]

By 1935, a number of studies of health problems as a function of age had demonstrated that older people made reasonably good workers. One of the first, a 1925 study of 1,819 factory workers of the Norton Company in Massachusetts, concluded that for every worker not able to work after age sixty, there were two that could. Older workers were generally in good health, and few had signs of degenerative disease [40, pp. 812-814]. Four years later, another study concluded that a worker's highest earning capacity could be significantly prolonged by medical supervision and skillful placement after age fifty [41, p. 12]. In 1930, employers who would use illness rates as an explanation for age discrimination had to contend with statistical evidence that employees between twenty-five and forty years old were more likely to be sick (defined as two or more days out of work) than those between forty and sixty. The lowest incidence of sickness was found in the fifty-five-to-sixty-four age group. A public-service company in Massachusetts considering compulsory retirement for those over seventy found that the illness experience of that group compared favorably with that of younger employees [42, pp. 385-386]. Research published in 1935 showed that up to age sixty-three, disabling diseases occurred most often among employees in their early thirties [43, p. 245]. Moreover, in the late 1920's studies often began to appear indicating that older workers suffered fewer, if more costly, accidents [44, p. 68-69].

CONTINUED DISCRIMINATION

Neither the demands of social stability nor the new health studies suddenly made an anachronism of age discrimination. Most employers continued to prefer younger to older workers. In the broadest sense, the choice was usually between a stable, conservative work force that blended youth with age and produced moderate short-term efficiency, and a more mobile, potentially more radical and militant work force made up largely of highly productive younger workers. The choice was between two kinds of efficiency—productive and social—and between two attitudes toward future profits, one more immediate than the other. Within this continuum compounded of control and productivity, employers were sometimes able to achieve one without sacrificing the other. This was the case with turnover reduction, for here the older worker offered both efficiency and stability. Group incentives, popular after Elton Mayo's Hawthorne experiments of the late 1920's, were similarly attractive, for they allowed corporations to maintain an older work force by stimulating slower workers to acceptable levels of productivity [45, pp. 92-93]. For the most part, however, the corporation operated on the efficiency end of the continuum, and personnel managers, unconvinced of the viability of an older work force, consistently practiced various forms of discrimination.

In the health movement, older workers remained pawns in larger games, their needs ancillary to industrial efficiency and control. Full of the typical Progressive passion for order and standards, statistician Hoffman had in 1906 called for the establishment of physical requirements for entry and continuance in different trades and occupations, as an aid in "eliminating the physically unfit from recognized unhealthful or injurious employment." [21, p. 13]

The absence of job-performance standards did not deter government and industry from developing and applying the physical examination, even though the technique implied that standards existed and workers were affected as if they did. Examinations were apparently first used in the 1890's; by the late 1920's about one firm in five put its workers through a physical [46, pp. 959-963]. These examinations served several purposes. They played a role in the administration of retirement and pension systems, for some employers used the exams to exclude unreasonably large numbers of older applicants from employment [47, pp. 20-21]. Railroad workers believed that their employers were using the physical to enforce age restrictions, neglecting its administration when labor requirements dictated, and as a weapon against labor organizations. During the 1930's, twenty-seven railroad employees in the vicinity of Council Bluffs, Iowa petitioned the president of the United States to sign the railroad retirement bill recently passed by Congress. They argued that railroads without pension plans were "at the present time giving a rigid physical examination and in many cases taking the old men out of service mostly on account of their eyes." [48] The Mid-Continent Oil Company admitted that it was one of many enterprises that applied the physical examination more rigidly to older applicants than younger ones, a practice justified, it said, because of "unjust claims" against the company by employees with physical defects. Through the rigid physical examination, the company availed itself of the protection available under state law, according to which claims were not allowable if the employer could show that the employee had the physical ailment before employment. The problem, concluded a company official, "is not so much with age as it is with physical condition." [49, pp. 23-24] Thus, older workers were often victims of an open-ended device that was seldom applied in the interests of health.

THE SALESMAN: A CASE STUDY

The experience of the salesman—the foremost occupational symbol of the twentieth-century economy of consumption, distribution, and mass markets—illustrates a variety of these phenomena. It also provides evidence for the hypothesis that older workers were more likely to suffer employment handicaps in industries where the development of new methodologies was abrupt and sporadic.[2] Neither an executive nor a member of the working class, the salesman remained outside the corporate and union bureaucracies, which by 1920 were beginning to protect minimal numbers of workers from unemployment and old age. He was uniquely vulnerable to change in fashion and consumer taste, to the competitive markets of the early twentieth century and the business cycle. Although the salesman's skills would seem to have been relatively easily transferable from one industry or firm to another, this aspect of the occupation was circumscribed by the increasingly sophisticated nature of products and sales training.

Between 1900 and 1930, salesmen, particularly those over forty, were victimized by changing definitions and requirements of their occupation, a revolution as real and disruptive as simultaneous developments in the technology of automobile manufacture. This revolution began in 1903 with the publication of *Salesmanship*, a self-styled first attempt to establish a literature on the science of selling. Almost from the first issue there was some recognition in the journal that older salesmen might be ill suited to this new professionalism. These early pieces at once denied that a problem had to exist and warned of its coming:

> Let me say that a man is only as old as he acts, and it is his own fault if he is shelved for a younger man [50, p. 143].

[2] This hypothesis was developed by Elliott Dunlap Smith, professor of industrial engineering at Yale University. In several forums, including an important meeting of the American Management Association in 1930, Smith argued that the obsolescence of older workers was not, as others had said, a function of the psychological deficiencies incident to the aging process, but in fact followed from management's own failure to apply its principles scientifically. Continuity was crucial. Forced unemployment was most likely to occur "when periods of managerial and engineering stagnation are followed by spurts of intensive progress."

In little more than two years, the journal had dropped its tentative approach and had taken up a full-scale attack on the unambitious men in the "Used-to-Be class," the old men with their anecdotes of crucial big sales.

The critique focused on the inability of older salesmen to adopt the methods of the modern corporation or to adapt to a changing economic and technological environment. These deficiencies were variously ascribed to a natural stubbornness that comes with age, to learning disabilities, and to prejudice against anything new. Older salesmen were further disadvantaged when, after 1920, corporations seeking people with technical training turned increasingly to colleges. Rather than educate thirty- and forty-year-old workers to market the new technology, General Electric hired engineers and Bristol-Myers recruited college graduates with training in pharmacy, medicine, or dentistry. It was commonly believed that older salesmen could be trained and retrained only with recently developed techniques designed to overcome inherent resistance [51, p. 507; 52, pp. 15-17].

These policies reflected real changes in marketing methods which emerged with chain stores, retail consolidations, industrial concentration, and scientific buying. As chemists, mechanical engineers, and other technical personnel replaced shop superintendents as buyers of industrial products, and as chain-store buyers, aided by statistical departments and laboratories, replaced the grocer and the druggist as purchasers of consumer goods, the old-time salesman who had succeeded on the basis of personal contact and the force of personality became an anachronism. Another technical consideration—the tendency, particularly after 1920, to market products toward youth—also induced employers to sell through younger personnel [53, p. 798].

Although stamina and endurance continued to be perceived as important qualities in the 1920's and 1930's, they were never as important as in the decade after 1905. After about 1915, however, the older salesman was faced with a related obstacle, one for which he could not prepare, even with regular exercise. Convinced of the crucial importance of matching person and task, and lacking objective standards to guide the process, personnel managers were drawn for at least a decade to a group of pseudoscientists who claimed that character (and therefore ability to sell) could be inferred from physical appearance. After Katherine Blackford, whose theories had considerable influence in the personnel field, Grant Nablo, with superb photos designed to demonstrate relationships between size and shape of the head and behavior, was perhaps the best known.

At the retail level, applicants who survived the initial contact with the personnel manager because of an unusually well-preserved countenance faced another, also presumably scientific, variant of age discrimination. The age of the employee was expected to be suited to the department within the establishment. This could benefit the aging job-seeker: "mature" women, for example, were considered ideal for selling infants' wear, coats, dresses, suits and expensive fabrics; toiletries salespeople, on the other hand, were expected to be young enough to reflect "youth, attractiveness, and all the other qualifications that the buyers of this merchandise hope to gain through its use." [54, p. 380]

Discrimination in sales began to ease after 1924. Customers as well as personnel managers were put off by too much vigor, enthusiasm, confidence, and pep. Employers found older salesmen less likely to irritate difficult customers and more likely to succeed with the abusive customers called "hardshells." Corporations increasingly desired career men, willing to remain with the enterprise and learn the new, often complex product lines [55, p. 46]. Sales executives in the printing trades seemed to agree that the more technical the product, the older the salesman could be and retain his efficiency; by the late 1930's they had also become firmly convinced of the excessive turnover costs that accrued to firms hiring younger salesmen. When *American Business* published its survey findings in 1937, demonstrating that the average age of "star" salesmen was forty-two and that older salesmen were the best producers in a number of lines, the problem would seem to have come full circle [56, p. 46].

AGE DISCRIMINATION BECOMES A SOCIAL AND POLITICAL PROBLEM

There were those, even in the late 1920's and early 1930's, who too easily dismissed age discrimination as a function of the youth fetish and pronounced its imminent demise [57], and others, of greater influence, who denied that a problem existed. Among the latter were Glenn A. Bowers and Murray Latimer, leading spirits behind Industrial Relations Counselors, Incorporated, a prestigious business advisory agency with links to major corporations. Bowers and Latimer shared the view that although hiring limits existed, they were related to demonstrable and legitimate job requirements [58, pp. 327-328]. In 1930 the Associated Industries argued that there was no general discrimination against workers over forty. Two years later the Bureau of the Census released a report based on 1930 figures which (given the massive problems with unemployment statistics) offered some legitimate evidence that age discrimination between thirty-five and forty-five was less severe than had been thought. Unemployment for the group was estimated at less than 2.5 percent. But the Bureau's statistics also revealed unemployment among the fifty-five-to-fifty-nine age group of 7 percent, and over 13 percent for those between sixty and sixty-four [59]. Those who argued that age discrimination should not be taken seriously because the forty-five-to-sixty-four age group was a larger percentage of the labor force in 1930 than in 1890 were misguided; the increase, though real, would have occurred naturally, for the population itself was aging. It was, moreover, in part the product of the elimination from the work force of those over sixty-five and under twenty; child-labor legislation and retirement had, for the moment, eased the pressure on the middle-aged [60, p. 39].

Nonetheless, in the five years after 1925, age discrimination came to be perceived as the serious social problem it had been for more than two decades. A study by the New York State Committee on Old Age Security, completed in 1932, found hiring discrimination began at age thirty-five for men, thirty for women. The first bulletin of the California Department of Industrial Relations concluded that arbitrary discharge of workers because of age was becoming general policy in the late 1920's. A problem that might have been tolerated had it remained within the industrial working class and the unorganized middle class of salesmen, had by this time aroused concern in the increasingly organized public sector and in those professions, such as accounting and engineering, most dependent on the private sector [61]. As the economic system either released older workers or refused to hire them, organizations with an interest in old-age dependency came to share the sense of urgency. The American Association for Labor Legislation and the American Association for Old Age Security saw age discrimination as a problem to be met through the fuller development of public pension systems [62].

This ferment produced the first intensive studies of age discrimination. These inquiries, lacking in historical insight, pointed to the technological environment of the 1920's and to a variety of short-term factors, particularly pensions, group insurance, and workmen's compensation, which as explanations of age discrimination conveniently ignored the historical needs of a capitalist economy for efficiency and control. Data from a massive study by the National Association of Manufacturers demonstrated that these short-term factors were less important in the decision to establish an age limit than the perceived physical problems of the older worker [63]. Insurance company figures, less reliable because the companies had a vested interest in demonstrating that the underwriting of group life policies did not lead to discrimination, produced the same conclusion. Nonetheless, the social insurance argument had considerable appeal. The American Federation of Labor, eager to shift pension controls from the private corporations to the more neutral hands of the state and national governments, and unwilling to come to grips with the potential long-term divisiveness of the age discrimination issue for its members, leaned heavily on the contention that private benefit programs were conducive to discriminatory practices. A major segment of the corporate community also welcomed the opportunity to trace social dislocation to welfare policy [64, p. 46].

SUMMARY

One cannot expect of an age that it possess a coherent, historically and culturally informed overview of its institutions; but one can expect that a society seriously interested in exploring the work problems of a major segment of its population would center its inquiry on the workplace. This did not occur. Instead, analysis focused on a series of short-term institutional factors that, once accepted as the cause of age discrimination, could and did serve as a vehicle for a critique of social legislation. The considerable interest in the 1920's in technology came closer to explaining discrimination, but the dominant view made of technology a liberating force, the progenitor of the "new leisure." Contemporary analyses ignored the matrix of conditions that had generated age discrimination in the late nineteenth century: a competitive economic system, primarily concerned with the intensification of labor and therefore in the speed of its technology, driven by market structures and a critical externality, the shorter working day; and depending for profit on superior workmen. The perspective of the late 1920's or early 1930's could not reveal that the new interest in middle-aged and older workers emerged as well from the economic system, as its compelling drive for efficiency was attenuated and supplemented by the desire for stability and control. It helped that research showed that older workers were not so terribly inefficient and that Americans had, by 1925, recovered from the worst fears of cultural senescence.

This analysis implies a good deal about the reform movement of the late 1920's: it was generated within the economic system; it served at least some employers; and the solutions implied in its own analysis were superficial and peripheral to the sources of age discrimination.

The solutions that might have made a difference—massive job creation; a willingness to continue production with older forms of technology; a reduction in the operating speed of the technology—were not considered viable options.

Retirement was one of several means available to a business culture committed to restructuring the age components of the work force. Workers might be fired outright, of course, but such a policy was difficult for most public and private employers to carry out. Retirement was impersonal and egalitarian in its application. It allowed the powerful turn-of-the-century impulse toward efficiency to coexist with a system of labor-management relations that was still permeated with personal and human relationships. After 1915, a minority of employers found older workers attractive. Overall, however, discrimination did not diminish. Most employers continued to favor younger workers, and after 1925 retirement came to be seen as a realistic antidote to unemployment in depressed industries and in the economy at large.

REFERENCES

1. *The Index*, September 1929.
2. W. Beveridge, *Unemployment: A Problem of Industry*, London, 1909.
3. J. S. Thompson, *History of Composing Machines*, New York, 1904 (reprint edition, 1972).
4. *Typographical Journal, 13*, August 1898.
5. _____, *26*, March 1905.
6. *Inland Printer, 39*, August 1907.
7. *Typographical Journal, 61*, October 1922.

8. H. W. Cooke, The Machine Operator and His Nerves, *Typographical Journal*, 26:1, January 1905.

9. J. O'Connell, The Manhood Tribute to the Modern Machine, *Machinists' Monthly Journal*, 18, May 1906.

10. H. David, *The History of the Haymarket Affair: A Study in the American Social-Revolutionary and Labor Movements*, New York, 1936.

11. L. M. Powell, *The History of the United Typothetae of America*, Chicago, 1926.

12. L. Teper, Hours of Labor, *Johns Hopkins University Studies in Historical and Political Science*, Series L, No. 1, Baltimore, 1932.

13. United Typothetae, *Proceedings of the 12th Annual Convention of the United Typothetae of America*, Milwaukee, Wisconsin, August 23-26, 1898.

14. O. Bates, What Is the Significance of the Eight-Hour Working Day?, *Railway Review*, 59, September 16, 1916.

15. *Iron Age*, 95, March 1915.

16. L. Brentano, *Hours and Wages in Relation to Production*, (W. A. Arnold, tr.), London, 1894.

17. From *Die Englische Fabrikgesetzgebung*, Vienna, 1871, quoted in L. Brentano *Hours and Wages in Relation to Production*, pp. 29-30. Emphasis added.

18. Quoted in C. Haber, Mandatory Retirement in 19th Century America: The Conceptual Basis for a New Work Cycle, *Journal of Social History*, 12, Fall 1978.

19. J. Schoenhof, The Economy of High Wages: An Inquiry into the Cause of High Wages and Their Effects on Methods and Cost of Production, 1892; reprint edition, 1974, New York.

20. A. Marshall, *Principles of Economics*. 8th Edition, New York, 1948. The first edition appeared in 1890.

21. F. L. Hoffman, Physical and Medical Aspects of Labor and Industry, *Annals of the American Academy of Political and Social Sciences*, 27, May 1906.

22. C. E. Rosenberg, The Place of George M. Beard in Nineteenth-Century Psychiatry, *Bulletin of the History of Medicine*, 36, May-June 1962.

23. M. J. Nadworny, *Scientific Management and the Unions, 1900-1932: An Historical Analysis*, Cambridge, Massachusetts, 1955.

24. H. B. Drury, Scientific Management: A History and Criticism, *Studies in History, Economics and Public Law*, 65:2, New York, 1915.

25. H. Braverman, Labor and Monopoly Capitalism: The Degradation of Work in the 20th Century, *Monthly Review*, 26, July-August 1974.

26. Quoted in S. A. Marglin, What Do Bosses Do? The Origins and Functions of Hierarchy in Capitalist Production, *Review of Radical Political Economics*, 6, Summer 1974.

27. K. M. H. Blackford, *Employers' Manual: Instructions to Employment Supervisors and Other Executives in the Use of the Blackford Employment Plan*, New York, 1912.

28. K. M. H. Blackford and A. Newcomb, *Analyzing Character: The New Science of Judging Men*; Misfits in Business, The Home & Social Life, 2nd ed., New York, 1916.

29. *Railroad Trainmen's Journal*, 21, December 1904.

30. J. Wrench, Speed Accidents: A Study of the Relation between Piecework and Industrial Accidents, University of Birmingham, England, Faculty of Commerce and Social Science, Discussion Papers, Series E.: *Social Science Methodology*, *17*:3, May 1972.
31. L. Erskine and T. Cleveland, Jr., New Men for Old: The Hiring and Firing Problem in Industry, *Everybody's Magazine*, *36*, April 1917.
32. F. H. Colvin, *Labor Turnover, Loyalty and Output: A Consideration of the Trend of the Times as Shown by the Results of War Activities in the Machine Shops and Elsewhere*, New York, 1919.
33. H. A. Hopf, The Planning Department as a Factor in the Modern Office Organization, *Efficiency Society Journal*, *4*, November 1915.
34. *Iron Age*, *96*, October 1915.
35. *Typographical Journal*, *31*, July 1907.
36. P. Friedlander, *The Emergence of a UAW Local, 1936-1939: A Study in Class and Culture*, Pittsburgh, 1975.
37. F. L. Ruch, The Differential Decline of Learning Ability in the Aged as a Possible Explanation of their Conservatism, *Journal of Social Psychology*, *5*, August 1934.
38. Philadelphia Industrial Relations Association, Report on Older Workers, *Personnel Journal*, *17*, 1938-1939.
39. *New York Times*, part 2, p. 1, February 20, 1938.
40. W. I. Clark and E. B. Simmons, Older Workers in Industry Remain in Good Health, *The Nation's Health*, *7*, December 1925.
41. _____, The Fate of Old Employees, *Journal of Industrial Hygiene*, *11*, January 1929.
42. D. K. Brundage, The Incidence of Disease among Wage Earning Adults, *Journal of Industrial Hygiene*, *12*, December 1930.
43. S. D. Collins, A General View of the Causes of Illness and Death at Specific Ages, *Public Health Reports*, *50*, February 1935.
44. C. S. Slocombe, The Dangerous Age in Industry, *National Safety News*, *22*, July 1930.
45. C. C. Balderston, Group Incentives: Some Variations in the Use of Group Bonus and Gang Piece Work, *Research Studies*, Vol. 9, Industrial Relations Department, Wharton School of Finance and Commerce, University of Pennsylvania, Philadelphia, 1930.
46. *Railroad Trainmen's Journal*, *17*, November 1900.
47. New York State, Senate Committee on Civil Service, *Second Report of the Senate Committee on Civil Service in Relation to the Standardization of the Public Employments of the State*, No. 29, Albany, New York, 1917.
48. Letter with petition, August 19, 1935, Franklin Delano Roosevelt Papers, Franklin Delano Roosevelt Library, Hyde Park, New York, Official Files, 1095, "Railroad Retirement Board."
49. A. S. James, No Hiring Age Limit is Fixed by Mid-Continent Companies, *National Petroleum News*, *28*, November 1936.
50. R. N. Hull, The Fourth Profession, *Salesmanship*, *1*, November 1903.
51. E. A. Means, Why Bristol-Myers' Men Stick, *Sales Management*, *32*, May 15, 1933.

52. W. A. Sredenschek, *et al.*, Sales Personnel Techniques, *American Management Association Marketing Series*, No. 39, New York, 1940.
53. *Sales Management and Advertising Weekly*, *16*, December 29, 1928.
54. J. W. Fisk, Organization of Retail Selling Force, *Salesmanship*, *4*, November 1916.
55. *Advertising and Selling*, *18*, March 16, 1932.
56. *Printers' Ink*, *180*, July 15, 1937.
57. *New York Times*, May 18, 1930, Part 3, p. 10.
58. G. A. Bowers, Employment, Wages and Industrial Relations, *Factory and Industrial Management*, *79*, February 1930.
59. *New York Times*, October 12, 1932, p. 20.
60. *Dun's Review*, *47*, February 1939.
61. *New York Times*, November 19, 1932, p. 17.
62. Mss. paper by John B. Andrews, January 1922, in American Association for Labor Legislation Papers, Labor Management Documentation Center, Labor and Industrial Relations Institute, Cornell University, Ithaca, New York, microfilm reel 65.
63. *New York Times*, March 21, 1929, p. 23.
64. *Iron Age*, *134*, July 5, 1934.

Reprinted with permission of Yale University Press. From William Graebner, *A History of Retirement: The Meaning of Function of an American Institution, 1885-1978*, Comm: Yale University pp. 18-53, 1982.

PART IV. AGING
AS A WOMEN'S ISSUE

Former Director of the National Institute on Aging, Dr. Robert Butler has pointed out that "the problems of old age in America are largely the problems of women." His statement holds true not only demographically, but also in terms of the harsh socioeconomic realities of growing old female in the United States, and in many other advanced capitalist societies.

This section begins with a chapter, now more than a decade old, in which Lewis and Butler pointedly asked why the women's liberation movement was ignoring older women. An earlier version of this material was rejected for publication in *Ms. Magazine*—perhaps because as the authors note, the issues of the early women's liberation movement were primarily the issues of young and middle aged women.

In the decade since Lewis and Butler's article was first published, women's liberation *has* embraced the problems of older women and movement founder Betty Friedman, at age sixty-three, has proclaimed "elderly liberation" her new cause. But much further movement in this direction is needed. Recent concern with the feminization of poverty, for example, must include an appreciation of the "graying" of the feminization of poverty, as women not only enter old age poorer than men but grow poorer with age as a consequence of widowhood, inequities in pensions and social security and higher health care expenditures.

In Chapter 13 Estes, Gerard and Clarke address women and the economics of aging, with particular attention to the economic and policy arrangements that assure the maintenance of gender based inequities through the life cycle. The interrelationships between women's roles as caregivers, workers and beneficiaries are examined, and are in turn related to issues of social policy and income.

Attention to the sources of previous socio-structural and policy inequities are seen as critical prerequisites to the amelioration of their negative impact and to the eventual development of new policies designed to avoid the furthering of existing inequities.

Of the many areas in which the current gender inequities are played out, few are as striking as that of women's retirement. The final chapter in this section addresses this topic, examining the ways in which the sexual division of labor and the dual labor market contribute to the shaping of the retirement experience of women in the United States. The meaning of retirement for different social classes of women is also examined, and points up again the utility of a political economy perspective for understanding the ways in which facets of the aging experience are shaped and conditioned by one's placement in the social structure.

CHAPTER 12

Why Is Women's Lib Ignoring Old Women?

MYRNA I. LEWIS
ROBERT N. BUTLER

There are more than fifteen million women in this country who are sixty-five years of age and older. Yet they are not yet being widely involved in the women's liberation movement. Neither the truly oppressed condition of old women nor their potential political and economic strength is firing the otherwise active imagination of the women's movement. The issues of women's liberation have been largely the issues of the young and middle-aged—day-care centers, abortion reform, educational discrimination, etc. Obviously these are not the most immediate problems for old women who have been discriminated against all their lives and as a result are frequently poverty-stricken, socially isolated, and culturally obsolete. The National Women's Political Caucus which first met in Washington, D.C., in July 1971 formed a policy council which included no women members over sixty-five years of age. Interestingly, only one member was under thirty-five years and the younger women immediately rallied to protest discrimination against youth. But there was no such protest from old women.

Why is a socially sensitive movement like women's liberation neglecting its older "sisters," leaving them to fend for themselves? Why aren't old women raising vehement protestations? The answer to such questions requires a look at a newly defined but very familiar prejudice called "ageism." Ageism can be described as a process of systematic stereotyping of and discrimination against people because they are old, just as racism and sexism accomplish this with skin color and gender. Old people are categorized as senile, rigid in thought and manner, old-fashioned in morality and skills. Ageism allows all of us to see old people as "different" from those of us who are younger. We subtly cease to identify with them as humans and thus we can feel more comfortable about their frequently severe social and economic plight. We can avoid the notion that our productivity-minded society really has no use for the nonproducers—in this case, those who have reached retirement age. There is an added factor in ageism: unlike the racists and sexists who never need fear becoming black or female, ageists are all too aware that if they live long enough they will end up being "old" and thus the object of their own prejudice. Ageism is a thinly disguised attempt to avoid the personal reality of human aging and death. The traditional buffers of religious beliefs are in a process of challenge and change. No general ethical or philosophical system has yet evolved to deal with human life and death as a whole. The individual fills the frightening vacuum with a self-protective prejudice, and old people are the victims. As is often the case with prejudice, the victims tend to believe the negative definition of themselves. Old people in this country are still silently accepting the treatment meted out to them. They have not yet reached the point of moral outrage and outcry but there are increasing glimmers of demand for "senior power."

For females, ageism has a special bitterness, combined as it is with the cultural denigration of the female. Little girls quickly are taught that in this society it will be much tougher to be an old woman than an old man. Fairy tales set the mood with depictions of old hags, evil crones, scary old witches, and nasty biddies of all sorts. In real life, unmarried aunts are scorned as "old maids." Even beloved grandma becomes a family nuisance as she outlives grandpa and experiences and expresses the emotional and physical facts of aging. The message comes across early in life that a woman is valuable in order to bear children and raise them, and perhaps to nurse father in his dotage, but after that it's clearly downhill all the way. Therefore it is no surprise that women's liberation is currently experiencing a blind spot with respect to age since ageism is a national habit which has yet to be challenged by even the old themselves.

OLD WOMEN AND WOMEN'S LIB NEED EACH OTHER

Our contention is that older women not only need the liberation movement but that they have the potential to add significantly to the strength and viability of the struggle for women. Consider for a moment that older women are growing rapidly in total numbers and in proportion to the rest of the population. Old men and women now represent 11,5 percent of the population. With medical breakthroughs in cancer and heart disease they could make up 25 percent by the turn of the century. The elderly have a far higher rate of voter registration (90 percent) and actual voter participation (two-thirds of those registered do vote regularly) than any other age group. Added to this is the fact that there are numbers of women who have inherited enormous wealth from their departed husbands—wealth which might become a resource for the women's movement if older women were encouraged to join. If this combination of voting strength and wealth were found in any other group, politicians would be trampling each other in the rush to gain their favor and support. But no one has yet been able to grasp the notion that old women can be anything but "old" and "women," not even elderly women themselves.

The Low Visibility of the Elderly Woman

One of the traditions of the American social system is to keep its "undesirables" out of sight. For years we knew little about the poor or the blacks until they were "discovered" with great alarm. Even today such elementary information as an accurate census count of Chicanos, Indians, and black males is not available. In the case of the elderly and specifically the elderly women, facts are gathered but they lie hidden in government reports and scholarly papers. A White House Conference on Aging comes along every ten years to dust them off, but then it's back to the shelf. Newspapers and magazines rarely see the condition of individual old people as news unless they are doing something extraordinary. Elderly women must be truly exceptional to be noticed—Helena Rubenstein at ninety-three running a business empire, Grandma Moses painting primitive art, Martha Graham still dancing at seventy-six, Helen Hayes performing superbly at seventy or Lil Hardin dying at the piano at seventy-one while playing a jazz tribute to Louis Armstrong. To be anything less than remarkable is to be invisible.

Profile of the Elderly Woman

What is the life of an average older woman like? In general being an old woman means living alone, on a low or poverty-level income, often in substandard housing with inadequate medical care and little chance of employment to supplement resources.

FINANCIAL STATUS

A small proportion of older women are well off financially and some few have inherited enormous wealth. At the other end of the spectrum are those women who have been poor all their lives and who can expect greater poverty in old age. But in between these two groups are a multitude of women who lived comfortably throughout their lives and first experienced poverty after they became old—they are the "newly poor." Poverty is not reserved for women alone since old men too are often in dire financial condition. Yet whenever poverty is found, it is generally more profound and of greater consequence for women. In 1982 according to the official poverty index of $4,626.00 yearly per person sixty-five and over (surely a stringent estimation of living needs), 3.9 million of the nation's 26 million elderly men and women lived on or below the poverty line. By a more realistic definition of poverty, almost 40 percent of the elderly or about 10 million are poor or near poor. It is a common misconception that Social Security and Medicare adequately provide for the elderly. In 1982 the average Social Security benefits for a retired man were $483.00 a month while women averaged $305.50. Single black women averaged only $254.00 monthly. Medicare covers about 38 percent of health needs, so available income must go not only for food and shelter but also for health expenses. Little is left for clothing, recreation, travel, or anything beyond bare survival items.

Even women with sufficient income have problems because many of them do not know how to handle money for their own benefit. It is here particularly that societal patterns of passivity and accedence to masculine financial management shows itself. Women tend to turn their money over to men to manage—bank representatives, guardians, lawyers, male children, etc. Those who do take care of their own often are ill-prepared and unable to make sound decisions. A study of business and professional women found that they were good savers but suffered badly from inflation because of the way they invested. These were women who were well above average in income, job level, education, and years of experience but they knew little about investments or how to increase capital. Money management was a passive activity in which they preferred the false security of savings, cash, and annuities over a sounder investment program which required an understanding of economics and finance. This seems to be typical of most older women and women in general.

EMPLOYMENT OPPORTUNITIES

Close to six million women aged 55 and above work to make ends meet and keep themselves active. Many had never worked before and are employed in dead-end unskilled jobs. Others may have worked previously but earned less money than men all along the life cycle. Both situations result in lower Social Security and private retirement benefits and, combined with a longer life span for women, produce a lower income which must be stretched over a longer number of years.

Employers are reluctant to hire older women because of the stereotyped attitude that older women are not adaptable to today's jobs and technology—old women are seen as cantankerous, sexually unattractive, overly emotional, and unreliable because of health problems—yet studies indicate that they make exceptionally good employees, with lower turnover, higher productivity, and less absenteeism than men or younger women. The government itself historically has been one of the worst offenders on employment. For example, in 1969 the Department of Health, Education and Welfare decided to close the door on any women over thirty-five years as potential appointees for high-level jobs in the Department. Later this was changed to age fifty. While this kind of overt discrimination on the basis of age is no longer legal in the United States, covert examples of age prejudice and discrimination are not uncommon.

The Social Security system discriminates against older women in a number of ways. We have mentioned that women earn less, and therefore receive fewer benefits. Many jobs held by women have only recently been covered under Social Security—agriculture, hotel and restaurant work, hospital jobs, and domestic work (the latter is still frequently uncovered). Much work done by women has earned them nothing—primarily work as housewives and mothers. In 1980, the divorced wives of retired workers received an average social security payment of only $177.20 per month. If a man and woman are married, they may receive less Social Security than if they were not married, thus some old couples live together without marrying in order to obtain the benefits they both have earned. The Social Security "means test," which limits the amount of income which can be earned, is especially hard on women since they live longer and use up their resources. Many are reduced to bootleg work to hide their income from the government because they need to survive. Finally, Social Security is a regressive tax with a base rate of $35,000.00; therefore, women pay more proportionately than men because of their lower incomes.

MARITAL AND FAMILY STATUS

Of the 15.6 million women age sixty-five and above, over 52 percent are widows and an additional 9.4 percent are divorced or single. Thus, 62 percent of all older women are on their own, an ironic fact when one remembers that older women, more than any younger group, were raised from childhood to consider themselves dependent on men. Most of them married early, had little education or career preparation, functioned totally as housewives for forty to fifty years and then, *shock!* Their job descriptions, already diminished when their children grew up, vanish completely with the death of their husbands. They are left both unemployed and familyless at a point when they are least able to adjust.

Why so many widows? Women are outliving men everywhere in the world where they no longer perform physical labor and where maternal mortality is reduced. In the United States more boy babies are born than girls, but girls begin to outnumber them at age 18 and by the time they reach age 65 there are 146 females per 100 males in the 65 and above age group. This increases to 176 females at age 75. The difference in life expectancy seems to be a rather recent and poorly understood occurrence. In 1920 men could expect to live 53.6 years and women, 54.6—only one year difference. But by 1980 a seven and a half year spread was evident, with a life expectancy for men of 70 years and women, 77.5 years. Women are given the dubious privilege of living longer than men, after years of financial and psychological dependency—ill-prepared to survive on their own, much less to use their added years with enjoyment and fulfillment.

Old men have tremendous advantage over old women when it comes to marriage. Because they tend to marry younger women who will outlive them, they are much less likely to be widowed. More than that, they can count on a fairly healthy spouse to nurse them as they age. Should their wife die prematurely, they have more options for remarriage. At age sixty-five when men number 11 million, the 15 million women already outnumber them by 4 million and the odds "improve" as men grow older. In remarrying, men can bypass their own age group altogether and marry women from sixty-five all the way down to girls in their twenties and teens. We can readily see what is happening to older women in all of this. Their chances for remarriage are small. Only 22,000 find a second husband each year and the rest must resign themselves to being alone or scrambling for the remaining unattached men. It is socially frowned upon for an older woman to date or marry a man much younger than herself, a blatant form of discrimination when men are freely allowed this option.

This leads to the question of what older women do about sex. There are problems other than just the unavailability of older men. Many younger people assume old women have no sexual interests whatsoever. They are the neuters of our culture who have mysteriously metamorphosized from desirable young sex objects, to mature, sexually "interesting" women, and finally, at about age fifty, they descend in steady decline to sexual oblivion. This is the way society sees it. But this is not the way a lot of old women see it. They don't understand why older men can be considered "sexy" but never older women. They are angered that old men can attract younger women and be commended for their prowess, whereas older women are seen as "depraved" or "grasping for lost youth" when they show an interest in sex at all, let alone, younger men. Biologically, the cards are stacked heavily in favor of women. A woman in reasonably good health can expect to respond to and enjoy sex in her seventies and eighties, and even nineties if she has maintained a frame of mind which encourages this. Orgasms are possible, but as with younger women, they are not essential to the total enjoyment of sex. The situation is necessarily more precarious for the older man. He cannot simply relax and enjoy sex with the same ease, since "performance" is a more crucial factor.

Yet in spite of their capacities, older women have limited sexual outlets. They have been trained and locked in by the culture to accept the idea that they are no longer desirable sexual partners and that only younger women have sexual prerogatives. We are all familiar with the origins of this idea—namely, that women are sexy as long as they are young and pretty and able to enhance a man's feelings of status and power. What would happen if women had equal access to status and power on their own? Presumably, they might suddenly appear much sexier and attractive, whatever their ages. At the very least older women should demand to be recognized for their true sexual interests and capacities. It is in their interest to insist that something be done about increasing the male life-expectancy as well as allowing women the same sexual and companionship possibilities now enjoyed by males.

LIVING ARRANGEMENTS

Thirty-four percent, of elderly women live alone, 18 percent live with husbands, 39 percent with relatives, 4 percent with nonrelatives, and only 5 percent in institutions. Many women never lived alone until old age. It is estimated that up to 60 percent live in substandard housing. Although two-thirds of all elderly own their own homes which were purchased forty or fifty years previously, many cannot afford to maintain them. Rising inflation, cost of utilities, taxes (for example, an average 30 percent increase from 1963-69), combined with a fixed income, leaves old people, and more often old women, unable to meet expenses—they scrape by, cutting corners on food and all other needs. Moreover, homes are often located in deteriorating sections of town as are the cheaper rental locations. Old women, white and nonwhite, are easy victims for robbery, burglary, purse-snatching, and even rape. Determined to remain in their homes, they will deny themselves food, medical care, and safety before they will move to unfamiliar surroundings.

HEALTH

Old women can't count on the medical profession. Few doctors are interested in them. A familiar medical school term for an old woman is "crock," and their physical and emotional discomforts are often characterized as "postmenopausal syndromes" until they live too long for this to be an even faintly reasonable diagnosis. After that they are assigned the category of "senility," which is an excuse for no treatment at all since senility is not seen as disease-based. Doctors complain about being harassed by their elderly female patients and claim that they are merely lonely and seeking attention. Yet old age brings realistic health problems which deserve careful diagnosis and treatment. Eighty-six percent of all older people have some kind of chronic health condition and both depression and hypochondriasis commonly accompany these many physical ailments. Perhaps one step toward assuring better medical care would be the presence of many more female doctors who could, if able to overcome their own ageism, identify more readily with the physical and emotional problems of old women. Another possibility is a geriatric subspecialty just for the problems of older women. Again old women must demand the kind of care they want.

OLD WOMEN ARE THEIR OWN WORST CRITICS

The phenomenon of self-hatred is found in most groups of people who are the victims of discrimination. If enough people tell you something bad about yourself for a long enough time, you end up believing it. Thus old women typically discredit themselves in both obvious and subtle ways. For example, the late Gloria Swanson, while in her seventies and with a successful film career of more than sixty years, admitted that men are favored as actors over women in old age. Yet she insisted she had no use for women's liberation: "No no no. I want a man to know more. . . . Physically I want him stronger, mentally I want him stronger." Simone de Beauvoir, in an allegedly autobiographical work called *The Age of Discretion*, writes of a woman, age sixty, who is brilliant, a leading intellectual, possessing acute sensibility and social purpose, but who is revealed to herself as deluded by her success, dependent on men, mean in spirit, and afraid of growing old. On another level, a representative of the Department of Labor's Women's Bureau said many older women have a "Uriah Heep attitude" about employment, feeling they must appear obsequious and obedient because they have little else of value to offer an employer.

There are women who profit from and exploit the insecurities of their contemporaries. Helena Rubenstein, one of the world's wealthiest self-made women, is a fascinating example of a female who maintained her power and influence until age ninety-two, but made her millions off the cravings of women to stave off their inevitable aging. Older women rushed to buy her products to delay their banishment to "neuter land," the realm of women who are no longer youthfully pretty.

EMOTIONAL ADJUSTMENT PROBLEMS

A pervasive theme in the efforts of old women to find a satisfying life is the preference for male company and the downgrading of female companionship. Many cannot see themselves as fulfilled unless they have a husband or at least some male to whom they can devote themselves, and this becomes more difficult as the male population thins out. Some women compensate with an overbearing idolization of a son or grandson. Others make sad, futile efforts to appear young and thus recapture the lost sex-rights of their youth and middle age. The top-heavy ratio of women to men encourages an already culturally established pattern of competition with fellow females for the few remaining men. The mother-in-law syndrome is another way women may express their disdain toward their own sex (their daughter-in-laws) as well as the envy an older women feels toward a young woman's youthfulness. The harsh experience of women during the aging process makes it understandable why they may see the young as rivals, not only for the attention of males but also for the very economic resources necessary for their survival in old age.

Some elderly women turn to religion in a passionately excessive manner which seems less of a spiritual search and more of a way of filling the void of the former family. If a man is not available, then perhaps a masculine God-figure can give some sense of comfort and meaningfulness. Religion can serve as a cover-up for terribly lonely women who have no relevant human beings in their lives.

WHAT'S GOOD ABOUT BEING AN OLD WOMAN? IMPLICATIONS FOR THE WOMEN'S LIB MOVEMENT

We have detailed some of the difficulties of old women. But there is more. Old women have much to teach the young and middle-aged about the double whammy of sex and age discrimination as well as pointing to future possibilities for all ages.

What, then, is good about being an old woman? They have the potential for being the most liberated group of women in terms of personal expression. In addition, with increasing good health and longevity, they don't have to fight the conflicts between mothering versus careers which plague younger women. They can function as the only adult females who are truly free of the demands of child responsibility and in many cases marital responsibilities. Old women, of course, want the life expectancy of males raised more nearly approximate to their own, but widowhood or lack of males need not carry the stigmata of failure. The idea of dependency on a male is deeply ingrained but old women may be responsive to challenges of this tired stereotype. Many women were forced into marriage by cultural and family pressures and might have been happier as single career or professional women. Educational programs should be designed especially for them to explore late-life careers. Other older women are lesbians who have been hiding as "heteros" for a lifetime and might be willing to "come out" if the climate were favorable. Numbers of others could have satisfied heterosexual companionship and maternal needs without marriage or children and still can. They could challenge the sex-age prejudice and obtain the options now reserved for men. We might, for example, be surprised at the number of secret liaisons between young males and older females which could surface if they became socially acceptable.

Older women by example could give younger women confidence to resist the beautiful face and body trap, with the knowledge that a rich life can await them as they age. Women of all ages may begin to refuse to be discarded and to demand recognition as humans. Young women and even the middle-aged are floundering for viable female models to follow. A considerable number of old women have forged unique positions for themselves in terms of identity, personal achievement, and even financial and political power but they need to be located and made visible.

Another unique asset of age is that most older women have adjusted in some way to the idea of personal death. It is characteristic of the elderly to fear death much less than the young. They may attain a certain degree of extra objectivity from this vantage point. There is a possibility for a greater sense of moral commitment and flexibility beyond their own egos. Old people are often thought of as conservative but in truth they are inclined to be dovish on war and liberal on political and social issues. In terms of flexibility this is the generation which indeed has, as Nikita Khrushchev so aptly put it, gone "from the outhouse to outer space" in one lifetime.

Politically, the older woman is in a most advantageous position and it is likely to improve. With a voting strength of eleven million, two-thirds of whom are registered voters, most of whom vote regularly, they represent a major and fast-growing constituency which already could elect their own congresswoman in those states where they reside in high proportions. They have the available time and energy to lobby, campaign, and promote candidates since 90 percent are retired from active employment. There is reason to suppose that women candidates for the presidency and supreme court may come from this age group since older people often fill these positions.

In spite of widespread poverty for many women, there are tremendous sums of money in the hands of widows and female heirs. It is time that women took up their own financial management, instead of entrusting it to surrogate husbands. Women of wealth could exert much greater influence in economic, social, and artistic spheres if they used the resources they already have. They could provide backing for the women's liberation movement and specifically for their own age group problems.

Many elderly women have lived out their last years as characterized by Edna St. Vincent Millay: "Life must go on—I forget just why." But there is a sturdy and hopefully growing group of old women who are undaunted and look to life with enthusiasm. Old women will not accept their bleak lot forever because they have the brains, money, and voting strength to do something about it. An eighty-three-year-old former suffragette who recently became excited by the women's liberation movement states, "I don't want to leave the world without being a part of this."

Editor's Note: This paper was originally published in 1972 and is reprinted here because it represents an important early look at the often "invisible" nature of older women's issues. While the women's movement has taken important steps to address a number of these issues in recent years, the position of older women in American society remains problematic. Indeed, while we have updated the statistics in this article to portray current trends, such figures continue to reflect the "double jeopardy" inherent in being old and female in the United States.

Reprinted with permission of Greenwood Press. From *Aging and Human Development*, *3*, pp. 223-231, 1972.

CHAPTER 13
Women and the Economics of Aging

CARROLL L. ESTES
LENORE E. GERARD
ADELE CLARKE

Dr. Robert Butler, former Director of the National Institute of Aging, has observed that the "problems of old age in America are largely the problems of women." [1, p. 1] This observation reflects not only demographic data predicting that there will be ten women for every five men over the age of seventy-five by the year 2000, but also, and more importantly, it reflects the distressing socioeconomic conditions in which many older women experience higher rates of poverty (60% higher than elderly men), differential pay and treatment in the labor market (averaging 60% of male wages), and consequently lower Social Security benefits (about two-thirds of the average male benefit) [2,3].

The National Advisory Council on Economic Opportunity has challenged the myth that poverty has been eradicated. This observation becomes more salient when one examines the economic status of American women. The phenomenon that "two out of three poor adults are women" has been called the "feminization of poverty." [4] For some women, this poverty is a reflection of the life-long experience of poor socio-economic conditions. For many others, however, it is a new experience resulting from the inequities of divorce. The question has been posed whether divorce, in effect, has created a class of "new poor" consisting of women and children who previously were in the middle income bracket [5]. It is likely that this "new poor" class of women will experience hardships as they grow older and seek income security benefits.

During the 1970's, families headed by women increased more than 51 percent, from 5.6 million to 8.5 million. Today, there are "9.4 million single-adult female-headed families and the number is growing ten times as fast as male-headed families." [6, p. 40] Because women usually earn less than men and these families generally lack the benefit of a second income, they face economic hardships [3, 7]. In 1978, the median income of families maintained by women was $8,540, or less than half of the $17,640 median income of all families. Among whites, 12 percent of all families were maintained by women, while females headed 20 percent of hispanic families and 41 percent of black families [8].

By any standard, the most critical problem facing older persons is the lack of adequate income. Retirement from the labor force often reduces an individual's income by about one-half. After years of declining poverty, the poverty rate of older persons is on the rise again—rising dramatically from 14 percent in 1978 to 15.7 percent (or 3.9 million people) in 1980. More significantly, there is a larger percentage of persons over sixty-five whose income levels are stacked just above the official poverty threshold. Almost 35 percent (8 million) of the elderly are estimated to be poor and near poor [9].

These economic realities are compounded for elderly women and minorities [10-14] who traditionally do not achieve social or economic status in society. Women, blacks, and other minorities are the most disadvantaged, with 38 percent of aged blacks and 30.8 percent of hispanic aged living at extreme poverty levels [15]. Today, half of all the aged poor are single women (never married or widows) who live alone [16]. As shown in Table 1, about one-fifth of elderly women are poor, with the highest rates of poverty concentrated among older black and hispanic females.

It is important to examine the factors underlying these inequities and how they relate to the economics of aging for women. Two major structural factors affect the economics of aging for women now and in the future: first, the explosion of the fourth generation; and second, the labor force participation of women.

Table 1. Incidence of Poverty among Persons Age 55 and Older, by Sex and Race, 1981

	Percentage of Persons with Income below Poverty Line	
	Age 55–64	Age 65 and Older
All groups, total	10.1	15.3
Male	7.8	10.5
Female	12.1	18.6
Whites, total	8.3	13.1
Male	6.6	8.5
Female	9.9	16.2
Blacks, total	27.8	39.0
Male	20.3	32.3
Female	33.7	43.5
Hispanics, total	19.1	25.7
Male	15.9	23.6
Female	21.2	27.4

Source: U.S. Bureau of the Census, "Money Income and Poverty Status of Families and Persons in the United States: 1981," Current Population Reports, Series P-60, No. 134.

EXPLOSION OF THE FOURTH GENERATION

More than 25 million people are sixty-five and over according to the 1980 U.S. census. This represents 11.3 percent of the total population, up from less than 3 percent a century ago when the first compulsory retirement policies were introduced. The concept of the fourth generation refers to the demographic boom of the very old and is attributed not only to greater longevity but also to earlier marriages and earlier childbearing reducing the average span in years between generations [17]. The percentage of aged who are seventy-five years and older, now comprising 38 percent of the elderly population, is expected to grow to 45 percent by the year 2000 [17, 18]. It is estimated that two-thirds of those over 75 will be women [1]. The oldest group—particularly women who are unmarried or widowed and without social supports—is most vulnerable because of dependence upon public resources and programs to offset social factors such as diminished finances, loss of spouse or family supports, urban relocation, and increased incidence of health problems.

LABOR FORCE PARTICIPATION OF WOMEN

Some attribute the economic plight of older women to the inadequacies and inequities of income maintenance programs. However, as the Task Force on Women and Social Security cautions, "there is no magic in Social Security." [3] Social Security payments merely reflect differential rewards and inequities in the labor market: in other words, the root of the income problem for women stems from the labor market, wherein differential pay, low-wage occupations, and episodic work participation due to familial commitments have a combined and often devastating effect in later years.

The social and economic inequalities experienced in old age, then, are extensions of individuals' earlier positions in relation to the labor market [19-23]. The economic security or insecurity that women experience in later life will be determined, to a large extent, by the relation of women in their middle years (45-64 years of age) to the labor market. This observation was affirmed by Congressman John Burton when he commented, "certainly we cannot erase all the inequities in Social Security until women achieve equality in the labor force." [2, p. 12]

There has been an enormous increase in labor force participation by older women over the past thirty years [24-26] and women now comprise about 40 percent of those forty-five years of age and over in the labor force compared with 25 percent in 1950 [26]. This dramatic increase in older women's labor force participation in the U.S. can be attributed to women's changing role in society, economic factors, the growth of the service industry, increased education, and efforts to provide equal employment opportunities [24]. However, older women's labor force participation is largely in the lower paid service sectors.

For example, women make up 80 percent of the employees in the health care industry [27], but they represent the lower paid workers within the industry.

WOMEN'S ROLES AND SOCIAL POLICY

An examination of women's roles in society as caregivers, as workers, and as beneficiaries is central to a social policy perspective. These roles are neither inclusive nor mutually exclusive; they form a complex and dynamic inter-relationship. Each of these social roles has corresponding institutional structures that mediate between the individual and society, schematically shown in Figure 1.

Attention is now being given to the family's and women's caregiving roles, particularly in light of growing concern about the public cost of long-term care for the elderly, disabled youth, and adults. The general thrust of recent policy proposals and political rhetoric has been to emphasize family responsibility with minimal subsidies or tax incentives. Home care and other assistance for dependents is often provided by unpaid adult women. The consequences for such care-takers in terms of their own economic and social well-being is largely ignored.

While the family continues to be the institution that assumes primary respon-sibility for the young and old, the family is not a system that operates in isola-tion. "It is deeply enmeshed in the social, political, and economic conditions of the times." [1, pp. 12-13] Interventions targeted at the family alone do not acknowledge the complexity of the problems of older women nor do they appro-priately address the need for intervention.

Few policy intervention measures are targeted at the second and probably most significant institutional structure that affects women's economic status throughout their lifespan—the labor market. Although the aged have been accused of "busting the budget" and of draining resources from the younger working population [28, 29], there are few public policies that lend support to the con-tinued and valued experience of older persons in the labor market, and virtually none address the particular labor market problems of older women.

Women's Roles	Institutional Structure
Caregivers	Family/Marriage
Workers	Labor Market
Patients/Beneficiaries	Public and Private Policy: Income and Health Programs

Figure 1. Women's roles and institutional structures.

The Age Discrimination in Employment Act[1] and the Age Discrimination Act of 1975[2] have had a very limited effect. While evidence indicates that millions of older people want to work, the Older Americans Act employment program has never employed more than 53,000 nationwide. Further, in both 1982 and 1983, the Reagan Administration requested reductions that threatened the survival of even this small program. The Civil Rights Commission has found discrimination against the elderly in federal training and employment programs, which are targeted to those seen as most employable, thus largely excluding the elderly [30]. The loss of many Comprehensive Employment and Training Act (CETA) jobs through federal cuts and other reductions in public funded employment and training programs seriously exacerbates the problem. In addition, the President's economic program has reduced jobs for women in multiple ways. For example, between April and June of 1982, 46 percent of the federal workforce reductions were female although women make up only 29 percent of the force. It has been estimated that 9,500 jobs disappear for women with every $1 billion increase in the military budget [6].

Ageism, sexism, the economic climate, and specific employment policies (e.g., superannuation or retirement) undermine continued work for older persons in general and for older women in particular. Even if work can be found, there are disincentives, such as the reduction of Social Security benefits ($.50 for every $1.00 earned) above a fixed minimum income. Although there has been substantial discussion about maintaining the productivity of older persons in the work force, the U.S. Joint Economic Committee has observed that the U.S. government and industry are unlikely to encourage older persons to remain in jobs or to take new jobs as long as there is widespread unemployment [24].

The third major institutional structure is public and private policy as it affects income and health programs. Publicly financed income and health programs are targeted largely toward those who are retired. At retirement age, an older individual can seek support from private savings, investments, employer pension plans, or public programs such as Social Security or means-tested Supplementary Security Income. In addition, Medicare (Title XVIII of the Social Security Act) is designed to provide health insurance to most individuals aged sixty-five and over and to disabled persons under sixty-five years who qualify. Cost-sharing and deductible features of the Medicare program, which finances the cost of acute, episodic illness requiring hospital care and some portion of physician services, result in Medicare coverage of only approximately 44 percent of an older person's health care bill. The limitations of such income and health programs and the consequences of the Reagan Administration cutbacks have been described as severe [31].

---

[1] Enacted in 1967, the 1978 amendments extended coverage by upper limit in the act from age sixty-five to seventy for private employment and non-federal public employment, plus other changes.
[2] P.L. 94-135, 1975, provides that "no person in the U.S. shall on the basis of any age, be excluded from participation in, be denied the benefits of, or be subjected to discrimination under any program or activity receiving federal financial assistance."

For persons under sixty-five years of age, access to medical care is almost entirely tied to group insurance plans negotiated at the place of employment. The only exception to this pattern of health care coverage in the United States is the Medicaid program, which is the nation's largest publicly financed health insurance program for the poor. Access to Medicaid is tied to a state's welfare criteria and consequently often has a high stigma associated with it. While women living at the poorest economic level can seek access to health care through Medicaid, many others who are "near-poor" (subsisting on an income just above the official poverty threshold) or on "moderate" incomes are caught in between without the financial means to secure adequate health protection.

There are some 30 million persons in the United States without any health care coverage. An overlooked segment of this population is women between forty-five and sixty-five years of age who are frequently without adequate insurance coverage to protect them against the risk of acute or chronic illness. This "invisible" group of uninsured women is estimated to be around 4½ million women in mid-life. The experience of these women is often one of dependent homemaker or parttime worker whose health insurance was lost (or nonexistent) as a result of a change in marital status. Also, mid-life married women may lose family health care coverage when their older husbands retire and can no longer afford to continue the insurance on a private, individual basis of payment [32]. Furthermore, many of those women who can afford to pay for private insurance will be subjected to careful scrutiny by the insurance carrier. For example, what is viewed as an "adverse health history" of a woman over forty-five years of age can be the basis for disqualifying an applicant from private health insurance protection [32].

In summary, health-related policy issues for women encompass older women in mid-life as well as those over sixty-five years of age. Major concerns are: 1) the effects of work on health status and the effects of health on work status [33]; 2) access to health care for those women in mid-life living on moderate to low incomes and for those older women over sixty-five years of age; 3) the effect of the women's caregiver role on poverty, health, stress, and labor participation; and 4) the inadequate and fragmented health care system skewed toward institutional services with few or no community care alternatives—a system which burdens the informal caregiving sector, the family and especially the older woman.

SOURCES OF INCOME FOR OLDER WOMEN

There are *four* potential sources of income in old age: 1) income from assets, 2) private pensions, 3) Social Security, and 4) income programs for the poor over sixty-five.

Income from Assets

Although approximately half of the older population receive income from assets, many units receive only small amounts and the proportion of total income it represents is low [10]. For example, the median amount of asset income for those aged sixty-five and over was only $870 in 1976. Evidence indicates that individuals whose lifetime income is high will accumulate more assets than will those whose incomes are lower. Thus, it is not surprising to find that men have larger assets than women, and that marital status is a critical factor in the distribution of those assets [34].

Private Pensions

Any attempt to determine the adequacy of income for the elderly must consider private pensions systems as well as the public system and the inequities that characterize them. There are about one-half million pension, profit sharing and stock-bonus plans. In 1979 it was estimated that over 30 million persons— about half of all wage and salary workers—were covered in private pensions. However, women are much less likely than men to be covered by a retirement plan [24]. According to the White House Mini Conference on Older Women, private pensions are not available to over 80 percent of retiring women workers [35].

Further, until 1983, it was legal for pension plans taking equal contributions from men and women to pay women retirees at lower rates based upon their greater longevity. Significantly, it was a Supreme Court decision (under the 1964 Civil Rights Act), rather than a legislatively enacted policy, that finally provided individual women pensioners with equal protection [36].

Social Security

The issues surrounding the treatment of women under Social Security have been and continue to be a topic of national importance, especially since Social Security is the major source of income for the majority of older women [2, 3, 24, 35]. Of particular public policy concern are those older women in the lower economic strata. Using data from the 1981 Current Population Survey, a recent study showed

> ... that single women over age sixty-five with incomes less than $5,000 depend on Social Security for more than 80 percent of their income. But half the older women in this country have incomes under $5,000 and almost two-thirds of all older women in the United States are single (widowed, divorced, separated, or never married) [6, p. 61].

While it is estimated that Social Security preserves two-thirds of the older population from *acute* poverty, it is insufficient to keep millions of retired persons from *real* poverty [8]. The 1979 *median* Social Security benefit was $290 per month [30]. And, as previously noted, women's Social Security benefits are only about two-thirds those of men.

Major gaps and inadequate benefits in Social Security are particular problems for women who are divorced and who have spent most of their working years as homemakers. The major adequacy problems are 1) lack of protection for women divorced after less than ten years of marriage; 2) inadequate benefit levels for aged divorced women, and 3) gaps in protection for women whose spouses die before retirement [37]. Divorced women who have not been consistent wage earners have little or no Social Security protection in their own right. Since aged widows tend to live longer, they are likely to have little or no income other than below-average Social Security benefits computed on outdated earnings, which may be further reduced if the widow finds she must draw benefits before age sixty-five [2].

The major inequities in Social Security are between married couples and single individuals and between one-earner and two-earner couples.

- Two-earner couples generally receive lower benefits than one-earner couples with the same total earnings.
- Because of the differences in the benefits of one- and two-earner couples, the surviving spouse of a two-wage-earner couple generally receives less than the surviving spouse of a one-earner couple with the same total income.
- Married women who spend time out of the paid labor force in homemaking and child care activities are not allowed to drop out child-rearing years from the averaging period used to compute benefits. (Both men and women have five drop out years.) This long averaging period generally results in lower average benefits to women than to men.

There are serious inadequacies and inequities within the Social Security system for millions of working wives, single working women, and homemakers [38].

> While recognizing the family as the consuming unit in need of income, the system failed to allow for the coordinated efforts of family members in income-getting. In the case of the house-wife's support services, the system has been faulted for not adequately protecting the homemaker's community property claim to husband's earned benefits, especially against a rising tide of marital disruption. In the case of the working wife's earnings, the system has been criticized for discounting the second earner's essential role in family finances [39, p. 571].

Income Programs for the Poor Over Sixty-Five

For those individuals who have been intermittently employed and for those who have had very low lifetime earnings covered by Social Security, mainly women and minorities, a federal minimum benefit had been established. Especially significant for women are the Reagan Administration and Congressional cutbacks in 1981 and 1982 that resulted in the eradication of the minimum Social Security benefit (which then was only a bare $122 monthly) for all but those already in the program and for those who would become eligible before January 1982.

In addition, Supplementary Security Income (SSI) is a cash assistance program enacted in 1972 for the poor aged, blind, and disabled persons. This federal-state program is a means-tested program, for which an individual's income and resources determine eligibility and the amount of payment. SSI provides a subsistence income to over four million needy persons, with the majority (three-fourths) of aged beneficiaries being women over seventy-five years of age. Of those aged families subsisting on the combined benefits provided by SSI and Social Security, 49.4 percent were still below the poverty line in 1977. For single persons in these circumstances, 59.5 percent were officially living in poverty in 1977 [24]. The maximum federal SSI benefit is $265 for an individual and $397 for a couple (as of January 1982). Once the minimum federal payment level is established, states have complete discretion in determining whether they will supplement this amount, by how much, and the standards. Among the twenty-five states that administered their own programs in 1980, the average level of state supplement benefit varied greatly from $20 in Wyoming to $206 in Virginia for poor, aged single individuals living alone. Thus, there are substantial inequities based on such factors as place of residence and living arrangements [31].

POLICY ISSUES CONCERNED WITH THE ECONOMIC AND SOCIAL WELL-BEING OF WOMEN

The status and resources of older women in the next two decades will be affected by the economic climate and health of the U.S. and world economy and the politically negotiated choices of how a "healthy" economy is to be achieved.

Health Policy

The two structural factors noted earlier—women's increased labor force participation and the explosion of the fourth generation—raise important questions pertaining to the issue of health and who bears the burden of its cost. We know enough to predict that the fourth generation will require a measure of family responsibility as well as possible monetary support in the form of private income transfers among family members.

What demands will a fourth generation exert on the social and medical supportt system funded largely out of public dollars? How, in turn, will this contribute to or hinder the labor force participation of older women? We must keep in mind that 80 percent of the care of elders is given by family members, primarily women. Given the knowledge that differences in social class, race, and marital status are crucial in determining women's economic status, can we assume more women will be better off in their later years as a result of increased continued employment?

With the push to reduce the federal role as well as publicly funded social expenditures, increasing attention has been given to approaches in social and health policy that lower the public costs. An example is the emphasis upon the family's assuming responsibility for the long-term care for family members (whether it be a spouse, parent, or child). Yet, often such words as the family or phrases as the "informal support system" have been euphemisms for women as daughters and daughters-in-law being the primary caregivers [40].

Clearly, the family is an important social institution in assuming responsibility for both the young and the old. We know that both the presence of a caregiver and the type of living arrangement are critical in determining nursing home entry [41, 42]. Nevertheless, a key issue is whether the current policy emphasis on the family in long-term care is commensurate with other social and economic demands on women in their middle and later years, and especially for those who are single, divorced, or widowed and without adequate income. Is it realistic to assume women (many of whom are in the work force) can still meet familial expectations and obligations assigned to them in the nineteenth century? The Task Force on Women and Social Security [3] has noted that the traditional belief that "woman's place is in the home" has persisted into the twentieth century in the face of so many contradictions and exceptions that it has become a "convenient myth." While the historical increase of women's participation in the labor force challenges this notion, the recent resurrection of such myths is useful in supporting public policies that limit state-sponsored services for such groups as the elderly, the disabled, and the young chronically ill.

Intervention strategies need to take into account these social-structural parameters so that "informal support" is not a rhetorical substitute for further inequitable burdens on women as caregivers. Consideration must also be given to the fact that a woman's role as a caregiver in a family unit may be quickly transformed into that of patient or beneficiary, dependent upon the state. The purview of long term care policy ought not to be limited to the poorest segments of society but rather should encompass a larger population of *all* women who are without adequate income protection and sufficient assets to offset the possible afflictions of chronic illness, depression, loss of spouse, the necessity to support a parent, and social isolation. A woman's economic and social well-being may very well be threatened by a configuration of any one of these factors as she grows older.

While much attention is afforded the public costs of long-term care, much less attention has been given to the financial impact on the remaining partner of institutionalizing a spouse [43]. Although the financial problems arising from this situation may indeed be devastating, public policy offers little or nothing to the middle class or near poor elderly spouse in this situation. For example:

> This individual, who is usually a woman, is forced to divide one income into two parts; one portion for the payment of nursing home costs and the second for her own living expenses. This not only keeps

the community-based spouse from maintaining her maximum level of functional independence, but it also increases the likelihood of her entering a nursing home [43, p. 1040].

There are several options open to a woman when faced with the dilemma of having a spouse who requires long-term care: 1) "spending-down" until Medicaid eligibility is achieved, thereby impoverishing herself; 2) getting a divorce; 3) continuing payments for long-term care [43]; 4) if she works, quitting her job to assume the role of primary caregiver to prevent the spouse's institutionalization.[3] Each of these "solutions" virtually assures poverty for the spouse. Because this is largely a hidden problem of the middle class married elderly population, very little is known about its role in the poverty of older women. A similar set of pressures and financial losses is incurred by millions of daughters and daughters-in-law in caring for older parents. This also is an under-studied and ignored phenomenon by public policy.

Current public policy provides strong disincentives for community-based family support in the following ways: the one-third reduction in Supplemental Security Income (SSI) for living in the household of another (thus depriving an elderly parent of essential income if they reside with their adult children): the prohibition in many states against payment through the Social Services Block Grant (formerly Title XX) to individual family members providing care to an elderly parent,[4] although homemaker help provided by non-family may be paid for; the Title XIX Medicaid spend-down provision that may impoverish both the patient and spouse; the almost nonexistent Medicaid-Medicare home health benefit coverage; and the tax structure that offers no incentives (i.e., tax deductions) to family members who assume some financial responsibility for their elders, regardless of whether they live in the same household.[5]

Income Policy

Historically, women have earned less than men—averaging 60 percent of men's earnings. Worse, the median income for women fifty-six to sixty-four years of age approximates *one-third* of the *median* income of males of the same age [7]. The median income for older men in 1981 was $8,173; the figure for women was $4,975, or just 58 percent of men's income. Since half of all older women have incomes below or within $400 of the official poverty level ($4,359), it is not surprising that 72 percent of the elderly poor are women [44].

---

[3] To avoid impoverishment due to an institutionalized spouse, it was found that welfare case workers in North Carolina were encouraging elderly married couples to file for divorce to avoid deeming of income [43].

[4] This is not the case, however, in California which does make payment to family members in support of a poor elderly individual; many other states in the U.S. do not make this offer.

[5] At the federal level, bills have been introduced in Congress that would allow a credit against tax for care of elderly family members. Currently there are tax provisions to offset some expenses incurred but because of rigid eligibility requirements very few families use them. At the state level, some states have proposed tax relief legislation to help families but few have actually enacted such legislation [30].

Table 2. Male and Female Differences in
Median Income (in Dollars): 1977

Years: 45–64	Male	$15,311
	Female	$ 5,670
55–64	Male	$12,243
	Female	$ 4,533
65–69	Male	$ 6,516
	Female	$ 3,010

Source: U.S. Bureau of the Census. *Statistical Abstract of the United States: 1979*. Washington, D.C.: U.S. Department of Commerce, 1980.

Table 2 breaks down the difference in median income for three age groups, 45–54; 55–64; and 65–69. As shown, women's median income is even less than half of men's prior to age sixty-five.

This disparity in earnings stems from "the social institutions of school, family, and economy and not within Social Security *per se*." [39, p. 572] It is important to note that serious issues of adequacy and equity in income security benefits exist for older women because these benefits are based largely on labor market experience that is disadvantageous to women of all ages. In analyzing the effects of mid-life work history and the retirement income of older single and married women, O'Rand and Henretta summarize several important features of women's participation in the labor market [45]. First, many women experience in-and-out-of work patterns (interrupted participation) over time. Second, women largely are concentrated in a few occupations such as sales, service, and clerical work, and a few professions such as teaching and social services. Third, women tend to work in industries characterized by high turnover rates, low wages and fringe benefits and the absence of a union. Furthermore, starting work after the age of thirty-five years can be particularly disadvantageous in terms of the level of retirement income unless work is begun in an industry with good wages and pension benefits [45]. Thus, a determining factor in the adequacy of retirement benefits is whether one works in the primary labor market (characterized by high-paying jobs with stability and benefits), or the secondary labor market (characterized by low-paying jobs with instability and poor working conditions). Women and minorities are overrepresented in the secondary labor market and as a result depend largely on Social Security benefits which turn out to be quite low.

SUMMARY AND CONCLUSIONS

Social policies are shaped largely by requirements of the economy and the economic climate. The position of women workers in the economy has been and continues to be systematically unequal. By failing to address these inequities, social policies affecting older women have perpetuated their disadvantaged economic situations throughout old age. Bluntly stated, public policy has reflected the myth that women have worked only for "pin money," assuring that elderly women did not then have a right to a reasonable or even decent standard of living. The value of women's labor in the home and in creating and maintaining the family also has been ignored or minimized.

Given the politics of fiscal retrenchment and its severe impact on young and old women alike the policy outlook for older women is grim. The bias against women and minorities of federal policy shifts, and of tax and budget cuts since 1981 has been extensively documented [46-48]. Tax cuts have dramatically benefited households with annual incomes above $80,000 (augmenting their income by more than $55 billion), while households with incomes under $10,000 are losing $17 billion between 1983 and 1985 [49]. Benefit reductions, on the other hand, have been taken in largest measure from the under $10,000 annual income category and next from those in the $10,000 to $20,000 income category. While 45 percent of the cuts will come from the under $10,000 group, and 25 percent from the $10,000 to $20,000 group, less than 1 percent of the cuts will come from the $80,000 and over group by 1985 [47-48]. Because women have lower incomes, they are incurring a larger share of benefit cuts and a disproportionately small share of the tax reduction benefits. Thus, the inequities in wealth distribution have been increased as there has been an accelerated shift of resources from females to males and from minorities to whites in the U.S. with the policy shifts commencing with the Reagan Administration [6, 49].

Despite retrenchment, policies continue to be reformulated. Attention to the sources of previous socio-structual and policy inequities is needed to ameliorate their negative impact and aid in the development of new policies to avoid furthering the already extremely inequitable economic situation of older women.

REFERENCES

1. U.S. National Institute on Aging (NIA), *The Older Woman: Continuities and Discontinuities*, Superintendent of Documents, U.S. Government Printing Office, Washington, D.C., October 1979.
2. J. L. Burton, Elder Women Suffer Frequently and Severely during Retirement, *Generations*, 4:4, pp. 12, 36, 1980.
3. U.S. Senate Special Committee on Aging, *Women and Social Security: Adapting to a New Era*, Superintendent of Documents, U.S. Government Printing Office, Washington, D.C., October 1975.
4. A. I. Blaustein, (ed.), *The American Promise: Equal Justice and Economic Opportunity*, Transaction Books, New Brunswick, New Jersey, 1982.
5. M. Culverwell, Are Divorcees the Nation's "New Poor?", Sheet 58:26, p. 1, University of California, July 12, 1983.
6. National Women's Law Center, *Inequality of Sacrifice: The Impact of the Reagan Budget on Women*, Washington, D.C., March 16, 1983.

7. U.S. Bureau of the Census, *Statistical Abstracts of the United States* 101st edition, Superintendent of Documents, U.S. Government Printing Office, Washington, D.C., 1980.

8. U.S. General Accounting Office, *Perspective on Income Security and Social Services and an Agenda for Analysis*, Washington, D.C., August 13, 1981.

9. P. Lehrman, Poverty Statistics Serve as Nagging Reminder, *Generations*, 4:1, pp. 17-18; 67, May 1980.

10. S. Grad and K. Foster, Income of the Population Aged 55 and Older, 1976, *Social Security Bulletin*, 42:7, pp. 16-32, 1979.

11. J. Abbott, Socioeconomic Characteristics of the Elderly: Some Black-White Differences, *Social Security Bulletin*, 40:7, pp. 16-42, 1977.

12. R. L. McNeely (ed.), *Aging in Minority Groups*, Sage, Beverly Hills, California, 1983.

13. M. M. Fuller and C. A. Martin, *The Older Woman*, C. C. Thomas, Springfield, Illinois, 1980.

14. R. C. Manuel (ed.), *Minority Aging: Sociological and Social Psychological Issues*, Greenwood Press, Westport, Connecticut, 1982.

15. U.S. House Select Committee on Aging, *Every Ninth American*, Superintendent of Documents, U.S. Government Printing Office, Washington, D.C., 1981.

16. U.S. House Select Committee on Aging, *Hearing: Poverty among America's Aged*, Superintendent of Documents, U.S. Government Printing Office, Washington, D.C., August 9, 1978.

17. P. Townsend, *Poverty in the United Kingdom*, University of California Press, Berkeley, California, 1979.

18. Data Resource, Inc., *Inflation and the Elderly*, Data Resource, Lexington, Massachusetts, 1980.

19. A. Walker, The Social Creation of Poverty and Dependence in Old Age, *Journal of Social Policy*, 9, pp. 49-75, 1980.

20. _____, Towards a Political Economy of Old Age, *Ageing and Society*, 1:1, pp. 73-94, 1981.

21. P. Townsend, The Structured Dependency of the Elderly: A Creation of Social Policy in the Twentieth Century, *Ageing and Society*, 1:1, pp. 5-28, 1981.

22. J. F. Myles, The Aged, the State, and the Structure of Inequality, in *Structural Inequality in Canada*, J. Harp and J. Hofley (eds.), Prentice-Hall, Toronto, Canada, pp. 317-342, 1980.

23. U.S. House Select Committee on Aging, *The Status of Mid-Life Women and Options for Their Future*, Superintendent of Documents, U.S. Government Printing Office, Washington, D.C., March 1980.

24. U.S. Joint Economic Committee, Special Study on Economic Change, *Social Security and Pensions: Programs of Equity and Security*, Superintendent of Documents, U.S. Government Printing Office, Washington, D.C., October 1980.

25. J. Kreps and P. Clark, *Sex, Age, and Work*, Johns Hopkins, Baltimore, Maryland, 1975.

26. Work in America Institute, Inc., *The Future of Older Workers in America*, Work in America Institute, New York, New York, 1980.

27. M. Urquhart, The Service Industry: Is It Recession Proof?, *Monthly Labor Review*, 104, pp. 12-18, 1981.

28. R. J. Samuelson, Busting the U.S. Budget: The Costs of an Aging America, *National Journal*, *10*:7, pp. 256-260, 1978.

29. _____, Benefit Programs for the Elderly—Off Limits to Federal Budget Cutters?, *National Journal*, *13*:40, pp. 1757-1762, 1981.

30. U.S. Senate Special Committee on Aging, *Developments in Aging*, Superintendent of Documents, U.S. Government Printing Office, Washington, D.C., 1980 and 1981.

31. C. Harrington, Social Security and Medicare: Policy Shifts in the 1980's, in *Fiscal Austerity and Aging: Shifting Government Responsibility for the Elderly*, Sage, Beverly Hills, California, pp. 83-111, 1983.

32. Older Women's League (OWL), *Health Insurance Coverage of Women in Mid-Life*, Older Women's League, Oakland, California, 1983 (unpublished paper).

33. E. Fee (ed.), *Women and Health: The Politics of Sex in Medicine*, Baywood, New York, 1983.

34. J. Friedman and J. Sjogren, Assets of the Elderly as They Retire, *Social Security Bulletin*, *44*:1, pp. 16-31, 1981.

35. White House Conference on Aging, *Miniconference of Older Women*, Superintendent of Documents, U.S. Government Printing Office, Washington, D.C., October 1980.

36. San Francisco Chronicle, July 11, 1983.

37. A. H. Munnell and L. E. Siglin, Women and a Two-Tier Social Security System, in *A Challenge to Social Security: The Changing Roles of Women and Men in American Society*, R. V. Burkauser and K. C. Holden (eds.), Academic Press, New York, pp. 101-123, 1982.

38. R. V. Burkauser and K. C. Holden (eds.), *A Challenge to Social Security: The Changing Roles of Women and Men in American Society*, Academic Press, New York, 1982.

39. J. Treas, Women's Employment and Its Implications for the Status of the Elderly of the Future, in *Aging: Social Change*, S. B. Kiesler (ed.), Academic Press, New York, pp. 561-585, 1981.

40. E. M. Brody, Women in the Middle and Family Help to Older People, *Gerontologist*, *21*:5, pp. 471-480, 1981.

41. L. H. Butler and P. W. Newacheck, Health and Social Factors Relevant to Long Term Care Policy, Institute of Health Policy Studies, University of California, San Francisco, California, 1980.

42. U.S. General Accounting Office, Entering a Nursing Home—Costly Implications for Medicaid and the Elderly, Report to the Congress by the Comptroller General of the United States, U.S. General Accounting Office, Washington, D.C., 1979.

43. R. Packwood, Long Term Care: Costs, Financing and Alternative Services, Public and Private Sector Policy Options, in *The Future of Health Care: National Journal Issues Book*, National Journal, Washington, D.C. 1981.

44. Leadership Council of Aging Organizations, *The Administration's 1984 Budget: A Critical View from an Aging Perspective*, Leadership Council of Aging Organizations, Washington, D.C., March 15, 1983.

45. A. M. O'Rand and J. C. Henretta, Midlife Work History and the Retirement Income of Older Single and Married Women, in *Women's Retirement: Sage Yearbooks in Women's Policy Studies*, volume 6, M. Szinovacz (ed.), Sage, Beverly Hills, California, pp. 24-44, 1982.

46. J. Palmer and I. Sawhill (eds.), *The Reagan Experiment*, The Urban Institute, Washington, D.C., 1982.

47. Congressional Budget Office (CBO), *Effects of Tax and Benefit Reductions Enacted in 1981 for Households in Different Income Categories*, United States Congressional Budget Office, Washington, D.C., 1982a.

48. Congressional Budget Office (CBO), *Effects of Tax and Benefit Payments Enacted in 1982 for Households in Different Income Categories*, United States Congressional Budget Office, Washington, D.C., 1982b.

49. R. Greenstein and J. Bickerman, *The Effect of the Aministration's Budget, Tax, and Military Policies on Low-Income Americans*, Interreligious Task Force on U.S. Food Policy, Washington, D.C., February 1983.

Reprinted with permission of Baywood Press. From: *International Journal of Health Services*, *12*:4, pp. 573-584, 1982.

CHAPTER 14

The Sociopolitical Context of Women's Retirement

ROBYN STONE
MEREDITH MINKLER

The current period in the social history of America recently has been designated "the era of working women." [1] While this label is a useful one in underscoring one of the most salient demographic and social phenomenon of our times, it by right should be expanded to include the "era of the female retiree." For the unprecedented increase in female labor force participation over the past thirty years, coupled with extended female longevity patterns [2], has spawned a burgeoning subpopulation of older women who will spend, on the average, close to two decades in retirement [3].

Women's retirement has been the subject of considerable research attention in recent years [4-7]. With the important exception of studies such as those by O'Rand and Henretta [8, 9] however, most of the research to date does not place the topic explicitly within a broad sociopolitical context. As a consequence, it generally fails to examine the sociostructural roots of those phenomena (e.g., women's location in a dual labor market and resultant disadvantaged retirement income) which may heavily influence retirement decisions and adaptation.

In this chapter, female retirement is examined from a political economy perspective. Such an approach is predicated on the assumption that the position of older working women and women retirees in our society, and the retirement processes which they experience, are shaped and conditioned by their place in the social structure, and by the social and economic factors affecting that placement [10, 11].

Following a brief discussion of the selective inattention to sociopolitical context in retirement research in general, women's retirement will be examined as a case example of the importance of considering such broader contextual issues. Gender differences in adjustment to retirement, as well as differences among subgroups of female retirees will be the foci of particular attention. Throughout this analysis, the political, social, and economic antecedents and consequences of female retirement will be stressed and utilized to highlight the importance of a political economic theoretical framework for our understanding of the differential impacts of retirement.

THE NEGLECT OF CONTEXT IN RETIREMENT RESEARCH

While Graebmer [12], Myles [13], and others [14, 15] have played an important role in placing retirement in a broad sociohistorical and sociopolitical context, such a perspective is virtually absent from most retirement research. As Guillemard has argued, retirement policies and subsequent sociological analyses of retirement have failed to consider the socio-economic conditions which govern access to resources and status in the social structure [15]. Retirement, therefore, has been perceived as a rupture whose effects would be common to everyone. In reality, as noted earlier, retirement has a differential impact according to prior or lifelong social status which allows varying degrees of access to occupational pensions and other similar rights to income based on the interaction of age, sex, and occupational status [11].

Socio-economic status based on prior labor market participation thus is important not only in determining post-retirement economic status but also in determining life changes during the retirement and post-retirement years. Elderly people in the lowest social classes are the most likely to be disabled and poor. A recent British study thus found that retired men who had been in skilled manual jobs for most of their working lives were two times more likely to be bedfast or housebound than men who previously had been employers or managers [16].

Similarly, a recent national sample survey of 1.8 million men retiring before age sixty-two in the United States revealed that 80 percent of the blacks and 66 percent of the whites interviewed left the labor force involuntarily largely due to poor health [17]. These early retirees with health problems were significantly more likely to have poverty or near poverty incomes, and most did not subsequently receive adequate pension or disability benefits. In almost every industry and occupation, moreover, blacks were more likely than whites to leave the labor force involuntarily and to receive lower retirement incomes.

Findings such as these underscore the importance of an approach to retirement research which would include an analysis of socio-structural determinants of how retirement is differentially experienced by social class, gender, race, and occupational category, as well as by cohorts retiring under different societal economic circumstances.

In the latter regard, for example, it has been hypothesized that retirement during a recession or depression may be perceived as significantly more stressful than retirement in a period of economic prosperity [5]. While recessions are likely to result in both increased pressures on older workers to retire and in the latter's increased resistance to retirement in the face of high inflation and economic insecurity [18], the effects of such economic conditions on the health status and adaptation of retiring or recently retired workers has been all but ignored in the literature.

The importance of considering such variables as the state of the economy at the time of retirement was pointed up in the findings of Barfield and Morgan's two wave attitudinal study of workers retiring in 1968 and 1976 respectively [19]. These investigators revealed that 75 percent of the earlier interviewees responded favorably to the idea of retirement, compared with only 56 percent of the latter cohort, a finding which Foner and Schwab have suggested may be attributed to the high inflation rates of 1976 as compared to relatively stable prices in the 1960's [20].

Brenner's research documenting higher mortality rates for cardiovascular disease in the two years following an economic recession provides an important illustration of the need for examining the effects of such broad socio-economic conditions on health status [21]. Further analyses of this type, taking a particular look at the morbidity and mortality rates of recent retirees in conjunction with such societal events as a major recession, would greatly expand our existing knowledge of the influence of retirement on health, post-retirement morale and related outcomes.

The neglect by researchers of the sociopolitical context of retirement is evident on another level when we examine the dominant conceptual approaches to retirement utilized in studies to date. Retirement thus has tended to be viewed either as a time limited "stressful life event" [22, 23] or as a process through which the individual may respond differently at different period prior to, during, and after the actual termination of work [24].

The strengths and limitations of the stressful life event and process approaches to retirement are examined elsewhere [24-26] in discussions which tend to reinforce the differences between these two theoretical approaches. For the purposes of the present chapter, however, it should be noted that the process and life events perspectives on retirement are in fact similar in their focus on the individual as the appropriate and sole unit of analysis while ignoring the larger sociopolitical structure within which retirement occurs. Both perspectives hence tend to reinforce the implicit assumption that retirement is a given to which the individual simply needs to "adjust" properly.

In the remainder of this chapter, the fallacy of this assumption will be pointed up as female retirement is examined in greater detail. As should be clear from this analysis, whether one looks at gender inequalities in a dual labor market system, or at class differences in the way retirement is experienced by differentially advantaged and disadvantaged subpopulations of women, the impact and meaning of retirement cannot adequately be understood except within a broad socio-structural framework.

WOMEN'S RETIREMENT: AN OVERVIEW

While retirement has traditionally been perceived as a phenomenon primarily affecting older males, policymakers and researchers have become increasingly aware that retirement also represents a significant life transition for older women. The dramatic increase in female labor force participation rates during the past thirty years underscores the need to understand the retirement process among older women. In fact, the percentage of women who are employed in the paid labor force has risen from 34 percent in 1950 to over 50 percent in 1980. Approximately 30 percent of these women are "mature" workers, a term used by the Department of Labor to categorize individuals forty-five years of age or older. In 1980, 59.9 percent of women aged forty-five to fifty-four were employed as were 41.5 percent of women between the ages of fifty-five and sixty-four and 15 percent of women aged sixty-five to sixty-nine. In addition, in 1978, 12 million women, or one-quarter of all employed females, were working part-time compared with 6.4 million men. Older women were disproportionately represented in this part-time category [27].

While trends in labor force participation have been well documented, the exact number of female retirees is currently impossible to ascertain because official data sources tend to aggregate housewives and retirees into a single "nonworker" category [6]. Nevertheless, it has been estimated that between 1952 and 1978, the proportion of retired women aged fifty-seven and over increased by 29 percent while the proportion of homemakers in this age group decreased by 31 percent [28].

Female longevity patterns also suggest that retirement and, in particular, the post-retirement period may very well represent a significant portion of an older woman's life cycle. Women who reach age sixty-five can expect to live about eighteen more years. If they reach age seventy-five, their expected longevity is an additional twelve years. In contrast, at age sixty-five older men have an average life expectancy of fourteen years; at age seventy-five, they can anticipate nine more years of life [2]. As will be discussed in more detail later, women who because of their longevity patterns will live as retirees for a considerably longer period than men nevertheless enter their retirement years with far fewer financial resources than their male peers.

The past decade has witnessed a proliferation of theoretical discussions and empirical analyses which have focused on issues surrounding female retirement. (See [4] and [6] for detailed reviews of the female retirement literature.) Several provocative critiques of the research relating to female adaptation to retirement [4, 29] have concluded that retirement is "no problem" for most older women and that more attention should be paid to the decision to retire. While we agree that the decision-making process is a critical issue warranting further investigation, the methodological limitations of studies to date and the equivocal nature of their findings suggest that conclusions concerning the consequences of female retirement are premature. In particular studies which have explored female attitudes toward retirement [6, 24, 30-32] and post-retirement behavior among older women [5, 24, 33-35] have relied almost exclusively on cross-sectional and retrospective data and have been based on small convenience or occupational samples of primarily white middle and upper class women. The diversity of subjective and objective measures which have been used to define and operationalize retirement [26] further raise serious doubts as to the reliability and generalizability of the findings. The one longitudinal analysis which did explore the consequences of retirement among unmarried older women [37] (N = 377) thus assumed individuals to be retired if they worked less than thirty-five hours per week and were receiving a pension. Such a loose interpretation of retirement tends to lump together those individuals who have completely withdrawn from the labor force, those who are partially retired, and those who have slightly reduced their work schedules. The study's conclusion that retirement is of no significant consequence to most older women therefore must be viewed with extreme caution.

A number of studies which have investigated gender differences in adjustment to retirement [9, 24, 30] as well as adaptation problems among specific subpopulations of older women [33, 35, 37, 38] support the notion that the retirement experience may represent a stressful life change for some groups of female retirees. These tentative findings of differential effects underscore the importance of examining retirement within the broad sociostructural context in which it takes place.

The disadvantaged economic status of many female retirees has been offered as one possible explanation for the differences in retirement adaptation patterns. While other factors, e.g., the loss of work based social ties [34, 35, 39, 40] and the concomitance of such life changes as widowhood and retirement [41, 42] also have been shown to influence retirement adaption and decision making, our analysis is limited to those broader structural factors which determine in large part one's economic condition on the threhold of retirement and one's chances for a positive experience in the post-retirement years.

ECONOMIC STATUS OF THE FEMALE RETIREE

Economic status on the threshold of retirement and during the post-retirement period has been identified as a major contributor to the well being of the female retiree [6, 8, 24]. Retirement income further has been perceived as an important coping resource that can lessen the impact of the potential stress resulting from the loss of the work role [42, 43]. While many women approach retirement with adequate financial resources, a large proportion of female retirees, particularly if they are unmarried and living alone, must depend on a meager retirement income [1, 44].

The disadvantaged economic status of certain groups of women has been used to explain gender differences in adjustment to retirement [7, 24, 30] as well as differences among subpopulations of female retirees [6, 33, 35, 38]. For example, in a study controlling for differences between employed and retired females with respect to age, income, and health, Jaslow found higher morale among the workers [33]. The pattern was reversed, however, among women with annual incomes of $5,000 or more, with the retirees in this income group reporting higher morale.

Differentials can be attributed, in part, to the single marital status of many older women, largely accounted for by the loss of a spouse, which frequently places them in a disadvantaged economic status. In 1978, among women aged sixty-five and over, 52 percent were widowed, 3.2 percent were divorced, and 6.2 percent had never been married. Only 36.7 percent were married and living with a spouse compared with 75 percent of older men. By the age of seventy-five, 69 percent of women were widowed compared with 23 percent of their male counterparts. For seven out of ten older women who do become widowed, the average duration of widowhood is sixteen years. Women over sixty-five further are seven times less likely to remarry than are their male peers [27].

Recent poverty statistics underscore the potential magnitude of these differentials. While the operationalization of poverty has been the subject of much controversy, the number of aged women living in poverty is excessive, regardless of the criterion (e.g., current income; intra-family and in-kind transfers and liquid net worth) or the index (e.g., official versus "near poverty" index) used to measure economic status [44]. For example, in 1978 one of every six women aged sixty-five and over had a below-poverty income, and women were more than twice as likely as their male peers to experience poverty in old age [44]. Moreover, the highest rates of poverty exist among unmarried females, with single women, primarily widows, comprising over 72 percent of this nation's aged poor [45]. While only 8 percent of the women sixty-five and older in families were below the poverty level in 1981, 28 percent of women in this age group living alone or with nonrelatives, lived in poverty as did 61 percent of single older black women. The figure for impoverished older unmarried women living alone increases to 50 percent if one uses the Census Bureau's "near poverty" index [46].

Social Security, which accounts for 83 percent of all government transfers, exacerbates poverty differentials between men and women because its benefit structure differentiates on the basis of marital status in a way which favors married couples over all other categories [44, 47]. Furthermore, 21 percent of all older unmarried women who received Social Security benefits in 1978 had no other source of income. Their median income was only $3,660 while the comparable figure for family/single units with more than one retirement benefit was $7,800 [48].

The single marital status of many female retirees, however, does not sufficiently explain the disadvantaged economic position of older women in retirement. In particular, it does not take into account aspects of a woman's pre-retirement work and family history which are critical in determining her retirement status. Two interrelated pre-retirement factors—the sexual division of labor which consigns women to certain family obligations [49] and the female worker's occupational location throughout adulthood [8] are particularly important in this regard and are examined here in greater detail.

THE DUAL LABOR MARKET

The political economy of aging perspective locates the heart of the problem of women's disadvantaged position upon retirement in the dual market structure of the economy [3, 14, 50]. According to this theoretical framework, the transition from competitive to monopolistic capitalism in America and other western industrialized nations produced segmented private labor markets composed of a core or primary sector and a peripheral or secondary sector [51]. The primary sector is characterized by relatively high salary and wage schedules, good fringe benefits including pensions, a high degree of job security and opportunities for mobility. In contrast, the secondary sector is characterized by relatively low earnings, few fringe benefits, poor working conditions, and little job security [52]. If pension plans exist at all, they offer a limited coverage, require at least ten years of service to be vested, and are not portable [53].

A primary feature of women's work careers is the tendency for females to be overrepresented in secondary sector industries. In particular, a large proportion of female workers is concentrated in retail trade and in service sectors where pensions are not available or attainable [8]. Similarly, women are frequently located in a few select occupations such as sales and clerical work and are limited to traditionally female-oriented professions like teaching and social services [54]. Blau and Jusenius have noted that this occupational gender segregation is often tied to lower earnings and pension coverage which places the older female retiree in a more disadvantaged economic position than her male counterpart [55].

Since pension income represents a significant factor in one's economic well being during the retirement years, the preponderance of women in peripheral sector industries and occupations suggests that many female retirees will be entitled to few, if any, pension benefits. According to a recent policy report on the economic status of women [27] 42 percent of married couples, 32 percent of unmarried men and only 22 percent of unmarried women receive private pension income. Moreover, even when older women accrue pension benefits their income from private plans tends to be lower than their male peers. In 1976, the median private pension income was $2,060 for male retirees compared with $1,340 for older women [56]. An analysis of retirement income levels among 1,041 unmarried women and 3,917 married and unmarried men participating in the Social Security Administration's Longitudinal Retirement History Study found that the number of pensions exerts the strongest influence on retirement income among female retirees. However, location in a favorable pension industry[1] increased a woman's retirement income by only $275 while her male counterpart enjoyed a $395 increase [56].

While the dual labor market approach calls attention to the fact that women are disproportionately represented in the secondary sector of the economy, it does little to explain how or why so many females are relegated to this industrial and occupational position [49]. Inadequate attention thus is paid to such structural factors as 1) sex discrimination in hiring and promotion which limits the occupational access and mobility of women, and 2) the sexual division of labor which assigns primary family obligations, including childrearing, to the woman of the household [49].

THE SEXUAL DIVISION OF LABOR

The sexual division of labor is of particular importance to an understanding of the differential effects of retirement since pre-retirement family responsibilities influence women's work lives to a much greater degree than they affect men's careers [58, 59]. In particular, interrupted and delayed career patterns, largely accounted for by childbearing and childrearing, may negatively affect the economic, emotional, and possibly even the physical well-being of female retirees [7, 8, 24, 38].

Chenoweth and Maret have identified three major career patterns among women: continuous labor force participation, interrupted participation, and nonparticipation, or "homemaking." [60] The interrupted or "in and out" pattern includes midlife career entry, intermittent employment throughout the work cycle, and frequent job changes.

Women who experience interrupted careers are apt to earn less retirement income because the "in and out" pattern decreases one's opportunity to achieve pension vesting rights and also insures lower wages upon which retirement income is based [8, 61]. Although the Employee Retirement Security Act of 1974 (ERISA) was intended to rectify some of the inequities in pension benefits, this piece of legislation did not address the problems emanating from the diverse work patterns among female employees. For example, in 1977 over 30 percent of female workers compared with 12 percent of working men were employed less than 1,000 hours per year [62]. However, ERISA did not require employers to provide pension plans for employees working less than 1,000 hours annually, thus denying pension coverage to a large proportion of female part-time workers. Indeed, it has been estimated that fewer than one-quarter of female workers are covered by pension plans in the private sector [8].

---

[1] Industries have been designated as "favorable" or "unfavorable" pension industries according to the extent and promise of final pension coverage. Favorable pension industries include government and public administration; finance, insurance, and real estate; manufacturing; transportation, communications, and utilities; and professional and related services. Unfavorable pension industries include mining; construction; wholesale and retail trade; entertainment and recreation; and personal and other services [53, 57].

The continuity and timing of one's work career may have a significant impact upon well being in retirement [8, 24, 38]. Atchley has hypothesized that women who interrupt their careers to have children or who enter the labor market following childrearing may perceive retirement as "off time" and stressful because they are neither financially nor emotionally prepared for the cessation of work [24]. Several studies lend empirical support to this argument. In a retrospective study of 179 middle and upper class female university alumnae, Block found that continuous work is associated with high retirement satisfaction, largely attributed to health, post-retirement income and retirement planning [38]. O'Rand and Henretta explored the impact of diverse work patterns on the retirement income levels of a national sample of male and female retirees participating in the Longitudinal Retirement History Study [8]. They observed a distinct financial advantage among women exhibiting a continuous work pattern. For example, unmarried females with interrupted work histories could expect $666 less than those who had worked continuously. Similarly, married women exhibiting an "in and out" pattern could expect, on the average, $667 less than their "continuous worker" counterparts.

Childrearing and delayed career entry were also found by O'Rand to have a significant impact on an older woman's economic well being [8]. Women were thus found to have started full-time work on the average five years later than men with approximately 15 percent of females assuming their first major job after the age of thirty-five. This delay not only limits one's earnings and pension opportunities but frequently requires women to work past the age of sixty-five in order to acquire financial resources. When women do retire, the tendency is greater for them to return to work in order to augment their income from earnings. Moreover, each child reduces a woman's chances of pension coverage by 2 percent and decreases annual retirement income by $94 [9].

A final key finding of this study was that women's perceptions of their health were negatively affected by retirement to a significantly greater degree than were men's. While O'Rand attributed this finding, in part, to increased social isolation resulting from the unmarried status of the women, she also conjectured that their disadvantaged economic status relative to men's further limited the female retirees' role options and perhaps encouraged these women to assume a sick role.

A final and often neglected dimension of the impact of the sexual division of labor involves the fact that older women workers are far more likely than older males to be forced to retire to care for an ill spouse or relative. This involuntary cessation of work, coupled with the added stress of caring for an ill spouse or relative, may be hypothesized to lead to an ultimate decline in the health of the female retiree. While studies have not been conducted which specifically test this hypothesis, findings of increased illness among aged female caregivers suggest the possibility of a synergistic relationship between retirement and caring for an ill spouse or relative [63, 64]. Such studies further underscore the fact that the sexual division of labor with regard to caregiving does not stop with child-rearing but continues throughout the life cycle.

CONCLUSION

While women's retirement has been the focus of increasing research attention, studies for the most part have failed to place the topic within a broad sociopolitical context. As such, they have tended to ignore such factors as the dual labor market and the sexual division of labor which may heavily influence women's retirement decisions and adaptation.

A broader political economic analysis of women's retirement reveals that the disadvantaged economic status of many female retirees may play an important role in determining retirement adaptation patterns. The disproportionate representation of women in the peripheral or secondary sector of the labor market and the sexual division of labor which encourages an interrupted and discontinuous pattern of female labor force participation, thus help explain the disadvantageous economic position of many women upon retirement. The financial burdens faced by single women retirees are particularly significant and may be seen to reflect in part inequitable benefit structures within Social Security and many private pension plans which favor married couples over single individuals.

While a variety of factors including the loss of work based social ties and the not infrequent concomitance of retirement with widowhood may influence the individual woman's retirement experience, that experience must, on a macro level, be viewed within the context of broader sociostructural realities.

By placing women's retirement squarely within such a context, the political economic perspective helps us better understand those structural inequalities which may be at the root of differential retirement outcomes both by gender, and within different subgroups of the female population.

REFERENCES

1. J. Treas, Women's Employment and Its Implications for the Status of the Elderly of the Future, in *Aging and Social Change*, Keisler, *et al.* (eds.), Academic Press, New York, 1981.
2. L. M. Verbrugge, An Epidemiological Profile of Older Women, paper presented at the 111th Annual Meeting of the American Public Health Association, Dallas, Texas, November 16, 1983.
3. L. Olson, *The Political Economy of Aging*, Columbia University Press, New York, 1982.
4. B. Gratton and M. R. Haug, Decision and Adaption: Research on Female Retirement, *Research on Aging*, 5:1, pp. 59-76, 1983.
5. R. C. Atchley, The Process of Retirement: Comparing Men and Women, in *Women's Retirement*, M. Szinovacz (ed.), Sage Yearbooks in Women's Policy Studies, Sage, Beverly Hills, California, pp. 153-168, 1982.

6. M. Szinovacz, Beyond the Hearth: Women and Retirement from the Labor Force, in *Older Women: Issues and Prospects*, E. W. Markson (ed.), Lexington Books, Lexington, Massachusetts, 1982.
7. A. M. O'Rand, Women, in *Handbook of the Aged in the United States*, E. Palmore (ed.), Greenwood Press, Westport, Connecticut, 1983.
8. A. M. O'Rand and J. C. Henretta, Midlife Work History and the Retirement Income of Older Single and Married Women, in *Women's Retirement: Policy Implications of Recent Research*, M. Szinovacz (ed.), Sage, Beverly Hills, California, pp. 23-44, 1982.
9. A. M. O'Rand, Loss of Work Role and Subjective Health Assessment in Later Life among Men and Unmarried Women, in *Research in the Sociology of Education and Socialization*, Vol. 5, A. C. Kerckhoff (ed.), JAI Press, San Francisco, California, 1983.
10. C. L. Estes, L. Gerrard, and J. Swan, Dominant and Competing Paradigms in Gerontology: Toward a Political Economy of Aging, *Ageing and Society*, 2, pp. 151-164, July 1982.
11. A. Walker, The Social Creation of Poverty and Dependency in Old Age, *Journal of Social Policy*, 9:1, pp. 49-75, 1980.
12. W. Graebner, *A History of Retirement*, Yale University Press, New Haven, Connecticut, 1980.
13. J. Myles, Conflict, Crisis and the Future of Old Age Security, *Milbank Memorial Fund Quarterly*, 61:4, Fall 1983.
14. J. Williamson, L. Evans, and L. A. Powell (eds.), *The Politics of Aging*, Charles C. Thomas, Springfield, Illinois, 1982.
15. A. Guillemard, Retirement as a Social Process, Its Differential Effects upon Behavior, paper presented at the 8th World Congress of Sociology, Toronto, Canada, 1974.
16. A. Hunt, *The Elderly at Home*, HMSO, London, 1978.
17. E. Kingson, The Early Retirement Myth: Why Men Retire before Age Sixty-Two, Report by the U.S. House Select Committee on Aging, U.S. Government Printing Office, Washington, D.C., Pub. No. 97-298, October 1981.
18. L. Harris, *The Myth and Reality of Aging in America*, National Council on Aging, Washington, D.C., 1976.
19. R. E. Barfield and J. N. Morgan, Trends in Satisfaction with Retirement, *The Gerontologist, 18*, pp. 19–23, 1978.
20. A. Fonar and K. Schwab, *Aging and Retirement*, Brooks Cole Publishers, Monterey, California, 1981.
21. M. H. Brenner, Economic Changes and Heart Disease Mortality, *American Journal of Public Health, 61*, p. 606, 1971.
22. F. M. Carp (ed.), *Retirement*, Behavioral Publications, New York, 1972.
23. C. Eisdorfer and F. Wilkie, Stress, Disease, Aging and Behavior, in *Handbook of the Psychology of Aging*, J. E. Birren and K. Warner Shaie (eds.), Van Nostrand, Reinhold, New York, pp. 251-275, 1977.
24. R. C. Atchley, *Social Forces in Later Life* (2nd edition), Wadsworth, Belmont, California, 1977.
25. S. Kasl, The Impact of Retirement, in *Current Concerns in Occupational Stress*, C. L. Cooper and R. Payne (eds.), John Wiley and Sons, London, 1980.

26. M. Minkler, Research on the Health Effects of Retirement: An Uncertain Legacy, *Journal of Health and Social Behavior, 22*, pp. 117-130, 1981.

27. Women's Studies Program and Policy Center at George Washington University and The Women's Research and Education Institute of the Congresswomen's Caucus, *Older Women: The Economics of Aging*, Washington, D.C., 1981.

28. F. C. Pampel, *Social Change and the Aged*, Lexington Books, Lexington, Massachusetts, 1981.

29. A. Foner and K. Schwab, Work and Retirement in a Changing Society, in *Aging in Society: Selected Reviews of Recent Research*, Riley, et al. (eds.), Lawrence Erlbaum Associates, Hillsdale, New Jersey, pp. 71-94, 1983.

30. G. F. Streib and C. J. Schneider, *Retirement in American Society*, Cornell University Press, Ithaca, New York, 1971.

31. D. Jacobson, Rejection of the Retiree Role: A Study of Female Industrial Workers in Their 50's, *Human Relations, 27*, pp. 477-491, 1974.

32. N. Kroeger, Preretirement Preparation: Sex Differences in Access, Sources, and Use, in *Women's Retirement*, M. Szinovacz (ed.), Sage Publications, Beverly Hills, California, pp. 95-111, 1982.

33. P. Jaslow, Employment, Retirement, and Morale among Older Women, *Journal of Gerontology, 31*, pp. 212-218, 1976.

34. S. M. Levy, The Adjustment of Older Women: Effects of Chronic Ill Health and Attitudes toward Retirement, *International Journal of Aging and Human Development, 12*, pp. 93-110, 1980.

35. J. H. Fox, Effects of Retirement and Former Work Life on Women's Adaptation in Old Age, *Journal of Gerontology, 32*, pp. 196-202, 1977.

36. E. B. Palmore, L. K. George, and G. G. Fillenbaum, Predictors of Retirement, *Journal of Gerontology, 37*:6, pp. 733-742, 1982.

37. R. H. Jensen, "After Retirement: An Exploratory Study of the Professional Woman," in *Women's Retirement*, M. Szinovacz (ed.) Sage Publishers, Beverly Hills, Ca. pp. 169-182, 1982.

38. M. R. Block, Professional Women: Work Pattern as a Correlate of Retirement Satisfaction, in *Women's Retirement*, M. Szinovacz (ed.), Sage Publishers, Beverly Hills, California, pp. 183-194, 1982.

39. C. Depner and B. Ingersoll, Employment Status and Social Support: The Experience of Mature Women, in *Women's Retirement*, M. Szinovacz (ed.), Sage Publishers, Beverly Hills, California, pp. 61-76, 1982.

40. R. S. Prentis, White Collar Working Women's Perception of Retirement, *The Gerontologist, 20*, pp. 90-95, 1980.

41. T. I. Wan, *Stressful Life Events, Social Support Networks, and Gerontological Health*, Lexington Books, Lexington, Massachusetts, 1982.

42. E. Palmore, W. P. Cleveland, J. B. Nowlin, D. Ramm, and I. C. Siegler, Stress and Adaption in Later Life, *Journal of Gerontology, 34*:6, pp. 841-851, 1979.

43. F. Elwell and A. Maltbie-Crannel, The Impact of Role Loss upon Coping Resources: Life Satisfaction of the Elderly, *Journal of Gerontology, 36*, pp. 223-232, 1981.

44. J. L. Warlick, Aged Women in Poverty: A Problem Without a Solution?, in *Aging and Public Policy*, W. P. Browne and L. Olson (eds.), Greenwood Press, Westport, Connecticut, 1983.
45. N. W. King and M. G. Marvel, *Issues, Policies and Programs for Midlife and Older Women*, Center for Women Policy Studies, Washington, D.C., 1982.
46. U.S. Senate Special Committee on Aging, *Developments in Aging*, Superintendent of Documents, U.S. Government Printing Office, Washington, D.C., 1980 and 1981.
47. S. Lapkoff, Working Women, Marriage and Retirement, report prepared for the President's Commission on Pension Policy, Washington, D.C., August, 1980.
48. S. Grad and K. Foster, Income of the Population Aged Fifty-Five and Older, 1987, *Social Security Bulletin, 42*:7, pp. 16-32, 1979.
49. V. Beechey, Women and Production: A Critical Analysis of Some Sociological Theories of Women's Work, in *Feminism and Materialism*, A. Kuhn and A. Wolpe (eds.), Routledge and Kegan Paul, London, pp. 155-197, 1979.
50. J. J. Dowd, *Stratification among the Aged*, Brooks Cole Publishing Company, Monterey, California, 1980.
51. D. M. Gordon, *Theories of Poverty and Underemployment*, Heath, Boston, Massachusetts, 1972.
52. R. D. Barron and G. M. Norris, Sexual Divisions and the Dual Labor Market, paper presented at the BSA Annual Conference, 1974.
53. W. W. Kolodrubetz and D. M. Landay, Coverage and Vesting of Full-Time Employees under Private Retirement Plans, *Social Security Bulletin, 36*, pp. 20-36, 1973.
54. V. K. Oppenheimer, The Female Labor Force in the United States: Demographic and Economic Factors Governing Its Growth and Changing Composition, Population Monograph Series, No. 5, University of California, Berkeley, 1970.
55. F. Blau and C. I. Jusenius, Economists' Approaches to Sex Segregation in the Labor Market: An Appraisal, in *Women and the Workplace: The Implications of Occupation Segregation*, M. Blaxall and B. Reagan (eds.), University of Chicago Press, Chicago, pp. 181-199, 1976.
56. A. M. O'Rand and R. Landerman, Early Family Role Effects on Women's and Men's Retirement Income Status, *Research on Aging*, 1984 (in press).
57. J. H. Schulz, T. D. Leavitt, and L. Kelly, Private Pensions Fall Short of Preretirement Income Levels, *Monthly Labor Review, 28*, p. 32, 1979.
58. C. J. Waite, Working Wives and the Family Cycle, *Journal of Marriage and the Family, 40*, pp. 401-411, 1980.
59. J. A. Sweet, *Women in the Labor Force*, Seminar Press, New York, 1973.
60. L. C. Chenoweth and E. Maret, The Career Patterns of Mature American Women, *Sociology of Work and Occupations, 7*, pp. 222-251, 1980.
61. R. L. Clark, *Retirement Policy in an Aging Society*, Duke University Press, Durham, North Carolina, 1980.

62. W. D. Spector, Women's Retirement Income, in *Women and Poverty*, (ed.), Sage Publications, Beverly Hills, California, 1977.
63. A. P. Fengler and N. Goodrich, Wives and Disabled Elderly Men: The Hidden Patients, *The Gerontologist*, 29, p. 175, 1975.
64. W. Satariano, M. Minkler, and C. Langhauser, The Significance of an Ill Spouse for Assessing Health Differences in an Elderly Population, *Journal of the American Geriatric Society, 32*, pp. 187-190, 1984.

PART V. FUTURE DIRECTIONS IN THE POLITICS OF SOCIAL POLICY FOR THE ELDERLY

Despite improvements in such economic indicators as inflation and unemployment, the politics of retrenchment continue to portent cutbacks in welfare state programs and policies for the mid 1980's. In the United States, federal cutbacks of at least nine billion dollars are anticipated in 1984, and come on the heels of earlier cuts which had the effect of dismantling major health and social service accomplishments of the last half century.

The final two chapters in this volume address the climate of fiscal austerity which has characterized the early 1980's, examining the meaning and significance of that climate for the elderly. In Chapter 15, Estes examines some of the specific social constructions of reality in the 1980's that have helped to shape recent public policy for the aged. Perceptions of old age as a social problem best addressed through individual level interventions are seen as having a profound effect on policy development for the elderly during the current era of fiscal conservatism. Similarly, the political declaration of a fiscal crisis and the perception of decentralization as a partial solution to economic problems in the United States are viewed as contributing to policy "solutions" that have had the effect of worsening the plight of the elderly, the poor and other disadvantaged segments of the society.

In the final chapter, Minkler looks further at the politics of scapegoating the poor and the elderly as "causes" of the fiscal crisis. In contrast to the victim blaming of the 1960's and early 1970's which defined the elderly as a social problem and devised solutions (e.g., Medicare and Medicaid) for dealing with that problem, the victim blaming of the 1980's is seen to define these earlier "solutions" as part of the problem. Thus, not only are the elderly perceived as a problem, but ameliorative programs are seen as "busting the federal budget" and in need of dismantling and/or shifting to lower levels of government or the private sector.

While both of these chapters focus on the United States, parallel developments within a number of other advanced capitalist and state socialist countries may be seen. As Minkler notes in Chapter 16, for example, the Thatcher Government's assignment of blame for Britain's economic difficulties to programs for the poor and the elderly closely mirrors victim blaming analyses of this type in the United States.

Although the victim blaming of the 1980's is seen as bearing important similarities to that of the 1960's, it is at the same time viewed as more devastating in the effects which it may have on the elderly and other oppressed groups. Effective coalition building among these groups, and the development of educational strategies based on political economic analyses are proposed as important approaches to fighting the scapegoat mentality and its "divide and conquer" tactics.

CHAPTER 15
Austerity and Aging: 1980 and Beyond
CARROLL L. ESTES

OLD AGE AND PUBLIC POLICY

The major problems faced by the elderly in the United States are, in large measure, ones that are socially constructed as a result of the dominant societal conception of aging and the aged. This conception emerges within, reflects, and bolsters the economic and political structure of the society. What is done for and about the elderly, as well as our research-based knowledge about old age and aging, are products of these conceptions. The key determinants of the standard of living enjoyed or endured by the aged are national social and economic policies, political decisions at all levels of government, the power of structural interests, and the policies of business and industry [1].

The policies that social institutions produce reflect the dominance of certain values and normative conceptions of social problems and their remedies. The value choices and definitions of existing conditions do not derive from consensual agreement of the members of society; nor do they result from a benign accommodation among different interests as the pluralists posit [2], nor from the definitions of older persons themselves [3]. In a class society, some individuals and groups have much greater power than others to influence the definition of social problems and to specify the policy interventions that address these problems [4, 5].

The politically organized elderly seek to influence socially determined priorities and public policies. They are, however, only one of a number of sectors of the society that have a vital interest in determining policy choices for the elderly. Growing in power are those economic and political interests that have the most to gain from the Reagan Administration policies of reducing domestic social spending and increasing tax benefits for corporations and upper-income Americans.

Definitions of the "social problem" of old age and of the appropriate policy solutions for this problem have reflected the ups and downs of the U.S. economy

241

and the shifting bases of political power during the past thirty years. With the economic rebound after the recession of the late 1950's, there was a period of rapid economic growth and corresponding political optimism in dealing with two difficult domestic social problems—racial discrimination and poverty. In gerontology, this optimism was reflected in the activity theory of aging which was predicated on the assumption that health, mobility, adjustment, and general well-being were realistic outcomes for most older Americans; and policies to foster socialization and recreation were to be commended. Optimism also was evident in the enactment of Medicare in 1965, which aimed to provide the elderly with access to needed medical services.

In the 1960's, the initial policy of treating the aged as a homogenous category was established under both Medicare and the Older Americans Act of 1965. Conceptually, all aged were lumped together as a general class with little specificity as to whether they were disadvantaged or as to how income, race, sex, or ethnic differences affected their status. The Older Americans Act provided limited funding, initially and mainly for senior center activities, reflecting a view of the problems of the elderly as social isolation and the lack of social activity (consonant with the activity theory of aging). Differences in hardship among the aged were downplayed in favor of social and recreational programs for which all the aged were equally eligible. The approach of the Older Americans Act obscured the visibility of the elderly who were poor, extremely disabled, or ill [1].

As economic growth and the Vietnam war fueled inflation, the optimism of the 1960's was replaced by disillusionment. The ensuing economic recession of the early 1970's and continued inflation were accompanied by a move on the part of the Nixon Administration toward retrenchment of federal programs under the banner of "new federalism" and decentralization. The consequence of this policy and the revenue sharing programs it generated was ultimately to shift political and fiscal responsibility for many domestic programs increasingly from the federal to state and local governments. President Nixon's intention was that the decentralization strategy would curtail the growth of federal programs, while shifting the political and economic pressure of social programs from the federal and state and substate arenas.

Consistent with this trend, Older Americans Act policies shifted from recreation to a major emphasis on state and local coordination, planning, and comprehensive service development. The 1973 Older Americans Act amendments assigned existing state agencies on aging the responsibility for designating local planning and coordination agencies (area agencies on aging), which, in turn, were assigned responsibility for generating local resources.

The decentralized planning-coordination policy of the 1970's largely ignored the widespread poverty of the aged, providing no direct economic relief. The emphasis, instead, was on the aged as service recipients and consumers, supporting the development of an expanding service economy and confirming Miller's thesis that the treatment of social problems during the 1970's mirrored the task of the decade—to put the economy on its feet [4].

Embarking on the decade of the 1980's, there are three dominant perceptions of reality that appear to be shaping public policy for the elderly under the Reagan Administration:

First, there has been a political declaration of fiscal crisis at the federal level which has generated a climate of intense psychological uncertainty and vulnerability of the American public to proposals to dismantle major social programs. The crisis definition of the U.S. economy, now incorporated into law through both the Omnibus Budget Reconciliation Act and the Economic Recovery Tax Act of 1981, has assured the objective condition of a fiscal crisis in many states.

Second, there is a growing perception that the problems of the elderly and other disadvantaged groups cannot and will not be solved by instituting *national* policies and programs; rather, the solutions must come from the efforts of state and local government, initiatives of the private sector, or initiatives of the individual. The rationale enunciated by many politicians [6] is that the problems that social programs address are either not remediable by, or are not the responsibility of, the federal government. In this context, the cost of government intervention in itself is characterized as harmful to business productivity and to the U.S. economy. There is a resurgence of the ideology that individuals create their own conditions and opportunities, and that they are to be held accountable for their predicament. There is also much rhetoric about the decentralization of federal programs as a means of getting government "off the backs" of the people.

Third, there is a popular perception in the United States that old age is a problem resulting largely from the biological and physiological decline of the aging individual [1]. Further, the dependency of the elderly is seen by many as a consequence of individual default (e.g., not planning well, not saving enough). Each of these perceptions has strengthened the support for policy intervention strategies aimed at the individual level rather than collective social change efforts.

DOMINANT PERCEPTIONS SHAPING PUBLIC POLICY FOR THE ELDERLY

The Perception of Fiscal Crisis and the Necessity for Reduced Federal Expenditure

Fiscal crisis is a concept that has had a major impact on the policies of local and state governments. Initially the term "fiscal crisis" came into currency in the United States in the 1970's to describe the problems of a local government that could not service its debts (e.g., New York City, Cleveland) or of a state whose expenditures exceeded its revenues. The term fiscal crisis is now being widely applied to describe federal expenditures for social programs and the U.S. economy.

Since 1975, there has been a decline in federal, state, and local expenditures as a percent of the gross national product (GNP) and a decline in per capita expenditures in constant dollars [7]. After intergovernmental transfers (i.e., federal and state to local, federal to local), the most significant declines are at the local level [8]. Since 1975, state and local expenditures have declined from 15.1 percent to 13.5 percent of the GNP, while federal expenditures have decreased from 12.3 percent to 11.9 percent of the GNP.

Fiscal crisis at the local level will be exacerbated because of the severe cutbacks in direct federal aid, as well as the community development block grants and the comprehensive employment and training block grants that have been eliminated, and others that have been significantly reduced [7, 9].

From *above*, there are federal limits on Medicaid expenditures for health care for the poor, and major block grant initiatives with a 20 to 25 percent reduction in the funding level of the prior categorical (targeted) programs that the block grants replace. Both of these conditions are shifting medical care costs to the states, to local governments, and to the elderly themselves [10].

From *below*, there are fiscal crises and tax revolts at the state and local levels. Caught in the squeeze, health and social services are involved in a fiscal crisis of their own. During the 1980's, all levels of government will seek to cut costs and to shift expenditures to other jurisdictions. For example, at least one-third of the states were planning Medicaid cuts before the enactment of the Omnibus Budget Reconciliation Act of 1981. Many more will follow suit as a result of federal reductions in social spending and the limits that the Act placed on the federal share of Medicaid costs.

These fiscal pressures at multiple governmental levels pose a particular problem for Medicaid-funded services because of the magnitude and rapid increases in these expenditures, now outrunning the capacity of states to raise the necessary revenues [11]. In view of the Medicaid expenditure escalation, and the fact that 20 percent of the elderly receive Medicaid and 39 percent of Medicaid expenditures are for the elderly, the cost-containing policy changes at the state level are likely to affect the elderly poor and near-poor directly.

The Perception that National Policies Should Give Way to Decentralization and Block Grants

Budget cuts have been made in the block grants which represent the major element in President Reagan's domestic social program proposals. In the 1970's, this policy concept emerged under the banner of "new federalism," which converted a number of categorical programs to block grant-type revenue sharing programs (e.g., Title XX of the Social Security Act). Designed to decentralize responsibility for domestic social programs to state and local governments through block grant-type funding and to limit federal involvement in those programs, new federalism augmented the fiscal and political responsibility of state and local governments for multiple programs, including those affecting health care [12]. Both the block grants of the 1970's and those created in the Omnibus Budget Reconciliation Act of 1981 ease the constraints of categorical funding and of federal requirements, resulting in increased discretion for state government decision making in multiple programs that affect the elderly, including such programs as community mental health centers, home health services, emergency medical services, and hypertension control.

A significant consequence of the block grant decentralization is that the wide discretion it provides individual states will augment the inequities in the same program across the states [1]. This, in turn, makes it impossible to assure uniform benefits for the same targeted population (e.g., the aged) across the jurisdictions or to maintain accountability with so many varying state approaches. Finally, because the most disadvantaged (e.g., the poor aged) are heavily dependent on state-determined benefits, they are extremely vulnerable in this period of economic flux.

The net result of the large-scale shift to block grants in health and social services, combined with the across-the-board expenditure reductions for Fiscal Year 1982 for the block-granted programs, is increased pressure on state and local governments to underwrite program costs at the same time that many states, cities, and counties also are under extreme pressure to curb rising expenditures. The result is likely to be serious for the elderly poor and for the poor of all ages.

The Perception of Old Age and Aging as an Individual Problem

Consistent with the liberal philosophical emphasis on individual responsibility, public policy for the aged in the United States has treated the problem of old age largely as resolvable through the provision of services at the individual level. Medicare and Medicaid policies, Title XX Social Services, and the Older Americans Act are all predicated on the notion that treating *individuals* is the way to treat the "problem" of aging. Further, the provider of service receives reimbursement under all of these programs, while the elderly are defined as "recipients," clients, or patients of service. Thus, the helping professions share—and benefit from—the individualized conception of aging, which is implemented through policies in ways that contribute to the further dependency of the aged. The medical profession has been the provider group to benefit most from this conceptualization and the U.S. health policies that flow from it.

In the United States, not only has aging been defined as an individual problem, but old people themselves have been specifically defined as "the problem." One important influence of this dominant perception is the research emphasis that has been given to the biological aspects of aging and the concern with disease processes rather than the causes of disease, particularly with the social, economic, and environmental factors that contribute to disease. Social and behavioral science research has been focused on studying the individual old person; it has been heavily concerned about the adjustment, life satisfaction, and morale of old people and with human development and the life cycle processes of aging.

The societal treatment of the elderly (through policies of mandatory retirement and reduced income) tends to be taken as "given" by most researchers. The research task has been to learn how the aging process works (implicitly taking for granted the existing policies and conditions) and how adult development and adjustment occur under given conditions.

Thus, while aging is typified as an individual problem, it tends also to be seen as one that occurs largely as a result of apolitical processes (i.e., individual physiological and chronological decline). The biological models and biomedical problem definitions of aging support the notion that aging is an *individual* problem and that it is largely a *medical* problem. This "medicalization" of aging at least partially explains the strong support for current U.S. health policies that have benefited doctors, hospitals, and insurance companies far more than they have the elderly, who are now paying more out-of-pocket medical care costs than their entire health bills before the enactment of Medicare.

An important consequence has been the expansion of the health services industry. Increasingly, in the 1970's, the formation of the problem of aging in America, as described, led to policies that are service strategies—with a highly medical character, and with power largely in the hands of service providers, through policies which provide them reimbursement. Medical care dollars outstrip social service dollars $30 to $1 [13]—this prior to the Fiscal Years 1982 and 1983 cutbacks that are expected to curtail social services far more than medical services [14]. The problem formulation has done little to address the root economic inequality of the aged or to directly alter the dependency status of the aged through policies that provide continued employment or adequate retirement income.

The policies that emerged also have the core characteristic of being largely separatist in nature—that is, separting the aged from other groups in society on the basis of their special need. As a consequence of this problem formulation and policy prescription, an "aging enterprise" has been created to serve the aged. The aging enterprise includes the congeries of programs, organizations, bureaucracies, interest groups, trade associations, providers, industries, and professionals that serve the aged in one capacity or another [1]. The concept of the aging enterprise is intended to call attention to how the aged and their needs are processed and treated as a commodity in our society. It also calls attention to the fact that the age-segregated policies which fuel the enterprise are socially divisive solutions, in contrast to those polcies which do not single out, stigmatize, and isolate the aged from the rest of society (e.g., national health insurance, full employment). The policies and political processes that surround the aging enterprise have engendered competition between disadvantaged groups and between the generations; in so doing, they encourage dangerous dichotomies.

Among many advocates and politicians, there is a firm belief that no equity is possible; there are just trade-offs. Such policies and politics do little to advance the cause of social justice; they perpetuate acceptance of the inevitability of scarcity, inequity, and intergroup rivalries.

DIFFERENTIAL IMPACT OF PUBLIC POLICIES

These definitions and policy prescriptions obscure an understanding of aging as a socially generated problem and status and divert attention from the social and political institutions that, in effect, produce many of the problems confronting the elderly today. Political economy analyses, emphasizing the interaction between policy and the economy, have begun to reexamine and challenge these dominant conceptions [1, 15-25].

The issue of the role and power of the state, constraints on state intervention, and its legitimating function in the distribution of benefits has not been examined extensively with respect to public policy for the aged, although Ginsberg [26], O'Connor [27], Gough [28], and others have addressed these issues indirectly in their analyses of the role and function of the welfare state. In the health field, major contributions to a political economy framework have been made [5, 29-32]. Drawing on the approach by Walton [33], the political economy of aging focuses on the nature of and intersections between aging status and class politics, which can be understood only in terms of their structural bases and how they are conditioned by the socioeconomic and political environment.

The political economy approach is distinguished from the dominant gerontological perspective by viewing the problem of aging as a structural one. The individualistic view assumes the overriding importance of the market in distributing rewards and in determining socioeconomic status. The dependency status of the elderly is explained by the individual and his or her lifetime (and work) behavior patterns. The theory, simply stated, is that "you get what you earned." Numerous U.S. studies on status and income maintenance adopt this approach [34-37]. Most policy interventions in the United States reflect this perspective nad, in the case of the aged, promote age-segregated policies and services for a detached and dependent minority.

In contrast, the structural view of aging starts with the proposition that the status and resources of the elderly, and even the trajectory of the aging process itself, are conditioned by one's location in the social structure and the economic and political factors that affect it. The dependency of the elderly is to be understood in the labor market and in the social relations that it produces—and these as they change with age. Policy interventions from this perspective would be directed toward various institutionalized structures of society, in particular the labor market.

Current old age policy in the United States reflects a two-class system of welfare where benefits are distributed on the basis of legitimacy [38] rather than on the basis of need. Old people may have more legitimacy relative to other disadvantaged groups in society competing for scarce public funds [39], but old age neither levels nor diminishes social class distinctions. Social class, status, and economic resources in old age are largely determined by lifetime conditions and labor force participation established before retirement age [17]. As Nelson [40] indicates, both income and services policies in the United States reflect different classes of "deservingness" in old age.

Public policies in the United States are very different for the aged who are considered "deserving" compared with those who are considered "undeserving" (see Figure 1). Three classes of the aged are entitled to some type of government program: 1) the middle- and upper-class (the deserving nonpoor) aged; 2) the newly poor in old age (the deserving poor); and 3) the aged who have always been poor (the undeserving poor). The nonpoor aged have the resources to permit

Policy Area	"Deserving Poor" (Upper Class/Middle Class)	"Undeserving Poor" (Lower Class)
Income	Highest social security payments to upper and middle classes Regressive taxation—no Social Security tax after $32,400 salary level Pensions Tax credits	$6,000 retirement test for Social Security hurts this group the most Supplemental Security Income payment levels are below poverty
Medical care	Medicare—hospital and medical expenditures are highest for upper and middle classes Private health insurance	Medicaid—approximately 50% of those below poverty level are not covered; states may have more restrictive eligibility than the federal government
Social services	Social services block grant (formerly Title XX of the Social Security Act)—$2.4 billion ceiling in 1983; no federally mandated priority to Aid for Dependent Children, Supplemental Security Income, or Medicaid recipients Older Americans Act access/socialization services—limited resources; all aged are eligible, but provides services most needed by the middle class (e.g., access)	

Note: There is one federal policy covering the "deserving poor," in contrast to 50 state variable policies covering the "undeserving poor." State variable policies emerge primarily from state-federal programs in which states have much discretion over eligibility and the scope of available services. State discretionary programs are fiscally vulnerable, unstable, and highly vulnerable to swings in state-level political and economic factors.

Figure 1. Class basis of policies for the aged.

access to public and private services without the necessity of government intervention. They also receive a disproportionate share of the benefits of the largest federal programs for the aged (e.g., Social Security, Medicare, and retirement tax credits). Most services policies tend to favor the newly poor in old age, largely because they are thought of as both deserving and deprived. Services have been designed largely to assist the recently deprived aged to maintain their lifestyles, rather than to provide the more crucial life-support services (e.g., income) needed by the poor aged. The aged who have been lifelong poor are assisted largely through inadequate income-maintenance policies, such as Supplemental Security Income (SSI), the Social Security minimum benefit (now available only to current, not future beneficiaries), and Medicaid (which is highly variable from state to state).

Deservingness in old age income policies is very much based on the principle of differential rewards for differential achievements during a lifetime. The social security system reflects the notion that there is no entitlement as a matter of right to those who have not earned it. For those individuals who have been casually employed or who had very low lifetime earnings covered by social security (mainly women and minorities), the minimum benefit has in the past guaranteed a basic monthly payment of $122. Since some estimated 3 million beneficiaries receive a higher monthly payment than would be payable under regular benefit formula, critics have pointed to the alleged welfare character of the minimum social security benefit. Successful Reagan Administration and congressional cutback efforts targeted at eliminating the social security minimum benefit for all future beneficiaries [41] is illustrative of the efforts to eliminate the "undeserving" aged from the social security trust funds. Proponents of this policy change argued that those who require income support beyond what they have actually earned in the labor market ought to go looking to the Supplementary Security Income (SSI) program or other state discretionary welfare programs for relief [42].

The important point is that most, if not all, of the policies that deal with the "undeserving" aged are "state discretionary policy"—that is, they are in the hands of the states. As such, the eligibility and benefits under these policies depend upon the variable willingness and fiscal capacity of states to fund programs at the state level. Not only are these state discretionary programs different from state to state, they tend to be easily politicized and certainly they are more economically vulnerable and variable than uniform federal policies. Thus, the most economically disadvantaged aged do not have the security of stable, uniformly administered federal policies (like social security and Medicare) that apply to those considered more deserving.

Health policy exemplifies the class basis of U.S. policies. While most aged are eligible for Medicare, research has shown that more Medicare benefits are provided to the upper and middle classes and to whites than to the lower classes and blacks [43]. Inequities in Medicare benefits appear on the basis of income, race, and region. In the southern region of the United States, where 56 percent of the nation's aged nonwhites reside, the disparities between white and nonwhite Medicare beneficiaries persist [44]. Further, upper- and middle-class aged can afford to supplement these benefits with private health insurance, and they are better able to meet the increasing cost of copayments and deductibles under Medicare than are the lower-class aged. The Reagan Administration and Congress have adopted policies in the 1981 Omnibus Budget Reconciliation Act and are proposing further Medicare reductions for Fiscal Year 1983 that will increase the hardship of medical expenses for the poor elderly. In 1982, both the costs of physician and hospital services have been increased under Medicare. Such increases are particularly significant in the context of the already high out-of-pocket costs borne directly by the elderly for their medical care—estimated to be in excess of $1000 per capita in 1979—and the increasing rate of poverty among the elderly [45].

For the poorest aged, Medicaid is available as a state program. Medicaid is a highly variable program whose state-determined eligibility standards are so stringent that it has been estimated (prior to the 1982 cutbacks) that at least 50 percent of the people below poverty level are not eligible because of the widely varying eligibility requirements across the states [46]. The effect of the most recent policy shifts in the United States toward capping the growth in federal Medicaid costs, block grants, and reduced social spending will be to increase existing inequities in programs for the poor across the states.

The lesson is clear. The states that are "generous" in terms of Medicaid eligibility standards and benefits must pay for it in large part themselves. It is not federal policy to formally address the needs of the most disadvantaged with a national policy that is uniform for all low-income aged across the country. Both medical and income supplementation (i.e., Supplemental Security Income) for the poor aged are left up to the states and their varying willingness and declining economic capacity to support these programs.

As economic problems have mounted at the federal level, more and more human service programs have been delegated to the states. These pressures are occurring simultaneously with other growing fiscal pressures on the states, including the loss of general revenue sharing at the state level, taxpayer revolts (real or threatened), and huge inflationary increases in state health expenditures.

The class-based policy treatment of the elderly just described may be affected by the new emerging strategy that would emphasize the adoption of "nonservice approaches" to the problems of the poor and aged. Consistent with the declaration of fiscal crisis, the aim of this approach is to redirect expectations from the national policy level to the local level where individuals can help themselves without public funding by such means as advocacy, self-help, administration, and tax policy changes [47]. However, these policies are not likely to seriously challenge the predominantly medical services strategy. How this will be played out and how it will affect the services strategy now in place remains to be demonstrated.

SUMMARY

Programs and policies for the aged will be affected by the major policy shifts emerging with the Reagan Administration in 1981. These comprise: 1) a reduction in federal spending for social programs, reflecting a major shift in priorities from nondefense to defense spending and from public to increased private allocation of resources [48], 2) increased decentralization and block granting of program authority and fiscal and political responsibility for social programs to the states; 3) deregulation and the promotion of procompetition approaches, particularly in the health sector [10]; and 4) a sharp reduction in federal revenues with the Economic Recovery Tax Act of 1981.

There will be increased competition and heightened tensions between the health and social services sectors as the cutback pressures mount on nondefense spending. States will be required to invoke stricter state-determined measures to limit their expenditures for health and social programs as a consequence of increased state and local responsibility and fiscal constraint.

Further, even the prospects for the most popular entitlement program for the elderly—social security—are under assault, to the extent that the aged are blamed for the fiscal crisis [35, 36]. The attribution of such culpability of the elderly is at least partly a result of the same separatist thinking that has fostered the aging enterprise. The consequence of such thinking appears to be dangerous in a period of economic retrenchment, for it is just as "special" and "different" groups (e.g., the aged) who may be used to explain the origin of the fiscal crisis— this in spite of the world politics and broad economic conditions and policies of which the aged are but a small part and which their policies only reflect.

ACKNOWLEDGMENT

The author gratefully acknowledges the assistance of Lenore Gerard.

REFERENCES

1. C. L. Estes, *The Aging Enterprise*, Jossey-Bass, San Francisco, 1979.
2. W. E. Connolly, *The Bias of Pluralism*, Atherton, New York, 1969.
3. C. L. Estes, Community Planning for the Elderly: A Study of Goal Displacement, *Journal of Gerontology*, *29*, pp. 684-691, 1974.
4. S. M. Miller, The Political Economy of Social Problems: from the Sixties to the Seventies, *Social Problems*, *24*:1, pp. 131-141, 1976.
5. R. Alford, *Health Care Politics*, University of Chicago Press, Chicago, 1976.
6. Interview with Ronald Reagan, *The New York Times*, November 1981.
7. Advisory Commission on Intergovernmental Relations, *Recent Trends in Federal and State Aid to Local Governments*, U.S. Government Printing Office, Washington, D.C., 1980.
8. Advisory Commission on Intergovernmental Relations, *Significant Features of Fiscal Federalism, 1979-80*, U.S. Government Printing Office, Washington, D.C., 1980.

9. State and Local Government in Trouble, *Business Week*, October 26, 1981.
10. C. L. Estes and P. R. Lee, Policy Shifts and Their Impact on Health Care for Elderly Persons, *Western Journal of Medicine*, *135*:6, pp. 511-517, 1981.
11. C. L. Estes, P. R. Lee, C. Harrington, R. Newcomer, L. Gerard, M. Kreger, A. E. Benjamin, and J. Swan, Long Term Care for California's Elderly: Policies to Deal With a Costly Dilemma, Institute for Governmental Studies, Monograph Number 10, Berkeley, California, 1981.
12. P. R. Lee and C. L. Estes, Eighty Federal Programs for the Elderly, in *The Aging Enterprise*, C. Estes (ed.), Jossey-Bass, San Francisco, 1979.
13. S. Brody, The Thirty-to-One Paradox: Health Needs and Medical Solutions, *National Journal*, *11*:44, pp. 1869-1873, 1979.
14. L. M. Salamon and A. J. Abramson, The Federal Government and the Non-profit Sector: Implications of the Reagan Budget Proposals: A Study for Independent Sector, the 510(c)(3) Group, and the National Society of Fund Raising Executives, The Urban Institute, Washington, D.C., May 1981.
15. C. L. Estes, J. Swan, and L. Gerard, Dominant and Competing Paradigms in Gerontology: Toward a Political Economy of Aging, *Ageing and Society*, 1982 (in press).
16. A. Walker, The Social Creation of Poverty and Dependency in Old Age, *Journal of Social Policy*, *9*, pp. 49-75, 1980.
17. _____, Towards a Political Economy of Old Age, *Ageing and Society*, *1*:1, pp. 73-94, 1981.
18. P. Townsend, *Poverty in the United Kingdom*, Penguin Books, Harmondsworth, 1979.
19. _____, The Structured Dependency of the Elderly: A Creation of Social Policy in the Twentieth Century, *Ageing and Society*, *1*, pp. 5-28, 1981.
20. J. F. Myles, The Aged, the State, and the Structure of Inequality, in *Structural Inequality in Canada*, J. Harp and J. Hofley (eds.), Prentice-Hall, Toronto, pp. 317-342, 1980.
21. _____, The Aged and the Welfare State: An Essay in Political Demography, paper presented at the International Sociological Association, Research Committee on Aging, Paris, July 8-9, 1981.
22. A. M. Guillemard, The Making of Old Age Policy in France, in *Old Age and the Welfare State*, A. M. Guillemard (ed.), Sage, International Sociological Association, New York, 1983.
23. _____, Retirement as a Social Process: Its Differential Effects Upon Behavior, presented to the 8th World Congress of Sociology, Toronto, Canada, August 21, 1974.
24. J. J. Dowd, *Stratification among the Aged*, Wadsworth, Brooks/Cole, Monterey, California, 1980.
25. L. Evans and J. Williamson, Social Security and Social Control, *Generations: Journal of the Western Gerontological Society*, *6*:2, pp. 18-20, 1981.
26. N. Ginsberg, *Class, Capitol and Social Policy*, Macmillan, London, 1979.
27. J. O'Connor, *The Fiscal Crisis of the State*, St. Martin's, New York, 1973.
28. I. Gough, *The Political Economy of the Welfare State*, Macmillan Press, London, 1979.

29. S. Kelman (ed.), Special Issue on Political Economy of Health, *International Journal of Health Services, 5*:4, pp. 535-642, 1975.

30. M. Renaud, On the Structural Constraints to State Intervention in Health, *International Journal of Health Services, 5*:4, pp. 559-571, 1975.

31. V. Navarro, *Health and Medical Care in the U.S.: A Critical Analysis*, Baywood, New York, 1973.

32. _____, *Medicine Under Capitalism*, Prodist, New York, 1976.

33. J. Walton, Urban Policital Economy, *Comparative Urban Research, 7*:1, pp. 5-17, 1979.

34. J. Henretta and R. Campbell, Status Attainment and Status Maintenance: A Case Study of Stratification in Old Age, *American Sociological Review, 41*, pp. 981-982, 1976.

35. R. J. Samuelson, Benefit Programs for the Elderly Off Limits to Federal Budget Cutters?, *National Journal*, pp. 1757-1762, October 3, 1981.

36. _____, Busting the U.S. Budget: The Costs of an Aging America, *National Journal*, pp. 256-260, February 18, 1978.

37. M. Baum and R. C. Baum, *Growing Old*, Prentice-Hall, New York, 1980.

38. A. Tussing, The Dual Welfare System, in *Social Realities*, L. Horowitz and C. Levy (eds.), Harper and Row, New York, 1971.

39. F. L. Cook, *Who Should be Helped? Support for Social Services*, Sage Publishing Company, Beverly Hills, 1979.

40. G. Nelson, Perspective on Social Need and Social Services to the Aged, *Social Services Review*, 1982 (in press).

41. U.S. Public Law 97-35, The Omnibus Reconciliation Act of 1981, U.S. Government Printing Office, Washington, D.C., September 1981.

42. U.S. House of Representatives, Committee on Ways and Means, Subcommittee on Social Security, Elimination of Minimum Social Security Benefit Under Public Law 97-35, U.S. Government Printing Office, Washington, D.C., September 1981.

43. K. Davis, Equal Treatment and Unequal Benefits: The Medicare Program, *Milbank Memorial Fund Quarterly, 53*:4, pp. 449-488, 1975.

44. M. Ruther and A. Dobson, Equal Treatment and Unequal Benefits: A Reexamination of the Use of Medicare Services by Race, 1967-1976, *Health Care Financing Review, 2*:3, pp. 55-83, 1981.

45. U.S. Congress, House Select Committee on Aging, Analysis of the Impact of the Proposed Fiscal Year 1982 Budget Cuts on the Elderly, briefing paper presented by the Chair, U.S. Government Printing Office, Washington, D.C., 1981.

46. K. Davis and C. Schoen, *Health and the War on Poverty: A Ten Year Approach*, Brookings Institute, Washington, D.C., 1978.

47. SRI (Stanford Research Institute) International, Nonservices Approaches to Problems of the Aged, Center for Urban and Regional Policy, Menlo Park, California, 1981.

48. U.S. Congressional Budget Office, *Economic Policy and the Outlook for the Economy*, U.S. Government Printing Office, Washington. D.C., March 1981.

CHAPTER 16

Blaming the Aged Victim: The Politics of Retrenchment in Times of Fiscal Conservatism

MEREDITH MINKLER

A hallmark of the current politics of retrenchment has been the tendency by many policymakers to scapegoat the poor and the elderly as "causes" of the "fiscal crisis." Social Security, Medicare, and Medicaid have been among the programs most under attack for "busting" the federal budget. By implication, the elderly beneficiaries of these programs have been the targets of special resentment, with young and old constituencies pitted against each other as competing interest groups fighting for limited resources [1].

It is the thesis of this chapter that the current era of fiscal conservatism in the United States has led to a new and more virulent form of victim blaming, with the elderly constituting a key target of attack. The ideology of victim blaming, as described by Ryan [2], will be reviewed, followed by an examination of recent sociopolitical developments which have altered this phenomenon and the ways in which it is manifested.

Several sociopolitical contexts will be presented, within which we may examine current budget cuts affecting the elderly in terms of both direct and indirect contributions to the perception of the aged as a primary cause of the fiscal crisis. These contextual lenses will provide a framework for analyzing those policy approaches which in turn have led to a new variant of victim blaming. Finally, the need for critical analysis and re-education will be stressed as a means to helping to recast the mislabeled "aging problem" in American society.

VICTIM BLAMING RE-EXAMINED

In his classic book, *Blaming the Victim* [2], Ryan described both an ideology and a subtle process applied to American social problems. Briefly, the steps involved in blaming the victim are: 1) identifying a social problem;

254

2) studying those most immediately affected by the problem and discovering how they are different from the rest of us; 3) defining these differences as the cause of the social problem; and 4) assigning a bureaucrat to develop "humanitarian action programs" that will "correct the differences." Writing in the 1970's, Ryan noted that the ideology of victim blaming was very different from the "open prejudice and reactionary tactics" of earlier times. Rather, "Victim blaming is cloaked in kindness and concern, and bears all the trappings and statistical furbelows of scientism; it is obscured by a perfumed haze of humanitarianism." [2, p. 7]

The victim-blaming ideology and its precursors (e.g., C. Wright Mills' [3] ideology of social pathologists) characteristically spawn "exceptionalistic" as opposed to "universalistic" problem-solving attempts. Thus, while fundamental efforts at solving such problems as poverty and unemployment would require major alteration of community and social arrangements, the victim-blaming ideology encourages far more narrow approaches which in turn evolve more limited and individually framed programs and policies.

Food stamps may be seen as an example of an exceptionalistic approach to a problem whose "solution" would in reality call for far broader and universalistic measures, such as full employment policies and/or a guaranteed income policy. Congregate housing, meals on wheels, and most other programs designed in part to help meet the needs of individual elders also fall into the exceptionalistic category.

Ryan's analysis is one of many contemporary critiques [4-6] of U.S. health and social policy which point up the problems inherent in focusing on the "pathology" of the deviant rather than on the unequal power relations and other structural bases of health and social problems. Yet as Gough has noted, when we examine the welfare state[1] and related policy we are focusing on a decidedly "contradictory phenomena." Thus, "To concentrate solely on its positive aspect . . . is to lose sight of its repressive, capital-oriented side. But equally to concentrate solely on its negative side is to lose sight of the very real gains that a century of conflict has won." [7, p. 14]

While Social Security and Medicare, for example, may be justifiably criticized as in part representing social control mechanisms [8-11] they also represent important albeit incremental gains for the elderly beneficiaries of these programs. The official poverty rate of the elderly in 1978, for example, while still greater than that of the general population, was only slightly more than half of what it had been a decade before [12]. The actual gains in income, access to medical care, and so on, that were a consequence of the programs of the 1960's and 70's

---

[1] While Gough, Myles, and others refer to the United States as a welfare state, it should be noted that we are relatively "underdeveloped" in this capacity. Thus, as Wilensky has noted, "Despite rising costs of pensions, Medicare and Medicaid, our spending on the social security package (including health insurance, pensions, etc.) puts us in the lowest quarter among the 19 richest democracies." [38]

cannot be lightly dismissed. These gains help explain why proposed and actual cutbacks in Social Security, Medicare, and related programs have been so vehemently opposed by the elderly and by aging advocates.

By the mid-1970's, and reflecting on Nixon's "New Federalism," Ryan was pointing out [2, p. 301] that the victim-blaming ideology ". . . has become somewhat less prominent, in part because it has been superceded by more vicious and repressive formulations." While Ryan did not go on to examine these more recent approaches, it is the present author's contention that such examination might reveal important relationships between the more recent formulations and earlier victim-blaming ideology and methodology.

The contemporary form of victim blaming is certainly not restricted to the elderly; consider, for example, recent attempts to "blame" undocumented workers for high unemployment in the United States. At the same time, the process is especially well illustrated with respect to the aged, and particularly the elderly poor in the United States. Consequently, our analysis will focus on the new victim blaming of this nation's "fastest growing minority." [13]

Several overlapping contexts will be presented within which we may examine sociopolitical and ideological trends that have led to and supported current budget cutbacks affecting the aged. Each of these contexts will be seen as fitting within the overarching framework of the current economic crisis and the intensified class conflict and related outcomes which it has generated. Together, these contexts will be used to help clarify the newer victim-blaming process and ideology and its relationship to the earlier phenomenon.

BUDGET CUTS AND THE ELDERLY: SOME THEORETICAL CONTEXTS FOR ANALYSIS

The elderly as a group have been among the hardest hit by recent federal budget cutbacks in the United States. While efforts to reduce Social Security benefits were thwarted by a powerful political backlash, Medicare and Medicaid and Social Services (Title XX) sustained severe financial blows. Further cuts in the 1983 budget will continue the process of shifting greater burdens for health care expenditures to the elderly, who already pay on the average more than $1000/year on out-of-pocket medical care costs [14]. Reductions in reimbursement rates to providers under Medicare and reduced eligibility for Medicaid, as well as reduced benefits for such optional services as home care, will further reduce access to needed services among the elderly working class and poor.

While a detailing of the budget cutbacks is beyond the scope of this chapter, it is worthy of note that of the approximately $31 billion cut from social programs in 1983, an estimated $11.8 billion was in programs serving the elderly [15]. Several analytical and sociopolitical frameworks will now be examined for the light they may shed on the rationale behind the cuts and the growing tendency to scapegoat the elderly as key contributors to society's economic ill health.

Fat Times, Lean Times: The Redefining of Social Problems

A first major context for analysis is the perspective on fiscal crisis developed by O'Connor [5], Miller [16], and others. This approach focuses on the cyclical nature of social problems, positing that when the economy is perceived in terms of scarcity, social problems are redefined in ways that permit contracted, less costly approaches to their solution. Thus, while the economic prosperity of the 1960's permitted us to "discover" and even "declare war" on poverty in the United States, the recession of 1973 and its aftermath have necessitated a redefinition of poverty and the subsequent generation of less costly "solutions."

Recent attempts to redefine poverty in the United States have included experimentation with methods of revising the poverty index which would count as income such benefits as food stamps and Medicaid [17]. These efforts differ importantly from earlier victim-blaming approaches in that the end product is not a bureaucratic action program designed to help "correct the differences," e.g., between the poor and the rest of society. Rather, bureaucrats—in this case, in the Bureau of the Census—are assigned to find new ways of adjusting official definitions of poverty such that fewer individuals may fall into this category.

An examination of recent and related attempts at redefinition of the "aging problem" in the United States is particularly informative. Critical to this process, for example, has been the propagation of the myth that the elderly constitute a major "success story" of the War on Poverty [12]. This belief has provided a key rationale for current efforts to cut major programs serving the aged.

In point of fact, while the number of elderly poor did decrease by 1.5 million over the period 1968-1978, the implication that poverty among the elderly has dropped precipitously is a dangerous misconception. Indeed, as the National Council on Economic Opportunity has pointed out [12, p. 15], "Beneath the appearance of a dramatic decline in poverty among the aged is the reality that most of those who have 'moved out' of poverty have in fact moved from a few hundred dollars below the poverty line to a few hundred above it." Thus, if one adds to the officially poor those elderly in the "near poor" category (i.e., those whose incomes fall within 125 percent of the official cutoff), approximately 25 percent of the elderly fit the poverty designation. That is, by adjusting the poverty index so that it more correctly reflects inflation [18], the proportion of elderly in poverty nearly doubles. It further should be noted that when women and minority elderly are examined independently, these figures climb still further. Over half of the black aged, for example, are poor or near poor, as are two-fifths of all elderly women who are single, widowed, or divorced [19].

The myth that poverty among the elderly was largely erased through the War on Poverty hides another fact with important implications for the current climate of austerity and budget cutbacks: to the extent that there *have* been substantive improvements in the economic health of the elderly over the past decade, these improvements have resulted almost entirely from the expansion of "income transfer" programs such as Medicaid and Medicare. Indeed, a Department of Health Education, and Welfare study [20] in the late 1970's concluded that "poverty will not continue to decline at the rate experienced in the late 1960's and early 1970's unless transfer payments continue to expand."

Recent budget cuts affecting the elderly have been most heavily aimed at precisely those income transfer programs credited with "lifting" many of the elderly poor out of poverty. While, as noted earlier, such crediting is itself problematic, income transfer programs such as Medicare and Medicaid *have* made important contributions to the well-being of the elderly, and particularly the elderly poor. Ironically, the myth of the near-abolition of poverty among America's aged has helped to create a climate permitting budget cuts in precisely those programs which have contributed most to the reductions in poverty that have been witnessed over the past decade.

Substantial budget cuts in programs affecting the elderly provide a classic example of the evolving of a less costly "solution" to a problem which, in times of fiscal conservatism, is redefined to become a more limited and hence more manageable one.

The Fiscal Crisis Mentality

A second contextual framework within which to view the budget cuts and their effects on the elderly is suggested by Estes [1] in the argument that the very declaration of a fiscal crisis can be a political event that may be relatively independent of objective economic conditions. As she has pointed out [1, p. 575]: "The crisis definition of the U.S. economy, now incorporated into law through both the 1981 Omnibus Reconciliation Act and the Economic Recovery Tax Act of 1981, has assured the objective conditions of a fiscal crisis in many states." In Estes' view, the rhetoric of "fiscal crisis" helped to create an intense psychological vulnerability on the part of the public to ideas not previously entertained, e.g., a radical dismantling of the welfare system.

A clue to this perceived increase in popular acceptance of the dismantling of the welfare state may lie in closer attention to the semantics used by the political representatives of the corporate class to garner support for this position. In a recent review of existing opinion poll data, for example, Ladd and Lipset [21] noted that those same polls that found that the public favored reducing "welfare" also showed negative public reactions to cuts for the elderly, special education, and services for minorities, the poor, or the handicapped, or needy. Such polls further suggested that the majority of Americans continue to support the very programs (Social Security, Medicare, Medicaid, etc.) which lie at the base of the "welfare state."

In a subsequent and more extensive review of national opinion poll data, Navarro [22] further demonstrated that "there is very little evidence to support the current statements that there is a popular mandate for cuts in health programs and in programs for the elderly and needy. . . ." Rather, public dissatisfaction with a perceived fiscal crisis and the felt need to balance the federal budget have resulted in calls to reduce defense spending and to increase corporate taxes without reducing health and social services.

The perpetration of the fiscal crisis mentality and of a concomitant spurious mandate for cutbacks in social programs also may be seen as constituting in part an attempt to increase societal eagerness to look for—and find—scapegoats for current economic difficulties. In this regard, expressions like "the graying of the Federal budget" and "the aged are busting the Federal budget" take on important meaning. Such phrases, which have achieved currency among many policymakers and the conservative media, both reflect and help to create divisiveness in the population, where "the elderly" are portrayed as a separate, homogeneous, and costly problem group for the rest of society. Such widely held perceptions, of course, leave little room for a focusing of attention on the social creation of the "aging problem" whereby people age 65 and over are systematically and structurally devalued [9, 14, 23, 24]. Yet such a focusing of attention, which "locates the elderly firmly within the prevailing social and economic structure" [24] and clarifies the social creation of their dependent status, is critical to any fundamental analysis of the "aging problem" in American society.

The declaration of fiscal crisis on the national level detracts attention from such analysis of the root causes of the "aging problem." Instead, as noted above, it has played an important role in creating psychological vulnerability to the felt need for major change, which the Reagan Administration in turn has accepted as a mandate for radical cutbacks in health and social programs. This apocryphal mandate in turn has led to further scapegoating of the elderly as a cause of current economic ills.

Victim Blaming and Decentralization

Ryan's ideology of victim blaming was developed in the late 1960's and early 1970's during what Miller [16] would refer to as economically "fat times." The final step in the victim-blaming process—assigning a bureaucrat to develop an humanitarian action program to "make them more like us"—hence assumed a prospering economy where federal-level action programs would continue to proliferate on a large scale. The mid-1970's, however, marked the end of the growth of social welfare programs and policies, not only in the United States but in Britain and Western Europe as well.

In the United States, a key response to the sagging economy and the need for less costly "solutions" to social problems has been to attempt to shift responsibility for many social problems from the federal to the state and local levels, and ideally to push them out of government and onto a supposedly vast and willing private and/or voluntary sector. Excellent descriptions and analyses of the new federalism and its accompanying decentralized block grants are available elsewhere [14, 25-27]. For the purposes of this chapter, however, it should be noted that "the across-the-board expenditure reductions . . . for the block-granted programs has increased pressure on state and local governments to underwrite program costs *at the same time that many states, cities and counties also are under extreme pressure to curb rising expenditures*" [1, p. 577, emphasis added].

In the latter regard, Estes has reported that at least half of the states were planning Medicaid cutbacks before the federal level cuts were announced in 1981 [1]. Since close to 40 percent of Medicaid expenditures are for the elderly [28], such cost-containment policies at the state level pose serious threats to low-income persons within this age group. As numerous critics have noted, the whole process of moving programs to block grants encourages the pitting of separate interest groups against each other, as they compete for approximately 25 percent less money than was available under the earlier categorically funded programs. Thus, the Social Services Block Grant consolidated twelve formerly categorical grant programs covering such disparate areas as Title XX Social Services, Child Abuse, Development Disabilities, Foster Care, and Rehabilitation Services. Under the 1982 budget, this block grant was funded at $3.8 billion, or only 75 percent of the 1981 funding level for the previously separate programs included in the block. The very nature of the block grant process forces aging constituencies and advocates to compete with child welfare advocates and representatives of other groups, each of which has a major and continuing stake in the outcome.

For the elderly, already at high risk for being scapegoated as a major cause of fiscal crisis, this forced and direct competition with other interest groups is unfortunate. Such forced competition builds on those pre-existing tensions between the elderly and the rest of society which were created in part through age-separatist policies, e.g., Social Security, Medicare, and the Older Americans Act [26, 29]. Negative stereotyping of the aged as a dependent group for whom such special programs could be rationalized [18] may be reinforced through the current struggles over block grant allocations. The victim-blaming process under decentralization indeed may take on another dimension: rather than assigning a bureaucrat to develop an action program, the perceived problem itself (e.g., the costly aged) is assigned in greater measure to states and localities whose expanded responsibilities include encouraging competition between different interest groups for limited and decreasing resources. The victim-blaming process takes on new visibility. Not only are the "differences" between the elderly and the rest of society cause for concern, but programs designed to correct those differences have been labeled as too costly for the federal budget to handle. These costly programs (e.g., Medicaid and Medicare) in turn are labeled problems and—where politically feasible—reductions and/or transfers to the state and local levels are suggested as a means of "saving" the federal government from budget busting "caused" by the aged.

Movement Toward an
Ideological Definition of Reality

As Blaustein has argued [12, p. xiii], a fundamental assumption that underlies larger policy formulation under the Reagan Administration is "the illusion that economic policy can be separated from social policy." He adds [12, p. xiii]: "By separating economic theory from social policy and pursuing the former at the expense of the latter, the Administration has adopted a strategy of brinksmanship that could lead to social chaos. Drastic cuts in basic social and human service programs will exact social and human costs and they will also appear as direct financial costs at future times in different ledgers."

It should be noted, however, that the "direct financial costs" of the current policies, not to mention the human and social costs, will be difficult—if not impossible—to measure. Indeed, another consequence of the current "ideological offensive" [30] involves our inability to carefully study the impacts of the budget cutbacks. In the words of Dr. Zvi Griliches [31, p. 27], Chair of the Department of Economics at Harvard, "The country is embarking on one of the largest macro-economic policy experiments in our history with very little research support for it, and they do not even want to measure its effects, to know how it is doing and what its consequences might be."

By drastically cutting funding not only for research but also for the gathering of census data [32], the Reagan Administration is preventing the collection of information that might allow effective evaluation of the impacts of the new policies. Moreover, even among programs not faced with funding cutbacks, e.g., the National Institutes of Health (NIH), stringent new guidelines have been imposed which may seriously curtail the conducting of critical research in "sensitive" areas. One such set of guidelines, for example, suggests that proposals not be funded by the NIH if their aim is to examine the effects of age, sex, race, or income on mental health.

Gerontologist Robert Atchley [33] has argued that the cutbacks in research monies "make sense" when viewed within the context of the Administration's move toward "an ideological, rather than a pragmatic, definition of reality." While research and a strong data base are necessary for the latter, an ideological definition of reality, by contrast, demands far less rigor in data collection and analysis. Indeed, the "facts" revealed through research may become an ideological impediment. Atchley's argument is, of course, an oversimplification, since "reality" is often socially constructed, particularly as it concerns such politically sensitive areas as the degree of poverty and other health and social problems in society. At the same time, to the extent that the current administration is committed to greater than normal "redefinition" of health and social conditions, the relative lack of attention to data collection and research poses a very real concern.

The inability to accurately measure the effects of the budget cuts on the elderly, and particularly the elderly poor, may constitute yet another manifestation of the new victim-blaming process and ideology. Thus, for example, the active discouraging of research on the influence of class, age, race, and sex on mental health paves the way for an even greater emphasis on the individual as the problem, and as the appropriate and sole target for ameliorative action. Similarly, failure to collect adequate data on the true numbers of impoverished elderly feeds into preexisting myths concerning the near-eradication of poverty in this age group. It further helps to rationalize the cutting back of programs and policies designed in part to help the low-income elderly gain access to food, health care, and other necessities.

If we are unable to document whether the billions of dollars in cuts to Medicare and Medicaid and other programs really have hurt the elderly, the assumption may well be that they have not and that such costly programs are merely another example of the ways in which the aged are "busting the federal budget." Furthermore, since many impoverished elderly are "known" only because of the service provider system, the dismantling of this system may well render them more invisible and voiceless than before.

AGING, SOCIAL CLASS, AND THE ECONOMIC CRISIS

The overarching context within which to view the budget cuts and their effects on the elderly is, of course, the current economic crisis—characterized by such symptoms as high unemployment, inflation, and slow growth—and the responses it has invoked by and on behalf of those in power. While the cause of the economic crisis lies most centrally in declining corporate profits [27, 30], a more popular explanation among the corporate class has been that growth of social expenditures, affecting largely the working class and the poor, has "caused" the crisis. This victim-blaming analysis is not limited to the United States. As Gough commented in examining the Thatcher Government's assignment of blame for Britain's economic difficulties, "The fate of the nation now appears to depend . . . on the number of home helps for the elderly or the price of school lunches." [7, p. 134]

In the United States, the nature and extent of the current budget cutbacks, expected to total $214 billion by 1984, has led some analysts [30, 34] to view this response as involving "an unprecedented class warfare." Not only is the welfare state being "restructured" to reduce collective consumption while supporting capital accumulation [30], but the state interventions utilized in this process are aimed in part at increasing divisiveness within the working class, thereby decreasing larger group consciousness and action.

One facet of the restructuring of the welfare state—the frontal attack on social expenditures—has been addressed in this chapter in the examination of decentralization, the fiscal crisis mentality, and other contexts within which to view the budget cuts and their effects on the elderly. Of equal importance, however, is the other key thrust of the welfare state restructuring, characterized by substantial growth in government interventions designed to strengthen the corporate class. Such interventions have included vastly increased military expenditures, large transfers of funds from the public to the private sectors (e.g., through increased privatization of services), and changes in the management and control of certain state apparatuses such that they better serve the needs of capital [30]. Indeed, an analysis of those tax cuts (totaling $286.1 billion by 1984) that work to benefit the capitalist class is every bit as revealing as a look at those budget cuts which adversely affect the working class [35].

Equally revealing is an examination of the net income tax gains from the recent tax cuts by income level. As will be seen from Figure 1, persons with incomes of less than $10,000 in fiscal year 1982 represented 22.5 percent of the

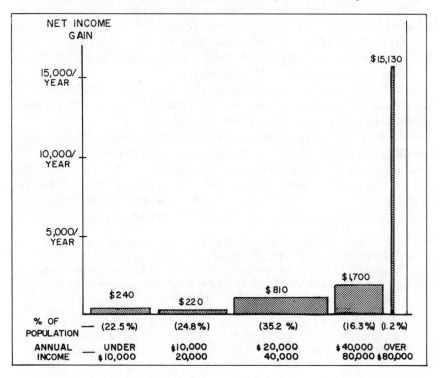

Source: Adapted from reference [36].

Figure 1. Net income gain from fiscal year 1982 tax cut by income level.

population and had a net gain in annual income of only $240. The comparable figure for the 1.2 percent of the population in the over $80,000 income bracket was $15,130 [36].

For the elderly, who are disproportionately represented among the working class and the poor, the shifting of tax cuts to further benefit the corporate class has combined with cutbacks in social programs to portend deleterious consequences. Moreover, the nature and scope of the reorganization of state interventions may serve to further contract options available to the working class and poor elderly for dealing with economic grievances and the conflicts to which they give rise. Indeed, as Piven and Cloward have noted [27, p. 132], the current constraints being imposed (e.g., in the form of decentralization) may "tend to become invisible as political issues and instead appear to be merely the limits of the possible." In the view of these observers, the tax cuts, for example, may be seen as "... [narrowing] the parameters within which future political struggles will be fought, because the prospect of large annual deficits will make social expenditures seem impractical. Under these circumstances, *fiscal austerity will not appear to be politics; it will appear to be the inevitable adaptation of a responsible government to the constraints imposed by limited resources*" [27, p. 134, emphasis added]. The fiscal crisis mentality and the ideological definition of reality accompanying the tax cuts in short may help make the latter a longer range victory for corporate mobilization than might initially be realized [27, 30].

The contracting of the arena within which political struggles may be fought is importantly tied to efforts to encourage divisiveness among the working class. If decentralization succeeds, for example, national constituencies that have been mobilized to fight for shared economic goals may break down as political efforts are diffused and redirected from the national to the state and local levels [27]. Similarly, as noted earlier, forced competition between "interest groups" within the working class may further mitigate against the growth of a broader class consciousness. That this outcome is an intended one is suggested by Navarro, who has noted that the dismantling of federal health interventions in the United States

> ... *aims* at presenting the needs of specific sectors of the working class (such as the elderly, the disabled, and the working poor) *as in contradiction* with the needs of other sectors of the same class (such as the young and able or white against blacks and Latinos or women against men). ... A climate of social hostility, tension and suspicion is thus created that, side by side with tensions triggered by the arms race and the threat of nuclear war, accentuates the feeling of crisis of national survival and security, a public feeling that is required for peoples' acceptance of the authoritarian state and its austerity policies [30, p. 184, emphasis added].

The scapegoating of the elderly as a primary cause of the fiscal crisis is, as we have seen, one of many manifestations of the new victim blaming which has had the effect of contributing to this polarization.

BEYOND VICTIM BLAMING: ON
THE NEED FOR CRITICAL
ANALYSIS AND RE-EDUCATION

The foregoing examination of some of the contexts within which budget cuts affecting the elderly may be viewed was geared at helping us to elucidate some new and old dimensions of the victim-blaming process using the elderly as a case in point. Yet this analysis itself reflects a common and problematic way of looking at the world by virtue of its examination of phenomena in terms of competing interest groups. By focusing on the budget cuts primarily as they affect the elderly, for example, one runs the risk of further perpetrating the narrow interest group perspective which can contribute to the pitting of one segment of soceity against the other in the competition for limited resources.

In defense of having singled out the elderly as a focus of concern, it was argued earlier that persons age sixty-five and over have been particularly victimized by the budget cuts, both directly and in terms of their having been made a primary scapegoat for the fiscal crisis.

While this scapegoating has had important precedents dating back to at least the Kennedy Administration,[2] it has reached a new nadir in the past two to three years, best typified by the stepped-up efforts of the Reagan Administration to focus public attention on the high cost of Social Security rather than on greatly increased military spending, high unemployment, inflation, and related problems.

The scapegoat rhetoric has coincided with what Estes [1, p. 575] has described as "a resurgence of the ideology that individuals create their own conditions and opportunities, and that they are to be held accountable for their predicament." Such an ideology is well embodied in the victim blaming of the 1980's, with its deemphasis on the development of federal "action programs" and its resurrection of the notion of individual, state/local, and private sector responsibility for ameliorative social programs and solutions.

The semantics of individual responsibility, coupled with the scapegoating of the elderly as a cause of the fiscal crisis, point up the need for re-educative strategies geared at focusing attention on the root causes of the current crisis and the nature and genesis of the "divide and conquer" strategies which have been employed to divert attention from more structural and fundamental problems. In particular, a recasting of the mislabeled "aging problem" is called for, such that it is seen for what it is—a convenient smokescreen for those underlying social

---

[2] The first Secretary of the Department of Health, Education, and Welfare under President Kennedy argued that too much money was spent on the elderly and not enough on youth—a politically unpopular position for which he later "atoned." Both Presidents Nixon and Ford attempted to cut funds to aging, and benefit-cutting proposals aimed at the elderly were considered under the Carter Administration. The Reagan Administration's budget cutbacks affecting the aged thus may be seen as culminating almost two decades of tentative and attempted movement in this direction.

processes through which the elderly are systematically devalued, "homogenized," and labeled as a social problem.

Critical analysis and re-education concerning the "aging problem" should focus, as noted earlier, on the social creation of the dependent status of the elderly. Integral to such an analysis would be an examination of the structural relationship between the elderly and younger adults and the socially constructed relationship between age, class, the division of labor, and the labor market [24]. As Myles has noted [9, p. 7]:

> ... "old people" as we now know them were an *effect*, not a cause of the welfare state. Withdrawal from the labor force in advance of physiological old age—the institutionalization of retirement and the creation of a new social category of superannuated elders, especially within the working class—occurred after and was made possible by the intervention of old age pensions and other welfare state programs.

While the welfare state in advanced capitalist societies is in fact organized primarily for the elderly [37],[3] such organization came about precisely because it was in the best interests of corporate capital to forceably unemploy chronologically older members of society in exchange for pensions and related benefits [9, 10]. As Navarro has noted [4, p. 87], "It was a function of welfare programs to integrate those sectors of the population who have felt increasingly alienated from the political system and to give them the feeling of being a part of the system in which those programs were introduced." It is an irony of our times that the social definition of old age which forceably "retired" the elderly and created the welfare state now is reified and made the villain in yet another socially lean time—the "fiscal crisis" of the 1980s.

In *The New Class War* [27], Piven and Cloward suggest that the current politics of retrenchment may well provide the stimulus necessary for poor and oppressed groups to fight for and ultimately win back major concessions lost with the dismantling of the welfare state. Such a victory, however, presumes the pulling together of oppressed groups which, as a consequence of block granting and other divide-and-conquer strategies, may in reality be more polarized than before.

The scapegoating of the elderly as a primary cause of the fiscal crisis is, as we have seen, one of many manifestations of the new victim blaming which has had the effect of contributing to this polarization. Political-economic analyses of such new victim-blaming efforts, their targets, and their consequences are needed in part to counterbalance the "ideological definition of reality" being put forward

[3] As Wilensky and others have observed [37], the largest items in the welfare state budget are pensions and health care—both directed in large measure at the elderly. For an excellent discussion of why the welfare state is so heavily focused on its aged members, see Myles [9].

by the current Administration and the corporate class. Educational strategies based on such analyses and directed at those oppressed groups (e.g., workers and unemployed/retired people, young and old) currently placed in competition with one another must be developed to help prevent further divisiveness. Finally, analysis and education must focus on the double-edged sword which the welfare state in fact represents.

To "trade" the victim-blaming approaches of the 1980's for those of the 1960's and early 70's is not a solution to problems which ultimately are grounded in the skewed distribution of economic and political power within the society. While fighting to restore budget cuts to health and social problems constitutes an important incremental step, real efforts to redress inequalities in society will require an understanding that such social programs also serve as effective mechanisms of social control, in part by structurally segregating and creating tension between different oppressed groups within the society [26].

SUMMARY AND CONCLUSIONS

The scapegoating of the elderly as a primary cause of the fiscal crisis has, as we have seen, deflected attention from the more compelling and deep-seated causes of the current economic crisis. At the same time, and fueled by such policies as block granting, it has been used as a political tool to stoke resentment of the elderly and has contributed to the forced competition of the aged and younger members of society for limited resources. Finally, the definition of the aged as a major cause of the fiscal crisis was seen as a classic example of a more pernicious form of victim blaming than that initially conceptualized. Indeed, the very "solutions" to social problems of an earlier era (Ryan's "humanitarian action programs") are themselves being labeled problems. New solutions, ranging from the redefinition of "people in need" to the dismantling and/or decentralizing of social programs, are being proposed and implemented within a context that places little importance on evaluating the effects of these actions.

The new victim blaming, while bearing important similarities to the old, may well prove more devastating in its effects on oppressed groups in American society, including, importantly, the aged. Recognition and critical analysis of this phenomenon are essential for the development of true class consciousness among those sectors of the working class against whom the new victim blaming is being utilized as a mechanism of divisiveness and social control.

ACKNOWLEDGMENTS

The author is particularly indebted to Kathleen Roe, Beverly Ovrebo, and Stephen Blum for their helpful comments and suggestions. Also deserving of thanks is Dr. Carroll Estes, both for her own research into the political economy of aging and for her encouragement of my work in this area. Finally, thanks are due to Dorothy Nelson for her help in the typing and retyping of this manuscript.

REFERENCES

1. C. L. Estes, Austerity and Aging in the United States: 1980 and Beyond, *International Journal of Health Services*, *12*:4, pp. 573-584, 1982.
2. W. Ryan, *Blaming the Victim*, Random House, New York, 1976.
3. C. W. Mills, The Professional Ideology of Social Pathologists, *American Journal of Sociology*, *49*:2, pp. 165-180, 1943.
4. V. Navarro, The Political Economy of Medical Care: An Explanation of the Composition, Nature, and Functions of the Present Health Sector of the United States, *International Journal of Health Services*, *5*:1, pp. 65-94, 1975.
5. J. O'Connor, *The Fiscal Crisis of the State*, St. Martin's, New York, 1973.
6. H. R. Kelman, The Underdevelopment of Evaluative Research on Health Services for the Elderly in the United States, *International Journal of Health Services*, *10*:3, pp. 501-511, 1980.
7. I. Gough, *The Political Economy of the Welfare State*, The Macmillan Press, Ltd., London, 1981.
8. J. B. Williamson, et al., *The Politics of Aging: Power and Policy*, Charles C. Thomas Press, Springfield, Illinois, 1982.
9. J. F. Myles, The Aged and the Welfare State: An Essay in Political Demography, paper presented at the International Sociological Association Research Committee on Aging, Paris, France, July 8-9, 1981.
10. W. Graebner, *A History of Retirement*, Yale University Press, New Haven, 1980.
11. H. S. Berliner, The Origins of Health Insurance for the Aged, *International Journal of Health Services*, *3*:3, pp. 465-474, 1973.
12. A. I. Blaustein (ed.), *The American Promise: Equal Justice and Economic Opportunity*, Transaction Books, New Brunswick, New Jersey, 1982.
13. H. Brotman, The Fastest Growing Minority: The Aging, *American Journal of Public Health*, *64*, pp. 349-352, 1974.
14. C. L. Estes and P. R. Lee, Policy Shifts and Their Impact on Health Care for the Elderly Persons, *Western Journal of Medicine*, *135*:6, pp. 511-518, 1981.
15. U.S. Senate Select Committee on Aging, Proposed Fiscal Year 1983 Budget: What It Means for Older Americans, U.S. Senate Select Committee on Aging, Washington, D.C., March 1982.
16. S. M. Miller, The Political Economy of Social Problems: From the Sixties to the Seventies, *Social Problems*, *24*:1, pp. 131-141, 1976.
17. U.S. Bureau of the Census, Technical Paper No. 50, Alternative Methods for Valuing Selected In-Kind Transfer Benefits and Measuring Their Effect on Poverty, Superintendent of Documents, U.S. Government Printing Office, Washington, D.C., April 14, 1982.
18. R. H. Binstock, A Policy Agenda on Aging for the 1980's, in *Aging: Agenda for the Eighties*, J. P. Hubbard (ed.), National Journal Issues Books, Government Research Corporation, Washington, D.C., pp. 4-10, 1979.
19. S. Grad and K. Foster, Income of the Population Aged 65 and Over, *Social Security Bulletin*, July 1979.
20. P. Gottschalk, *Earnings, Transfers, and Poverty Reduction*, Technical Paper No. 16, Department of HEW, Office of Income Security Policy, Washington, D.C., October 1978.

21. C. Ladd and S. M. Lipset, The United States in the 1980's.
22. V. Navarro, Where Is the Populate Mandate? A Reply to Conventional Wisdom, *New England Journal of Medicine,* December 9, 1982.
23. M. Minkler, Research on the Health Effects of Retirement: An Uncertain Legacy, *Journal of Health and Social Behavior, 22,* pp. 117-130, 1981.
24. A. Walker, Toward a Political Economy of Old Age, *Ageing and Society, 1*:1, pp. 73-94, 1981.
25. National Health Law Program, People Under Pressure: The Administration's 1983 Health Budget, Los Angeles, 1982.
26. C. L. Estes, *The Aging Enterprise,* Jossey Bass, San Francisco, 1979.
27. F. F. Piven and R. A. Cloward, *The New Class War: Reagan's Attack on the Welfare State and Its Consequences,* Pantheon Books, New York, 1982.
28. P. Butler, Financing Non-Institutional Long-Term Care Services for the Elderly and Chronically Ill: Alternatives to Nursing Homes, *Clearing House Review, 13*:5, pp. 335-376, 1979.
29. A. Etzioni, Old People and Public Policy, *Social Policy, 7,* pp. 21-29, 1976.
30. V. Navarro,The Crisis of the International Capitalist Order and Its Implications for the Welfare State, *International Journal of Health Services, 12*:2, pp. 169-190, 1982.
31. Hearings Before the Subcommittee on Science and Technology, Committee on Science and Technology, U.S. House of Representatives, 97th Congress, 1st Session on HR 1520, 1982 National Science Foundation Authorization, January 1981, p. 27.
32. Chopping the Fingers Off the Census, *New York Times,* February 3, 1982, p. 1.
33. R. Atchley, The Federal Budget and the Challenge to Aging Research and Training, Panel Presentation at the Western Gerontological Society 28th Annual Meeting, San Diego, California, February 27-March 3, 1982.
34. A. H. Raskin, Lane Kirkland, A New Style for Labor, *The New York Times Magazine,* October 28, 1979, p. 91.
35. The Winners and the Losers Under Reagonomics, *The Washington Report,* (United Automobile Workers of America), *21*:33, pp. 1-3, 1981.
36. *San Francisco Examiner,* February 28, 1982.
37. H. Wilensky, *The Welfare State and Equality,* University of California Press, Berkeley, 1975.
38. H. Wilensky, Evaluation Research and Politics: Political Legitimacy and Consensus as Missing Variables in the Assessment of Social Policy, in *Policy Evaluation,* S. E. Spiro and E. Yuchtman-yaar (eds.), Academic Press, New York, 1982.

Reprinted with permission of Baywood Press. From: *International Journal of Health Services, 13*:1, pp. 155-168, 1983.

Epilogue

Reassessing the Future of Aging Policy and Politics

CARROLL L. ESTES
LENORE E. GERARD
MEREDITH MINKLER

The decade of the 1980's is characterized by economic uncertainty and political ambiguity regarding the direction of American public policy for the elderly. Although great progress has been made in the past twenty years, we are facing a time of unprecedented fiscal constraints and a changing national commitment. The concern is not only with the present but also with the future. Indeed, we are looking into the 21st century when the nation's older citizens will live a longer and, in many cases, healthier life. By the year 2050, 67 million persons, or 22 percent of the population, will be over age sixty-five—a fact with major ramifications for young and old alike.

The austerity cutbacks in domestic social spending which were initiated by the Reagan Administration in 1981 reflect more than temporal change and will have far reaching effects on the adult working population, their families and future generations of retirees. Public policy choices will influence tax burdens on the younger adult population, their opportunity for savings, their personal responsibility for aged relatives, and their own economic security in the 21st century.

As this book goes to press, the nation is faced with a November 1984 Presidential election and a reassessment of Reaganomics and the policies of the "new right." The President's FY 1985 budget proposal reflects a continuation of prior fiscal policy, namely, substantial increases in military spending, reductions in domestic spending, and tax reductions for both business and individuals. Thus, there will be a deepening of the cutbacks and, more importantly, an effort to change expectations regarding entitlements and the citizen's right to adequate income and health benefits.

The first major change in this direction came with the attack on the solvency and expectations of the nation's income security program, Social Security. As a result of recommendations of President Reagan's Social Security Commission adopted in 1983, the Social Security program already has undergone major revisions (including, for example, a gradual raising of the retirement age from sixty-five to sixty-seven and greater disincentives to earlier retirement) which may negatively impact on many future retirees.

A second prominent budget issue that promises to increasingly and more predominantly shape future budget debates is the crisis in health care costs. In addition to the $19.5 billion cut in the Medicare and Medicaid programs during the FY 1982-1985 period, the Reagan Administration's proposed budget for 1985 would reduce federal health care spending by another $2 billion. If these cuts are enacted, we may anticipate growing out-of-pocket expenses and reduced access to health care for the elderly, the poor, the low-income worker and the unemployed.

While such cutbacks and the fiscal crisis mentality which they reflect are cast in sharpest relief in the United States, they are not geographically confined to America. Indeed, as several contributors to this volume have suggested, visions of fiscal crisis and accompanying austerity measures are also likely to dominate the political economy of aging in Great Britain and much of Western Europe in the foreseeable future.

The critical perspective reflected in this Reader is intended to be a tool for re-thinking the relationship between the policy, the economy and the society. Beneath the exterior intergenerational tension is a greater conflict of priorities and allocation of scarce resources reflected in the federal budgets of the United States, Great Britain and other advanced industrialized nations. In the United States in particular, the aged, as beneficiaries of entitlement programs, are in direct conflict with the interests of the military-industrial complex and hence with a defense budget that is projected to total $1.5 trillion between 1982-1986. As the 1984 Democratic and Republican debate has sharpened its focus on federal spending and high deficits, the ideological conflict between welfare and warfare has intensified.

A major issue underlying recent public resource allocation decisions concerns the trade-offs created by the shift in priorities from domestic social to defense spending. In the United States, this shift was initiated by the Carter Administration in the late 1970's, but was dramatically accelerated under the Reagan Administration. Reagan's strategy differs from previous efforts, however, in seeking not only to modify existing trends, but also to shift policy into a fundamentally altered ideological framework. The most significant feature of the Reagan strategy is a dramatic redefinition of the role of the federal government, involving a significantly larger commitment to defense spending and a corresponding reduction in domestic spending.

These domestic policies continue unabated into the mid-1980's. In spite of a much-touted economic recovery, the United States faces the highest federal deficit in world history; high unemployment; almost uncontrolled growth in health spending; a highly redistributive tax burden that works in favor of corporations and high income individuals; and shifting capital investments overseas.

Clearly, the administration occupying the White House in January, 1985 will inherit these structural and political problems and will have to devise reasonable solutions. We would hope, however, that the only viable solution would not be seen as one of shifting more of the burden on those least able to bear it. The attempt of Reagan policies to transform the welfare state, and, indeed, the role of government and public priorities is unsurpassed in ideological fervor since the Great Depression. Reagonomics is more than one administration's view; it represents the new right perspective, which is nothing less than an attempt to alter the relationship between the state and the economy upon which the welfare state is constructed. In this intense historical struggle, vested interests, aging advocates, the intergovernmental lobby, corporate power, and the general public all are vying for the power to influence outcomes.

The character of the economic crisis raises important and critical questions concerning political strategy and advocacy. Can conventional interest-group pluralism succeed? In the past four years, the political initiatives commonly employed by interest groups have been neutralized by the reality of fiscal constraint and its political environment, as well as by the resurgence of corporate power and supply side ideology.

In the United States, state and local governments have been "under siege" since the 1978 taxpayer revolt resulted in the imposition of spending and/or taxing limits in at least two-thirds of the states. Further, by 1983, thirty-nine (78%) of the states projected their year-end bugets as either in a deficit or under three percent (although a surplus of at least 5% is deemed necessary to allow for unexpected revenues or loss of state revenues). By 1984, only ten states projected a year-end balance in excess of 5 percent of annual appropriations. These recent state budgetary profiles contrast sharply with 1978, when approximately two-thirds of the fifty states reported a year-end surplus of 5 percent or more. By 1984, the total fifty-state year-end budget balance, estimated at $3.3 billion, can only be described as unfavorable when compared with the more than $11 billion year-end balance recorded four years previously. As a result of all these factors, efforts and activities aimed at ameliorating the fiscal crisis itself, are critically needed in the 1980's. These will require intergenerational and coalitional efforts to preserve and to expand available revenues for governments under financial stress and to address issues of tax inequities.

There are four major questions for the future of aging policy under the current conditions of austerity.

The first question for the future of aging policy concerns the extent to which aging interest groups, professionals and individuals will ally with a broader base of action and expand their concerns to encompass generic issues rather than simply those which are identified as aging issues. Examples of these broader concerns are: revenue reform, equity in taxation (particularly between corporate and individual taxation), and labor control of pension funds. Single-interest, aging-based politics may have been an efficacious strategy to follow over the past thirty years. Yet there is evidence that unless advocates for the elderly now address broad policy issues, many of which may not deal directly with aging issues, the elderly are likely to find their future shaped by the advocacy of others.

The second question affecting the future of aging policy in the United States concerns the extent to which state and local elected officials will continue to "accept" the federal retrenchment and shift of governmental responsibility to state and local government, especially as their political futures are increasingly jeopardized by untenable political choices in the context of shrinking fiscal resources and growing social problems associated with the projected disappearance of the economic recovery. As the full impact of federal and state cutbacks reverberates "at home," and especially with the serious projected economic downturn for 1985, we predict that these representatives of the "intergovernmental lobby" will begin to resist further domestic retrenchment and decreases in fiscal aid to state and local governments.

The third question about the future of aging policy is whether the interests of the wealthy and the middle class (particularly the mythical average worker who theoretically will have the opportunity for a long, steady, secure, and uninterrupted work career) will continue to dominate public policy for the aging; or whether the interests of all working people (the marginally employed, those disabled in the course of their working lives, the working poor, and women) will be given due consideration.

A fourth question involves where the aging organizations, professionals and individuals will stand in the struggle over the future direction of public policy. It is well known that few national aging organizations have been identified primarily with the low income elderly, and that those that do are the least powerful such organizations.

When times were better, it was easier for most aging organizations and advocates to provide constituency support for improving benefits to a broad base of elderly—including the poor, female and minority older persons. But what will these organizations and advocates do as financial and political pressures mount? Will the retired middle-class who are dependent on the benefits of Social Security, Medicare and favorable tax treatment work to ensure the survival of the welfare state? Or will what survives be a more distinctly and deeply divided welfare state that further increases the gap between rich and poor? Will we see an intergenerational coalition between the economically disadvantaged elderly and the younger adult population who are equally hard-pressed by current fiscal and monetary policy in the era of tight economic conditions and constraints? Or will we see, as the popular press is fond of suggesting, a heightening of intergenerational conflicts and rivalries?

While some suggest that the prospects for coalition building have been dimmed by the divide and conquer strategies of the current administration, such intergenerational and inter-group efforts would seem critical if we are to reverse those policies and trends which have set into motion a dismantling of major health and social service accomplishments of the last half century. As stated by Maggie Kuhn in her special introduction to this volume, aging is a life process and, as such, the life chances of the old and the young are tied together. As Navarro further has argued, the vast majority of men and women, young and old and black, brown and white people in the U.S. are members of the working class, and hence similarly should have a shared stake in reversing those policies which have resulted in dramatic increases in allocations for defense and equally dramatic decreases in domestic spending.

It is hoped that this book has helped to provide some of the political economic analyses upon which effective educational strategies for coalition building and change can be based.

Contributors

Robert H. Binstock is Henry R. Luce Professor of Aging, Health and Society at Case Western Reserve University in Cleveland, Ohio. He formerly was Louis Stulberg Professor of Law and Politics and Director of the Program in the Economics and Politics of Aging at Brandeis University. A former President of the American Gerontological Society he also has served as Director of the White House Task Force on Older Americans. Dr. Binstock's many books and articles in aging and political science include *Handbook of Aging and the Social Sciences* (with Ethel Shanas, Van Nostrand Reinholt, 1976), *The Politics of the Powerless* and *Feasible Planning for Social Change.*

E. Richard Brown is an Assistant Professor of health education and behavioral sciences at the School of Public Health, University of California, Los Angeles. He received his Ph.D. in the Sociology of Education at the University of California, Berkeley in 1975 and subsequently worked as a health planner and taught courses in the social and political economy of health on the Berkeley campus. Dr. Brown's major publications include *Rockefeller Medicine Men* (University of California Press, 1979).

Robert N. Butler, M.D., is Professor and Chair of the Department of Geriatrics and Adult Development at Mt. Sinai Medical Center in New York. He served as the first Director of the National Institute on Aging of the National Institutes of Health, and as a special consultant to the United States Senate Committee on Aging. Dr. Butler's many books and publications include the Pulitzer prize winning, *Why Survive? Being Old in America* (Harper and Row, 1975), *Sex After Sixty* (with Myrna Lewis, Harper and Row, 1976), and *Aging and Mental Health* (C. V. Mosby, 1982, with Myrna Lewis).

Adele Clark is currently a doctoral student in the Department of Social and Behavioral Sciences, University of California, San Francisco, where she is doing research in the sociology of science on reproductive biology, 1900–1940. She was previously coordinator of women's studies at Sonoma State University.

James J. Dowd is Associate Professor of Sociology at the University of Georgia. He received his Ph.D. from the University of Southern California in 1976.

Dr. Dowd is the author of *Stratification Among the Aged* (Brooks/Cole, 1980) and of numerous monographs and papers on socialization across the life cycle, capitalism and the phenomenon of mid-life crisis, and mental illness and aging.

Carroll L. Estes, Professor of Sociology, is Chairperson of the Department of Social and Behavioral Sciences, School of Nursing, University of California, San Francisco, and is Director of the Aging Health Policy Center, University of California, San Francisco. Dr. Estes, whose Ph.D. is from the University of California, San Diego, conducts research and writes about aging policy, long-term care, fiscal crisis, and new federalism. She is the author of *The Decision-Makers: The Power Structure of Dallas* (1963) and *The Aging Enterprise* (Jossey Bass, 1979), and co-author of *Fiscal Austerity and Aging* (Sage, 1983) and *Political Economy, Health and Aging* (Little Brown, 1984). Dr. Estes is a past president of the Western Gerontological Society and of the Association for Gerontology in Higher Education.

Linda Evans is Associate Professor in the Department of Sociology, Central Connecticut State University. She received her Ph.D. from Boston College in 1977 and has co-authored and co-edited several books in the fields of aging and sociology including *Strategies Against Poverty in America* (Schenkman, 1975), *Aging and Society* (Holt, Rinehart and Winston, 1980), and *The Politics of Aging* (Charles C. Thomas, 1982).

Lenore E. Gerard is a research staff associate in the Department of Social and Behavioral Sciences, Aging Health Policy Center, School of Nursing, University of California, San Francisco. She is involved in research and analysis in medical sociology, the political economy of health care and health policy, and is co-author of *Political Economy, Health and Aging* (Little Brown, 1984).

William Graebner is Professor in the Department of History at Fredonia State University College in New York. He received his Ph.D. in History from the University of Illinois at Urbana in 1970. In addition to his recent book, *A History of Retirement: The Meaning and Function of an American Institution 1885-1978* (Yale University Press, 1980) he is author of *Coal-mining Safety in the Progressive Period* (University of Kentucky Press, 1976) the research for which won him the Fredrick Jackson Turner Prize in 1975.

Charlene Harrington is Assistant Professor in the Department of Family Health Care Nursing and Associate Director of the Aging Health Policy Center, University of California, San Francisco. She received her Ph.D. in Social and Higher Education from the University of California, Berkeley in 1975 and subsequently served as Deputy Director of the Department of Health Services and the State Licensing Certification Program for the State of California. Dr. Harrington's major publications include her co-authored books, *Fiscal Austerity and Aging* (Sage, 1983) and *Public Policies and Long Term Care* (Sage, in press).

Maggie Kuhn is founder and national convenor of the Gray Panthers, a 50,000 member coalition of people of all ages who are committed to fighting age discrimination and to activist approaches to social change. She has written two books, *Get Out There and Do Something About Injustice* (Friendship Press, 1972) and *Maggie Kuhn on Aging* (Westminster Press, 1977), as well as numerous monographs and articles on aging, work, older women, religion and health care. She has appeared on numerous radio and television programs nationwide, and recently was named one of the 25 most influential women in America.

Myrna I. Lewis is on the faculty of the Department of Community Medicine, at Mt. Sinai School of Medicine in New York, and is also a psychotherapist in private practice, and a gerontologist, social worker and writer. She holds an ACSW and is presently earning her doctorate at Columbia University. Ms. Lewis is co-author of several books including *Aging and Mental Health* (C. V. Mosby, 1982) and *Sex After Sixty* (with Robert N. Butler).

Meredith Minkler is Associate Professor in the Department of Social and Administrative Health Sciences, School of Public Health at the University of California, Berkeley. She received her doctorate in Public Health Education from the University of California, Berkeley in 1975 and was a Kellogg National Fellow from 1980-1983. Dr. Minkler served as a special consultant to the Technical Committee on Health Promotion and Disease Prevention of the 1981 White House Conference on Aging and has published numerous monographs and articles in the areas of community organization, social support and health, the health effects of retirement and the political economy of aging.

John F. Myles is an Associate Professor in the Department of Sociology and Anthropology at Carleton University in Ottawa, Canada. Dr. Myles' research centers on comparative class politics and comparative class structure in North America and Western Europe. His recent publications include his new book, *Old Age in the Welfare State: The Political Economy of Public Pensions* (Little Brown, 1984).

Vicente Navarro is Professor of Health Policy at Johns Hopkins University and founder and editor-in-chief of the *International Journal of Health Services*. He has written extensively on sociology, political sociology, and the political economy of medical and social services. Dr. Navarro is the author of *Medicine Under Capitalism; Social Security and Medicine in the USSR: A Marxist Critique*; and *Class Struggle, the State, and Medicine: An Historical and Contemporary Analysis of the Medical Sector in Great Britain*; and editor of collections *Health and Medical Care in the U.S.: A Critical Analysis* and *Imperialism, Health and Medicine.*

Robyn Stone is a doctoral candidate in health policy at the School of Public Health, University of California, Berkeley and a Research Associate at the Aging Health Policy Center, University of California, San Francisco. She received her MPA in Public Administration in 1978 at the University of Pittsburgh and worked for several years as a project officer and policy analyst in the Department of Health and Human Services. Ms. Stone has published several monographs, book chapters and articles in the areas of women's retirement, the feminization of poverty and aging health policy.

James H. Swan is Assistant Research Sociologist, Aging Health Policy Center, University of California, San Francisco. He received his Ph.D. in Sociology from Northwestern University in 1981. Dr. Swan's major publications include his co-authored books, *Fiscal Austerity and Aging* (Sage, 1983) and *The Political Economy of Aging* (Little Brown, 1984).

Alan Walker is a lecturer in social policy at the University of Sheffield, England. He was previously a senior research officer at the National Children's Bureau and research officer at the University of Essex. He is the author of *Unqualified and Underemployed* (Macmillan, 1981) as well as numerous articles and pamphlets on poverty, disability, social policy, and old age. He is currently researching the care of elderly people by families.

John B. Williamson is Associate Professor in the Department of Sociology, Boston College. He received his Ph.D. in Social Psychology from Harvard University in 1969. Dr. Williamson has authored and co-authored several books including *Strategies Against Poverty in America* (Schenkman, 1975), *Aging and Society* (Holt, Rinehart and Winston, 1980), *Growing Old* (Holt, Rinehart and Winston, 1980), and *The Politics of Aging* (Charles C. Thomas, 1982).

Additional Titles in . . .

POLICY, POLITICS, HEALTH AND MEDICINE Series
Series Editor: Vicente Navarro

Volume 1— *Health and Medical Care in the U.S.: A Critical Analysis*
Edited by Vicente Navarro

Volume 2— *Organization of Health Workers and Labor Conflict*
Edited by Samuel Wolfe

Volume 3— *Imperialism, Health and Medicine*
Edited by Vicente Navarro

Volume 4— *Women and Health: The Politics of Sex in Medicine*
Edited by Elizabeth Fee

Volume 5— *Health and Work Under Capitalism: An International Perspective*
Edited by Vicente Navarro
and Daniel M. Berman

Baywood Publishing Company, Inc.
120 Marine Street, P.O. Box D, Farmingdale, NY 11735

122580